EFFECTIVE
GROUPWORK

EFFECTIVE GROUPWORK

An Introduction to Principle and Method

ALAN F. KLEIN
State University of New York at Albany

Association Press
𝒻 Follett Publishing Company/Chicago

EFFECTIVE GROUPWORK

Copyright © 1972 by Alan F. Klein
Association Press, 291 Broadway, New York, N.Y. 10007

All rights reserved. No part of this publication may be reprinted, reproduced, transmitted, stored in a retrieval system, or otherwise utilized, in any form or by any means, electronic or mechanical, including photocopying or recording, now existing or hereinafter invented, without prior written permission of the publisher.

"At a Window" is from *Chicago Poems* by Carl Sandburg. Copyright 1916 by Holt, Rinehart and Winston, Inc. Copyright 1944 by Carl Sandburg. Reprinted by permission of Holt, Rinehart and Winston, Inc.

"An Illustration of a First Meeting in a Primary School Under the Auspices of a Youth-Serving Agency" is from *Group Work with Young School Girls* by Edith Miller Tufts, Camp Fire Girls, Los Angeles Area Council, Inc., 1968 (NIMH Project MH 01268-01), pages 38–40.

"An Illustration of the Use of Program" is from the same source, pages 45–49. Both records were dictated by Wynn Tabbert, groupworker and research assistant, and edited by E. M. Tufts.

The epigraph is from *The Redemption of Democracy* by Hermann Rauschning. Copyrighted by Alliance Book Corp.

The excerpt in Chapter 12 by Professor Emanuel Tropp is from "The Group: In Life and in Social Work," *Social Casework*, May, 1968 by permission of the Family Service Association of America.

The record "An Illustration of a First Meeting with Young Adults with Epilepsy" on pages 83–88 and the record "An Illustration of Termination" on pages 289–293 are reprinted with permission from *Concepts and Methods of Social Work*, edited by Walter A. Friedlander and published by Prentice-Hall, Inc. in 1958. They were written by Dr. Gisela Konopka and appear in her chapter "Method of Social Group Work" on pages 156–161 and 289–298 respectively in that book.

International Standard Book Number: 0-695-81077-4

Library of Congress Catalog Card Number: 79-51126

Fourth Printing

Printed in the United States of America

There is one conclusion that we are bound to draw today from our past experience of a reversion to barbarism unconnected with the idea of progress: we must avoid any developments sure to lead once more to forms of totalitarian coercion. This conclusion is rejected by certain important political elements, perhaps with the Machiavellian reflection, avowed or not, that there is bound to be coercion, and so at least it had better be used for good purposes.

The interpreters of the new civilization reckon in tens of centuries. They compare to the centuries the few bitter decades of transition. But what we have experienced is the bitterness of the present. The tens of future centuries are not yet a reality. On the contrary we believe it is our conclusive experience that if the masses have the elements of self-discipline interpreted away from them; if they are degraded to the level of unreasoning herd animals; if they see all ethical values unmasked as remnants of bourgeois ideas in disguise; then there is nothing left but to keep them forever behind the bars of totalitarian coercion. Possibly a class of the "free" may remain above these masses as heirs to something like a substitute for civilization. But it may justly be doubted that the existence of such a new class or of a new society dominated by a tiny class has any advantages over late-capitalistic forms.

But if, as cannot but be the case, civilization and higher probity are possible only when they grow from the morally responsible individual nature, and then only as far as the individual is allowed freedom of co-responsibility and joint decision on a universally valid basis—if this is so, then there is only one thinkable conclusion. The conclusion is to resist the temptation toward all-powerful machineries of coercion, even though it be in the interest of so-called progress, or would make that progress easier. The conclusion will be that we had far better give up such supposed progress than expose ourselves to the mortal peril of a coercive system.

HERMANN RAUSCHNING, *The Redemption of Democracy*

Contents

CONTENTS

CONTENTS

Introduction

Effective Groupwork is about method; it is a book that explains and describes how a groupworker practices effective groupwork. It is a sequel to *Social Work Through Group Process* which contains the philosophy, theory, and basic framework of groupwork.[1] This book is a textbook and is designed primarily for students. It is written for undergraduates taking social welfare courses in colleges and community colleges, and for graduate students who require a knowledge of groupwork but are not concentrating in this area. It is suited also for generic methods courses in graduate schools of social work as well as for use in elementary courses in groupwork at the graduate level. Paraprofessionals and other persons in the helping professions who work with groups but are not trained specifically in social work will find the book valuable. Step by step, it proceeds to elaborate differential ways of working with groups for different purposes and at different stages of their development.

The material does not purport to be the only viable way to practice groupwork. I have little patience with authors who claim that theirs is the only way to achieve positive results, and I have less tolerance for dogma. There is no *one* way to work with people. Groupwork is useful because it offers the groupworker and the group members many options and allows both or either to innovate and create means that are appropriate and effective in the unique situations at hand. This is its appeal, its strength, and its promise.

My approach to working with human groups is predicated on the belief that it is the mission of every person to improve himself, to enjoy his faculties, to strive to reach his potential, and to live in a nutritious society; in a word, to be human. To move toward such goals, each man must find himself and be free to do so.

I do not look with favor upon social scientists who regard man as a machine to be managed, or a creature to be trained. As I observe the current state of knowledge about human nature, I do not think we will learn to understand more accurately and sensitively the world of another person unless we are willing to listen, to hear,

xiii

and to engage ourselves with him. To stand off and objectively observe him defeats the enterprise before it begins. Neither is it possible for a person to grow or find himself in a group that is dominated, controlled, managed, or exploited. Freedom to be one's own self is essential if one is to become what one can be.

Democracy is more than freedom of action, speech, or belief in the political sense. It is more than voting or representative government. Democracy requires a society and hence groups in which the individual's right to be himself is accepted genuinely and his worth and dignity are valued. We cannot permit *anyone*—poor, black, ill, or disadvantaged in any fashion—to be unnecessarily deprived, injured, humiliated, neglected, exploited, or manipulated. We cannot condone anyone being used as a tool, no matter how unimportant that one may seem to be, no matter how righteous the cause, or no matter for whatever expressed justification, because we know that anyone so neglected, mistreated, controlled, or put down will be blocked in growth, prevented from improving, and be less capable of participating in a free, democratic society.

Too much of what is written in the literature of both the helping professions and the disciplines, and too much of what one observes in practice is a denial of man's right and need to be free of domination. Too many experts think that they know what is best for other people and are overly zealous in their willingness to plan for them, even though the efforts of these professionals contribute to the development of dependency, the undermining of the ego, and the disintegration of communities.[2]

Much of the unhappiness, malfunctioning, and copping out is a result of alienation, frustration, and the thwarted efforts of people to achieve closeness with others. These conditions stem from the absence of positive object relations and the incapacity to relate oneself to others. When this is combined with constant pressure to mold one into the image that others create for one, human misery and tragedy ensue. The group in groupwork is a viable and fertile culture in which freedom and self can grow within a context of social responsibility.

The model of groupwork which is presented rests upon fifteen premises. They are stated here and will be explained and elaborated in the text.

These premises are:

1. Behavior is a response to need, and how a need is met or thwarted gives rise to still other kinds of behavior. The resources that are available and how they meet or frustrate a need are secondary stimuli to behavior. Responses can become habitual and, therefore, can become modes of adaptation.

2. A person's position, status, and role determine, in part, what resources will be available to him. These and other aspects of his location in the group determine his behavior by virtue of the kinds of responses he receives to his need-seeking behavior which are provided by the social situation.

3. Coping and adapting are learned behaviors as is maladapting. Socialization into a culture, i.e., conformation to its norms and expectations, is learned; deviance is also learned. Just as behavior is learned and becomes part of habit patterns, feelings and attitudes also become habitual. Social learning is effected through the recurrence of rewards and punishments by resources and responses.

4. It is not enough for one to learn to cope and adapt to the environment; social action is essential so that a person can make the environment more suited to his needs and the needs of others.

5. Groupwork is one means of facilitating a matching of individual needs, responses, the resources for these needs, and the requisites of society in order to improve the consequences for both the person and his environment.

6. A person must learn to cope, adapt, master, and match his environment, but of equal importance, as much mismatching as possible must be prevented.

7. In groupwork, the group is a system of mutual aid wherein each member assists every other member to meet his needs, to create a maximizing environment, and to achieve the group goal (which, if achieved, is perceived by each member as helping him to achieve his personal goals). This concept is not the same as cooperation. In mutual aid, each member helps the others and expects that he will be helped also.

8. The desire for human closeness is innate and its achievement is essential for health and survival. Experiences in closeness are possible only if trust has been established and external control has been minimized. The member-to-member and member-to-worker interactions must be experiences in closeness.

9. Directly related to the desire for closeness is the thrust to be free. Manipulation and control by others shut out potentials for growth; creativity does not develop in authoritarian systems, and self-realization is not facilitated when one is being controlled by others.

10. Choices and options must be available for there to be freedom.

11. Responsibility must go along with choice so that the group members are confronted with the ultimate in freedom: that each man is responsible to himself and that he cannot escape his responsibility by projecting onto others.

12. If the members are free and responsible, the groupworker can ask them what they are going to do about the group's concern or task and the goals of the members. It is their responsibility to do something about them, they are free to do something about them, and they have the other members and the worker to help them.

13. The important learning through groupwork is not primarily cognitive or intellectual. The addition of an experience along with an awareness of what is happening, and a clearly known and understood goal is the significant factor.

14. The groupworker is not the change agent; the group is the medium for change.

15. The function of groupwork is to free the members to be themselves. This means, for instance, free them from inhibitions, free them from old conflicts and the residues of old conflicts (mistrust, shame, guilt, doubt, anxiety, fear, and so forth), free them from the effects of previous domination (fighting against father and mother figures, transferences, rebellion), and free them from current domination.

The book is designed on a pedagogical rationale. Concepts which are presented in earlier sections are reintroduced and elaborated later in more complex forms—they reappear and are applied in the chapters on method. In this plan, there is a continuity of material in an orderly sequence which then is integrated and applied. Some of the most important premises and propositions are repeated for emphasis and to provide bridges to methodological applications.

The book is organized in fifteen chapters beginning with a review of objectives, purposes, and typical applications of groupwork. Chapters 2 to 5 present what are essentially behavioral-science concepts about people and groups; Chapters 6–12 use these and other concepts to inform the practice of groupwork; Chapters 13–15 move into related subjects.

The organizational principle for the ordering of these chapters is the sequence of phases through which groups progress and then how a groupworker functions within them. In the second chapter, I discuss how to compose a group. This is followed by a chapter that details the processes by which a group forms. It develops structure, norms evolve out of values and beliefs, subgroups emerge, and patterns of relationship and communication begin to form. The major theme in the first phase of group development is the establishment of mutual trust. This theme is illustrated by an excerpt from a group record.

There follows an analysis of the dynamics of group process in first meetings and the characteristics of the first phase of group development. A record is used to illustrate them.

All of the excerpts from records in the book are actual practice records and were written by different people at different times. They are longer than the records which usually appear in books of this kind so as to permit the student to understand how the worker is functioning; the essence of groupwork does not lie in specific acts of a worker but in his whole approach, that is, his stance. The records are included as examples of practice and as exercises for the reader, not to illustrate recording. They are not prototypes of perfect groupwork to be copied, but are only examples of practice to be examined, analyzed, understood, and used as a basis for the reader's own creative efforts in similar situations in his own experiences.

The components of group structure are examined in detail in Chapter 3. Most of the content in this chapter is culled from writings over some years in small-group dynamics and research. This chapter discusses the role concept and seeks to differentiate this descriptive concept from the essence and meaning of the true self.

Social-systems theory and analysis have become popular recently in the social sciences and in social work education. It is a powerful construct for understanding groups and for analyzing group processes. Basically, it is descriptive not explanatory in nature and hence it is not a theory in the true sense of the word. Like many other popular ideas in social science and social work that have just found their time, many of the concepts in social-systems analysis have been known and used by social groupworkers since about 1925. The small group is a social system and about the easiest one to appreciate; it functions within the larger systems of the agency, the neighborhood, and the culture. Subgroups were recognized as subsystems and the inputs and outputs were systematically studied and used by groupwork theorists and practitioners. These concepts are discussed and described in Chapter 4. This discussion of social systems rounds out the content about group structure and processes and sheds light on interactions and relationships which are the major components of a group, i.e., a social system. The systems components and processes are used in Chapter 8 to inform method. Chapter 5 resumes the examination of the phases of group development. The theme in the second phase revolves about authority and fear of the groupworker. Coping with these concerns calls for negotiation which results in a re-formation of group structure; this, in turn, opens the way for a resolution of purpose and a formulation of a treatment goal. In this period and in the third phase one begins to see the development of commitment and motivation. This facilitates interpersonal transaction at a meaningful level and permits the member to experience closeness which, in turn, opens the way to mutual aid and the finding of oneself.

Groupwork in the first three phases is detailed in Chapter 6 and records are introduced to illustrate the worker's stance and functioning. Chapter 7 explains the basic components of groupwork and in Chapter 8 the way a worker uses these concepts is elaborated. These three chapters constitute the core of the book and set forth in some detail the essentials of helping a group through the stages of group development and helping the members by means of groupwork.

The two chapters that follow, Chapters 9 and 10, are part of this latter subject matter. They discuss the specific modalities of program utilization and the use of agency function. Chapter 11 follows the group development through to its conclusion and discusses various aspects of termination. Here, also, emphasis is placed on the function of the worker.

I profess that my explanation and conceptualization of groupwork is not the only viable one, nor is it suggested that in all instances it is preferred. Chapter 12 sets forth briefly six additional ways of working with groups that are worth the reader's study and attention. I admit that I have not done them justice in the brief space allocated to them, but hope that students will be stimulated to pursue them in the original sources and extended writings.

The book then branches away from the direction it has been taking to a consideration of important and related matters. In Chapter 13 intake into an agency is discussed; this differs from intake into a group. Chapter 14 examines groupwork practice with committees, delegate councils, and neighborhood groups wherein the main purposes are task oriented. Chapter 15 takes a behind-the-scenes look at T-groups, sensitivity groups, and encounter groups. The insights in Chapter 15 are derived from my experience in the use of these devices from the nineteen forties to the present as well as from theory.

The title of this text is *Effective Groupwork*, which may sound presumptuous to some. One might question the authority for such a contention. The methods explicated in this book have been effective for me. I have practiced in all of the situations which I have discussed and have seen their effects. They have been evaluated and validated by experts and others, such as schoolteachers of children who have been in the groups, by the experiences of students whom I have taught, and by research studies. The studies have been conducted in a children's treatment center in Toronto, Canada; in several public primary schools and in a university experimental school in Pittsburgh; in a youth-development center with acting-out adolescents in Pennsylvania; and in a family group-counseling project funded by N.I.M.H.

The nature of the method is such that not everyone will be able to use it because it requires a worker who has become a person in his own right. The means rests upon a concept that used to be honored, began to erode in mechanistic approaches to groupwork, and is in favor once again in many circles and especially with students; that is, the use of self. In contrast to some other models of practice, the one that is presented here is humanistic. I am less interested in altering behavior, effecting conformity, or imposing values. I have as a major purpose the growth and development of the self and the evolution of human environments. It is by these criteria that I present the book as an exposition of effective groupwork.

I am indebted to those groupworkers who wrote the recordings which appear in the book; some of whom were students, others were colleagues. In the course of many years of teaching and conducting institutes as well as attending courses and seminars, I have collected dozens of recordings which do not bear the names of their writers. Their identities never were revealed, hence they remain unknown to me, and the sources from whence the records came are obscure. It is with gratitude that I thank these workers and apologize for being unable to attribute each illustration to its author.

It is especially pleasant to acknowledge the invaluable assistance of my wife who edited and typed the manuscript.

ALAN F. KLEIN

Loudonville, New York
Fall, 1971

NOTES / READINGS

1. Alan F. Klein, *Social Work Through Group Process* (Albany, New York: School of Social Welfare, State University of New York, 1970).

2. Donald C. Klein, *Community Dynamics and Mental Health* (New York: John Wiley & Sons, Inc., 1968).

1

❖❖❖❖❖❖❖❖❖

Roots and Branches

The effectiveness of a group as a means of achieving human goals has been known for many generations. Historians note that if the last 50,000 years of the existence of mankind on earth were to be divided into lifetimes of sixty-two years, we would be living now in the 800th lifetime. The first 650 lifetimes were spent in caves and yet it was at that time that group life evolved as a means of providing man with certain basic needs and satisfactions. The tribe, as a social structure, developed as a means of survival and also as a medium for human interaction.

History also tells us that the ancient Mayans, the Hebrews, and the Greeks used group catharsis as a means of therapy, and that the commune, as a form, precedes the Christian era. It was elaborated upon by that religious group. It is only in the last six lifetimes, however, that written communication has become ubiquitous. When one realizes that the study of the small group and its uses is only about 140 years old and the accumulation of knowledge about group process goes back only two lifetimes at the most, it begins to be apparent that groupwork is a very modern development.

One could date the beginning of the quest for information about man and his society from approximately 1830 with the work of Comte who founded sociology as a formal body of knowledge. Early sociologists investigated man and his society by looking for and at the elements, processes, and consequences of group experience. These early concerns were mainly with large social groupings and the basis of their theory was social philosophy. The early philosophical premises were that a human infant is helpless without the group, and that ways of thinking and acting and the nature of the social order man creates are products of group life. As a matter of observable fact, from infancy on a person can only meet his basic needs with and through other people. As a matter of demonstrated fact, personality is conditioned by others, self-image is formed from the reactions of others to oneself, and attitudes, values, and norms are products of group involvement; the individual and the group are an inseparable unit in reality. People live their entire lives in groups.

The conscious use of knowledge about group life in order to influence human behavior has existed for little more than one lifetime. The social worker and other helping professionals apply this knowledge. They must understand social phenomena and social process; they involve themselves in social process toward purposeful goals to improve social functioning and in the interest of human betterment. The helping professions are concerned with social values and are based, as were the early sociologists, in social philosophy. As of this point in time, much of the substance of the social helping professions is based upon a system of beliefs. More and more evidence is being presented to support a contention that cultural beliefs about behavior—that is, good or bad, ill or well, and so forth—are the basic criteria which we use to evaluate people and to establish "treatment" goals.

It is social philosophy that defines the good life and designates good mental health. It is also social philosophy which tells us what a good society is. In the United States, as an example, most people believe that it is wrong for people to suffer from starvation and poverty while a few people have far in excess of what they can ever use and engage in conspicuous consumption, waste, and exploitation. A majority in the Far East believe that it is wrong for people born to an elite status not to have a huge surplus of material things and that it is wrong to equalize resources because the difference in economic wealth and power among people properly maintains the structure of society; everyone in his place.[1] As hard as it is to believe, even the deprived person at the bottom of the social scale thinks that equality is wrong and elitism is right.

In the helping professions, philosophy and practice are not separate things. The philosophy that guides social work is not removed from life. Our social services achieve their purposes only when those who administer them and those who make them possible understand the underlying beliefs that inspired them. That which makes social work distinctive is the fusion of philosophy with goals and means. The basic philosophy and principles of human relations have their origins in the yearnings of man for a good life. The principles that inform groupwork practice flow from the same foundations.

I am not discounting the importance of knowledge in this formulation. The practitioner applies knowledge to achieve goals, but the choice of goals and means rests upon beliefs. The concepts of social welfare spring from a sense of social responsibility and a respect for people. Practice is made more effective by scientific observation and testing as it aims to improve the common good and to continue the humanization of mankind, but means and ends are inextricably joined and hence the means one chooses must be based on the same values as are the ends sought.

Social work is based on a belief in the dignity of man—dignity meaning the quality and state of being worthy. A man has intrinsic worth because he is a man. He need make no more case for his entitlement to meeting his needs than that he is a person. It follows that he is also entitled to be free and to live in a nourishing society unburdened by fear, want, ill health, and oppression. A nourishing society is one that is enhancing rather than depriving and endangering. In such a society he is able to develop his individual abilities, use them, and have access to happiness. Social work is based on a belief that no human being should be hungry, uneducated, unnecessarily ill or ill without care, or in want. It follows also that society is enhanced by strengthened members and that members grow in an enhancing society.

The question of means in the practice of social work, and particularly in groupwork, is crucial. When a person is in need of treatment, the social service should aim at his habilitation and seek to help him reach what he is potentially capable of achieving. This should be done by his own efforts with skilled help and support which foster his independence. No longer is there any question about the interrelation of positive health and the availability of societal resources. Requisites for normal, healthy development include good physical nurture and the assurance of affection, a sense of self-worth and accomplishment, stimulation, and a sense of security. These requisites support the premises of practice that a social worker seeks to understand, not "judge"; accepts the person; and treats his trusteeship confidentially. An additional corollary especially important in groupwork is the idea that each person is responsible for himself as well as the others. Then, undeniably, it follows that those affected by plans (or treatment) must participate in the decision-making about those plans.

I reject the theory of rugged individualism, of undirected struggle for survival, and of so-called free competition. Those who hold that such is the American way are deluded. The frontier was opened by groups of mutually interdependent people and the industrial developments in this country were subsidized by land grants, franchises, and government cash. Today, we provide huge subsidies to

agriculture, mining, shipping, and a multitude of production indus-
tries. The American way has been to provide subsidies to business
and industry out of the common treasury, a communal and group
philosophy which to all intents and purposes is public welfare.
Americans prefer a socially directed struggle to protect and
strengthen such characteristics as they deem desirable.

It can be said that knowledge about small groups began with
the work of Georg Simmel. He proposed that a primary concept
in group life is a consciousness of self and established that there
is relationship between the behavior of individuals and social control
by the group, that is to say that individual behavior is influenced
by the group with which one is identified.[2] Simmel originated the
idea of mutuality in social relations, a conception that has been
built into groupwork.

Simmel was interested in internalization, which is how an individual takes in group values and incorporates them into his self-
governing. He saw this process as taking place within the small
group, as indeed it does. It has taken us fifty years or more to
see the relevance of this for group treatment and its importance
in understanding gangs, the youth culture, and current social
movements.

Emile Durkheim introduced the "social fact" concept. He found
that while thoughts, beliefs, and feelings are facts which are internal
and individual, they are also external and are transmitted through
the social groupings to which one belongs, such as occupational,
religious, professional groups, and so forth. Max Weber carried this
further with his concept of "social behavior." Social behavior is
behavior, he argued, that is carried out in direct reference to the
behavior of others.

It was Charles H. Cooley who refined these ideas by developing
the relationship of individual personality and the social system. It
was he who defined the primary group, discussed "we feeling" or
bond, and introduced the idea of mutual identification in groups.[3]

Cooley postulated that the primary group is a social fact and
its existence must be recognized if one is to understand individual
behavior. He taught that the self is always a social self and it cannot
be separated from relationships with other people. Cooley's concept
of the "looking-glass self" is a very basic idea because it establishes
the tremendous influence the group has on individual growth and
development since a person thinks of himself as he imagines he
appears in the eyes of others judged by their reactions and behavior
to him. This is a most important contribution foreshadowing modern
feedback-control system theory. We are returning to the insights
of Simmel, Durkheim, Weber, and Cooley in the development of

current small-group theory and in the most up-to-date conceptions of group therapy. Some of Simmel's early ideas sound very new today. He stated that groups develop structure; that subgroups arise in groups; that dyads and triads form; that group bond is in inverse ratio to the size of a group, and so forth.

George Mead's work foreshadows role theory and communication theory. He conceived that to take the role of another is the basis of cooperative action. It is through taking the role of another that one is able to actualize oneself and feel one's own role. A person must perceive how another person feels and thinks in order to communicate with him. A leader is one who can enter into the attitudes of the group and also can become an intergroup liaison, entering several groups and interpreting each to the other. The "generalized other" has taken on many other-roles or he has taken on the typical other-role and thereby is the epitome of the norm.

It was Durkheim who established the truism that a man needs a goal and that the goal should be reachable. He also noted that society or the group acts as a controlling agent. To make life tolerable, society determines what are attainable and appropriate goals. The group provides a setting for the person which takes him out of isolation.

It is both interesting and encouraging to note that many modern psychiatrists discuss mental illness as alienation, a disorder in social (interpersonal) relationships, and that a recent survey of pertinent research concluded that positive mental health is directly correlated with a person's being anchored in a reference group.* To generalize these findings, it would be fair to say that anyone belonging to a small reference group, sharing common goals and values in which there are structured roles, would seem to be provided with an element of protection against emotional disabilities no matter what kinds of stresses he may have to face. This seems to be true even though we know that some strong and creative people lead lonely lives.

This very brief review of early history has not been to look at the past in order to comprehend how we got where we are but to understand the premises for effective groupwork. The study of the group has been going on for but one lifetime and it is the one in which the reader and I are living. The historical insights mentioned in the last few pages remain the current fundamentals of group dynamics and inform existing practice. As this book unfolds, the reader will see again and again that modern groupwork rests on the belief system inherent in a humanistic and democratic phi-

* See note 10.

losophy and on the fundamental themes developed by the sociologists whom I have been discussing.

Groupwork method and group experiences are influences which help the members and that help takes place through mutual aid. The dynamics through which this occurs, in part, is through the development of a self; a self develops through interaction with others. A healthy self evolves within a significant group; a reference group.

Groupwork is a method of helping people through a group experience—a form of social helping directed toward giving people a constructive experience of membership in a group so that they are able to develop as persons and be better able to contribute to the life of the community. A group is a social system consisting of two or more people who are in face-to-face interaction at both the cognitive and psychic levels within which the people perceive that they belong to the group. By virtue of it being a social system, it is understood that there are common goals, common norms, reciprocal relationships, social structure, and cohesion. It is also agreed that the interrelationship of all of the components of the system are so interdependent that change or action of any one component influences every other.

A reference group is a group to which a person belongs or thinks he belongs (that is, aspires to) and which he uses to guide his behavior by adherence to its norms, values, and general social culture. For a group to be a reference group for a member it must be significant to him. Its importance is contingent on whether or not it meets his needs. Such a group guides one in relation to the central values that are perceived, however dimly, as basic to one's very being. These concepts will be discussed later in this chapter in greater detail.

The primary consideration here is whether the group is significant; whether it gives something important to the member. If it does, it will influence his behavior and growth, but if it does not, it is unlikely that it will have influence. Group cohesion correlates with how attractive a group is to a member and, again, this depends upon how significant it is to him. As simple as these ideas are, they are rarely maximized in practice to alert agencies and staff members to an awareness that for groups to be effective for the growth of members they must be giving and need-meeting.

Human Needs

There are some human needs which are considered to be universal. The importance of each such need varies from life-stage

26

to life-stage. Any need varies in intensity and in its influence on behavior, depending upon the age and predisposition of the person. People of course are different. If needs vary in time-stages, the need-meeting within a reference group must also vary so as to match or cogwheel with the needs of the individual member if that group is to be significant to him.

Needs are assessed differently by different theorists; for example, Adler postulates behavior on a need to feel important, Sullivan on interpersonal relations, Fairbain on object relations, White on a relationship with the environment. Maslow provided a continuum of needs based upon self-realization. These range from (1) basic physical, survival needs through (2) security, (3) belongingness, (4) love and esteem to (5) self-realization needs. Needs occur in importance, according to Maslow, in that sequence of priority. He argues that an individual is not concerned with esteem, nor can he be appealed to in these terms until he has a minimum and continuing satisfaction with his survival, security, belongingness, and love needs. At any given time all five needs are present but only one need is dominant or most powerful. The individual's first unsatisfied need in this order of relative priority becomes his dominant need. Any critical change in the individual, in the external situation in which he finds himself, or in both, may cause a shift of that individual's dominant need along that continuum. Parenthetically, if the groupworker or group is offering need-meeting resources which do not fit the dominant need, it is not really a referent. This has important connotations in social work practice.

The individual directs his behavior toward satisfying the need that is dominant at any given time. Motivation is based upon needs, actions, the goals toward which behavior is directed, and the energy released in the individual to accomplish these goals. Maslow's five needs enumerated above merge into each other and there is no clear demarcation between them. A person's need, however, may change from situation to situation. His behavior generally gains at least partial satisfaction of more than one need at a time. The fact that many basic needs are present and that all of these influence the behavior of a person helps one to explain the reciprocal interaction between needs and behavioral responses.

If the components of the social system change, this can threaten or calm the need responses related to survival, security, love, and belongingness, and by so doing bring into dominance different needs. Also, people in a group are at different levels in their need dominance and hence the change in system variables will impact differently on each member.

It may be that needs are arranged on a continuum and that

their position in a hierarchy is fixed, as Maslow suggests. I prefer to think of them as related to each other in a different way. The needs most often identified in the helping professions are to be loved, to be recognized, to have status, to be secure, to belong, to be accepted, and to feel adequate. These are not listed in any significant order. To some people to belong means that one is accepted, important, and liked by others. Depending on to what one belongs, status may accrue. To have status makes one feel adequate and recognized; it connotes acceptance. To be loved affords security.

I am not placing them in any fixed relationships but suggesting that they vary in their importance to individuals, and that in given situations the effort to satisfy one need may imply the striving to satisfy another need. Needs vary greatly from person to person and from social situation to social situation. We can relate this to the important conclusions that love, recognition, and a sense of belonging are important needs which are susceptible to provision or deprivation in the social environment with notable effects upon mental and emotional well-being. However one looks at a hierarchy of needs, it would seem that the striving for any one of them ultimately relates to the yearning to be loved, that is, to object relations. Stripped of all of the semantics, the presence of love is the only healer.

The Social Groupworker's Beliefs

The social groupworker believes in and dedicates himself to service to his fellow man in the context of helping him to meet his needs, within a climate of love, in a manner conducive to the enhancement of others. He is dedicated to this concept of service because he knows that the well-being of any individual depends upon the impinging environment within which he lives, and hence upon the health and safety of others. The goals of the groupworker are, therefore, always person centered. A significant groupworker believes that the democratic process is inherent in groupwork, group therapy, and family group counseling, and that effective treatment cannot be practiced in any agency or setting which thwarts the basic rights of people to be involved in making decisions which affect their lives.

The mandate for these helping efforts is derived from society and the ultimate goal is the welfare of the total population of the community. To achieve this end requires the effective participation of individuals and groups of individuals. One task of the groupworker is to assist them to acquire effective skills in social participation. Social action is, therefore, an essential element of practice and it is the task of the groupworker to promote the abilities of members and groups to perform their roles as socially competent citizens in a democracy. This concept of democracy is meaningless except on the premise of the inherent worth and dignity of all people, and an abiding belief in the potential right of people to govern themselves and to determine their own destiny. This principle is crucial in community development and in groupwork where the primary objective is the growth and development of the group members. It is also indispensable in treatment, be it social work or psychiatric. This fundamental *sine qua non* must be the basis of and major guideline for practice, and hence it follows that poverty, deprivation, endangering environments, racism, and all forms of exploitation are anathema to the effective groupworker whatever the context, be it clients, patients, members, students, colleagues, supervisees, neighbors, and in general.

The groupworker believes in the right of individuals and groups to preserve their cultural heritage so that different cultures, existing side by side, may strengthen the total society and the individuals who live therein, and to develop a sense of identity as well as a creative and mutually enriching unity in diversity. Such norms are dynamic and deviations which do not deprive or endanger others are the right of all people.

Concern for the person and attention to his needs involves recognition of the importance of the family and its relationships in the development and growth of its members. The family is, after all, the primary reference group. It is in the family that the foundation of personality is established. Healthy personality growth is dependent upon the meeting of needs, qualitative and quantitative, in the formative years. Poverty and injustice which result in malnutrition, frustration, and psychological poisoning in infancy and latency are noxious and intolerable in American society.

The World in Which We Live

It is an obvious fact that the world in which we live and the society which comprises our immediate environment are not enriching or enhancing for many infants and their families, and that this is endangering and insulting to large numbers of citizens. The experiences of growing up in such families and in certain neighborhoods block or frustrate normal growth and work against individuals' realizing their potential. The self which emerges is often a self-deprecating self wherein the self-image is one of worthlessness beset with doubt and shame. For some, doubt and shame are handled by a what-is-the-use attitude to the world which results in a lack of motivation, copping out, the use of alcohol and narcotics, and self-defeat. To others, it gives rise to anger and hate, sometimes acted out against society or other individuals, or internalized against oneself. While these results are more likely to happen in low-income families, they are also prevalent among the more privileged as well. The effects of superindustrialization and increased mobility are more and more evident, and become apparent in tenuous interpersonal relationships and the modular concept of man. Imagine the idea of the male breadwinner who, when being moved by his firm, leaves his family where it is and "plugs into" a new family living where he is transferred. The possibility is being entertained today by futurists.

In this discussion we are more interested in the more current effects: the deprivation of any need-meeting resource, be it food, love, security, or validation of self. Many people grow up in homes where these resources are in short supply. It is axiomatic that such deprivation at an early age interferes with the establishment of basic trust which is essential to the development of good interpersonal relations. If one has never been loved one does not learn how to love. If one is not given to, one does not learn how to give or how to receive. The real self develops in a climate wherein one can find identity, the identity of who one is. It is postulated here that an important basis of faulty social functioning is the failure to become or find oneself. By the same token, one of the objectives of groupwork is to enable individuals to become themselves.

It is suggested that many families and other social institutions superimpose a role-carrying self upon the child and later the adult, and make of him what someone else expects him to be. This is, in part, a process of socialization, but socialization which occurs through control and a demand for conformity often breaks the will of a child, and in so doing renders him plastic in the hands of those who would manipulate him. In such a process, he does not grow and mature; instead he is forced into a mold. Such a process denies freedom and fosters guilt. It not only creates an ego-weak person who lacks basic self-security, and hence retards his ability to relate himself to others in meaningful ways, but it also feeds the worst aspects in the psychic being of the one who does the controlling and fettering. It is the objective of groupwork to help people to free themselves to be themselves and to facilitate interpersonal closeness by reaffirming basic trust. The thesis is that many people need help to develop social competence and that the most prevalent social disabilities are correlated with unfound or underdeveloped selves.

A little earlier, it was noted that persons who are frustrated often feel that there is no use in trying, or they cop out, or they may act out. There are attitudinal and behavioral responses when roadblocks are placed in the way of need-meeting. Examples of such reactions are apathy and lack of motivation, the use of deadeners like alcohol and narcotics, and the use of violence or acting out against others. Some people avoid the roadblocks and go around them by the use of deviant or illegal means, goal displacement, and by changing themselves to conform, thereby selling their souls for a mess of pottage.

Some people retain their perspective of reality, keep their eyes on the goal, and with great effort fight their way through the block. In our culture we honor such people and laud this as the American way and say that they have great ego strength. Seldom do we stop to assess the psychic cost of such an endeavor to the self and to others, the deflection in values and goals, or the changes that occur within the person as a result of the mobilization of so much aggression. Love rarely is served in such enterprises.

Objectives for Groupworkers

Some writers postulate different kinds of groupwork predicated on a variety of objectives. Some think that groupwork methods also differ in accordance with the objectives. There are, generally speaking, the following objectives in groupwork:

1. *Rehabilitation.* This means to restore to a former capacity. Rehabilitation can refer to emotional or mental difficulties, or to behavior, and it can also be used to mean attitudinal or value orientations.
2. *Habilitation.* This is a developmental concept and implies growth and development rather than treatment. To be precise, some people who have difficulties may never have learned how to behave when they were younger and hence they cannot be restored as rehabilitation implies. In this instance, habilitation is more accurate.
3. *Correction.* This usually means helping people who are having problems with social laws or mores and are offenders or violators.
4. *Socialization.* This means helping people to learn how to do what is socially expected and how to get along with others. Resocialization implies that one has regressed and needs to be trained again. As in the case of rehabilitation, it is used incorrectly often as many clients were not socialized in the first instance and, therefore, cannot be resocialized.

5. *Prevention.* This implies anticipating difficulties before they occur and providing the necessary environmental nutrients that individuals need. It can also mean anticipatory inoculation, that is, helping people to learn how to cope with events that are likely to occur.
6. *Social action.* This means helping people to learn to change their environment in addition to coping and adapting.
7. *Problem-solving.* This means helping people to use groups to achieve tasks, to make decisions, and to solve social problems.
8. *Social values.* This means to use groupwork as a means of helping members to develop viable social values which are relevant to living.

Using the above generalized objectives, it is possible to become more specific about the usefulness of groupwork to achieve social goals.

A major function of an effective groupworker is to help the group and its members to accomplish their purposes. The worker's efforts are guided by their purposes. The worker is called upon to understand the needs of the members so that his own behavior is helpful to them according to each person's need and the needs of the group. He seeks to affect the interacting process so as to facilitate an increase in social competence. He seeks to help the members handle problems related to social tasks. He shares appropriate knowledge and skill but, above all, he helps them to help each other.

What, then, are the constructive potentials that inhere in a group experience? Many writers have addressed themselves to this question and what follows is a summary of their contributions.[4] The group can provide an experience in human closeness through encounter and through meaningful communication. What occurs in and through the group is experiential and this experience is the growth and change ingredient.

A group experience based on closeness facilitates a sense of belonging and security which permits one to release the energy which has been diverted in defense and fear to a more satisfying use. Some writers hold that there is a reduction of anxiety through the substituting of group standards for individual superego or for anomie. While this may be true and in some instances desirable, to practice on this premise is dangerous as it condones dependency and externalized social control. A more desirable concept is that of emotional support from peers and worker through which a person develops his own values and can find himself while others are finding him.

There is also more to be said for negotiation among peers and commitment to the group goals than for the imposition of a group conscience.

A few writers, especially of the classical psychoanalytical school, believe that group relationships encourage sublimation. One should examine sublimation with great care. In many instances, sublimation is a restrictive solution to one's internalized conflicts and merely reduces anxiety without meeting basic needs or coping with one's genuine yearning. It is too easy to become a simulation instead of a real self by being conned into a socially imposed and hence socially accepted activity. Sublimation of basic drives has been known to result in neurotic suffering.

It is more important to be aware of the potential within a group experience for loosening the façade of defense mechanisms to avail oneself of the opportunity to test fancied fears by comparing them with the reality of the perceptions of others. Perhaps, of all of the possibilities within a group, this is the greatest because it is through this experience that one can begin to free oneself of past and present hangups.

Old-school theorists still postulate in therapeutic terms the desirability of utilizing a group experience to (1) help individuals to curb infantile desires and behavior, and to internalize group standards in exchange for the love and protection received; (2) to direct undue aggressiveness onto real evils and use it for purposes of developing self-control and defense.

The *quid pro quo* which permeates our societal norms naturally seeps into our treatment protocol. I contend that the group member needs to feel unconditional love and protection and not be obliged to purchase it in exchange for anything. To be loved and accepted because I am me is different from what you direct me to be. It is granted that one must learn to do, in a social sense, what one must do in order to be accepted and to survive, but one must learn to want and choose to do these things. One can choose to be part of society when one's environment induces one rather than forces one. The group can provide that kind of experience; it should and can be the place where one gains status and self-respect because others respect one.

The group experience can encourage self-expression, foster catharsis, provide an atmosphere wherein it is safe to relate to others. It can encourage the expression of suppressed anger, fear, and yearning and release deep-seated tensions as well as help the member to acquire better perspectives of his problems and feelings. Such a group experience is recommended on a reality level. Here, the idea is one of cognitive problem-solving, reality-testing, and the experimentation with alternative means of coping. Such purposes are not restricted to work with persons having emotional problems; it is also applicable to work with offenders in correctional settings, for example. It may apply to any other kind of groupwork where it is deemed appropriate.

The group experience in groupwork helps the member to achieve greater harmony between inner needs and impulses and outward social behavior. As such, it is the channel through which one can develop a matching between the impinging environment and the intrapsychic needs of the person. This is the essence of the matching model which was elaborated upon in *Social Work Through Group Process;* namely, that the over-all objective in social maturation is to achieve a matching of significant elements in coping patterns and the environmental elements so as to enhance both the individual and his environment.[5]

In a society wherein alienation and isolation are rife, the group provides the setting which can relieve the feelings of uniqueness, loneliness, and abandonment through the facilitation of relationships. We say "can" because in many worker-dominated groups it does not accomplish the purpose stated. Moreover, if basic trust is not facilitated, it will not relieve feelings of isolation and alienation. This point must be underlined. Members will not reveal problems easily, growth will not be accelerated, defenses will not be diminished unless freedom of atmosphere is allowed and examples are set by peers and worker to permit each to function with decreased self-protective restraint and fear. Self-revelation is presumed and agreed to be the way in which each member can make it possible for the group to help him. It cannot take place unless there is an atmosphere of confidentiality, freedom from sanctions, and a demonstration of acceptance.

The potential for the use of the group in helping people find themselves is great. Participation in group life in associations with others psychologically is a life-giving necessity. The "life space" of the group is the here-and-now. It is the stuff of reality. The group sustains self-identity, but by like token it can enhance self-image. The group can be responsive, supportive, and validating. The group is the setting in which the helping process can focus actively on social interaction and peer relations in current reality.

The Concept of Purpose

In the previous section I have been discussing objectives in general. The specific purpose for which a group is organized by a worker is a primary determinant of the composition, size, structure, and choice of methodology. The specific purpose for which it is formed or is to be utilized must be absolutely clear in the mind of the groupworker and, hopefully, also the administrators of the agency. If the purpose is not clarified consciously, the worker (and the group) will float directionless and will move in such confusion as to make consistency impossible and opposing means which contradict each other probable.

Purpose is an indispensable element in any practice with groups. The social agency, hospital, school, organization, or other sponsor must know why, as a strategy of choice, it wants to use a group before a group is chosen. Purpose acts as a determinant of size. The larger the group, from about five on, the less effective it will be for enhancing behavior, self-image, adaptation, coping mechanisms, attitudes, and the like. Small groups have greater impact than large ones, permit more interactions for each member, and provide a milieu for closeness. Some authorities write that groups should have odd numbers of members so as to eliminate the possibility of stalemate due to equal votes for each side in a split decision. This kind of thinking has no place in groupwork. Decision-making based upon superiority of numbers, power, or parliamentary concepts works against closeness and good interpersonal relations. Moreover, the very idea encourages polarity rather than consensus and loses sight of the importance of commitment to agreed-upon goals.

There is no intent here to imply that a groupworker cannot be effective in large groups; he can. The important thought is that size is related to purpose. Some purposes can be achieved less readily in large groups and others can be more appropriate to relatively large groups.

Purpose guides composition. The groupworker chooses members and arranges composition, to a large extent, based upon purpose. Writers who give blanket prescriptions for grouping, such as demographic data, problem homogeneity, diagnostic labels, degree of remission, and so on are failing to recognize that group purpose affects group process and hence is crucial in relation to outcomes. Decision-making groups such as those involved in social planning are more likely to be influenced by heterogeneity of education, language, age, and so forth than a group of persons who are hurting inside because they are the parents of damaged children. One composes an educational group differently from a treatment group, for instance. Some guidelines for composing a group will be offered later.

Structure flows from purpose. A diagnostic group should have a minimum of structure because structure organizes relationships and standardizes norms for behaving. The lack of structure makes it more likely that people will behave as they usually would outside of the group and hence present themselves as they are. Also, the lack of structure creates anxiety and, therefore, a worker would be able to see defenses and modes of adaptation more readily than he would if there were structure. If purpose is goal directed, structure appropriate to the task should evolve. In a similar way, once purpose is clear, the group members can know what they are to do in order to carry out the purpose. This is called function. Function as well as structure flow from purpose.

Method can be viewed as on a continuum of strategies; some have argued that there is only one method and that one has a variety of emphases. There are a great many variables which can be influenced when working with a group. The choice of the variables which are significant must be related to the purpose for which the group has been formed. Change in some variables is more likely to produce some desired outcomes than change in others. Some may be more easily influenced or may be more accessible. Work with groups is applicable to a wide variety of group purposes ranging from development to treatment, rehabilitation, correction, and social change. There are a variety of modes which comprise group method. Mode means a manner of doing something or performing a particular function or activity. The battery of modes that are available within groupwork gives the worker options which provide a differential approach. The selection of modes depends upon a conscious choice related to purpose and to the assessment of which variables are significant, where the impact will provide maximum growth for the minimum effort, and what is accessible within the setting and situation.

Groupwork is not by any standard a unified, bounded, and well-defined entity. There are many interpretations of what it is. Groupwork as used in this text is a method. The word "method" is used in the collective sense to mean an orderly procedure or process, a regular way or manner of doing something. It is characterized by regularity or habitual practice in action. Since groupwork is a method which is composed of a large variety of modes or specifics, a worker selects those which are appropriate and effective for the purposes desired within the professional context of his work.

In summary, the variables which are significant for influence and change by a worker will differ from system to system and in relation to the proximate purposes and desired outcomes. Proximate goals determine the significant variables to be influenced; ostensibly to induce change in a given subsystem and thus, in turn, help to determine the means. Group methods are useful for achieving social outcomes in a multiplicity of settings which include treatment groups and goal-oriented groups. They apply also to groups where the purposes are education, correction, growth, and community action. With this in mind, let us look at some typical settings.

Some Typical Applications of Groupwork

Public Assistance

One finds an increasing use of groups in public assistance programs. This will grow as maintenance functions are separated from personal social services. The purposes most often cited are: (1) to orient clients to the service—this is to inform and to lower anxiety; (2) to prepare people to use the resources; (3) to help unwed mothers understand their situation—this is both a matter of awareness and treatment; (4) to enhance motivation for employment—this is education, training, and treatment; (5) to improve family relationships and coping mechanisms—this can be treatment, problem-solving, and training; (6) to help parents discover strengths in themselves, to develop social relationships, and to engage in mutual help to change their situations; (7) to resolve marital conflicts; and (8) to resolve parent-child conflicts.

Less often cited, but of profound significance, are purposes related to the clients' situations and the power and authority of the agency. To the client, the public assistance agency represents governmental power with the authority to withhold and all of the attributes of control. The client, or most clients, see themselves as powerless, little people; as born losers. To a client, the power of the worker is momentous. The client perceives himself, no matter how unconsciously, as caught in a conspiracy of industrial giants, cybernation, restrictiveness, racism, and social dependency. He, the client, is reduced to diminished social functioning characterized by immobilization, withdrawal, and depression. The black, Chicano, and Indian client especially has been exploited and put down in the past; he cannot plan for the future and hence he tends to be disinterested in the opportunities (if any) in the present. Understandably, he has poor impulse control because if he does not "take" what he can at the moment there is no assurance that it will wait or that he will be afforded an opportunity to win it.

The undeniable fact is that the client suffers from a chronic situational depression and some use aggression to cover or defend themselves against that depression. Rage and hostility are basic defenses against depression. It is inevitable that the agency and the worker are likely to be identified with a depriving society, with the punitive overseer, and with the denial of respect and friendliness.

Unfortunately, all too often the client's perception is reality. Many social institutions are responsive to political and social constituencies rather than to clients, and it is apparent that the majority opinion of Americans in the nineteen seventies is not sympathetic to the poor, the coloreds, or the different. Such a public remains distrustful of clients and hence tax-supported social agencies remain eligibility focused and budget shy instead of problem focused and client centered.

This kind of atmosphere reinforces fear and dependency and accentuates anxiety. Pure survival fuses financial assistance with emotional dependency for the client and results in infantile role performance. Dependency flows from the denial of resources, deprivation, and from the excessive frustration of striving toward independent ego functioning. Wiltse and Fixel say:

Out of our experience we developed a working concept of "situational depression" which seemed to characterize most of the adult members of the client families. The features of this "situational depression," it became clear, appeared primarily in reaction to the buffetings of an unfriendly social environment, unfortunate life experiences, and dismay at their own inadequacy and ineptitude in handling life's problems. An unusual number of ANC parents had had a history of relatively severe deprivation, either of an economic and cultural type or of a more specifically material type. It is difficult to point to specific details or to say which factors were the most important. Rather it seems best to describe the clients as typically engaged in a vicious circle of frustrating and ego-diminishing experiences which made them depressed, dependent, and inadequate. They were characterized as being typically withdrawn and immobilized in their close interpersonal relationships, in neighborhood and community, and in relation to any activity that would eventually yield them financial independence from the public assistance agency.

Modern, progressive, governmental social services see groupwork as a means of dealing with these feelings and assisting clients on the road to self-respect and independence. The group provides mutual support and help; specific suggestions about management of personal and household problems; the opportunity to express anxiety and fear; and most important, to express safely hostility, rage, anger, and the concomitant feelings of worthlessness, shame, doubt, and guilt. Slavson has said:

The ego debilities that result from the feelings of being unique and isolated are overcome through group relationships. Instead of relying solely upon himself in bearing the stresses of life, the individual shares his burdens with others who support and guide him. His capacity for relationship, trust, and faith in people is thus increased through fellow group members whose basic intent is one of helpfulness and support rather than hostility and destructiveness. With this added strength, the individual can deal with reality with more satisfying results which, in turn, again strengthen his ego powers and favorably alter his self and social images.'

The purposes which are being discussed here illustrate the relationship of purpose to practice. Obviously, the worker must not control, represent authority, use coercive power, restrict, oppress, nor deprive if the group members are to benefit from the group. The group must not increase fear and anxiety, dependency, rage and hostility or reinforce the powerlessness of the member. What is being said here about the public assistance worker's function is wholly applicable to other settings as well. Perhaps it is clearer here than in so-called treatment settings but we shall see that it is nonetheless no truer.

Child Welfare Settings

In child welfare settings, public and private, the most usual purposes cited are: (1) to assist foster parents to learn management techniques, to feel less isolated, and to be helped to grow into better parent surrogates; (2) to help house parents learn and gain sensitivity; (3) to help children in protection cases with their problems of adjustment, rejection by parents, the trauma of placement, and also grief and depression; (4) to help children cope with group-living in the institution; (5) to help children cope with school and neighborhood adjustments; (6) to help children grow and find themselves; (7) to assist children with cultural and value orientation.

Parents' Groups

Parents' groups which are in settings such as Aid to Dependent Children and Families, abandoned and divorced mothers, and Parents of Exceptional Children are especially useful. The purposes most often cited are: (1) to explore and ventilate their problems; (2) to counteract isolation and social withdrawal; (3) to offset guilt and shame; (4) to learn how to cope with children and the problems specific to the function of the agency; (5) to deal with dependency; (6) to handle hostility to the agency and society; (7) to identify with an ego-strong worker; (8) to handle fear, anxiety, and feelings of failure; (9) to handle grief; (10) to enhance self-image; (11) to learn how to use oneself better.

Corrective Settings

The NASW Practice Committee in its Frame of Reference for Social Group Work says:

> In instances where there has been social or personal dysfunctioning or breakdown within individual members, or within their social situations, the group experience may be utilized to provide corrective experiences. In these instances something may have gone wrong or never developed within the person or within the social situation. A group of people may have similar problems or be affected adversely by their social situation. Examples of such problems include delinquents, emotionally retarded people who need social experiences guided by a strong adult, people suffering from physical or emotional breakdown or social isolation, or people who are demoralized by socially, economically, and culturally deprived situations. Examples are not intended to be exhaustive but merely illustrative.[8]

In this context, one cites six major categories of purpose. These are:

1. Social malfunctioning because a person does not know what behavior is expected or is acceptable. This deficit may result from cultural deprivation or difference, faulty learning, inability to read cues, or distorted communication. The remedy lies in educational and training experiences primarily.

2. The person knows what is expected but does not know how to perform; that is, he lacks the skill or competence. The remedy lies in training through experience, role-playing, and practice.

3. The person knows the expectations, has the competence to perform but lacks the ego strength to perform. The remedy lies in enhancing ego strength in those specific areas which are related to the malfunction. The kind of specifics referred to are such things as reality-testing or postponement of gratification, for example.

4. The person knows what is expected, has the skill to perform, has sufficient ego strength but is blocked emotionally. One is concerned here with modifying the person's attitude and patterns of behavior by increasing an understanding of self, of one's problems and one's part in creating them, in addition to supporting or maintaining his strengths by helping him to mobilize his capacity to cope with the current situations.

5. The person may not be troubled with any of the preceding

disabilities but he may not want to behave in other ways or change his behavior. This is a question of attitudes and of cognitive and conscious decisions to defy societal norms. The remedies lie in attitudinal change, in cognitive decision-making based upon assessing consequences, in choosing alternate means of gaining satisfactions or in different strategies for coping and adapting.

6. The basic problem may lie in the social situation which frustrates, endangers, exacerbates, and thereby evokes antisocial or self-defeating behavior. The remedies lie in social action, environmental change, and in different forms of advocacy.

It would appear from the record of experience with corrective efforts that so-called therapeutic methods, especially those predicated on psychoanalytical modalities, are not the most effective. Greater success, such as it is, seems to come from training, reality therapy, operant conditioning, and opening doors to opportunities for rewards to change behavior.

Treatment Groups

Treatment groups are of many kinds and varieties and in many different settings. The use of the group for treatment has grown by leaps and bounds and continues to burgeon. The cited purposes that guide the use of groups for treatment are many and only a few will be discussed. These include: (1) to enhance self-image; (2) to share anxieties and test judgment; (3) to learn to communicate; (4) to learn to relate to others; (5) for catharsis; (6) to resolve the conflict between wish and fear by reducing fear—this is the so-called enabling solution as contrasted with the restrictive solution; (7) to externalize suppressed feelings; (8) to improve reality-testing; (9) to aid in socialization; (10) to motivate for therapy.

A more vital purpose for the treatment group—one that is returning to the importance that it deserves—is that the treatment experience helps the client to develop a real self, to find himself, and to start him on the road to becoming somebody.

Over the years, certain assumptions have been made about the use of groups for treatment purposes. They will be summarized here: (1) treatment groups are recommended for psychotherapy; (2) social hunger, that is, a desire to relate to people, must be present in the members; (3) group relationships encourage sublimation; (4) groups loosen defenses; (5) the ego of members must be strong enough to withstand group pressure; (6) members must have a minimum of superego; (7) members must have had some satisfying experiences in infancy; (8) treatment groups afford support.

41

Preventive Purposes

From its inception, groupwork has been the one specialization in social work and in youth work which has promoted prevention as a major aspect of its practice. Groupwork, in its traditional settings, has always adhered strongly to its role of prevention, which is a credit to group-serving agencies. Prevention means not only the provision of need-meeting nutrients, the elimination of endangering elements, the making available of growth-inducing group experiences, the training of interpersonal skills, and the like, but it also means inhibiting deterioration processes and keeping things from getting worse. It means also "anticipatory inoculation," providing both an awareness of what is to come and some help in anticipating how to cope with the eventualities.[9]

The group may provide experiences which bolster mental health, provide alternatives for dealing with crises, explore alternative values, provide motivation for change, or provide an opportunity for early detection of emotional problems. In this context, the group can be an excellent support for persons under stress, contagion, or continuing environmental insults.[10]

The Developmental Groups

The type of group which one most usually thinks of in the traditional groupwork setting is the normative, social-growth group. This kind of group can provide experiences which facilitate progression through the normal developmental stages and extend the capacity for social relationships. Groups of this kind can fulfill their purpose or their potential but, unfortunately, too many of them do not.

In addition to the usefulness of the typical club for normal youngsters, the normal-growth group also is helpful for people in stress periods. Such groups can help to provide preparation for new situations such as intake, moving into a new job or school, preparation for marriage or parenthood, or the developmental crises of adolescence, retirement, old age, and the like.

There is still another kind of group experience which falls into this category. This includes interest groups such as creative arts, social clubs, discussion groups, action groups, and so on. Herein, the group experiences help participants to develop social competence, express latent potentialities, and provide enrichment. An individual can find a fuller life experience which is growth-inducing through such groups.

In summary, one can see group experience as a means to provide primary relationships with others and with nonhuman objects, and as an opportunity to use and develop adequate ego adaptations and depersonalized controls.

The Group

From time to time in this book, reference will be made to the misconception that natural friendship groups are the most viable groups for promoting social growth in the traditional groupwork sense. Mobilization for Youth relied heavily on the use of such groups for all or most of the purposes set forth in this chapter, and it concluded that groupwork was the least successful part of its program.[11] Let me suggest why.

A group is a social system consisting of two or more persons who stand in status and role relationships with one another and possessing a set of norms or values which regulate the attitudes and behaviors of the individual members in matters of consequence to the group. A group is a statement of relationship among persons. Such object relations and the identification of each with and by the others is internalized into the ego. The ego is a precipitate of object relations. Social attitudes are formed by persons in relation to group norms. A person becomes a group member to the extent to which he internalizes the major norms of the group and other members become part of him, and carries on the responsibilities and meets the expectations for the position and status he occupies. His identity, his self-image, his security all are related to his status and role in the group and these determine his attitudes.

When the groupworker has no involvement in group composition, the group will form around complementary norms and values of the members. When the groupworker has no function in relation to the environmental inputs into such a group system, it is probable that the group culture will reinforce the norms around which the group formed. In such instances, both the internal group culture and the environmental culture will operate against attitudinal and behavioral changes, at least so far as the groupworker is concerned. This is another affirmation that purpose informs composition.

Crisis Intervention Groups

Crisis intervention has become a major treatment modality in a variety of settings, or so it appears from the literature. It is believed that a little help given at the proper moment is more effective than more extended help over a period of less emotional stress. As with most popular themes in casework, groupworkers have attempted to adapt it to practice with groups.

In crisis theory, the essential components are the occurrence of a hazardous event, a person in a vulnerable state, some precipitating factor, and a resulting active crisis or disequilibrium. When the usual equilibrium mechanisms or the usual problem-solving methods do not work and the problem is such that other methods that might be used to cope cannot be used for whatever reason, tension increases and the processes that lead toward disequilibrium become accentuated.

Crisis intervention is most appropriate for people with strong egos who require help for but a short period of time. It is also useful for those who are not well motivated for continuing treatment. It has been demonstrated that such a modality is viable for those for whom the onset of the emotional problem is clearcut and for those whose previous vital balance was stable. In addition, the person must have some awareness of both the behavioral and social problem for which he is seeking help and also know the precipitating stress. Groups tend to be very useful for such people. They are seeking primarily a reduction of stress and some relief from the symptoms. They want relief from suffering. It is doubtful that crisis intervention through a group is a good idea for people other than these.

In many ways a group can be a substitute for the family. It can provide a sense of belonging—that "we-ness" which is an antidote for isolation—and it can counteract the real family's contribution to the decompensation of the suffering person. The stress question in crisis theory must be assessed as a failure in object relationships and hence significant others can be a source of support. The precipitating factors are usually familial and object-relations problems. The group is the ideal place to find peer support and acceptance.

The etiology of such a crisis lies in the interpersonal relations of the person, his self-image, and the image others have of him. A mutual-aid group lends itself admirably to such causalities. However, one should be cautious about using this approach with most clients or group members. The fact is that for most people with emotional problems, the course of the social malfunction is insidious rather than sudden. The symptoms are long-standing. The person has had a low level of social function over the years. In many instances, the family has functioned without him, excluded him, blocked him out, or has programmed him in a distorted family system. These are but continuations of a long series of insults. The original sources of the conflict have been long forgotten by the family members but the disappointment and bitterness remain.

However, for the many reasons which have been discussed in the preceding pages, an intake group is a most desirable strategy. The newly arrived person can be oriented, anxiety levels can be lowered, the person can be involved as a participant in his own treatment, there is full opportunity to have peer support, and diagnostic assessments can precede introduction into a treatment modality. The group process affords protection as a person can listen but not speak if he so chooses. He can recognize his own feelings in others, and he can maintain both touch with reality and also ego recognition as a person. The group is a personal experience rather than an institutional one.

No attempt is being made to discuss all the kinds of groups there are from the physically handicapped to the chronically disabled, from the aged to children, from those discharged to aftercare, from socialization to rehabilitation, and more. The thrust of this section has been to emphasize the need for clarity of purpose in forming a group or using groupwork as a strategy of choice and to stress the importance of identifying the needs for service which can be implemented within and through the group. One must answer the question affirmatively, "Can our purposes be met through a group and in this group?" before one can proceed.

The Reference Group

A reference group is one to which an individual relates himself as a member or to which he aspires to relate himself psychologically. One does not have to belong to it for it to be a reference group so long as one aspires to be part of it and sees reward therein. The importance of this concept is twofold for our purposes. First, attitudes, values, and norms have a major source in one's reference group; that is, one looks to the reference group for how to feel, believe, and act. The reference group, therefore, has great influence on members. It provides major anchorage in self-identity, levels of aspiration (personal goals), judgments, and concepts of what is right and what is wrong.

One's anchorage contributes materially and at all times decisively to the way one organizes experience and behavior. Reference groups are one's major anchorages, which means that one's ego attitudes are formed in relation to the standards or assumed standards of reference groups. However, the flow is not in one direction only. A person chooses his reference group because its value system is compatible with his own and because in some way he sees it as meeting his needs. Reference groups are usually considered to be a positive influence but they also can be negative in two ways. One can know that one does not wish to be identified with a certain group and hence reject all of its values. If a youngster does not like the influential and favored clique in high school, the one the principal prefers, he may reject completely all that the group does and values. He may then join a deviant or antisocial reference group. In this sense, the reference group guides one in what not to value or what to eschew.

The second important feature of the reference group concept is that one selects a reference group, consciously or unconsciously, because it meets one's needs; it gives something important to the individual. This has several notable aspects. It explains why some people join deviant groups and conform to their antisocial values even when these values conflict with those they might have held previously or privately. For example, a boy may join a gang because it accepts him and gives him a sense of belonging, an experience which he may not have had before from family, peer groups, or schoolmates. He sells out his own values for the psychological rewards the group affords. On the other side, many social agencies, religious groups, and school groups have little or no influence on the values, norms, and behaviors of their members precisely because they give nothing that is felt to be meaningful by the participants. For a group to have real influence it must be significant; for a worker to have influence he must be significant. Significant means that it or he meets the basic needs of the members. Hartshorne and May demonstrated this fifty years ago, but the importance of these factors often seems to be neglected in practice today.

A peripheral factor to be mentioned is that when one studies groups in the laboratory, such groups are not reference groups and, consequently, it is a mistake to extrapolate the findings to real groups that have cohesion and permanence.

For a worker or group to have significance thus differentiates momentary or situational influence from the lasting impact of a reference group. A person is influenced by any group in which he is interacting. As an individual moves from one group to another he reacts to the demands, pressures, and rewards of each different group situation in terms of past experience, need priorities, values, and the kind of person he considers himself to be and his aspirations, that is, his goals and future orientation. He reacts, therefore, to the intensity of his belongingness in respect to past and present identifications and future goals for security, identity, status, adequacy, expression, and the like. He operates, of course, in response to values or goals that are outside of and beyond the immediate group situation.

How one relates in any group is a function of the social norms of one's reference group. This tends to become consistent and transcends momentary needs. When an individual who is identified with a reference group is participating as a member of another face-to-face group, his cognitive mapping of the immediate group will be in terms of his guideposts in his reference group.

However, as a group becomes significant to a member, the group standards are internalized and become part of one's superego. Many problems in social functioning can be traced to uncertainty and insecurity stemming from the lack of a stable anchorage in a reference group. This leaves one without a sense of personal identity and bereft of the security of guideposts. The marginal man, a familiar figure in our society, is one who is caught between conflicting referent groups, often none of which really provide for his needs. Moreover, many groups in our fragmented society are joined for social status, prestige, and as an antidote to loneliness and, therefore, are not reference groups.

People who are enmeshed in positions wherein they are subjected to conflicting or inconsistent demands, exhibit stress reactions. These are seen best in anomie, alienation, withdrawal, and psychological collapse. Some redefine their norms and sell out for whatever gains are available; some cop out; some become agitated and can proceed to open conflict; some retreat to symptoms which are either calls for help or solutions to alleviate stress. In all instances, the resultant behaviors are designed to reduce stress.

One of the greatest forces for change in attitude, values, and behavior is a change in reference group or perhaps the introduction into a reference group. The concepts that have been set forth in this section are of the utmost importance in formulating those methods called groupwork and group therapy.

The Significant Group in Groupwork

The desire for human closeness is innate and its achievement is essential for positive health and survival. It is rooted in the human animal's collective unconscious which began in the caves when survival of any individual was dependent upon being part of the group. It rests in the helplessness of the human infant at birth and its complete dependence upon others for continuation of life. It is built upon the obvious fact that all of our psychological needs are met through others and our self is essentially a social structure. Closeness is necessary because it is the only medium for validation and identity. In all probability it is also a learned value and hence its affirmation is reinforced.

People do need what other people have to offer and people are the resource through which human needs can be met. Healthy growth occurs when human closeness has made such need-meeting resources available and enabled the growing person to utilize them. Maladaptive behavior, stunted growth, failure to realize potential, and unhappiness result from a lack of closeness and, in turn, perpetuate the inability to achieve closeness. The problem of life is really the problem of intimacy. Many people are deprived of closeness in their primary families and have never felt that they belonged to the primary group. Many adults lack intimacy in their marital relationships and with their children. Many children are isolated in children's groups and in the classroom. Many teenage boys and girls feel alienated from human contacts. Youth seems to be saying that even in college and in communes it is difficult to get close to people. Those who prognosticate say that in the future society of superindustrialism, relationship and intimacy will be even more difficult to achieve than it is now. Men are able to reach the moon but seem to be unable to reach one another.

Anxiety, fear, the inability to risk, distorted communication, and the inability to reach out to others or accept the reaching out of others are attributable to the punishment experienced and perpetuated when the person reached out in his past. Ego function—which includes perception, memory, intelligence, judgment, reality-testing, and self-control—is limited also in growth potential by threats that one experienced in seeking favorable response and validation from significant others.

There is a deep and all-abiding yearning in everyone, unless it has been destroyed by tragic experiences, to mean something to some person or persons and to reciprocate. One wants to appear important in the eyes of others and to know that others care. Everyone wants to feel that it matters to someone whether he lives or dies, is happy or depressed, is pleased or pained, and, in turn, everyone wants to be of use and consequence to others. It is important to be missed and important to have someone who can be missed. The opposite of love is not hate; it is to be ignored. As unpleasant as hate may be, it is a relationship that confirms one's being, but to be ignored means that one just does not exist. The birth of a real self depends upon the look in the eyes of others, the softness of their touch, and the warmth of their feelings toward one. People learn how to love by being loved. They learn how to care by being cared for and if one does not have that experience it is difficult, if at all possible, to acquire the capacity to be close with people.

48

It is a misuse of words to speak of falling in love. People do not fall in love, they grow into love. As Carl Sandburg said so well in his poem "At a Window":

. . . .
Give me hunger, pain and want,
Shut me out with shame and failure
From your doors of gold and fame,
Give me your shabbiest, weariest hunger!

But leave me a little love,
A voice to speak to me in the day end,
A hand to touch me in the dark room
Breaking the long loneliness.
. . . .
Let me go to the window,
Watch there the day-shapes of dusk
And wait and know the coming
Of a little love.

Since learning to care about others is learned through experience, the group in groupwork must be an experience in mutual caring if it is to fulfill the purpose of helping people to maximize their potential. In any helping relationship, the experience must be congruent with the purpose. In groupwork, the group—the member-to-member and member-to-worker interactions—must become experiences in closeness and mutual aid. Interaction means mutual or reciprocal influence; people act upon each other and become part of each other.

Distance and closeness are affected by the degree to which group members reveal themselves to each other. The ability to share affect with others is the *sine qua non* of social competence and also of personal need-meeting. Such an experience is possible, as we shall see, if trust has been established and authoritarian control has been minimized.

From what has been said so far, one can deduce that there are three basic skills that must be learned for one to live in the world as it is and is becoming. These are to learn how to relate oneself to others (relate is a reciprocal verb). It means and includes making and maintaining rewarding human connections, mutual need-meeting, and communicating. A second skill is the capacity to choose. The very essence of adaptation involves the making of successive choices. Decision-making rests upon the ability to make choices and to see the relationship among goals (values), means, and end results. The third skill is the essence of ego functioning. It is learning how to learn. This includes reality-testing, value-testing, and coping. These three basic skills should be the syllabus for groupwork in the group-serving agency. They form the trinity for informal education.

The salient point about emotional disturbance and social malfunction is alienation, which is a derangement of social (interpersonal) relationships. The primary index of mental health is the capacity to form relationships with others. A healthy person responds freely and engages actively in transactions. He enjoys close relationships and acknowledges that he needs them. He belongs and participates in group activities. He recognizes his interdependence with others and is capable of love and compassion.

The functional objective of group treatment is the provision and restoration of a person's capacity to enter into relationships. The person must be helped to free himself from the conflicts of the past and to assume responsibility for himself and others. The groupworker's function is to facilitate conditions in which this can happen. He seeks to encourage the person to risk relationships with others, to cooperate, and to find security with others instead of in alienation.

This book is about how the worker proceeds to accomplish these end results.

Two record excerpts follow; the first illustrating the importance of group acceptance to a person. In it Walter tries to buy friendship. In the second record, Bruce learns that people care.

An Illustration of the Importance to a Person of Group Acceptance

AGE: Eleven
SETTING: Community Center
SESSION: Tenth

Walter is a boy who apparently has been unable to establish close and satisfying peer relationships. He is the eldest son living at home. He has a sister ten and a brother four. He told me once that he spends most of his time reading and plays with his brother a great deal of the time because he is not allowed out of the house. His father seemed to be very concerned that if he allowed Walter to mix with boys his own age he might get into some kind of trouble. Walter has a history of being easily bullied by other boys at school and for a while his lunch money was being taken by some boys for "protection." He attends a different school than the other boys and has been referred to the Community Center by the school because "he needs friends."

Since the club had already voted to limit their membership to fourteen, it was necessary for me to work with them in gaining entrance and acceptance for Walter as a new member. This was accomplished, objections being raised principally by Leo on the grounds that the club was too large already.

The first meeting that Walter attended, the boys were decorating the center's Christmas tree. Walter pitched right in and worked with Lark and Roger in putting the tree up. He told me later on that night that he had enjoyed himself and that he thought, "These are a nice bunch of guys." The boys played a little game of basketball before they left. Walter, Kerry, and I watched. Walter said he didn't know how to play but showed some interest in learning how. He commented on how good a player Frank was.

The following week, Walter came into the center with a cake which he said he had baked himself and had brought to the club so that the fellows could have a little party. The boys had planned to have a brief meeting and then go to a dance which was being given by a girls' club at the center. Those who were not interested in going to the dance were to go upstairs and play some basketball. Later on Al, Alex, Terry, Walter, and I ended up playing a game of "Clue" and eating the cake, which was heartily welcomed by these three boys. The following week the boys had decided to just have the punch, which was provided by the center, for the refreshments at their Christmas party. Walter came in with two half-gallons of ice cream. I asked him why he had decided to bring some ice cream and he said that he thought it would be nicer to have something more than just punch. Later on, Walter and Frank pooled their money and went out and bought some cookies. I made comments in front of the others twice as to how nice it was of Walter to bring this ice cream on his own, but I did not hear any comments of appreciation from the others.

An Illustration Regarding Closeness

AGE: Latency
SETTING: Treatment Center
SESSION: Eighth

The boys had continued meeting during November and December and had made plans for Christmas. As a group they voted to exchange gifts, the names to be chosen from a hat box. Everyone was anxious to pick Mike's name, least anxious to pick Peter and Bob. Joel, Scott, and Bruce had similar status in the group. The boys were planning their activities a little more thoroughly now, participating with each other to a greater degree. Peter was trying to form a tentative relationship with one member or another by inviting them to play "Xs and Os" on the board with him. Bob usually agrees to play with him but receives more satisfaction from playing Monopoly with Bruce. Bruce's aggression continues to come out sporadically. For the past three weeks it has been mildly controlled. Mike has been talking of leaving the group after Christmas. He was quite positive that he could get along outside of the club and told the others that although he would miss them he thought he was ready to leave the club now. This initiated a discussion as to what constituted being ready to leave the group.

Mike thought he would leave the club because the kids always argued, played rough, had no rules, and didn't listen to ideas, whereas he liked order and rules and thought you could talk things out rather than push your own ideas. The worker wondered how the others felt about Mike's statement. Strangely, no one questioned its validity. Scott said that he didn't feel ready to leave just yet because he still felt "funny" about outside kids, but here the boys were his friends and he knew even if he bossed them, they liked him. In fact, he had a new motto for himself, "I will try to do my best to help myself and cheat the rest." This evoked laughter with Bob saying he bet Scotty did feel this way. Scott said that he knew he shouldn't but he guessed he did. The worker said that maybe he thought he shouldn't because of the way we were told we had to feel about other people, nice and kind and all that, but that actually most of us felt two ways about people, we liked them and disliked them just as we liked some things about ourselves and disliked others. Scotty said yeah, he disliked plenty about himself. Like someday he wanted to be a research chemist but he knew he couldn't because he wasn't always smooth and polished like guys were supposed to be, like his dad was sometimes. He then said with a look of surprise, "You know, most of the time my dad looks smooth but I know he tries to fool people. I wish he wouldn't do that. I wish he would just be honest like a research chemist." The worker believes that Scott senses the false standards held by his parents and the *Death of a Salesman* attitude which his father exemplifies. The worker believes that Scotty is trying to find standards for himself. He is sensitive and knows that these exist. He is beginning to see the differences between his own standards and those of his parents in a more realistic manner. The worker said that sometimes we didn't appreciate our own worth. Being honest with ourselves was just as important as being honest with others. Scott thought that he didn't really believe his ditty. He only said it to see what kids would say and to cover how scared he felt. Bob interrupted him to say that he felt Scott could be what he wanted to because kids really like him. The worker wondered whether Bob felt that kids did not like him, when Joel in his halting manner said, "We like you too." Bob hung his head saying, "I wondered if you do." Mike added, "Why shouldn't we?" Bob said, " 'Cause I'm always bossing you around and I laugh at you when you do things wrong." The worker said we seem to enjoy finding fault with ourselves and others, but how about the good things? Scott and Bob talked of the good things about Mike—his fairness, his good fun, Scott liked Bob's sharing and his being so kind to the others. All agreed to this, even Bruce. Bob thought Scott "just swell" but also liked Bruce's ability to do things and play good games and the way Joel did things like climb on the ladder. Bruce looked both depressed and thoughtful now and said, "Gee, I didn't know any of you cared." The worker asked,

"About what?" and Bruce said about us kids and what we do. Scott looking agitated said he guessed he didn't like Peter (Peter left early). To the worker's "Why?" Bob said, " 'Cause he is a kind of funny kid, different." Mike thought maybe we didn't understand him and worker thought maybe this was true. To the worker's "What seems different about him?" the boys said, "He's touchy with kids, he thinks he's a martyr." To the worker's "Do you think he thinks this on purpose?" they answered, "No, we don't know what he thinks, but he sure is funny." The worker admitted that Peter was a bit different—like he didn't trust us. Maybe we needed to try harder to understand him, to show him we care about him too. The worker wondered how we could do this and Mike said, "We could let him act a little silly and still play in our games." "But he never wants to," said Bob. The worker thought that he might need more encouragement than is now given and the boys talked about ways of encouraging Peter to be one of them.

How to Conceptualize About a Group

There are various ways to conceptualize about a group of people. It can be thought of as an environment or a milieu. In such a conception, the group surrounds the member and impinges upon him. It may be true that anything that is external to a person's epidermis is environmental, but this view places a member *in* a group rather than *of* a group and it does not include in its purview the important point that the other members become part of the person and the group also is internalized by each member.

Viewing the group as a milieu allows one to suggest that the group in groupwork can be a microcosm of an accepting social environment in which to experiment with social relationships. The member is free to interact with the environment, test himself and also test reality. An accepting environment helps to mobilize latent strengths, to reinforce them through rewards, and to foster adjustment to role demands and expectations. Such an environment helps a member to accept certain desirable social values and hence there is a connotation of influence to change, that is, one can be changed by inputs from the group environment. In concepts such as these, the use of the word intervention seems appropriate to describe what a social worker does.

Webster's Third New International Dictionary defines *intervene* as "to enter or appear as an irrelevant or extraneous feature or circumstance; to come in or between by way of hindrance or modification; to occur or lie between two things. . . ."[12] The group and the members must be perceived as separate and discrete in this use of the word intervention. This is the implication in the social work phrase "person-in-the situation." But the person and the group are not separate and discrete, nor is the human group a situation. It is a system, a structure of relationships and a process.

Mead wrote, "If mind is socially constituted, then the field or locus of any given individual mind must extend as far as the social activity or apparatus of social relations which constitutes it extends; and hence that field cannot be bounded by the skin of the individual organism to which it belongs."[13] Gardner Murphy states the concept as, "I have believed for a long time that human nature is a reciprocity of what is inside the skin and what is outside; that it is definitely not rolled up inside us but is our way of being one with our fellows and our world. I call this field theory."[14]

In a social system, a person and his environment are of one piece; the outline of a person is the inline of the group; the worker can facilitate a matching of the person and the environment which maximizes transactions between them that nourish both. He can help both to keep the line that bounds them contiguous and encourage the processes of input and output from each to the other to be free flowing and healthful for both.

The concept which the student of groupwork must understand is that every organism that is to come to full fruition must be embedded in its soil. A person cannot be helped to grow and mature by emphasizing his separation from his surrounding world. Practice must rest upon the reality of the interconnections of man and his environment. A person and his society are halves of a whole and are what they are in relation to one another. The parts are interdependent, ecologically and systemically. Each nourishes the other if life-sustaining processes which interchange the need-meeting ingredients between them function properly.

It is possible to view the group in social work as a tool and I have been guilty of using that concept in previous writings. The tool concept means that since a group has influence on members, it could be used as an instrument to change people. The concept, as such, is an acceptable one but it has deteriorated into a manipulative device rather than an enabling one. It connotes control rather than freedom.

It is possible to speak of the group as a unit. Unit means "a single thing or person or group that is a constituent and isolatable part of some more inclusive whole. It is a member of an aggregate, that is, the least part to have clearly definable separate existence and that normally forms a basic element of organization within the aggregate."[15] Groups do have boundaries and their own organization. In addition to boundaries, groups have goals, values, norms, group cultures, internal structures and organization. As part of internal organization, groups are said to have three networks.[16] They have networks of affective relations, which means that some people are attracted more or less to others and can enjoy them or work better with them. Cohesion in a group is a function of how attractive the group is to its members as compared with how attractive things or people other than the group are. Groups have networks of communication patterns of who talks to whom, about what, and in what manner. Groups have networks of relationships centered around such concepts as power, status, position, role, and the like; and these are the components of group structure. Also, there are three main themes in a group's existence. These are: a cultural theme which defines values, beliefs, and patterns of behaving; a program theme which exposes members to a variety of learning experiences; and the emotional theme which is the psychic interaction from whence comes self-image, self-and-other perceptions, basic meeting of needs, support, and the internalization of others into oneself.

Finally, the group can be conceptualized as a social system. This will be discussed in detail in Chapter 5. A social system functions within certain imperatives. These are also essential aspects of any group, namely: a social system is made up of structured relationships which endure over time, one of which is the complementarity of roles; there are commonly held values; the members are motivated to keep the system surviving; there are system goals; there is a means of attaching the parts of the system to each other; there is some degree of tension; and the members perceive that the system meets basic needs, real or imagined. A systems designation assumes structure and stability within a given period of time. A social system is not a collection of individuals but a set of relationships between and among people. A group is all of the things described: a milieu, an instrument or modality, a unit, a structure, and a system.

A social group operates on two levels, the external which is organized and interrelated on the basis of content, rationality, and task; and the internal which is organized on the basis of the relationships between people. In this book a group is conceptualized as a social system and, as such, it is a structure and a process. It is also a subsystem of the larger system of its impinging environment and the suprasystem for its members.

We will now turn to how groups are composed.

NOTES / READINGS

1. Dennis Bloodworth, *An Eye for the Dragon* (New York: Farrar, Straus and Giroux, 1970).

2. Kurt H. Wolff, *The Sociology of Georg Simmel* (New York: The Free Press, 1951). For a review of the origins of small group theory, see Edward A. Shils, "The Study of the Primary Group" in Daniel Lerner and Harold Lasswell, eds., *The Policy Sciences* (Stanford: Stanford University Press, 1951), pp. 41–69.

3. Charles H. Cooley, *Social Organizations, A Study of the Larger Mind* (New York: Scribners, 1909).

4. Saul Schledlinger, Marion Sloan, S. R. Slavson, K. T. Wiltse and J. Fixel, Gertrude Wilson, and others.

5. Alan F. Klein, *Social Work Through Group Process* (Albany, New York: School of Social Welfare, State University of New York at Albany, 1970), p. 50.

6. Kermit T. Wiltse and Justine Fixel, *The Use of Groups in Public Welfare* (San Diego: California State Department of Social Welfare, September, 1962), p. 9.

7. S. R. Slavson, *The Fields of Group Psychotherapy* (New York: International Universities Press, Inc., 1956), p. 8.

8. November 1, 1963, National Association of Social Workers.

9. See Alvin Toffler's. *Future Shock* (New York: Random House, 1970), p. 140. Toffler discusses an idea he credits Dr. Herbert Gerjuoy with called "situational grouping" which he says sounds obvious once it is described but that it has never been systematically exploited. He calls "situational grouping" groups for people who happen to be passing through similar life transitions at the same time, i.e., families in relocation, parents without partners, those who have just moved into a community, or those facing imminent retirement. Like so many social scientists who are ignorant of social groupwork, an idea is said to be new if they have not heard of it. Such so-called "situational groups" have been stock in group services for a long time. Nevertheless, the idea is still valuable in the context of this section.

10. "Our best generalization at present seems to be that anyone bound to a small group by common goals and shared values may be provided with one element of protection against mental illness, no matter what kinds of stresses he must endure." Elaine Cummings, "Unsolved Problems of Prevention," *Canada's Mental Health*, LVI, Supplement (January–April, 1968), Department of National Health and Welfare, Ottawa, Canada, p. 12.

11. Harold H. Weissman, ed., *Individual and Group Services in the Mobilization for Youth Experience* (New York: Association Press, 1969).

12. *Webster's Third New International Dictionary* (unabridged), 1961.

13. A. Straus, ed., *The Social Psychology of George Herbert Mead* (Chicago: Phoenix, 1956), p. 257n.

14. Gardner Murphy, *Human Potentialities* (New York: Basic Books, 1958), p. viii.

15. *Webster's Third New International Dictionary* (unabridged), 1961.

16. Michael Olmstead, *The Small Group* (New York: Random House, 1959).

2

❖❖❖❖❖❖❖❖❖

A Group Begins

Groups with which one works in group-services programs are usually either natural or formed. Natural groups are those which are made up of friends. They are usually psyche groups—peer groups, gangs, and the like. They form by natural processes around a nucleus of kindred spirits. Formed groups, as the name implies, are formed by someone for a specific purpose. However, natural groups also form; they just do not come into existence full-blown. It is one of the functions of a groupworker to help groups form.

Natural groups may be said to have formed when a bond develops among the members to each other and also to a collective entity with which each identifies enough to refer to it as "my group" or "our group." When the persons so refer to themselves and to each other, a bond is being established and the members also are defining a boundary which separates the group from its surroundings. Two things then are evident as criteria for group formation: bond and boundary. In the latter, the members select and accept those who will be included. Bond may come into being because of affectional ties of attraction, because of mutuality of interest and goals, because of commonality of values and beliefs, as a means of defense against an external aggressor, because the members select one person as a love object or ideal, through psychological symbiosis, or out of a deep sense of being in the same boat. For bond to be possible, the members must have some social hunger, a desire to relate themselves to others.

The purpose or goals around which bond develops may be either overt and stated or covert. Examples of covert goals are the sanctioned release of aggression, escape, a leave of absence from reality or superego, and others. As we have seen, the establishment of bond, purpose, values, and boundaries is almost simultaneous with the formation of group structure. The presence of these elements indicates that a group is forming. Encouraging the development of these elements is the way a groupworker helps a group to form. For a groupworker to be effective in helping a group to form he must know about group dynamics, styles of organization, personal needs, generalized knowledge about that type of group, and knowledge of the culture and environment. All of these things are important but if he does not know himself he will not be effective.

Principles for Composing a Group

It is one of the functions of a groupworker to compose groups. There are almost as many ideas about group composition as there are authors in groupwork. The paucity of documentation about the effectiveness of various approaches in the selection of members is startling when the importance of this question is realized.

As a first and most important principle, how one composes a group depends upon the purpose. Many of the rules of thumb or the generalizations about composition in groupwork have been borrowed from the literature of psychotherapy or sociometrics, and even this latter school of thought came out of the work of Morino, a psychotherapist. Sociometric choice—that is, who selects whom in the choosing of friends—is a splendid method when the purpose is to develop (1) friendship groups, (2) clubs in a group-serving center, (3) patrols in a scout troop, (4) work groups in a classroom, and the like.

There are serious dangers in using a sociogram to form treatment groups, developmental growth groups, committees, and groups designed to produce specified results. The reasons are that people who are prone to neurotic coalitions choose people who reinforce their own hangups, thus dysfunctioning people tend to form dysfunctional groups that perpetuate their own dysfunction. Developmental groups reject isolates who may need the group experience badly, they scapegoat, and they limit the growth of low-status members. Committees, on the other hand, need to place emphasis on the committee task and not on the meeting of interpersonal needs which can and often does weaken the energy output of the group. Also, it often produces decision-making that is based upon favoritism or friendship instead of the merits. These thing are operative in the task-production group but such a group also needs skill diversity which is not synonymous with friendship patterns or sociometric choices.

Other reasons could be listed that contraindicate the use of sociometric choice of membership for many of the types of groups with which we work. Two concrete illustrations may help us to see the problem. A training school for boys uses sociometrics to set up cottages, sleeping rooms, and work details. The institution is open and group centered. The boys themselves prevent eloping because the norms are that to elope causes the whole group to lose privileges and the member who runs breaks up the group. Phil is Jack's best friend and he knows that Jack is going out the window. He does not stop him because his loyalty and needs lie with the friendship, not with the group.

In a treatment group, Mrs. Albert wants to confront Mrs. Bernie with her secretive drinking and knows that she should. However, she is unable to do this because they are friends instead of being mutual aiders. (Your best friend will not tell you.)

The generalizations about grouping or composition which appear in the psychotherapy literature may offer some points of departure for thinking about grouping for groupwork, but the reader is cautioned against accepting them as principles. Social groupwork is not the same as group psychotherapy; this may be a hotly debated question in some circles but in this book they are not the same. Psychotherapy is the art or science of treating mental diseases or disorders. This professional function is the province of psychiatrists and some clinical psychologists. Social workers are engaged in social treatment.

Many reading this book will be involved in educational groupwork where the objectives are to promote positive personality growth and development, to teach role behaviors, to develop positive attitudes and values, and in some instances to foster religious or ethical ideologies. These are certainly not psychotherapy. While it is true that other practitioners who work in hospitals, clinics, or other treatment facilities work with people who have been diagnosed as disturbed, the function of the groupworker is to help people to be free to be and to become, and in these endeavors to find themselves, that is, to find identity. Groupworkers do not treat mental diseases and disorders.

When the purpose of a group is to help members to help each other because they have social problems, such as parents who have disturbed children, spouses of alcoholics, one parent absent, diabetics with the problem of controlling their eating, those with heart ailments which restrict normal activities and the like, demographic criteria are not important variables for grouping. Persons who are in pain because of such problems usually can relate and form groups where they are of both sexes, of wide difference in adult ages, of wide variance in educational levels, of different socioeconomic backgrounds, of different ethnic origins, and of different races.

A general principle is that there must be ability to communicate with each other, motivation to work on their problems, no behavior so bizarre as to frighten the others, and no wide differences that are personally or culturally beyond acceptance, such as a known prostitute in a group of ladies who would be appalled at this, or a black in a group of white supremacists.

The principle calls for a preliminary assessment of potential members. If persons are put into groups for which they are not suited, the experience can be harmful to the person, to other members, to the group, and also to the purpose of the group. The questions to be answered are: Will the person benefit from this group? Will he be able to participate? Will he interfere with the realization of the purpose of the group and the needs and purposes of others?

The group must be homogeneous enough to insure stability and heterogeneous enough to ensure vitality. There should be no extreme differences among the members. The more external to oneself or one's deep personal needs the group purpose lies, the more relevant demographic variables become in group composition. Generally speaking, therefore, demographic variables are not of prime importance in composing a group in a child guidance clinic, for example, but they are for a club, a sorority or fraternity where relationships are not based upon common problems. Also, people can come together around a disaster, a crisis, or an external threat with little regard for demographic variables. However, people seem not to want to live and play together with people who are very different from themselves.

Principles for Composing a Treatment Group

As a principle, demographic variables are not crucial in composing a treatment group. There are several principles that apply for treatment grouping.

1. *Compose the group so that there is homogeneity with regard to the developmental task.* Another way of conceptualizing this is to assess the stage in which social dysfunction (if any) arose. Erik Erikson's eight stages of man can provide groupworkers with viable scales for grouping. Basic developmental tasks, such as trust and autonomy, can be the foundation for homogeneity in grouping. For treatment groups, the scales are represented, for example, by behavioral manifestations that focus on lack of trust, conflict with authority, apathy and lack of motivation, doubt, shame, guilt, and absence or confusion of identity as in ego diffusion. Persons who are struggling at one level of ego development are not well suited

for mutual aid in a reciprocal fashion with persons who are struggling at another level.

2. *Compose the group so that there is heterogeneity of coping patterns and defenses.* This provides a range of behaviors, the variety of which stimulates a comparison and assessment of those behaviors exhibited. The variety opens the eyes of members to options, choices, and alternatives, and makes it possible to learn from one another and to see the misperceptions of another person even though one is blind to one's own. It demonstrates that one does not have to do anything in only one way because there are many ways to handle a problem. It also provides a vehicle for testing the consequences of different behaviors and probing the motivations that underlie the different patterns.

3. *Compose the group so that there is balance and at the same time so that it is weighted toward the positive.* Depending upon the age of the members, their problems and behaviors (and the purpose), a groupworker will select to scale the variables which he regards as the important ones upon which this group will work. Usually three scales are enough, although sometimes more are desirable. For example, the scales might be such as aggressive–passive in behaving toward authority, rigid–flexible as to allowing oneself to express one's feelings, self–punishing–punishing others. When placing the potential members on each of these three scales, the over-all weight on each scale should overbalance in favor of the direction which the worker perceives to be desirable. The group should be composed with the emphasis on strength.

Maloney and Mudgett use a concept of relevant-problem homogeneity such as rejection by parents, degree of internal controls, and amenability to external controls as scales for composing a group.[1]

William Shalinsky suggests a shyness–aggressive scale involving behavior toward others and ability to cope with behavior from others. He also refers to a scale of social skills, meaning the ability to get along with peers as a grouping method in a summer camp for children. In an article in which he laments what he calls practice wisdom in grouping and pleads for a systematic approach through the use of a tested, theoretical approach to composition, he presents three scales. These are the basic interpersonal-need areas of affection, control, and inclusion. Shalinsky seeks groups of compatible members, by which he means relations that lead to the mutual satisfaction of interpersonal needs and to harmonious coexistence.[2]

He assumes that groups of compatible members will perform better than groups of incompatible members because of the greater satisfaction of interpersonal needs. His study is worth noting. His first hypothesis was that more members in groups of compatible members will like each other than would members in groups of incompatible members. His second hypothesis was that groups of compatible members will be seen as more attractive by those members than would groups of incompatible members. Hypothesis three predicated that groups of compatible members will show more co-operative behavior among the members than would groups of incompatible members. Finally, he guessed that groups of compatible members would be more productive in competitive tasks than groups of incompatible members. The study does illustrate how one can utilize scales that the worker considers to be relevant for the kind of group he wishes to compose.

While the study is useful from that point of view, the reader is cautioned against using Shalinsky's conclusions for composing all groups or any groups that do not fit the goals he had for his groups. His goals may be suitable for cabin groups at camp, clubs in traditional youth-serving settings, teams in competitions, or production-oriented groups. They are less appropriate for my conception of social groupwork, especially when we note that many of our members have problems in interpersonal relations and social incompetence is one of the problems for which they come for help. Many of the same weaknesses inherent in sociometric grouping apply to Shalinsky's assumptions. Of special concern is the scaling with regard to control because often some members need to control and others need to be controlled, a very familiar game that is played in many "compatible" groups.

The distance between extremes on any one scale should never be so great as to predict that a person will be an isolate, be regarded as bizarre, be too frightening to those at the other end of the scale, or create deep schisms.

4. *Compose the group so that there will be both stimulus for interaction and movement toward change in behavior.* An example of this is to group several very active members with others who are quiet and passive and, in reverse, several passive catalysts in groups of actors. Compose it so that there are role models such as placing several people with positive social values about stealing with those who are thieves. Avoid grouping by labels or by diagnostic categories.

5. *Compose the group so that levels of remission are not very different.* This refers to the degree of appropriate social functioning or malfunctioning of each potential member. In treatment settings, the criteria include the abatement of symptoms and closeness to reality. In nontreatment settings, the criteria include successful coping and adaptation, indicia of the strength of ego-functioning, levels

of deviance, the ability to form meaningful relationships, and degrees of alienation and loss of self.

6. *Assess and predict the probable role behaviors one can expect each potential member to enact.* This principle makes it possible to try to provide the roles necessary for group maintenance, to avoid major role conflicts, and to minimize injury to members due to assignment of roles that support maladaptive behavior. It allows the worker to try to avoid introducing members who will reinforce harmful behaviors in others or develop symbiotic coalitions. Experienced groupworkers also try to predict the possible role behaviors that may result from the group experience so as to anticipate future interactional patterns and their effects upon the outcomes relative to purpose.

7. *Avoid bringing people into a group when their behavior will be palpably ego-alien to any other member,* that is, excite another unduly, raise anxiety excessively, or trigger a breakthrough of their repressions to their detriment or the detriment of the group and its purposes.

8. *For groupwork to be a treatment of choice, the members must have some degree of social hunger.* Social hunger connotes the desire to be with other people and to relate oneself to them in the group. It is the motivation to invest oneself in the group. If there is no desire to interact with others, to gain favorable response, or if individuals fear people so much that social hunger is absent, the main influence and value of a group experience is lost and groupwork is not a treatment of choice.

9. *For groupwork to be indicated, potential members must be able to communicate with others in the group in a meaningful way.* (It is impossible not to communicate.) Successful or meaningful communication is that process which, through exchange of messages, leads to the establishment of correspondence of information between two or more people. It is the channel or medium for interaction between and among people and the way in which people relate, influence, meet needs and become part of each other. If one is unable to communicate with some degree of fidelity, whether because of faulty transmission, hearing, or interpreting, he will be unable to become part of and function within a group. This is not to say that people with communication problems are not suitable candidates for groupwork, but that people who are unable to communicate are closed off from others and have no media for interaction in a group or for involvement in the group process. Group treatment is not a form of therapy for the acutely ill.

As a general criterion, one applies the principle of purpose—that is, can the purpose be achieved in this group?

Age and Sex as Determinants for Grouping

In adult groups which are formed for treatment purposes, age is not usually a very important variable, but there are exceptions. An obvious exception is the Golden Age or geriatric group. In this instance the range is sixty-five and up. Other exceptions are the young marrieds, premarital counseling, and young adult groups. In the case of parents, age per se is not the factor, but the age of the troubled child is because parents find it difficult to relate if the ages of the children being discussed differ widely.

Sex is usually not a variable to reckon with in composing adult groups. Age and sex are important when forming children's groups. In general, groupwork is not a strategy of choice for children younger than eight or nine. Children who are younger (their maturity age, not chronological age) do not develop relationships with peers that have much continuity or permanence. Their relationships tend to be momentary and for the immediate interest. The grouping age follows the final stages of the oedipal resolution in psychosocial terms, or the initiative stage. Grouping with one's kind is said to result at this time as an essential response to the need for allies.

The age span which is recommended for children is a difference of two years between the oldest in the group and the youngest. This generalization changes at pre-teen where one identifies the "tweeners," those whose development is still quite childish in that they have not begun to enter adolescence. These children should not be grouped with those whose interests have become heterosexual. By like token, adolescents who have not resolved the problems associated with that stage should not be grouped with the maturing young adult.

Coeducational groups are not recommended for children where the purpose of the group is either developmental or treatment oriented. One must learn to relate to and cope with people who are similar to oneself before being ready to handle those who are different. Consequently, the principle is that boys must be comfortable with other boys before they are ready to learn to relate intimately with girls and vice versa. Obviously, some adolescents are ready for coeducation and some are not.

I have been discussing composition from the standpoint of preferabilities. Many practitioners work in settings where the number of potential group members is either not large enough or the range is too limited to have the kind of choices one might like. When these conditions exist, one does the best one can but even so one should never group to support malfunctioning or to the detriment of any member.

The Number of Members

Optimum size is determined in relation to the nature of the interaction desired. The smaller the group the more it demands involvement and the greater is its potential for intimacy. The smaller the group the greater are the group pressures, the easier is the access to the worker and to each other, and also the greater is the flexibility in modifying goals. As size increases, the potential for combinations of interaction increases geometrically.

Larger groups allow greater anonymity and hence a person can hide, withdraw, or get lost in the group. The larger the group the more formal the structure becomes, the more fragmentation into subgroups occurs, the more formal leadership patterns evolve, the more reliance there is on parliamentary procedures, and the more communication patterns become star-shaped rather than a totally connected network where each member is linked directly with every other member. The larger the group is, the less the members know each other and the less the worker can know them.

However, young people need experiences in large groups as well as in small ones. Large groups are necessary also where organizations have the need for many workers, diversification of functions, and multivarious representations within them. The larger the group the more difficult it is to achieve participatory democracy but it is not impossible. It is possible to utilize group methods with large groups and it is also possible to utilize groupwork principles.

It is difficult to work effectively when the group is too small. While the figure five to seven is often given as ideal, such groups almost require that everyone attend regularly. For general purposes, the number can be larger and developmental groups of fifteen are viable while some treatment groups of nine or ten can be very comfortable. Parents' groups, and other groups that meet once a week and must travel to the center should be larger to compensate for the usual absences.

One finds repeated reference in the literature to the numbers being uneven to forestall tie votes. This is an unfortunate misapplication of cultural mores about groups to groupwork where one seeks cooperation and mutual aid instead of the usual polarity and decisions based upon numbers and power. Majority rule is a political modality and has no relevance to treatment climates. The shortcoming of majority rule is that it does not foster a pluralistic democracy wherein the needs of the minority members are safeguarded. Outvoted minorities (the scapegoat, the isolate, the least chosen, the most needful) are unable to have their needs met and they are forced to accept crumbs, or resort to despair or disruption. This is verifiable in developmental groups as well as in treatment groups. When groups are composed as has been suggested above, the question of odd or even numbers should not arise.

Procedure for Grouping

Where it is possible or can be made possible, the worker should see each prospective member before selection. This might be thought of as intake, although the term is used usually to mean becoming a member of the agency or being taken into the agency for service.

The reasons for using such an intake interview are manifold: to acquaint the prospective member with the purposes of the group and why he is being asked to participate; to allow the prospect to voice anxieties or other feelings about group service and to ask questions; to begin to develop a contract; to begin to establish a relationship with the worker; to have a person with whom he is familiar the first time he comes to the group meeting; to know something about what to expect; and to be free to refuse or accept the offer.

The groupworker has an opportunity to begin to know (study) the prospective member and to assess his interpersonal reactions with a person perceived to be an authority figure; to have a beginning awareness of the prospect's modes, defenses, and possible role behaviors; to interpret the group and the service; to explore the prospect's anxieties and reservations about group services; and to prepare the prospect for the first meeting. This contact should be made by the groupworker and not left to a caseworker who may be referring the person for groupwork.

There are many instances where intake should be done through an intake or diagnostic group. Such groups provide the groupworker with an opportunity to observe and study the prospective members as they really behave in their interpersonal relations, how they cope in reality situations, and what roles they assume. It provides the worker with the specific information which we have been discussing as useful for composing a group. Intake or diagnostic groups are not composed according to the principles outlined above. They are random and unstructured. In such situations where there is no direction, no stated purposes, and no structure, anxiety and anger are generated quickly thereby stimulating reactions that disclose the members' modes of adaptation under stress. This, of course, provides a wealth of firsthand information (with less distortion) which might take weeks or longer to educe in an interview situation. Such a procedure is the basis for a relevant study in the here-and-now in a reality-based situation.

Diagnostic groups are short term and are used to help determine a person's suitability for group service and, if so, for which group and which fellow group members.

Having composed the group, we turn now to how a group begins to develop.

How a Group Begins to Develop

Group Process

Group processes are initiated as soon as people convene to do something together. A process is a series of actions and operations definitely conducting to an end or ends. Group process is that constellation of actions, interactions, and decisions whereby a group moves from one state of being to another. When people come together for the first time, there are immediate reactions of attraction and repulsion. Basically, each person wishes to engage himself with others. He seeks object relations or closeness. He wants to know others and to be known. He wants to touch and to be touched psychologically.

His view of the initial encounter in a group is based upon security, for he will join the group if security seems to be in the offing. However, his response to the others in the group will be influenced by transference—that is, of whom and of what each other person reminds him, his past experiences with others of either punishment or satisfaction—and by his perception of the realities in the immediate situation. His first response to all of these various factors will be one of testing to trust or mistrust. Because each person in the group will be in approximately the same emotional state, the group culture will be one of suspicion, caution, random testing, probing and withdrawal. One should expect this to be the climate in a group which is beginning and anticipate that the behavior of the members will be in response to anxiety and fear about security or trust. Persons wo have no such anxiety or who are willing to reveal themselves immediately to the others may be said to be unrealistic or unusually undefended.

On the other hand, the more immature the persons are (that is, the more they are fixated in the earliest stages of development or regressed to them), the more one can expect mistrust to be a group theme for many weeks. The same may be said of persons who have been traumatized by a grossly depriving social environment and whose experiences have conditioned them to mistrust. Why should anyone be willing to reveal himself, his weaknesses and problems, and lay himself open to attack, exploitation, or unfavorable response from strangers upon casual acquaintance? Why would anyone disclose himself to a groupworker merely because he is designated "worker"? In the beginning, the member or client must, if he is at all cognizant of reality, test and seek to confirm trust. This significant factor which has been affirmed by Garland, Jones, and Kolodny explains behaviors observed in groups when they are beginning such as random, noisy, withdrawn, tentative, seeking structure, and so forth.[3]

There is a difference of opinion among competent authorities about the sequence in the group process. Some believe, for example, that positions stabilize first; others think group norms are the forerunners of structure; and several believe that the first consideration is the formulation of goals. The question of which emerges first is usually dependent upon why the group formed and the homogeneity of the composition. When the members are drawn together because they believe alike or come from the same social and cultural strata, probably values and norms show first. When the group is formed around tasks, probably goals come first. But when persons are brought together for help with problems of social competence, it is probable that the phases will more readily follow ego states such as trust, autonomy, purpose, industry, and identity. We will look at these various possibilities and the probable emphases in the group processes.

It is my thesis that the quest for security and the heightened anxiety which is caused by the fear of closeness creates a demand for structure. Structure is not only an organizational medium which provides for division of labor and facilitates the development of internal machinery for conducting the business of the group, but it also provides known channels for interpersonal relations.

It is probable that most groups move to structure very quickly. This can be a serious barrier to social work in the group because it sets up differential access to resources, control over persons, status within which some people can meet their needs (often at the expense of others), influence which tips the balance in decision-making, and also can reinforce neurotic and other pathological problems of the persons involved. Positions probably emerge first because some members feel a need to exert control over others and validate themselves by becoming leaders, some feel a need to be controlled and hence support leaders, and some validate their own low self-images by gravitating to the foot of the social ladder.

In the early stage, the nature of the tasks undertaken and the immediately perceivable characteristics of persons are more influential in determining status and the trends of group process; hence, those who talk more tend to be chosen as spokesmen or institutionalized leaders.

Writers of articles and books about group dynamics and group-work tend to look at and describe group process in accordance with their own theoretical orientations which predetermine what they see and how they interpret what they see.[4] Those who think of groups in structural terms are prone to see the emergence of structure; those interested in task are likely to emphasize this aspect of group life; and those who are steeped in psychology are quick to describe the psychological dynamics in group process. Theorists in social psychology and sociology seem to remain wedded to monolithic conceptualizations when analyzing group phenomena. Most articles on group development describe what happens in the group; few attempt to explain it. It is imperative that groupworkers see both the psychological and sociological aspects as part of one integrated process. These have been isolated and described separately for the convenience of the particular social scientists working in different disciplines. *The groupworker is not being asked here to put the different aspects of group process together. They are together in reality; he is being asked to stop taking them apart.*

To illustrate this very important point, let us return to the beginning phase of a group. The potential members who come together seek human contact. They want closeness and the experience of being able, with freedom, to relate to each other. The urgent desire for human closeness has been thwarted often in a person's past experience by punishment or rejection when he reached out to others. As a consequence, the act of approaching others has been coupled with fear, anxiety, and pain. It is learned that people are not to be trusted and groups are not trustworthy.

The underlying fears may seem odd when looked at consciously, but it is not difficult to relate them to experiences we all have had. For example, people fear being eaten or incorporated. This is not only a physical matter but it also means losing oneself by being ingested by others. People also fear devouring others and thereby losing them. There can be a fear of being excavated or emptied and also of excavating others; of being abandoned or of abandoning others; of being castrated or of castrating others. There is the fear of being destroyed or of destroying others and especially of destroying others whom one loves. The connotations here are that when one becomes close to others, the danger of these eventualities occurring becomes great. For example: "Whenever I love someone, I become vulnerable and I am consumed by them."

These underlying fears are unconscious or preconscious. They are, however, learned. More obvious fears are: getting one's hand or face slapped when one reaches out, being rejected or snubbed, being ridiculed or laughed at, being made to feel inferior, being exploited, and being "put down." In psychological terms, we are talking about trust and hope; about shame, doubt, and guilt; about loss of self and lack of identity; about loneliness and alienation.

With these underlying themes in mind, we can begin to explain such behaviors in the beginning group as approach and orientation, as testing, as random behavior. These persons are seeking security and some answers to the unknown qualities of the new group; that is, they are testing for safety and for some routes to safety islands so that they can run to "home free" when risking tentative human relations. They probe for likely responses to different behaviors. These observable phenomena are not entirely conscious.

Values and norms do come to the fore early because to know the standards of behavior in a group affords security and lessens the risk. To reach some beginning agreement on values also opens the possibility for alliances with others and provides a bridge to interpersonal cooperation. For example: "If we believe alike, perhaps you will be favorable to me and less likely to hurt me." Agreement on values and norms provides a frame of reference for behavior and hence guidelines.

The early emergence of group goals which we will examine in more detail later has similar sources. The conscious determination of agreed-upon goals for the group permits any member to relate to any other with some assurance of acceptance based upon the assumption that they agree on going in the same direction together and also that they need each other to accomplish a group goal. It is easier for many people to relate to others around a goal or task than on an interpersonal basis. The ostensible goal is a means to reach others or a defense against having to be close to others.

Youth today resent the use of goals as a means of "making people." They are seeking more honesty in human relations and argue that perhaps it would be better to get instrumental goals out of the way quickly so that human relations are not used as means to ends but are the avowed end in themselves.

Group Goals as a Factor in Group Formation

The literature about groups tells us that group formation is a process by which people come together for an interacting experience directed toward some end. This is a socio-concept and the end that is emphasized is both a means for creating interacting experience and a result. In this way of looking at groups, goal is a prerequisite in group formation.

This concept is lamented by many psychologically oriented theorists because it epitomizes the impersonal nature of group life in America and highlights the fact that communities are composed primarily of task groups such as civic clubs, parent-teacher associations, chambers of commerce, taxpayers' groups, and the like. Also our schools foster such extracurricular groupings and our group-serving agencies have followed suit. There is a diminution of expressive groups in American society and this is a symptom of increasing alienation, of the growing impersonalization of a superindustrial society, of increased mistrust, and of fear of people.

One reads that members are attracted to groups because of overt conscious goals such as to learn skills, to achieve social change, to make friends, and the like. People are attracted to groups also, it is said, by implicit or unavowed goals such as the need to belong or to gain status. This latter idea can be generalized as: people join groups to meet their needs and these needs exist on a hierarchy of importance to different people.[5] It is also suggested that people are attracted to join groups because of unconscious personal goals such as identification, self-actualization, and so forth. These purposes can be classified as: immediate personal gratification, creation of conditions for personal gratification, pursuit of a common goal, provision of a situation in which people can set goals and pursue them, i.e., self-determination, and growth.

Inherent in these statements is a general definition of what constitutes a group goal. Mills writes, "What sets the concept of group goal apart is that in content and in substance it refers to the group as a unit—specifically to a desirable state of that unit. The concept resides in the minds of the individuals; the referent of the concept is the group as a whole."[6] Group formation is a social fact and rests upon the need in all societies to come together in groups because people perceive that if they participate in the achievement of a group goal their own personal goals will be more likely to be met than if they pursued them individually. A group goal, in this context, is a result of group effort which if achieved will help the individual members to meet their own personal goals in a way that they could not by themselves.[7]

The attraction of any member to a particular goal for the group may be expected to be influenced by individual motives, judgment of rewards and costs of involvement in the activities that are relevant to the goal, and one's subjective assessment of the probability that the group can and will attain the goal. It should be clear that the group goal is influenced materially by the social environment of the group and of each member. The group goal is, then, the group's product which emerges from the systemic inputs in interaction with what the members bring into the group with them—values, experiences, needs, and hopes. The group goal motivates and influences behavior. It creates tension and also it relieves tension. The degree of commitment to the group goal is the key to the effort and relevance of each member's involvement in the group and its activities.

A member will accept a group goal to the extent that his satisfaction is dependent upon the achievement of that group goal and to the extent that he predicts the probability of its achievement by the group since his satisfaction depends upon it. Those who have a clear picture of a group goal have close involvement in the group, are affected more by the group mood, and are more ready to accept the influence of the group.

These various social concepts which have been discussed above rely on some of the following explanations:

The primary group, the family, sets a behavioral prototype and by the process of socialization, teaches its offspring to value sociability and task achievement as interrelated. One result of this is that to participate in groups becomes an ego ideal in our society. The validity of this usually accepted premise is dubious as families are becoming less and less goal oriented, and also are losing much of their warmth and sociability. It would seem more in keeping with the facts to hypothesize that people are drawn to social groups as a substitute for what many modern families fail to provide.

Other reasons that one finds in the literature for why people form into groups include personal attraction (that is, because one likes the other people and also wants to be like them); as a prestige conveyer so that one's own prestige is enhanced; because the group task is suited to their interests; and for self-preservation as in such cases as gangs, labor unions, and welfare rights groups. Of course, all of these approaches are overlapping and blending.

There are manifest goals which are overt and latent goals which lie in unexpressed purposes. There are immediate or proximate goals and long-range goals. One must be aware also that while the members have personal goals, the agency has goals, the worker has goals and that sometimes these three are not congruent. Parenthetically, in social groupwork the goals of the members are given precedence.

When one speaks of the personal goals of each member, there is sometimes a semantic problem, but usually one means conscious achievements. However, personal goals that are conscious are steps to goals which are need-meeting and basic. To achieve conscious goals in some way satisfies self-validation and self-actualization. Conscious goals tend to be instrumental as they motivate behavior and help to reduce tension and achieve personal satisfaction.

Usually it is said that group effectiveness can be measured by an analysis of how well the group functions in reaching a collective goal. Inversely, ineffectiveness is measured in terms of the lack of an agreed-upon group goal and an inability to reach group goals. Effectiveness is said to be the extent to which a clear goal is present, the degree to which the goal motivates members to participate in activities, the degree of conflict or its absence among members, the degree to which members' activities are coordinated and appropriate to the group task, and the availability of necessary resources to the group.

All of this volume of information about group goals and group formation is good, as far as it goes, but it lacks the necessary synthesis for it to be useful for groupwork where the purpose is the growth of the members. They are less than useful for groups that are formed for specific purposes other than the fulfillment of tasks—that is, sociogroups.[8]

Let us, therefore, return to the thesis with which we began this discussion. People want and need to achieve intimacy and have learned in the process of seeking it to be afraid of other people. As they become part of a group they also resist becoming part of it in response to fear. People seek to find themselves and desperately hope to find "self" with the help of others. Conscious task-oriented goals can be means to these ends but they also can be defenses because they obscure the fear of people. One can look as if one is involved with others while working together toward a group goal and still be insulated from genuine personal contact.

Manifest group goals show themselves early in a group's life and can hide the common human yearning for personal relationships. A methodological question appears here and will reappear from time to time: Should the effective groupworker collude with the members and thereby reinforce their defense against intimacy? The answer depends upon the purpose of the group, and where the purpose is to help the members to grow and to find themselves, he should not enter into the collusion. It is easy to see how a failure to search out the dynamics of group life can lead the worker astray and can result in his observing the emergence of manifest group goals, group values and norms, and structure as the more important dimensions of group development. These are the natural events that occur even when an effective groupworker is not present. We subscribe to the inclusion of the groupworker to help the members be aware of and work on their real agenda; to understand that the agenda is interpersonal relations. In the beginning stage of a growth-oriented or treatment group, the immediate group goal should be the development of conditions that promote mutual trust among the members. We will return to this subject when we examine the third phase of group development in Chaper 5.

The following excerpt illustrates how a group fails to form until trust begins. When Anderson shows a willingness to reveal himself, the other members can risk more readily.

An Illustration of How a Group Materializes: The Development of Trust

AGE: Adults
SETTING: Child Guidance Center
SESSION: Fortieth

This excerpt is a record of an open group of middle-class fathers of emotionally disturbed children. River has been in the group several months, Mahler one month, Anderson six weeks, Lansing nine months, Wallace one year. The turning point comes when Anderson demonstrates the beginning of trust.

Mr. Wallace, during the course of the discussion in trying to bolster his point of view around the fact that the group was more or less impersonal, used the fact that there were times when he was not present and that he was fairly confident that he wasn't really missed and that the group proceeded anyhow, even though when he was there he did a great deal of talking and that perhaps it was even better when he stayed away. To this Mr. River, with a great deal of feeling, looked right at Mr. Wallace and said in a fairly strong and loud voice, "I miss you when you're not here and I can tell when you're not here. It makes for a difference in what we talk about. It's not that I don't get anything when you're not here, because I do but we talk about different things sometimes when you're not here." To this I summarized pointing out that there have been times when several of the men have been present with others absent and pointed out how just before the Christmas vacation when Mr. River and Mr. Mahler were present the topic under discussion was quite different and that the week preceding the three men who were present seemed to have some common feeling around the effect of treatment on other children in the family and that tonight we seemed to be dealing with an altogether different kind of concern. I pointed out that they seemed to be saying that discussing how they felt did not aid the group in its purpose but that some people in the group were regarded as more important than others and some they felt better about. I pointed out that this was something that I would expect to find in a group and that as we had talked they were able to recognize that it was with a great deal of feeling that they came to the group and that these feelings were not related specifically to the content; they had really an investment in each other as well as in the clinic.

Mr. Wallace again started off and reacted in a very surprised way to Mr. River's statement that he really had missed him and could see in looking back over his own participation in the group that he had similar feelings about people being present or not being present. Mr. Anderson too felt that there were differences in how he felt about other men in the group and that while he didn't want to talk specifically about which ones they were, he knew that this was so. He went on to say that, however, in spite of the differences most of his feeling was in a positive direction and he did like most or all of the men in the group. Mr. Mahler entered the discussion at this time trying hard to make a point; when I recognized him he said that he could now get an idea of what I had been driving at when I focused the discussion as I did on how people felt about each other in the group. He said that he can see where some of the feelings he has at times about contributing to the group or just listening are similar to how he thinks the children feel in wanting to get his attention at home. At home he says that now he's aware of the fact that he is very much a part of what the children are doing and that it isn't so much that he is the one who has to be right and there is no question about it beyond that point. I wondered how this would relate to the group and he said that here was a little bit different in that he wasn't in that position and that he was more like what the children were doing. I wondered how he could see this, for example, and his participation or lack of it in the group. Mr. Mahler said that he knows that at times he's quiet and wants very much to listen to what other men in the group have to say and that this helps him because first he wants to make sure that they might have some of the same feelings that he does before he ventures his own opinion and that at this point he feels enough similarity with other men in the group so that he doesn't have to wait every time for this to happen. He could sense some of the competition because when he first came into the group, he said it was sometimes very difficult to break into the discussion when he felt that it wasn't quite to the point or that he wanted to inject a comment or a question of his own and that at these times, he tries very hard to do so on his own, but then began to see that if he could look to me that I would help him in becoming more directly involved in the discussion. He, too, felt as Mr. Wallace did, that there are times when he participates by listening and this is a very important form of participation for him and that he has taken a great deal from it. He sees this as different from those times when he might withdraw from the situation at home and hide behind a newspaper and that really, here it doesn't represent running away or hiding, but rather that one plays a different part in the group.

I wondered if perhaps now we might begin to look at some of the other feelings that operated in the group. I wondered again whether there wasn't some competitiveness in the group and if they could recog-

nize where this came out. Mr. River needed to emphasize the point
that while he could accept the fact that there were many feelings that
each of them brought to the group, it wasn't nearly like the family
situation, in that things weren't "as emotional," and Mr. Wallace reiter-
ated his point about the impersonality of feeling. Mr. Wallace then
corrected himself and said that he wasn't trying to say that people
didn't really have an attachment to the group and have fairly strong
feelings about one another, but that it was different from the kinds
of situations in which one was involved at home and at work and
that he, and he felt all of the men in the group, knew where this
relationship ended. He said that one of the things that helped him
was to know that they did not see each other socially and that the
group was limited to Thursday nights to an hour and a half or so.
I accepted these points and added to them, pointing out that while
we might recognize that some similarity of feeling existed, that there
wasn't nearly the intensity, nor the degree of involvement that one
would expect in a family. I emphasized, too, the professional nature
of the relationship that while there were many personal feelings involved, the purpose for their being present in the group and the use
that was made of them was directed toward their goal in coming to
the clinic for help. I also pointed out that there were probably other
feelings that played a part in the group as well and mentioned briefly
some of the times when we could laugh together at things and how
the group had really begun to develop a humor which related to incidents
with which all of them were familiar, which made it sometimes difficult
for someone new to come in. I looked at Mr. Mahler for confirmation
on this and he said it had taken him about three or four weeks before he
began to catch on to some of the jokes that the men used and in particular
felt that Mr. River's concern with his daughter's piano playing had
very much helped in this regard. Just with the mention of the piano
playing Mr. River led the group in laughing, saying that he thought
for once this would not come up but could laugh at it when it did.
Mr. Lansing jokingly said that he wouldn't have let an evening go
by without bringing it up and was ready to do so had Mr. Mahler
not. Mr. River promised the group to let them know if there was any
change in their arrangement of Leslee for piano lessons, but at the
present time, everybody was quite pleased with her continuing.

Mr. Wallace then came back to the idea that there was competition
in the group and while they acknowledged that there might be, he
wasn't quite sure where it would come out in the clearest form. I asked
the general question of what they might be competing for and while
there was a momentary pause, Mr. Anderson said that he thought perhaps
we might be competing for the most amount of attention in the group,
needing to talk most about one's own problems. Mr. Mahler completed
that this was similar to what children did at home and that usually
at home this led to a great deal of rivalry between the children and
really put the parent in the middle. When I wondered who in the
group might be put in the middle by this kind of competitiveness,

Mr. Wallace directly answered by saying that it was for my attention that the group probably competed the most. I then wondered what my role in the group was as a consequence of this feeling in particular. Mr. Wallace said that while I was many times the target for some of the competitive feelings, that I also played the role of keeping the group from getting out of hand. It seemed to him that there was enough in my limiting, in my directing discussion, so that this was minimized and as a consequence of this, he felt more in touch with the other men because he could really understand the problems with which they came. He said that he tends to run away with the discussion. There were several immediate responses to this, particularly from Mr. River, Mr. Lansing, and Mr. Mahler, who said that their feelings were that when he, Mr. Wallace, did talk, that he really had something to say and that they were very much interested in it. Mr Wallace was a little embarrassed by this, thanked the men, then went on to say that there were times when he knew that what he was talking about really wasn't of interest and at those times he counted on my helping him to move on to something else. Mr. Anderson agreed with this and said that now that we had discussed what had happened in the group he had something else that he wanted to bring up.

In a very sharp contrast, he said that as long as we were talking about feelings, he wanted the group's opinion about something that he was struggling with. He said that in his contacts from the clinic, he had been "accused" of withholding a great deal of his feeling, particularly in regard to his children. He wasn't quite sure about this and what effect it had on the children, but that he was just wondering if any of the others had ever felt the same way. When I asked what it was tonight that enabled him to ask the group this, Mr. Anderson replied that he sort of felt that all of the men would really understand and would be able to help him to look at this. Mr. River, Mr. Lansing and Mr. Wallace all reacted visibly to this, each looking up, Mr. River smiling, Mr. Lansing nodding his head and Mr. Wallace leaning back in his chair and looking directly at Mr. Anderson. Mr. River responded first with a broad grin and in a very pleased and warm tone, welcomed Mr. Anderson to the group. When Mr. Anderson wondered what he meant by this, Mr. River went on to explain that it seems that Mr. Anderson no longer had to hide the fact that he really has some problems of his own. Mr. River said that it seemed to him that any time Mr. Anderson had talked before this, he talked in a very general way and that it was really hard for him to feel that he had any real problems and that now it seemed that he was bringing them out in the open more. Mr. Lansing confirmed this, saying that if nothing else, tonight he could really tell that Mr. Anderson was concerned about his feelings with his children as well as "what the book says one should do." Mr. Wallace looked up, paused, and then asked Mr. Anderson if he could say more about what he meant, to which Mr. Anderson replied that what he thought he was asking about had to do with the difficulty or the ease with which one really showed how he felt. He said that tonight the group seemed able to do it and this is what encouraged him to bring his concern and the question that had come from the caseworker and that at this point he wanted really to understand how this might influence his son and his daughter as well and his own participation in his family life.

The Evolution of Group Structure

We are still discussing the beginning of a group and what seems to emerge early in the group process. We are also still illustrating the importance of seeing the group as a system wherein the interaction of psychological variables and social variables is the basic unit of study. This means that we cannot be effective unless the unit of our concern is how the person transacts reciprocally with his impinging environment. Both the person and the social system in the transaction change through feedback and self-adjusting mechanisms, and both are and become part of each other. To try to explain the group or its members through sociological terms alone or through psychological terms alone is of little value to the groupworker in practice.

Very early in the life of a group, one observes that the members ask for and, in fact, develop group structure.[9] A cycle evolves in which social interaction creates social structure which influences and limits the patterns of future interaction. There are two important ways of viewing the formation of group structure and the groupworker cannot afford to confuse them. In the first view, social interaction which begins as random and diffused communication tends to take on patterns. As social roles are ascribed and functional aspects are delineated, social structure emerges; social experience and social needs interrelate to form a structure of relationships. In his view, as social interaction becomes patterned—becomes habitual and repetitive—behavioral norms or expectations develop; expected behaviors become designated by all in the group as appropriate or inappropriate.

What tends to occur is that these patterns become institutionalized and hence become norms which are solidified by routine, usage, sustained tradition, sentiment, and opinion. These habits and norms may be expressed or may be tacitly accepted.

Groups develop formal and informal structures as do larger organizations. The formal structure is the explicit organizational pattern which may appear as detailed written statements in a constitution and bylaws with designated officers who have prescribed functions, and so forth. Parenthetically, this ubiquitous use of constitution, bylaws, and parliamentary structure which we find in most groups in our social agencies is inappropriate to the purpose and function of treatment or growth groups and in its elaborate forms is not necessary for most groups in the helping professions. Trecker advised many years ago that a groupworker should encourage only the amount of formal structure in a club that is necessary for it to operate. Some authors argue that the use of formal structures teaches democratic process and prepares youngsters for the adult organizational world. The first premise is debatable and the second is lamentable. O'Gorman in "Storefront" writes that such education as preparation for the "grown-up world" is genocide.[10]

The informal structure may exist alone or parallel a formal structure. In the former, these are stable relationships which emerge without formal agreement or explicit description, while in the latter (where they parallel a formal structure), they represent members' expectations for interaction which operate in addition to the explicit statements of relationships and sometimes are even contradictory to those stated ones. These are illustrated by the grapevine, clique formation, and the indigenous leader who is not an officer. There is a general hypothesis which holds that informal structures tend to emerge more frequently in organizations where formal structures do not provide opportunity for the need satisfaction of members. The proposition is not applicable to groups where the enhancement of social functioning is the purpose.

Group structure is a dynamic concept. Although it tends to become patterned and self-perpetuating, group structure is capable of change. One way in which groupwork can help people is by enabling changes in group structure. This is an aspect of method which will be discussed in Chapter 8. Structure varies when there are changes in group size and composition. It is more usual for structure to be modified by changes in interpersonal choices, by alterations in communication patterns, by the creation of new interactional networks and through the introduction of program, a new group goal, or when the worker brings his influence to bear. The major aspects of structure will be discussed in greater detail in Chapter 3. They are position, status, role, power hierarchies, norms, subgroups, and communication patterns.

The difficulty with this first viewpoint regarding structure is that, while it is true that structure is capable of change, once it stabilizes it is difficult to alter and hence structure resists change and seeks status quo. The group members tend to structure relationships as replications of their past experiences to affirm self-images; those, for example, with poor self-images place themselves low on the status scale. The members tend to duplicate roles learned previously and thereby to reinforce maladaptive behaviors. The replay of these old scripts often supports pathology or, at least, malfunctional coping mechanisms. This also can be a way of controlling others. The development of structure favors the stronger over the weaker as well, and denies access to the needed resources to those who are weak and often need them the most. This is a re-enactment of the story of their lives and a reflection of the depriving society in which they live. However, all groups develop structure early in their life cycles because structure in this view, by definition, is the solidifying and stabilizing of whatever relationships do develop.

The second viewpoint about structure is of great importance to the groupworker. When a number of people come together for the first time, although there is an underlying yearning for person-to-person psychic communication, we have seen that there is fear of this occurring. The largest percentage of people, and especially those who seek our help, become very anxious in the presence of others, particularly in an unstructured situation. But even more socially competent people who can put aside their anxiety about human relationships or have skill in finding avenues for social intercourse because of their positive social experiences, begin to seek guides for ascertaining who is who, how to act to gain favorable response, what behavior would be acceptable, and in what relationships each member stands to any other, that is, higher, lower, nearer, farther, more-or-less powerful, important or unimportant, accepted, rejected, liked or disliked, and so forth. If one knows these and other similar things, one has guides or clues to how to function to meet one's own needs; this knowledge affords security. Some people are skilled in finding this out quickly and some are not.

Let us picture the situation by comparing it to one's entry into a dark, unfamiliar room. Ignorance of the room's size, shape, and its furnishings leads one to be very cautious and to grope about, feeling for stumbling blocks and open areas. The stranger looks for the switch so that he can turn on the light. This period of feeling one's way can be both frustrating and, to some, frightening. However, how would one feel if every time one's hand found the switch it was moved out of reach and the impediments in the room appeared to be in motion so that their positions changed repeatedly? It would be a nightmare. What could one do? One could continue to systematically map the room to ascertain patterns and trends by which to understand the situation and predict the layout; one could sit down and refuse to participate, thereafter to withdraw; one could rush about unmindful of barked shins and the overturning of tables and chairs in the frantic hope of finding one's way; or one could also call out for stability, a map, and a light, that is, for structure.

It is most usual for people to request the stabilization of relationships; that is, to look for, develop, and demand structure. Structure,
in this view, is a defense against anxiety. Structure relieves anxiety
because it informs the participants how to act toward each other.
The advent of position tells one who is the president; for example,
one can act appropriately to Mr. A because he is a president but
one may not know how to act toward Mr. A if he is just Mr. A.
The ascription of status to a person guides one in knowing how
to communicate with him, what social distance to assume, and how
much influence to accept from him.

The location of oneself in the structural network also tells one
what to expect from others and what they expect from him. In
other words, role behaviors are assigned and one is thereby given
direction for acceptable performance. Role behaviors become norms
and are reflective also of norms and values. These norms and role
expectations, in turn, tell one what personal goals are feasible and
what hopes one can entertain for oneself.

While on the one hand these structural prescriptions limit one
and can be seen as onerous, they are guidelines that give most people
a sense of security. They can successfully protect a person from
direct interpersonal relations. They mask person-to-person responses
and instead allow people to perform as actors who have donned
costumes and follow a script. They can prevent a person from being
himself. We must not confuse one's identity with one's social role.
They defend one against the fear of closeness and inhibit one from
realizing one's underlying wish to know others and be known by
them.

Phase I—First Meetings

All groups pass through sequential stages of development. They
are described and analyzed in the following pages as stages of growth
and are called phases to connote that the stages are based upon
sequences of time, task, and accomplishment. Groups form, develop,
mature, and terminate. Phase I covers the first meetings of a group
and is characterized as the orientation phase.

Orientation

The behavior in first meetings can be deceptive and frustrating.
On the surface it appears to be either polite and passive or very
active and disorganized. The climate of Phase I must be understood

by a worker if he is to be appropriate and responsive. Both behaviors, quiet and withdrawn or active and rowdy, are reactions to similar underlying feelings of the members. The reactions are an attempt to orient oneself, to feel out and test the social situation. The overt behaviors vary from age to age, from culture to culture, and from situation to situation, depending on the personality characteristics of the persons.

The underlying theme is anxiety and the action is a means of coping with it. Some people respond to anxiety by remaining passive, watching and waiting; this is a flight reaction. Some become hyperactive and flail around in random acting; some become aggressive and fight. In each instance, the action proposes to avoid coming to grips with the real concerns and fears. The behavior is tentative, wary, and exploratory. The members hope to be able to test how others respond and how to be safe in the new group while they seek to meet their needs and attain personal goals. Sometimes the first meeting is very quiet, the people seem to be unresponsive and sullen, or perhaps very cooperative, even enthusiastic, and the following meeting is raucous. Sometimes the first meeting is unruly and children run about and then the following meeting is subdued. Sometimes the initial atmosphere continues for several sessions, or changes at random. There seems to be neither rhyme nor reason to the actions of the people.

The people are leery of one another and of close interpersonal relations. They mistrust people. They fear rejection and consequently they reject. Some fear being hurt and as a defense they attack. The atmosphere is not friendly, it is cautious and hostile even though it may appear to be accepting and sociable. The climate is cool and there is social distance. In this state, the people seek to set up a frame of reference that is familiar and comfortable to them. They may use routines and pastimes—social conventions—to become familiar with each other. They may seek to be accepted or to make contact by revealing personal histories carefully tailored to gain a desired response. They may begin to map the situation in order to conform and get along. One moves toward others and at the first sign of danger or embarrassment one runs back. One lays a feather on the table and watches to ascertain how the wind blows. One tests for commonness to locate potential allies. One overacts to test for reaction; these are called feints in sports.

The questions that are bothering them include: What will it be like? Will I be liked? Will I be hurt or put down? What do I have to do to be accepted, to meet my needs? Can I find a friend here? What will this cost in psychic terms? Where can I hide? Can I trust the others; can I trust the worker? Will I be helped?

The wish is to involve oneself and gain the gratification it promises; the fear is to avoid the demands and frustrations that seem inevitable.

The themes in the first phase are anxiety, a desire for but fear of closeness, a desire to reveal oneself and be known but a fear of being vulnerable, a desire to be helped but a reluctance to pay the price. The worker must be responsive to these feelings as he conducts himself and as he considers program. This phase may last for several weeks or it may go on for a long time depending upon how mistrusting the people are and also how trustworthy the situation proves to be.

The excerpt from a record which follows illustrates a first meeting. In this illustration the worker tunes into the concerns of the members and sets a climate for future meetings.

An Illustration of a First Meeting with Young Adults with Epilepsy

AGE: Young Adults
SETTING: Community Center
SESSION: First

It was at about this time that Joe entered. Joe continually held his head down during almost all discussion, but mostly when he was speaking. He looked away from the person to whom he was directing his words. He threw his books down and said that it was difficult to find any place at this university. There was some discouragement and some cynicism in his voice. Both Lucy and I asked him about his study and he told us that he was taking business administration and right now a great deal of accounting. He enjoys mathematics and accounting, but he again said with some disgust that he was doing it the hard way because he was going to school longer than he should need to. Lucy entered this discussion with him in a lively fashion and said that she probably had no mathematical skill, but that she would be very much interested in learning more about psychology and psychiatry. She said that she herself is very tense, and she knows that this has not helped her and she would like to know more about what makes people tick.

Marge entered with a smile. She looks like a little girl who is always a little bit apologetic and feels that she has to smile continually at people to be accepted. She expressed her delight at coffee and cookies being available. When I poured the coffee half of it went on the floor. There was delighted laughter among all three of them and a very definite loosening up of the atmosphere.

It was at about this point that Fern, a very pretty nineteen-year-old-girl, entered. Fern and Lucy found out that they live in the same

direction and they talked about the distance from the university and
the poor streetcar service. This led into talking about how long one
has to wait at the clinic until one is seen by the doctor and Fern
said with some anger that it takes sometimes from ten o'clock in the
morning until four o'clock in the afternoon. And then immediately
jumping into the whole purpose of this meeting, Fern asked the others
quickly how often they had to go for their medical appointments. Lucy
and Fern said that they were going regularly, and it was interesting
to hear the two students say that they should go regularly but that
they do not do so any more because they find that there is no use.
Marge said that she had not had any seizures for almost two years.
Fern said that she had not had them for eight months, but at that
time she had four in a row, and she was certainly very unhappy about
this. Joe rather evasively said that he had them quite often, and Lucy
said that she has them at periods that she cannot quite determine but
quite often too.

We closed the door at this point since we did not any longer expect
the other two members to arrive, and I began to interpret the reason
for the meeting. I said that we don't know everything about their sickness
but that there was a point in discussing some of the things that they
would like to know. At the same time we think that there might be
some help if one loosens up and that maybe then seizures would be
a little less frequent, but that we were not sure about this. They are
our first group to try this and, therefore, we will come together to
find out how much we can be helped. Lucy said that she thinks this
is marvelous and that we should try to find out as much as we can,
and the more freely people are able to talk with each other about
it, the more they may know about it. She also felt that all the time
she is so much under an inner strain that it would be very helpful
for her to talk to others about it and get some indication of what to
do. She said that her husband first had thought that she should not
have a second baby for it would be too much strain on her. She hopes,
though, that she can relax more and that this will improve her seizures.
Anyhow, she wants to try.

FERN: If only people would not always think that we are just crazy,
that we are something like mentally sick. You have no idea how my
brothers treat me. You know, I did not grow up with my brothers
because my mother died very young, but when they see me they just
stare at me all the time, and they watch me, and I hate this. I have
a very nice roommate at the place where I am, and we got along
very well, but when I had my last seizure she was present, and she
was very good about it. But now she, too, is watching me all the time
and always so cautious and says, "Fern, sit down," and "don't get so
excited," and I hate to be treated that way.

LUCY: Yes, this is true, and very often even your own family doesn't
understand. But it is amazing how well my husband knows it, and
how good he is about it and understands it. It certainly is terrible
when it happens all the time when your relatives are present, as for

instance, just for the first time when my brother-in-law came to visit, it happened right away that night and one hates to be seen like that by one's own family.

MARGE: You feel that way because people always make us so dramatic. I will never forget the first time that I had an attack, when I was seven or eight years old. I was in school and when I woke up my teachers were all standing around me and the very frightened faces they had! Then one of my best friends went around shouting all over the whole place, "Marge had a fit, Marge had a fit." This made me so embarrassed. People would not shout that somebody had headaches like that, would they? I know that that is the reason I never again wanted to be together with so many kids.

JOE: People in general are quite kind to me. All my friends just lay me down and then they don't talk much about it afterwards.

Fern brought up the question of the type of seizures they had, whether it was petit mal or grand mal. Joe asked about the difference, he had never heard those words. I asked whether anyone knew the difference. Fern was the only one who tried to explain it, and then I gave in more detail the difference between petit mal and grand mal. That opened up everybody to describe their symptoms. Fern was clear that hers was grand mal for people had told her that she was falling down, foaming at the mouth and threshing around somewhat. Joe described his the same way. Lucy thought that hers was probably a combination of the two since she does not know how it happens, and because it happens only at night. Her husband says that she sounds like a little child crying, and he always gets up, thinking that the baby is hurt. Fern said that most people think that they cry like children and Marge said that she had heard herself moaning like a little baby. That aroused everybody's interest because they said that they had never though that anybody could hear himself, so they were quite interested in this fact, that Marge could be somewhat conscious during the situation. They explained that they felt that Lucy was extremely lucky in having it only in bed because she is lying down anyhow. Lucy explained though that she threshes around very much and that her husband holds her down and that she sometimes bites her tongue. Marge said that she had not had her grand mal attack for a long time but she wonders whether she doesn't have petit mal attacks once in a while. She said that at one time she had to talk to one of her advisers at the school and while she was standing there her books suddenly dropped on the floor and for a minute she did not know what happened. Again she expressed what a terrible embarrassment this is and how she does not know how to help herself. I explained at this point that there would not be anything wrong with letting the teacher know or just sitting down for a minute. They said that they also think that in general it is good to let people know but very often one is too embarrassed to do so. They wondered why most of the attacks do not start in babyhood, and they all seem to think that they started after a fall.

I had the impression that all of them were so filled with so many problems that we did not discuss one point at a time but I let them talk about anything they wanted to in this first meeting. They immediately went into the whole question of drug treatment. They described the symptoms, they said that the most horrible thing was the headaches right after the attack. The drugs did help but they made them terribly drowsy and they were yearning for a drug that would avoid this. Fern and Marge were able to describe a combination of drugs that they were taking, and that they too hoped for a discovery that would do something to get rid of the terribly drowsy effect. I said that at some future date I would ask Dr. Van or another one of the physicians to come in to talk to them and this was greeted with great enthusiasm.

Fern then said with strong feeling that she would certainly like to know whether, for instance, this disease is hereditary. Her sister right now is pressing her terribly, saying that she should not get involved with any fellow because she should never marry and have children. At this point Lucy spoke with great conviction and strength, that this was all wrong, that there was not a hereditary factor in this, but that one should discuss this with the future husband beforehand. She said, "You will live with this man day and night and he will find out anyway. It is better to tell him beforehand, and if you both decide to go along with it, then you just make up your mind not to be so worried about it and you can have children and raise them happily. I have my own child and I know that it is a healthy child." Lucy continued talking about how she met her husband, and said that as a youngster she did not dare go out at all like other girls did. Marge interrupted her at this point and said smilingly that she should not think that others dared to go out. She never has gone out with any boy either, because she is much too afraid of what might happen. Fern said that she especially felt very strongly about it and wanted to know the answer, because one of her brothers is spastic. So many people think that it is the same thing and they regard her family as a very poor bet for having children. I explained that being spastic or having seizures are two completely different sicknesses and that the one has nothing to do with the other. I gave some of the symptoms of the spastic patient and Fern was very delighted to recognize her own brother in them. I also gave Lennox's explanation of the fact that having seizures is not hereditary but that there might be some predisposition for it in some people. This was very well understood by the group and even Joe joined in at this point to try to explain it and said that there is maybe a "strain" but this does not mean that it will be transmitted to the child. Lucy again added with great conviction: "You simply cannot live always thinking about it all the time. I began to see that it is impossible to live that way, and I began to think about other people and somehow the sickness did not matter that much." Marge added at this point that her mother was very much in favor of such a group, that it was such a relief to be with others who have the same problems. Joe was comparatively quiet during this discussion and I encouraged him to say something also about his friends, and he said that he has quite a few.

Everybody in the group felt that they have to talk more about this, but they were already interested in the next aspect of the sickness. Fern said, for instance: "Why does everybody act so 'hush, hush' about our sickness? Why is nobody talking about it?"

Lucy said: "I think it is because nobody has enough knowledge about it and they think it is something so horrible."

I joined in at this point and explained how not so long ago cancer, for instance, was also a "hush, hush" sickness, and that it has a great deal to do with the symptoms and the fact that people don't know too much about it. Fern said with great conviction, "Then people should know and we should help them to know, and we should know ourselves." Marge asked shyly whether there is a law against marriage between seizure patients in the state and I could say that there is not. Joe at this point joined in with some resentment saying, "But there is a law about not being allowed to drive a car," and Marge felt resentful about that too. (I had called Fern "Ferny" at one point and she said with great resentment that I never should do that because her family calls her that.)

I interrupted at this point saying that we had run over the hour and that Joe was due for a class, therefore we would close for today but I wanted to ask the group some questions. The first one was: Do they feel that they want to go on? There was a generally enthusiastic response that this was very necessary and that they wanted it very much. My other question was whether they wanted to have some more members and whether it would be all right to bring in some older members since we did not have many more in their own age group. Fern said very seriously, "I think it will be very good if we have as many as possible to talk things over with, and if we have some older people, these older people have gone through things that we might still have to go through and we can learn from them." Joe underlined this very strongly and Lucy added that there is not such a great difference when people are adults. Marge said that the more people we have in the group the more people will know what to do and understand themselves better.

It was about time for Joe to leave at this point and he began to collect his books. The girls were ready to help with cleaning up the place and they all wanted to help me bring the coffee and so on to the other department. While they were getting up, Fern said that we should not be so formal with each other in this group and that we certainly could call each other by first names. Each one introduced himself in this way again. It was also Fern who added that she certainly thought it would be good if more fellows were in the group because poor Joe must feel very strange. Joe for the first time smiled at this point.

Lucy suggested that at some meetings she would like to bring her husband because it would be good for him "to see others who are in the same boat as I am, and see that we can explain some of the things we are thinking." With very nice feeling for the others, she added,

"Don't think that you are funny or crazy. He knows me, and he understands this." The others thought that this would be a good idea and I suggested that we just wait a little longer on this until we had talked among ourselves a little more and then we certainly could invite anyone of their friends or their relatives they wanted to bring in. Lucy agreed readily with this and Fern said that she would like to bring her sister and several others, but only "when we know a lot, and can tell them, and I sure hope that we can tell them." I kidded her a little bit and said that she would like to "show off." Fern said quite seriously that she certainly would like to tell an awful lot of people about this but that she always felt that we should hold back for a while. There would be a point when this group could start making people a little bit more understanding of epilepsy. Marge said at this point that maybe they should not use that word, and I agreed that the word had an unhappy meaning for many people, and they all said that they would prefer that another word be used. Marge added that she wanted to bring her mother.

Other plans that were quickly discussed at the last minute were that they would like to go out sometime together and they were looking forward to Lucy having the baby in April.

All three of the girls helped me to bring the materials back to the office. Fern and Lucy, who seemed to have established a friendship already and who live in the same direction, left together.

The group has begun to develop structure almost from the beginning. We will return now to elaborate on group structure in order to understand its consequences.

NOTES / READINGS

1. Sara Maloney and Margaret Mudgett, "Group Work—Group Case Work: Are They the Same?" *Social Work*, Vol. 4 (April, 1959), p. 32.

2. William Shalinsky, "Group Composition as an Element of Social Group Work Practice," *Social Service Review*, Vol. 43, No. 1 (March, 1969), pp. 42–49.

3. James Garland, Hubert Jones, and Ralph Kolodny, "A Model for Stages of Development in Social Work Groups," *Explorations in Group Work* (Boston: Boston University School of Social Work, 1965).

4. James K. Whittaker, "Models for Group Development: Implications for Social Group Work Practice," *Social Service Review*, Vol. 44, No. 3 (September, 1970), pp. 308–322.

5. Alan F. Klein, *Social Work Through Group Process* (Albany, New York: School of Social Welfare, State University of New York, 1970), pp. 63–68.

6. Theodore M. Mills, *The Sociology of Small Groups* (Englewood Cliffs, New Jersey: Prentice Hall, Inc., 1967), p. 81.

7. Dorwin Cartwright and Alvin Zander, *Group Dynamics: Research and Theory* (Evanston, Illinois: Row, Peterson & Company, 1960).

8. L. K. Frank, "What Influences People to Join Organizations," *Adult Leadership* (January, 1958).

9. Sources for the material on structure include:

Frederick L. Bates, "A Conceptual Analysis of Group Structure," *Social Forces*, Vol. 36, No. 2 (December, 1957), pp. 103–111.

The work of Robert F. Bales.

Paul Hare, Edgar F. Borgatta, Robert F. Bales, *Small Groups: Studies in Interaction* (New York: Alfred A. Knoff, 1955).

Hubert Bonner, *Group Dynamics: Principles and Applications* (New York: Ronald Press, 1959).

Edwin J. Thomas, ed., *Behavioral Science for Social Workers* (New York: The Free Press, 1967).

10. Ned O'Gorman, "Storefront," *Columbia Forum*, Vol. XIII, No. 3 (Fall, 1970).

3

❖❖❖❖❖❖❖❖❖

Components of Group Structure

Social structure can be understood primarily as a solution to the functional problems of a group of people. Their interaction becomes institutionalized, reducing the tensions that grow out of the uncertainty and unpredictability of the action of others. One's place in the structure can provide access to resources, control over persons, status, and identification with the group as a whole, thereby providing security. The stabilized expectations for behavior delineate the roles in the group.

Interaction

Interaction or social interaction is the reciprocal responses of people to each other. It is carried out at the most direct level of communication, both verbal and nonverbal. It is the continuous and reciprocal series of contacts between two or more human beings. Interaction involves an initial act or stimulus and the reactions to it, and it carries influence with it. Both or several parties to the interaction influence each other and in a very real sense become part of each other.

Position

Position is the location a person has in the structure. It relates to a function or functions such as husband, sergeant at arms, leader, follower, or isolate. It therefore defines functional behaviors. All positions are not attractive to everyone. The functional prescription, the degree of satisfaction one gets from one's location and the degree of ease or frustration one has in filling that position, influences behavior, morale, and health.

Positions define what one can have and can control in the group. They guide communication and what and how much information one can receive and send. They influence how one codes or interprets information. Those in positions of centrality receive much information which enhances their power and status while those on the periphery tend to become alienated. Position can afford affection, security, and freedom. Persons in important positions are envied and imitated. People who occupy no acceptable position or are isolates, scapegoats, or victims are deprived, put upon, despised, feel they do not belong, are worthless, disliked and they tend to become ill or perhaps disciplinary problems. Moreover, it would appear that, all other things being equal, followers remain followers.

To become able to participate as part of any system of relationships such as a group, one needs to have some definite position in the group which sets one's function. The absence of any idea of one's position is tantamount to anomie, or alienation, or lack of any anchor. This state disorients one and supports one's perception of being nonexistent, a phenomenon that some children have experienced and then re-experience later in some peer groups. One's self-image is very much influenced by the position one thinks one occupies. For some, there is no opening in the structure which can allow for success or opportunity to attain personal goals and these people, where they can, form their own substructure which tends to be deviant or against the established structure.

Position, then, is a means to need-meeting and also can allow or deny the right to behave as one wants or has to. By having access and control of resources, a person can have many more options than those who do not. However, this is not all positive because high position can also be frightening, anxiety-producing, and need-defeating. The high gastric acid producer, as an example, in a high and responsible position has increased chances of suffering from an ulcer.

Position, to be enhancing, must match the need dispositions of the occupant of the position. If one has a position and cannot produce that which the group demands, the person can be damaged easily. Some positions are high risk and fit competitive, skilled, hyperactive persons but are devastating to others. If a person has a low self-image and is peripheral in the group, his position confirms or enforces that image. Some people may revel in unhappiness, if that is their nature, or they may prefer being isolates, especially if they are afraid of relationships.

If a person never really belonged in his family and has had little sense of belonging all through his life, he may settle into a peripheral position in a group and be content to seem to belong. How much one needs to belong, to have high position, or to be recognized may determine how one responds to one's position, or how one strives for position, or how one frustrates others' occupancy of positions. If a person does not need to be reaffirmed by position— does not have any primacy of need for status, power, importance, or a sense of belonging because he is secure in knowing that he has or can have these things at will—high office may mean nothing and he may be happy, useful, and even motivated in an unimportant position. The meaning of position varies considerably from person to person, setting to setting, and culture to culture. What a position connotes or affords for a person is more important than the position itself. All men are not economic men. Some are more interested in art, service, freedom, love of fellow man, or being loved. Group structure is effective when it rewards the universal needs and desires, but when it fails to match the need dispositions of its individual members, it wastes human potentials.

In and of itself, the concept of position has little meaning. The important considerations are the need dispositions of the members and whether their positions are rewarding or frustrating. Important ways to help people are to help them to change their positions, alter the functional prescriptions of the positions they occupy, change the status of the positions, or for them to learn how to perform better in their positions.

Status

Status is related closely to position but the two are different and should not be confused. Status is the rank or importance that other people give to one, and it connotes also the rank or importance that one believes others afford to him or that one thinks one has. Sociologists define status as the sum total of obligations and rights one has as a person. These are the indicia or consequences of one's status. It is a relative or relationship term because one has status in relation to someone else, that is, higher or lower than another or others. Status can apply to a position. For example, the position of father can be high in one family or in one culture and low in others. It can apply also to a person or to a function.

A person's position, previous position, or cultural bias about his position may lead him to think that he has high status (or deserves it) and yet he may be regarded lowly by others. Obviously, one's self-image, bearing, aggressiveness, verbalization, energy output, and production will be influenced by one's status. One's performance depends in part upon the kind of status one has. If one thinks that one has high status but others do not respond, one will be frustrated, angered, in conflict, and might behave in fight, flight, or dependency fashions. If one has low status, it may lead to despondency and a sense of worthlessness. Although this feeling is uncomfortable, people who have low status still may tend to behave in a way that confirms and reinforces their low status. A client or patient will often seek a worker who is controlling and who acts as an expert because such behavior affirms his own low status. People of low status perform below their potential in most situations and will hold themselves back unconsciously from beating a person of high status in a game or for that matter in life.

People tend to attribute characteristics to those with high status as better or more skilled than others even though in reality there may be no evidence of this being so. In remembering an event or in writing minutes, people tend to give credit for acts with which they agree to people with high status and attribute acts with which they do not agree to those with low status. Status people are contagious; others take on their moods, adopt their attitudes, and follow them in voting, choosing, or making decisions. Majorities in organizations usually vote in accordance with the stated preferences of status members. People listen to high-status people and often tune out those with low status.

Often one can observe that a suggestion made by a low-status member in a meeting is ignored and then later the same suggestion made by a high-status person is acclaimed and adopted. The more a person represents the goals and ideals of a group the higher he ranks, and vice versa. High-status people are permitted to innovate and to feel free to do so. Those with middle status conform because they have more to gain and to lose by not doing so. Those with the lowest status either follow blindly or are less conforming, more bizarre and deviant. They have nothing to lose and no hope of gaining.

People with high status who have gained position or authority and hence high status through the performance of a skill, once that skill is no longer required by the group, tend to retain their status. Access to information confers status which in turn increases one's access to still more information. These cycles confer power. Low-status people inhibit both their own communications and their access to information, which results in reducing their own power. High-status people criticize more those who are lower in status than they criticize each other. Low-status people often express confusion, do not feel that they can make a contribution, and know that they do not have support. The more unpleasant one's position and status (together) are, the greater will be the amount of irrelevant speaking and acting one will do. Obviously, the attractiveness of a group to a member and hence cohesion is related to his perception of his own status and whether it is congruent with his own image. An example of this is that people tend to drop out of task groups such as committees when they feel that the demands made upon them are not appropriate to their sense of their own status.

Since low status inhibits persons from performing up to their potentials, reduces and maintains low self-image, fosters conformity, and so forth, it is inimical to growth, to self-actualization, and to success in treatment. Clients and patients are not helped when the worker or therapist confirms their low status. The weakest and most needful people in a group tend to be kept in these states by the group structure which restricts upward status movement.

One responds to the kind of status one has in direct relationship to the meaning status has for one. If one's need for status is primary, high status in a group can meet the need and help to produce adequate social competence. If one needs to feel important, needs to be bolstered, needs to be validated, one's behavior in the group will vary with the status one has in that group; that is, one will strive to improve one's status, will react negatively if it is threatened, or will be comfortable and productive if it is high. If one feels insecure, high status may produce feelings of high risk and be threatening. Different people respond to status and status-seeking differently. Status has no real meaning as a variable independently of the meaning it has to the person and to the other people in the group who are responding to him.

All people do not need status in the same way; status means different things to different people, that is, it can mean recognition to one, adequacy to another, and a chance for realization to still another. At different stages and times it has a different meaning to the same person and, in any case, the responses to it differ. Status has meaning only insofar as it meets the need dispositions and goal orientation of a person and is the proper resource for him. However, consistently low status has deleterious effects upon anyone because feelings of adequacy and acceptance are important, common human needs. High status connotes worth and competence in the eyes of others and confers other need-meeting resources.

Therefore, status in the structure is desired for a given person to help that person maximize his potential and in so doing he can in turn maximize the potentials of all of the other members. When the structure or the worker freezes a person into low status, and

94

this happens often, that person's opportunity to be habilitated is negated.

Viewing position and status together, it can be seen that if a group is to be effective in achieving its group goal (task) it needs to have certain positions and also certain status allocations because, theoretically, these provide for division of labor and functional diversity. In a task-oriented group, for example, it is said that the group requires encouragers, harmonizers, gatekeepers, standard setters, leaders, followers, and so forth. If a person is placed in a position or given a status that he does not want or that fails to meet his needs, he will not contribute as much as he is able and he may become a blocker or a dropout. This prevents the group from achieving its goal. It is incorrect and dangerous to apply these conceptions to the growth group or the treatment group and, perhaps, the education group as well. The ideal group for the enhancement of the members is one in which people are not controlled, exploited, or inhibited. The ideal group is one wherein all members have equal access to need-meeting resources; where growth is encouraged, not thwarted; where potential is rewarded, not punished; and where the member is not viewed as lower or inferior, even by the worker. Such a group is made up of equals and its *modus operandi* is mutual aid.

The usual hierarchical structure in group life based on an ordering where those who are low on the totem pole are deprived, is contraindicated for helping purposes and hence I contend that such structure inhibits growth and treatment. It is the function of the effective groupworker to block such hierarchical structure. Stated in positive terms, it is his function to facilitate egalitarian structure and to maximize interaction and communication among all. It is the worker's function to enable interpersonal closeness which most formal group structures hinder. This will become even more evident as we continue to study the dynamics of groups.

It is the function of the effective groupworker to help the group members develop a group structure that is appropriate to the purpose of the group and the needs of the members.

Social Role

The concept of social role is one that exists in all organized societies. It is not a new idea; the ancient Greeks used it. Many of the present meanings of role in the social sciences derive from the writing of Jung. Although some writers elevate role concept to the level of a theory, it is not a theory because what it does is to describe certain phenomena in human behavior and organize the descriptions into a neat format, but it does not explain the dynamics of what it describes.

The role concept is useful and it helps one to conceptualize behavior in social situations, as we shall see, but it is being applied in the helping professions and in human relations writings in ways which are stultifying. The next few pages are a summary of what is said about role in the literature. As usual, various disciplines such as sociology and psychology use the same terms to mean different things and different terms to mean the same thing. I shall not attempt to sort this out but, instead, try to relate a consistent story about role. Later in the section I will discuss its implications and applications in groupwork.

The word "role" is used in several ways. It means the behavior that is expected and also the actual behavior that is acted. Role is a relational concept. It applies to more than one person and implies reciprocal relationships. A husband to be a husband must relate as such to a wife and vice versa. A professor must have students, parents need children, a buyer needs a seller, a caseworker needs a client, and so forth. The expectations that define what is acceptable behavior for a role are determined by social norms, therefore role is a subset of social norms. The expectations are standardized by the group, society, or the culture. Role behavior is a system of actions in response to a set of expectations established by the group in which one has membership. Group life can be conceived of as a dynamic process of role assumption and behavior. Role enactments are prescribed for positions, statuses, and functions. It is said that roles are evolved to maximize gratifying positions and statuses in a group. This is patently untrue.

In any society and its groups, certain positions are assigned and these are accorded statuses on the basis of age, sex, family, appearance, skill, habit, and exploitive interest. In a real sense, one's personality is a combination of roles into which an individual is cast in his social relationships. It must be stressed again that social roles always exist in relation to others.

Roles in the society and in groups are required, permitted, or demanded. The role-carrying person has little to say about it except that (1) people tend to gravitate to roles which express their personalities in the sense that they choose unconsciously roles they have learned and into which they are usually typecast and (2) people play their roles in their own individualistic ways. Since roles are reciprocal, people behave in part because of how others behave toward them, that is, in response to the impinging social environment. The patterns of behavior tend to become consistent because they are conditioned responses and, reciprocally, the responses of one become the habitual stimuli for similarly consistent (learned) responses of others. They lock each other into customary, regularized interactions. Normal social functioning, therefore, depends upon widespread acceptance of ascribed status and corrsponding roles. If there were no such stabilities and agreed-upon role expectations, people would be forced to improvise behavior instead of following accepted role prescriptions. However, some roles are more highly valued than others.

We find, therefore, that one must learn one's role or roles when entering a new situation or a new group. This may induce stress. While there is a range of tolerance for deviation in a group, there is a limited range for any alternatives. Within each group, the behaviors of its members are perceived and judged by the norms of the role prescriptions and, as such, role behaviors represent familiar ways of communicating. Each comes to know the judgments and attitudes of the other members in advance and can count on their role partners to follow the script and not ad-lib. Therefore, one's self-other expectations and attitudes, self-images and self-concepts are prescriptions within a role system. If one adheres too rigidly to role prescriptions, one can be viewed as neurotic; not rigidly enough, as deviant; or caught between two sets of prescriptions which contradict each other, one can be viewed as marginal or conflicted. Does a new role relationship make possible a new self-perception? Does one maintain role regularity as a defense against growth, social change, and innovations?

According to the usual precepts, freely shared acceptances of roles, one's own and that of others, together with anticipation that others will abide by the script, makes for maximum communication and high morale. Therefore, change in the behavior of any member is a serious threat to the others and to the role system. That does not augur well for change or for treatment. This is further complicated by the general principle in the role literature which states that to fulfill a role which is understood by others and mastered by oneself offers an ease of communication and security of relationship which is not forsaken easily.

One can see that there are serious conflicts and issues involved in the contradictions between freedom and socialization. For example, not to have skill and motivation in taking on prescribed roles retards socialization and leads to role enactments which may be punished. The absence of opportunities to learn to enact roles appropriately leads to deviant conduct. Hence, adult role behavior depends upon prior acquisition of role skills and the willingness to perform these skills. This means that social functioning is evaluated by one's adjustment to role expectations. To adjust requires skill in reading the social cues and skill in mapping in a group. It also seems to require a willingness to conform. There is a strong implication that the absence of role-taking skills or an unwillingness to perform them influences our definitions of psychopathology and finds its way into social diagnoses.

Another aspect of role-taking relates itself to the psychology of roles. There are several aspects of this. (1) One identifies, gains identity, or achieves an identification of personality and social self with one's role sets; however, this is not necessarily one's real self. (2) Personal failure is often equated with being unable to perform in accordance with the expectation for particular roles. When a person is unable to live up to the role expectations others have for him or he has for himself, or to an ideal role perception, anxiety results and there will be compensatory activity and frustration. (3) Where a person occupies positions in two social situations or cultures at the same time and the expectations in each are not compatible with the other, a high psychic price is exacted. (4) The more role enactments a person has in his repertoire, the better will be his psychological adjustment, all other things being equal. (5) Interpersonal competence requires the ability to perceive the behaviors of others as if they were one's own. It is through this ability that one learns how to behave socially because as one grows up one "plays at" social roles by observing and internalizing the role performances of others. Therefore, one cannot take the role of another without being able to "play house," "play postman," and play the roles of "you be and I'll be." The perception of the other is the essence of empathy and empathy is an essential ingredient of intimacy. It is a *sine qua non* also for the effective groupworker.

It has been demonstrated that psychopathic personalities are less able to empathize than others. Ethnocentric persons enact authoritarian roles easily. Ethnocentric persons have difficulty in knowing how others feel. They tend to project their own feelings. Persons with a low ability to empathize tend to have interpersonal problems. Persons who are committed to egalitarian philosophies are basically empathizers. The quality of role enactment is a function of self, that is, human conduct is a product of self and role. To put these concepts into perspective, *role is a unit of culture, position is a unit of society, and self is a unit of personality*.

As we have noted earlier, self arises out of social interaction. The self is what a person is, an expression of identity. The ego is the perceiving object. The ego consists of the enduring characteristics of a person. Role is what a person does. The self arises out of phenomenal experience and includes the internalization of many others. Role and self are neither synonymous nor necessarily congruent. Since I postulate that the important function of the helping professions is to enable people to find themselves, these distinctions are vital.

Some Role Problems[1]

While role is offered as an important device for providing security and gratification, it is also a source of anxiety and threat. This aspect of role must be understood well by a groupworker. Role demands and how one performs in response to them do relate to self-image. They do threaten one's sense of self-identity as well as beliefs and values and, obviously, threaten one's capacity to perform in accordance with these expectations and one's own needs and desires.

There are a variety of classical role problems created by role expectations. When demands exceed a person's capacity to perform, the stress can become intolerable. Equally tension-producing are situations where a person is unable to fulfill his own needs and drive satisfactions because the role prescriptions for his position and status deny him the resources and freedom to do so. This is the plight of the weak, the low-status person, the black, the client, the low-income patient; in effect, those very people who need our help. In this context there is the problem of positions not being available or being denied to people and hence certain role outlets being inaccessible. Equally frustrating is the failure of a system to provide a function for a member as, for example, the aged person or grandparent who has no functions in family life.

There is a serious problem when the role expectations are ambiguous as they tend to be for the adolescent in our society. It was noted earlier that some people are caught in a situation where several positions which they occupy demand noncomplementary or contradictory role behaviors. There is discomfort when a person moves from one position to another or from one status to another and roles change. An example of the former is the change in the behavior which is expected of a worker when he becomes a supervisor; and of the latter, the changes which occur in the expectations of others for the behavior of people at different ages as they grow from infancy to old age.

A most stressful event occurs when one finds one's role discontinued as in the case of involuntary retirement or job elimination. There are various ways in which these stress-producing situations are handled by different people. Some give up the role, some create a new role which did not exist in the group before. In some instances, the group redistributes roles, such as in a family when the mother is ill a daughter prepares the meals. Some people assume disapproved-of roles or role behaviors. Some people become ill and assume a sick role, a dependent role, or a client role. Some regress to earlier or more comfortable roles and role behaviors, and some set up role compartments so that they can perform differently in different settings and remain personally uninvolved and uncommitted. This is not unusual.

More usual and distressing is the prevalence of role conformity. By this is meant not only rigid adherence to expectations, but also to expectations which do not buttress self-adequacy or guide behavior appropriately so as to be flexible as social conditions change, or which do not meet the person's needs. In this adaptation to stress, the person loses himself and becomes what others make of him. Some respond by a radical departure from old roles to new ones but become as slavish to the new ones as they were to the old.

The question is who is one—his self or his role which is dictated by others? The basic problem becomes that of the "false self," a ubiquitous component of neurotic behavior. The impersonal quality of a superindustrial society condones and reinforces the loss of self into social roles. The actors wear masks, as in the Greek tragedies, only now it is a modern tragedy.

Roles in the Socio-group

Concepts of position, status, and role are especially relevant to the socio or instrumental group as such groups are perceived in our society. Let us recapitulate the important aspects of role for the group when the purpose is to decide something or do something.

In a societal sense, some social roles are ascribed and relatively fixed. These must be enacted with reasonable accuracy. In this context, persons know what society expects of them. (This is a generally held view; but today, nurses are unsure, professors are confused, students are upset, parents are beset, and spouses are vague. Perhaps people used to know what was expected of them. Then, the role prescriptions were definite and people did not have to be as responsive, flexible, and creative as they do today. It is possible that our changing world is making these role sets obsolete.)

Because roles are reciprocal they not only prescribe the expected behaviors of a person but also the behaviors of others toward him. Once the role is ascribed, the person can incorporate the social expectation and develop a concept of a social self. He can take on the emotional reactions of others and react accordingly, and so the person who behaves himself becomes a "good me." (The minority person, the social-welfare client, or the handicapped person may be thrust into an unenviable position and role in this formulation.) Soon the roles become institutionalized; well defined as to function and expected enactments, and supported by tradition and values.

In small groups with informal structure, group roles develop in the same fashion. In the large group, the group maintains itself through functional delineation. One can argue that the same is necessary in the small group. It is said that without defined functions and appropriate roles, there would be incessant conflict. (If people never learn how to work together in close harmony as human beings, this is probably true. Instead of placing emphasis on leadership training, an investment in how to be a group member might pay off.)

Some groups solidify roles in a formal structure but they also develop informal roles, such as an indigenous leader, a follower, a scapegoat, and the like. Thus, groups in our society move as they organize into a process of differentiation and stratification of functional roles. (Why is there less mention of empathizer, helper, friend, and sympathetic listener?)

It is said that as a group forms, these structures emerge because a group needs social order and that there are obvious advantages to this development. It is said that chaos would result if all members attempted to perform the same functions. (Could functions not be shared, rotated, or ascribed on the basis of a person's need?) It is said also that not all members are qualified equally to perform all of the roles and hence personal capabilities indicate a hierarchy of functions so as to allow more effective group action. Thrasher indicated this when he wrote, "One fits the niche which the group determines for him." Thrasher also identified that "an inner circle," "a rank and file," and "fringers" develop.

The Role Concept Scrutinized

These views of man, the group, and role are vestiges of the concept of the divine right of kings and other autocratic rulers, and were reaffirmed in the Reformation. They have been glorified in the name of order. They are built upon a view of society and the group as a "community of obedience," and have been used to justify the idea of keeping people "in their place." Unwittingly, these perceptions of social role have kept minority members subjected, poor people poor, sick people sick, and the exploited powerless. Role, as deified in small-group literature, has concealed the damage which groups do to people who are locked into roles that stunt their growth, destroy their motivation to raise themselves on the social scale, deprive them of hope, and place them in situations where their needs are not and cannot be met.

The concept of role is an important and useful one as long as it is kept in perspective and is kept true to its definition; there are functional imperatives for position and also for statuses in society and in task groups in general. This also holds true for organizatons and families, for role is a viable concept in analyzing any social system. The concept begins to cause trouble when value judgments are introduced into the application of the concept.

Some of these difficulties are discussed here. To accept the idea that role performance is evaluated by its congruence with what others expect is the seat of many problems of alienation, shame and doubt, conformity, loss of self, false self, "bad self," and internal conflict. The concept is ingrained in ideas about socialization. A person is said to be socialized when he performs a role in the way others expect him to and if he fails to do so, by cultural definition, he is thought to be mentally or emotionally disabled. It also makes it possible and socially acceptable to expect everyone to act "as we do" and for anyone else to be viewed as either deviant, sick, or inferior. The result is often to punish change, innovation, creativity, or the speaking out against injustice. To be only what others want one to be is to cease to be one's own man. This is ego-deflating.

The assignment of roles helps to bring stability to group life in that people learn to know how to act appropriately. As long as the word "role" can be descriptive of that situation, it is useful. When it is divorced from all of the human aspects of the actor, it becomes mechanistic and restrictive. "Ultrabehavioristic philosophy which underlies today's psychology tends to see all individuals simply as machines, managed by reward and punishment."[2]

The concept of role is useful in ascertaining what reciprocal actors expect from each other and by identifying discrepancies in these expectations so as to isolate the frustrations and disappointments that cause conflict and unhappiness in a relationship. Modifications in expectation and performance so as to effect adjustment and congruence can bring harmony and happiness. However, the question is not that of making one actor conform to the demands of another or to diagnose as sick behavior the failure to conform. As long as one expects a person to conform, adjust, cope (or whatever word one uses to describe social demand, regardless of the justice of the demand or the consequence to the person), and as long as one perceives that truth or right is decided by consensus, there is a basic denial of human potential.

Dr. William Gordon puts the matter precisely: "I suggest simply that the social approach or strategy by whatever method or means in approaching the person-in-situation complex is to achieve a matching of significant elements in coping patterns and environmental qualities in order to improve the consequences for both the individual and his environment."[3] Such matching may require changes in either or both, but most likely in both.

I spoke of the "community of obedience" as an earlier concept and one that is not useful. A more viable way of regarding the group, and also group life, is as a "community of will." The basic premise here is that freedom is the norm.

Role is a useful concept as long as it is not used as the medium for relationship nor the criterion for evaluating a relationship. Relationship is primarily a matter of competence, the quality or state of being functionally adequate, rather than of roles. To be functionally adequate means that goals are facilitated and achieved. Human relationship becomes a different matter when viewed as interpersonal competence rather than as a matter of performing roles in response to an expectation or demand.

The very important point in discussing behavior in this context is to see the group as a network of relationships which provide close, human, communicative interaction between real persons rather than among positions, statuses, and roles. It is more difficult to relate oneself to others as just people and the major objective in groupwork is to develop the interpersonal competence to do so. Carl Rogers writes, "The immature person cannot permit himself to understand the world of another because it is different from his own and therefore threatening to him. Only the individual who is reasonably secure in his own identity and selfhood can permit the other person to be different, unique, and can understand and appreciate the uniqueness."[4]

This discussion of role has exceptional relevance to the current impressions about the role of the social worker, teacher, or other helping person. The worker is said to have a role and that, of course, means that there is a reciprocal role of client, group member, student, or what have you. It is presumed that each must carry his role appropriately and if each does all will be well. It is not necessary then to meet as persons and human communicative interaction can be avoided. This concept is inimical to the purposes of the educational enterprise and is lethal to social treatment. We will explore this further later.

The Interrelationship of Person and Role

I have said that the role expectation which is held for a position and/or a status may or may not be compatible with the needs and capabilities of the occupant of that position, and if the role does not provide the actor with satisfaction, frustration may result. If the role expectations exceed the capabilities of the actor, anxiety will follow as well as the probability of a failure to achieve. Such a failure influences one's sense of adequacy and also one's self-image. Rogers and Dymond have given some convincing arguments which correlate mental health to self-image, and one could extrapolate the possibilities inherent in a role for a given person as the role enhances or depreciates his image.[5]

If the role expectation for a position or status does not meet the needs of the occupant, or frustrates him by too little or too great a demand, he will experience grave discomfort. On the one hand, his role enactment may meet the expectations and be satisfying in most ways, but afford the person no status or no recognition; on the other hand, it may suit his personality but not his economic needs. The social environment and his needs do not match in such instances. Through past experience or value orientations, the individual misreads the expectations, or he may have an ideal expectation for himself which he is unable to fulfill in the position or status. Measured against his own standard he falls short of his own expectations; self-image suffers, frustration ensues, and a sense of achievement is lacking.

It is possible that a social structure denies access to certain role enactments because of the person's lack of power, lack of status, class, or caste. The roles that might most meet his needs or provide maximum satisfaction are not made available. That person's potential cannot be maximized because of these social restraints or limitations. It might be that the role needed does not exist in that group or social structure and, again, the person is denied a need-meeting and growth-producing experience. Such social deficiencies and limits by habituation can warp the person's personality, restrict his development of role repertoires, set behavioral patterns which repeat themselves and thereby freeze the person into inappropriate or thwarting life situations. People tend to re-enact habitual group roles so that each new group setting finds them redoing what they have done in recent, previous groups. Such behavior seems to be reinforced even when it has failed to be satisfying in the past. It seems to be reinforced because it gives security, or often because it permits one to belong, or to think it is the ticket for belonging, to the group.

Quite often the group casts people into roles because the powerful and high-status members need to have others perform certain roles, or because these roles express the group's psychological conflicts, climate, or culture. Kai Erikson has demonstrated, for example, that groups may cast persons into a deviant role. We know that group emotion will sometimes unconsciously direct a member to challenge authority, act out, be smutty to meet the group urge, or act to release group tension. Such group phenomena may meet the actor's desires by triggering the behavior, but at the same time they may cause a breakthrough of his repressed urges and hence unsocialize the person and cause him to be punished or to punish himself through his guilt feelings.

The role enactments and the group's influences on role enactments, therefore, can be matching or discordant. A person's need dispositions may be served or thwarted and in being served may be growth-producing or socially punishable. We are discussing role then as the transaction between the person, his psychological needs and habits, the demands of the group (social situation), and the opportunities it affords.

It is also true that in addition to groups assigning roles to members, members choose roles through habit or in response to needs. Such choices are usually not conscious or cognitive but are made because the person is seeking to meet his needs or because his preferences are influenced by his personality based upon past experiences, social learning, and modes of adaptation. Such choices are not necessarily rational and they may be maladaptive, self-defeating, or based upon distorted perceptions.

As I have said before, a person may not know what is expected of him but he can be shown or taught. He may know what is expected but lack the skill needed to perform it. The skill can be taught or he can be trained to perform as expected. He may know what is expected and have the skill but not want to perform. Attitudes, values, and desires can be changed through identification, group experience, re-education, goal changes, and so forth. He may know, have skill, and want to perform but be blocked or psychologically unable to change. Each of these situations requires a different approach but all, in one way or another, depend upon the person and how he thinks, feels, and functions. Role-teaching, or casting people into roles without regard for the compatibility of the role expectations with a person's physical and psychological predispositions, can precipitate unhappy results. A corollary follows that social work through group process must utilize group roles in the service of the members.

Suppose that a high gastric acid secreter who is ulcer prone is elevated to a position fraught with tension, conflict, and insecurity. Suppose that a woman who is dependent, lacking in self-confidence, abandoned by her spouse and, therefore, must become the breadwinner and head of her household of several small children, is selected to be a delegate to a citizen's neighborhood council. Suppose that a Cuban-refugee physician is denied a medical license in this country and must become an orderly in a hospital. All of these situations have counterparts in group life, organizational life, on the ward, on the board, on the staff, and in the social work practice group. I am trying to illustrate that such easy solutions as teaching a role, or changing positions and statuses and hence role expectations, can throw some people into states of anxiety, physical difficulty, withdrawal, or acting out. In contrast to the circumstances where a person is pressured to perform a role that is incongruent with his needs, treatment through psychological insights and a restructuring of his psychic system may enable him to perform social roles that now are congruent but previously were malfunctional to him. However, he may exist in a social situation which will not condone his new behavior, may punish him for it, may frustrate him, or may undo the influence of the treatment.

Socialization into the life-styles adopted by a culture is tantamount to educating or training for roles which the culture prefers or requires. The social group life molds the personality in this way. For example, it can be said that lower-income fathers displace their frustration and hostility on their sons. These men work at unsatisfying jobs wherein they are subject to repressive and capricious authority. In order to survive in their environmental and occupational settings, they must be either submissive and accept the authority of harsh foremen, or they must be hard and very aggressive to get and hold jobs. Certainly, the men do not reason out and consciously plan to create sons who can follow in their footsteps but, actually, this is what happens. By displacing their own disappointments on their sons, the sons become accustomed to dictatorial bosses and either to submitting or fighting. In some grand design, a society tends to create the kinds of people it needs to make it run. Our industrial and stratified society needs the cog type of workers; fathers train their sons to fit into this complex and enact roles that are available to them.

The fact is that these roles do not meet the needs of the fathers. They perpetuate destructive life-styles and exploit people for the so-called good of the group. These men are unhappy and unfulfilled; they are cast into self-perpetuating roles.

Further Observations about Group Structure

Some people think that simply manipulating the variables of position, status, role, and power will enable poor people to change their behaviors and become self-supporting, middle-class workers.

This is an offense against the deep and all-abiding respect for people which ought to characterize social work, and which is the significance of the emergence of the concept "transaction" in current discussions of human behavior. Transaction means an exchange between people, each giving something and each taking something, reciprocally affecting or influencing each other. The kinds of programs that are predicated upon single-purpose change such as those advocated through job training, occupational opportunities, or role change are not kind or in the best interests of the people because they fail to take into account the interrelationship of social and psychological variables. As roles are changed, people must be helped to fit these roles and also must be fitted to roles they can perform with beneficial results to themselves as well as to their communities.

People do not transact with a society or with a community. A culture is not transmitted or coped with through such large conceptual units. People transact with small groups in which they love, work, play, and acculturate. What has been said in this section about social role in general applies basically to group roles, for it is in small groups that one lives one's life and they are one's impinging environments. In social work the group is a medium, an environment, a milieu, a life space, a stage, and a laboratory. As such, it is a slice of life and is the setting in which the learning, the action, and the matching can take place.

As with position and status, role is a psychosocial concept and in groupwork practice cannot be dealt with in any one dimension alone. Structural variables permit access to resources; they are environmental. In groupwork they can be altered by the group as a means of enhancing the functioning of the member. (See Chapter 8.) Such modifications are not only ends which may help the group function better, but the modifications are the means whereby the members are helped.

Some people fail to negotiate life's maze and are unable to interact appropriately with others or transact with the environment because they are unable to perceive or assess their own position and that of others, their status and that of others, the role expectations and demands of themselves and others, and are naive about their own performance. Through feedback and group experience, they can learn some or all of these things and, especially, they can learn to "map" the group. They can learn to know the group components and to assess feelings and attitudes as well as beliefs and values. They can be helped to gain self-awareness, to learn appropriateness, how rewards are gained, how status is earned, and how adaptive their own behavior is; that is, how appropriate their behavior is, how successfully they are coping, and wherein their behavior is malfunctional or self-defeating. In these ways a person can be helped to alter behavior. In addition, such experience provides a means of validation for who one is, what one is, and how worthy or adequate one is. It provides identity conformation and can be the means to identity change.

Behavioral change of any kind requires adaptation to change and also requires adaptability. It is axiomatic that if an organism does not or cannot adapt it cannot survive. In its struggle for survival, its failure to adapt causes pain, frustration, and eventual disintegration. At the same time, life requires conflict and struggle with recurring crises that are negotiated and overcome in order to gain strength, skill, and increased capacity to cope with more challenging problems. Adaptation is not the achievement of a static balance. It is a constantly spiraling process in which changes occur in the person and in the situation. The essence of helping through group process is *adaptation to change.* This is accomplished through feedback networks. The group feeds back to the members and with help the members can self-adjust to the realities of interaction and transaction with the world. It is through this process that the person is kept in touch with reality and through which his reality-testing can be improved.

Three aspects of feedback are important to practice in this context. The first is goal-seeking feedback. This helps people to ascertain whether their behavior moves them toward or away from their goals or the meeting of their needs. The second aspect concerns the internal arrangements of the person or group. These include structure, modes of adaptation, habits, beliefs, techniques, and the like, and their matching with reality. Such information is important if there is to be a conscious change in structure; a modification of attitudes, beliefs or values, or change in ways of coping. The third aspect involves a person's or group's awareness of self, their self-image, and a knowledge of how they behave as well as what effect it has on them, on others, and on the environment. These three facets will be implied, although in different combinations, when the term feedback is used when discussing method.

Group structure is the variable we have been discussing. Structure—it cannot be stressed too often—is relationships. Groups must develop a structure through which they function and the structure should be appropriate to the purpose of the group for the most efficient operation. Task groups need a good deal of structure, usually because they function best when there is a clear-cut division of labor and responsibility, and when communication networks channel information and feed back most efficiently to those who need it to perform the group roles. Structure informs the member about who he is and how he and the other members of the group can relate to each other—how to behave in interactions. Structure prescribes, dictates, and sets the rules for the interaction. Structure provides security, the security of knowing how to act.

People who need such security as a primary or dominant need require unambiguous and formal structure. For them, loose structure is anxiety-producing and frightening. The greater the level of anxiety there is, the more demand for structure there will be. This is so because structure formalizes relationships. People can then confront one another as role players rather than as human beings. They can hide behind positions and statuses and avoid being themselves. This use of structure, however, may represent flight and may reinforce social incompetence. If the purpose is to facilitate achieving a group task, such structuring may be desirable, but if the purpose is to enhance social functioning, perhaps the members need to learn to deal with each other as people and not to escape as role carriers.

The less structure a group provides, especially at its inception, the more the members will enact their usual modes of behavior, adaptation, defenses, and games because they will be reacting to stress, anxiety, fear, conflicts, and human contact. Bereft of structure, they must be themselves, unprotected by a script. Such a living situation may afford maximum social learning.

Both learnings are essential: one must learn a wide repertoire of roles and the appropriate behavior for such positions, statuses, and given roles in order to be able to function in our society. However, one must learn also how to relate to others as people with intimacy and human warmth. Careful attention to structure and its use is essential in working with groups. One must be wary of universalized prescriptions and practice based upon group structure as the major medium for growth and change.

Structure represents at best a convenient way of codifying and talking about certain apparent consistencies in social phenomena before their internal processes and dynamic laws are fully understood. Parsons cautioned that when we make structure the primary focus of our attention, there is a danger that we will somehow deify it and bypass more basic questions about the processes which generate and maintain these apparent consistencies. Structure presupposes frozen process but, in reality, process never freezes.

This book is committed to change, adaptation, and the freeing of people to be and to become. The unprincipled use of structure in working with groups can be a serious block to freedom and it also can defeat change. Once a group becomes structured, those in power resist change because they do not want to give up their access to resources and control over others. We have seen that persons with high status support one another and are not sensitive to the needs of those below them; they do not listen to them but send directives down to them. They cast others into roles needed by the high-status people with little regard for the role needs of the low-status people. Information is restricted to those in control. Such structuring develops subgroupings which then place barriers against the development of acceptances and affectional ties. As a result, those who most need acceptance, a sense of self-worth and belonging are deprived of these need-meeting resources. Group structure, when it is allowed to formalize as it usually does, can foster a most undemocratic process, become a subterfuge for control of others, a means of putting down, and a device for majority control to the detriment of the most incompetent, self-defeating, or powerless members of the group.

If the people who need help are to get help in our groups, the question of group structure needs to be reviewed in groupwork. Moreover, positions that carry power, status that validates oneself, and roles that allow people to exploit others may be exactly the experiences in which many people should not be reinforced. Such experiences may be detrimental to them and to the common good. Also, it is obvious that such structuring does not help maximize the potentials for the others in the group.

All of these occurrences in groups have been documented and validated by social research and group dynamics. This is how groups act. The literature abounds with reports and examples. People should not be perpetuated in a need for structure to alleviate anxiety or as a channel to guide their interpersonal relations. Interpersonal relations, to be growth-promoting and need-meeting, require human encounter and closeness. When these are anxiety-producing, then what is lacking is trust not structure. One can learn to trust structure, to be sure, but that does not help one to learn to trust people.

The group in groupwork must be a place where people can meet each other as people to explore their feelings and attitudes toward each other, to become more aware of themselves and the effect that they have on others. It must be an opportunity for mutual feedback so that each can improve his interpersonal communication and develop and grow as a person.

Similar viewpoints are being voiced in education. Silberman, in a Carnegie Foundation study, suggests that educators do not think carefully enough about what they do. He believes that there is a need for more emphasis on the education of feelings and imagination and for slowing down in the cognitive realm. He is for more effort in the affective area with greater concern for personal growth and fulfillment. He finds that there is too much stress on the transmission of specific skills, intellectual discipline, and bodies of knowledge instead of on human-relationship skills.[6]

The motivation to take roles is to gain favorable response in order to gain satisfaction, but the price one pays is conformity. The roles demanded in school, for example, may be unsuited to one's personality, contradictory to one's culture, against one's experience, and counter to one's satisfaction. A teacher or groupworker may conceive of the roles for children within her own motives and values and since the child sees them within his own, the real meanings of his behavior are missed. The same applies in groupwork and in group therapy. On the other hand, the worker or therapist is role cast also as judge, expert, helper, referee, cop, limiter, supporter, target for hostility, friend, love object, and so forth. On the whole, people of average mental ability or slightly above average have the best opportunity to be accepted in our culture, and people who take the roles which the society assigns get along best. However, not everyone is willing to knuckle under and this may result in detour behavior.

Power

Power is related to position and status; but while they are related, they are not to be equated. A mayor has position and he must have had status to have been elected. High status is also ascribed to his position. However, power may lie with a political boss who holds no office and who is hardly known to the electorate. In a group, it often happens that the person with the power to influence it holds no position and has little observable status. In some groups, a person who is elected to the presidency may have low status personally and, also, that position may be regarded by the members as having low status. He may have no power to speak of and the seat of power may lie elsewhere in the informal structure. There are times when being elected to office is a form of scapegoating. Power can be related to who one is, such as the clique to which one belongs; the family name, connections, or background; a person's psychological drive which awes others or triggers their own fears; the control of needed resources; the support of followers who need to identify with force, aggressiveness, or control; and one's adherence to group norms so that one becomes a spokesman or symbol of the needs of the members.

Power is an important structural variable in group life. The elementary battle in parent-child relations around autonomy and

111

will is a prototype of interpersonal relations in which authority forces people into molds and often stamps their future self-image with guilt, shame, and doubt. The power of people over other people, of leaders in a group, or of the groupworker or teacher is an important consideration because control and domination lead to a loss of self and a failure of self-realization. There are few opportunities for a growing child to experience self-determination and freedom from stultifying control. If people are to be able to grow and to approach their potential, they must be freed to be and to become. There can be no finding of oneself if one is bound into the plan that someone else has drawn and if one is forced to be what others model him to be as one models clay. There can be no therapy without autonomy.

It can be, and usually is, as restrictive to substitute power of a teacher or of an indigenous peer leader for a parent's domination. It is also thwarting to try to grow under the thumb of a dominating camp counselor, recreation director, coach, or club leader. The same is also true, although less often realized, when the power of a group is invoked in order to induce change in the behavior of individual members. Groupwork has used and honored this property of the group to enforce conformity and to mold behavior. While the method may be appropriate and useful for some people, it should not be accepted as a universal mode or principle of groupwork.

Let me summarize what is known and written about power. Power influences opinions and beliefs, and it gives credence to information. It may restrain communication between status levels and heighten the tendency for sociometric choices to be made from only one level. People with power tend to be contagious. The lack of power affects a person's feeling of security, heightens anxiety, and reduces one's self-worth. People with power can innovate and also can resist change.

People having power are likely to be regarded by others as productive and are more likely to be able to satisfy their own needs, though possibly at the expense of others. Many people will kowtow to others if they think it will help them rise in the power structure. This is instrumental behavior and is viewed as the way to succeed. People with power talk to others with power, talk down to people with less power, and tend to give directions to them. On the other hand, those with less power talk up to people with power and try to tell them what they think these people want to hear. This is not an uncommon occurrence when a client talks with a social worker.

People with status and power originate activities in which they excel while those who lack power are not expected to excel. They are put in their place and must accept roles assigned to them. If they fail to perform them, they may be punished. People having power tend to exert influence on matters that do not necessarily fall within the established relationship. For example, medical personnel who are knowlegeable about physical problems may tell people how to handle psychological problems or give advice on matters of political policy.

People who lack power completely are seldom healthy. They are the first to be sacrificed and the most likely to accept their lot. They rarely get help in a group and their powerlessness is reinforced by the power structure. When the worker wields power, the client or member is put in an untenable position. He is reduced to a nonentity.

Earlier, I identified closeness, trust, and hope as primary themes in group life which come to the fore in the first phase of a group's existence. The acquisition of these requisites are basic to positive health and are essential if people are to be free to achieve self-realization. A second major group of themes clusters around power, authority, and manipulation. These evolve in the second and third phases in a group's development and are discussed in Chapter 5.

Norms

Norms are said to be the attitudes and behaviors expected of one which are held in common by members of a group. They are learned responses. Norms denote not only that behavior which is expected but also the range of behavior which is tolerated. They are not a sum total of the expectations of the members because they are new emergent products of a group and as such they cannot be predicted. However, they do serve to make the behavior of others predictable. A person, it is said, becomes a group member to the extent that he internalizes the significant norms of a group, carries the responsibilities that inhere, and meets the group's expectations. When he conforms to them it is thought that a person feels content and secure. This is an essential point found in theories about socialization, but it does not take into account their thwarted hopes and their surrender which may cause them to hate themselves as a result.

The word "norm" means several different things in the literature. It means a shared frame of reference, uniformity of behavior, or social pressure, that is, role obligation. In the concept of a shared frame of reference, what is shared is a mode of perception—a perceptual consensus. To become socialized then means to internalize a shared mode of perceiving or, in the last analysis, to internalize someone else's perception. This process is probably necessary if there is to be any communication between people. As a uniformity of behavior, it connotes that the members have similar opinions and modes of behavior. As social pressure, it means that the group induces or forces certain behavior on a member. A norm becomes, therefore, a "should" or an "ought."

Norms evolve as a group progresses in its formation. The members in interaction develop sentiments or feelings about one another and feelings about what they are doing as a group. A person's sentiments determine how he evaluates himself and others, and whether he approves an action or decision within the group. These sentiments are based initially on his own values which derive from his physical, social, and moral frames of reference. These are his individual norms which he brings to the group from his previous life experience and which were first learned in the family. Once he is in the group, a person considers his behavior with respect to that of the others, that is, compares his norms with the expectations of the other members and, if they are the same, they are commonly shared norms. If they differ, a person may make the others' norms his, internalize them, or just conform to them. He may be subject to group pressure to which he may feel he must yield if he wants to remain in the group and if he sees the group as worthy of the demands it makes in respect to his needs, that is, if the group is significant to him.

It is postulated that the values or behavioral norms that a person learns in a group carry over beyond the group and it is a premise that groupwork has importance in shaping positive, lasting norms through this process. (If norms and values are learned so easily, it would seem that people can become facile at norm adaptation and act the same as chameleons, changing color to suit their surroundings.)

Norms arise around position, status, and role and a group culture develops as "we do it this way." Thus, norms become the standard meanings through which group members communicate with each other. The norms provide both meaning and goals. A person depends upon group norms to give meaning to his actions. Norms provide goals because a person reacts to the approval or disapproval of others which is implicit in a norm. Of course, norms and values of a small group are worked out against the backdrop of the broader culture. Often the requirements for a therapeutic climate for a group are at odds with that broader culture or contraindicated for education, supervision, or in-service training. In these kinds of situations, norms and values tend to be superimposed. Over a period of time, members develop in a group a common set of words and usage, common agreements, physical arrangements, ways of getting work done, rules, and collusions. These are extremely difficult to alter once they become set because people, especially those with position, status, and power, have a vested interest in the status quo. It is, therefore, important for the worker to be involved in the formation of norms from the very outset of the group, beginning with the contract before norms become solidified.

As a by-product of stabilized interaction, members use catchwords, jargon, nicknames, slogans, customs, traditions, and a script. In a real sense, they are programmed. Stabilization of norms is a necessary by-product of group formation but how they are arrived at or imposed is an important question. Strong imposition may result in overly rigid adherence, in dropout and copout, or in conformity without commitment. In another sense, it may result in the "false self." A failure to have or perceive any norms may result in anomie or normlessness and all of the ills that are concomitant to that state.

The process of norming is complex and it has moral and ethical implications as well as those for psychic health. When persons become members, there is a reciprocation of norms and goals among them if they relate themselves to the group. When this occurs, a person is likely to accept willingly demands and instructions from others in the group who are higher up in the hierarchy. That being so, norms become a reference scale for aspiration, longing, selection of resources for satisfaction, the development of personal tastes, and so forth.

At first the norms are external restraints, then through reciprocal interaction they become mutual agreements and as one continues to participate, they become one's own rules. When this happens, a group expects even its leader to follow the rules. If one fails to abide, the price is strain and rejection, hence adherence to group norms is one index of solidarity within a group and is also a characteristic of the ingroup. Small deviations from a norm begin to unstabilize a norm and this readies a group for change.

Piaget's observations are important to groupwork practice as he notes that participation in games and activities with peers helps a child to develop a grasp of reciprocal human relationships. Through cooperative participation, a child comes to accept a group norm as his own and to develop inner loyalties and responsibilities toward the group norm. The premise is that internalization of standards or norms in this way is a major step toward autonomy of behavior in group relations. It does not take into account, however, that such norms may not necessarily meet the needs of the most vulnerable members or that norms held by the majority are not necessarily designed to be enhancing for minority members. The kind of reasoning that pervades Piaget's observations fails to perceive the plight of the child in a disorganized family, the child in the group who comes from an alien culture, or the discomfort of the deviant who believes in truths that as yet have not been discovered by his peers. It does not even raise the question of whether that which is called mental illness may be so designated by cultural definition since the behavior associated with it is a deviation from a social norm. Perhaps certain so-called pathological behaviors could be the rejection of group norms as a person's response to social group pressure or to an intolerable life situation.

The kinds of norms that are appropriate to foster through groupwork are those that honor freedom, that abhor manipulation of others for one's own ends, that oppose domination and control, and that regard the group as a system of mutual aid. Since such norms tend to be different from those in the surrounding culture, they must be introduced into the group at the outset and the effective groupworker, himself, must behave in accordance with such norms.

Some Aspects of Values

Norms, as we have seen, are one of the determinants in group formation because people tend to associate or choose others whom they perceive as sharing their own norms and values. Once they get together, the members learn that one must conform to the norms that are central to the group's concerns and purposes.

The ideas being discussed here give a group power over a member and make a group influential in either changing behavior or keeping it constant. The more a person needs to belong, the more power the group has over him; the more the group is a reference group, the more the individual is likely to look to it for his values. There are serious implications here for members of a group who want to get ahead. When one needs to belong or needs to rise in the hierarchy, one tends to become part of the establishment and become sensitive to the power structure. It has been said that the way to get along is to go along. If one aspires to achieve status and position in an organization, one is reluctant to oppose or antagonize powerful members. There is a breed of people who will risk such opposition and who are loyal to their ideological commitments. They act upon their minority convictions at the expense of getting ahead. In other contexts, people will conform at the expense of getting well. This has most serious connotations for practice.

The interrelationship of the person and the social group is observed, be the group the family, a peer group, a school class, a treatment group, or what have you. If one does not need to belong, a change in group norm may result in his dropping out, whereas one who needs to belong will conform. If the group is a reference group he will look to it for his values, otherwise he may not. The more central a person is in the affectional and communication network, the more he is likely to conform or internalize the values; the more peripheral he is, the less likely he will be to accept or act upon the norms.

Norms and values that are held by at least three high-status people tend to dominate in a group. However, people with strong convictions, great self-confidence and security, or who are challenging for position are not likely to conform. They will think for themselves.

It is easy to see the importance of group experience as an influence on norms, standards, values and hence on behavior. It should be apparent also from one's own experience that psychological sets, modes, and needs influence norms, standards, and values. Rigid people like tight norms. Cold people like values which deny the importance of human relationships. Sadistic people tend to applaud brutality. Frustrated people hate minority groups. People who have problems with relationships subscribe to the norms of a group that provides a constitution, bylaws, officers, and rules even where these have no possible validity for the particular group or its purpose. (Parliamentary procedure was formulated for parliaments and not for groups of eight or ten people.) Once again, the question of appropriateness and group purpose is pertinent.[7]

Subgroups

All groups seem to subdivide and form dyads, triads, and cliques. One way to defend against anxiety is to find allies. Subgroups usually form around common values and attitudes or interests. They also are based upon personal attraction and repulsion.

Subgroups can be based upon symbiotic relationships, can hold different perceptions of group goal, and can result from collusions that involve complementary needs.

Attempts to force the goals of a group on a subgroup will probably be futile and result in hostility and resistance. Subgroups can fragment group effort, cause conflict which may interfere with the attainment of group goals, and often result in the rejection or isolation of the needy members of the group. Dyads and triads usually are composed of friends, but subgroups are not always made up of friends. They may coalesce around individual leaders or points of view. However, when subgroups form, they establish the scales of social distance. Social distance is a phenomenon one tries to minimize in groupwork, especially where the purpose is mutual aid. Belongingness in a group is predicated upon one's acceptance by others.

Wilson and Ryland pointed out that belonging requires some giving of oneself as well as restraint in taking. The insecure person fears closeness and the possibility of self-devastation if he belongs, yet his growth needs motivate him to join and be part of the group.[8] There is a correlation between the acceptance of the members by a person and the acceptance of that person by the members.

In the usual type of group found in a center or settlement, there are various techniques used to bring the members closer together and to reduce the subgroup phenomenon. These will be mentioned here for the purpose of clarity. They include feedback so that the members become aware of what is happening and develop tolerance for each other; invoking the contract so that helping each other becomes more of a norm; seeking commitment to the group goal and to the means for achieving it; cutting across subgroup lines in establishing task groups, subcommittees, and work teams; the use of self as a central point for identification; helping individuals to learn cues and modify behaviors that cause their isolation or rejection; the use of program to facilitate team play, group loyalties, and group responsibilities; and the use of self as a role model.

In treatment groups, mechanical techniques per se are less important than the contract, feedback, and the group climate which is set by the stance of the worker. This will be elaborated upon in a later chapter.

Communication

The essence of interaction among people is communication. In no small measure, it is communication that holds a group together. When analyzing communication, the unit of study is not a person but the context in which an exchange of messages occurs. The exchange includes verbal communication, nonverbal communication (body language and psychic interaction), and also cues that lie hidden within the exchange. Like role, communication is an integrating concept because it is both internal and external to the person, that is, it is part of the social system and, at the same time, part of the psychology of each member.

Reduced to fundamentals, communication is a request, that is, an entreaty for personal need-meeting. It asks others to validate one, to attest that one exists, and to offer favorable response. One *is* because others react to one. In this context, it is essential for one to be in touch with reality-based communication, that is, in communication with reality. People learn to communicate in ways which will secure survival. Communication is learned and it can be learned as real, as distorted, or as part of a special code or language. Its distortion can be taught by one's parents or teachers; distorted communication can be "spoken" at home; distorted communication may be the only medium through which one can gain the desired or necessary response which ensures one's survival or gives one the needed emotional nutrition. Games are often played through the use of distorted communication. This is particularly true of family games.

In all communication, the elements consist of the source or sender, the transmitter, and the destination or receiver. In groupwork, as in other aspects of human relations, the major consideration is the message. What did the sender wish to convey and what did the receiver interpret the message to be? There are messages contained in the social situation itself as well as those from the people involved, messages that tell of norms, of limitations, and of directions. The receiver (a member of a group) must be able to decode the messages so as to recognize the limitations and understand the social reality. The social reality can be inhibiting as well as enhancing and growth-inducing.

Knowing who and what the sender is in all group situations is important to all in the group. In interpreting the message, the receiver assesses the sender's position, status, role, and power in relation to himself before he can decide how to respond. Failure to be able to do this can result in inappropriate behavior and also in a distortion in assessing the sender's intentions. The structural location of the receiver also determines how the message is heard and how it is decoded.

It is a true communication when the intent of the sender is correctly interpreted by the receiver, but in human relations it often happens that the sender does not relay his message properly, that is, he does not say what he means. Senders often convey their intent through gestures, facial expression, intonation and inflection and thereby send instructions as to how their messages are to be interpreted. On the other hand, the receiver can make assumptions about the sender's intentions which may be false.

There are opportunities for misunderstanding at every step. The sender may be unable to say (verbally or nonverbally) what he wants to say because he is "trained" not to; because he is afraid his "bleat" will go unheard, unheeded, unresponded to, responded to in a manner different from what is desired or needed, or that actually he will be punished. The sender may be unable to convey what he wants or needs to because he uses a code that is unknown to the receiver or he has learned different meanings (actual and emotional as in a semantic-differential sense) from those of the receiver. He may have learned a different relationship between communication, action, and consequences, and he may expect his communication to result in a response different from that which the receiver understands he wants and therefore gives. He may also lack communication skill and not know how to say what he wants to say or he may not even know the reality of what he is conveying through the inflection, tempo, and intensity of his speech, his facial expression and body language. A receiver can also have similar problems with being unable to hear true meanings, being unable to decode, or lacking the skill to read cues correctly.

Communication not only conveys meaning or content, but it consists also of metacommunication which tells the receiver how the sender wants him to use the message. Communication defines the relationship between and among the interactors. The way in which one communicates with another tells the receiver what status the sender has, the relative power they have vis-à-vis each other, their role prescriptions, the sentiment between them, the norms which govern their relationship, and perhaps also their goals. Distortions in communication are very crucial in interpersonal relations, are satisfying or endangering, and are central to the group process.

Distortion in communication can be frustrating to the sender or the receiver and can result in behavior which seems to be grossly deviant. For example, the sender may ask for help but use the wrong code and consequently feel that the intended receiver ignores him or does not care; the receiver may fail to hear the intended plea, that is, does not interpret it as such and cannot understand the sender's distress and, therefore, the self-image of the sender may be deflated because the receiver does not validate him. In reality, however, the receiver may not have intended to deflate him but the sender conveyed one set of meanings by his words and a contradictory set by his actions, both at the same time. The sender sent contradictory metacommunications and created a double bind; the sender did not convey a message that could produce the desired response, that is, the communication could not achieve the desired goal, and so on. This is not intended to be a complete detailing, but is only illustrative and as such throws light on why teaching communication is so important and also how groupwork can be very helpful in this regard. It also helps to show how faulty communication can explain emotional disturbance, seemingly inappropriate behavior, poor goal achievement, and systems breakdown.

The feedback from the communication will indicate whether

120

the receiver seems to respond as the sender wishes and will cue the sender to correct distortions, if any, in the communication. Successful communication is the process through which messages lead to a correspondence of information among people.

Communication is not only a person variable but also a group variable. People tend to speak in a meeting in relation to the position they occupy, the status they think they have, their commitment to the group and its goals, and where they think they are in the affectional network. People communicate as they think their role requires and also in response to a favorable or unfavorable climate which includes such things as trust, sanctions, support, anxiety, and the like. Communication in a group can be constructive or destructive. Ignoring, misinterpreting, denying acknowledgment, or returning something other than what was asked for is a "put down." When a person learns how to acknowledge the messages (requests) of others and to be validated himself without escaping from human contact, the group is achieving its purpose in groupwork.

However, although learning to communicate is requisite, improving communication in a group in itself is not enough because relationship is conveyed through communication and, therefore, the full force of position, status, power, control, and the like is transmitted by words, gestures, acts so as to enforce the hierarchies.

An essential skill or area of sensitivity is the groupworker's ability to hear and properly interpret the messages and not to be fooled into thinking that what is being said is what is going on in the group. To be an effective groupworker, one must be able to hear what the group members are working on. The effective groupworker also responds to the total message and not necessarily to the overt cognitive content.

We have seen that there is greater communication in a group between persons of similar status, that is, high-status people talk more to high-status people, also high-status people tend to talk more often. People tend to communicate more with members of their own subgroups and thereby tighten the ingroup which supports their sense of belonging while those outside of the group are not communicated with and their isolation is confirmed. More often, people who enter subgroups hold similar norms and through communication reaffirm and reinforce these norms, heightening the differences between the ingroup and the outgroup. The communication patterns draw the boundary lines, including some and excluding others. In groups, the most active initiators of communication are also the most active receivers. One receives to about the same degree that one sends. High communicators are most often mentioned by others but they are not necessarily more influential.

One observes in groups that leaders tend to address the group as a whole rather than specific members. Those of lower status tend to address specific members and more usually the leaders. The leader tends to become central in the communication network.

Group cohesion is a function of the efficiency of communication. High-cohesion members work hard to negotiate agreements while low-cohesion members are more preoccupied with their own needs and problems. Communication is high in a congenial group but in a noncongenial group communication is poor and there is distrust, suspicion, and jealousy. In groups where communication is good there is mutual understanding so that goals and objectives have relevance and meaning for each member. With better understanding, members make better adjustments. Where communication is blocked, those who do not participate have low status and make poor adjustments.

People will rarely hear messages which represent a viewpoint which is different from their own. When they do listen, they tend to accept those facts which are consistent with their previously held opinions or they reinterpret the message so that it will have a meaning different from that which was intended. In lieu of these reactions, some people will treat the message as inconsequential or irrelevant. Even when people are exposed to and accept as fact ideas which conflict with those they originally held, they do not necessarily act on them.

A group is influential because it can define reality to a person through an infinite variety of sense data and by the definition which a group gives to those data experientially. Once members become involved in the group goal and in an awareness of the need for cooperation, they become motivated to correct communication distortions. People are influenced by a group in their perception of events and members alter their perceptions when there is explicit group support for such change.

Once committed, people will attend to communications which are consistent with group norms. For example, when a group of people commits itself to mutual aid, communication patterns also tune themselves to those ends. Persons who participate in the communication and decision-making process are more likely to be committed to the message. It is primarily through group participation that one can ensure diffusion of a message, hence one of the basic objectives in groupwork is decentralizing the communication process.

When a person's overt behavior becomes different from his private opinions, there is a tendency for his private attitudes to change to coincide with his behavior. A change in behavior as a result of new learning in a group or because the climate allows it, will result in attitudes and motivations which were in harmony with the old behaviors being dissonant with the new ones. Such a clashing between behavior and attitudes often will cause one to change one's attitudes to be in keeping with the new ways of acting. Messages which point out errors as a lesson of what not to do may actually defeat the purpose. Action rather than knowledge is primary in producing attitudinal change. Since action is the teacher, it is the experience in the group, not insight as such, which is most effective.

Communication patterns influence goal-attaining activities by either affirming or denying latent objectives and by negotiating between personal goal orientations and the group goals. Such processes facilitate commitment and hence achievement. It is through communication which defines the relationship between members that power is explicated and this, in turn, regulates control. A person learns to communicate, learns the codes, and learns the relationship between the communication and its consequence through his experience with a significant communication network. The group can provide an arena for learning, especially through feedback, awareness, skill-training, and the opportunity to engage in reality-testing.

A person's communication patterns can help him to meet his needs or they can thwart him. These patterns can be reinforced in a group by affirming status, role, position, power, adequacy, and belonging by virtue of the communication patterns within the group. On the other hand, the group can provide a "script" which is different from the one the person (or family) habitually re-enacts and by so doing reorient the person and give reinforcement to new communication options which establish him differently in the system. Such a communication switch can offer new resources, reset relationship alignments, and elicit a new set of behaviors by meeting needs. Communication is the major process through which the person and for his environment transact.

I have approached the influence of communication on behavior by indicating that faulty communication may exist in the person's transmitters, decoders, and receptors. These can be affected by skill-training, awareness, alleviation of anxiety and fear, goal reorientation, and similar approaches. People communicate in a group through the group structure. In this regard, we observe that structural realignments, changes in communication patterns, and feedback can serve to reinforce individual behavior patterns or alter them.

If we put these two ideas together, we can influence the group (treat the system) in order to improve its communication patterns in the service of personal needs. By design, the group can move more readily toward its goal achievement and, more importantly, it can help the members to communicate so as to maximize their growth and functioning. In this way, both the individual and the group are helped.

In the following chapter, structure will be discussed in the context of social systems.

NOTES / READINGS

1. The content in this section is derived primarily from Henry S. Maas, "Behavioral Science Bases for Professional Education: The Unifying Conceptual Tool of Cultural Role," in *Proceedings of the Interdisciplinary Conference on Behavioral Concepts which Can Be Applied to Education for the Helping Professions* (Washington, D.C.: Howard University School of Social Work, 1958).

2. Carl Rogers, *Freedom to Learn* (Columbus, Ohio: Merrill Publishing Company, 1969), p. 183.

3. William E. Gordon, "Constructs for Organizing Social Work Knowledge," a working paper for the *Sub-committee on Knowledge Building, National Association of Social Workers, Commission on Practice*, October, 1966. (Mimeographed.)

4. Carl Rogers, *Freedom to Learn*, p. 192.

5. E. R. Rogers and R. F. Dymond, *Psychotherapy and Personality Changes* (Chicago: University of Chicago Press, 1954).

6. Charles Silberman, *Crisis in the Classroom* (New York: Random House, 1970).

7. See Judith Blake and Kingsley Davis, "Norms, Values, and Sanctions" in *Handbook of Modern Sociology*, edited by Robert E. L. Faris (Chicago: Rand McNally & Co., 1964), pp. 456–483, for a more detailed treatment of norms and values.

8. Gertrude Wilson and Gladys Ryland, *Social Group Work Practice* (New York: Houghton Mifflin Co., 1949), p. 50.

4

✦✦✦✦✦✦✦✦✦

A Group is a Social System

Groupworkers were aware of and using system concepts long before social-systems theory became popular in social work. A group of people is a classical example of a social system. The main elements of a social system are the same as those which were discussed in Chapter 3 under the heading of Group Structure; namely, role, status, position, norms, power, beliefs, sentiments, goals, relationships, interaction, and so forth. The processes are also similar; namely, communication, decision-making, boundary maintenance, attraction and repulsion, tension reduction, movement toward goals, and the like. The recognition that the principles which apply to social systems also govern group dynamics is important in any discussion of practice although it is often overlooked. We will look at the dynamics of social systems in this chapter and assay their relevance for groupwork practice.

What Is a Social System?

A social system consists of a number of people who have established more or less regularized patterns of interaction with each other based upon a defined social structure and operative through shared expectations and symbols. Group interaction, as we have seen in previous chapters, tends to develop uniformities or habitual modes over a period of time, and the relationships between and among the people tend to become structured. Therefore, social systems have structure and some degree of stability. Interaction herein means events in which one member influences the actions, emotions, and thinking of another. In a social system, it is always reciprocal and interdependent, and as there are common feelings and goals, usually some degree of intimacy ensues and results in group bond.

A system is maintained through some internal source of tension and within any group there are mutual attractions, repulsions, conflicts, agreements, and pressures, such as pressures to conform, to adjust to systemic changes, to adapt, and/or to resist.

Open social systems do not exist in a vacuum; they are part of and transact with an environment. They are, in fact, in constant transaction with their surroundings and are interchanging sentiments, thoughts, actions, and resources as well as developing and alleviating tensions with the environment; hence social groups are "open" systems.

Let us stop here to discuss the implications of what has been said so far. Every person in a group, through interaction, influences every other person in the group and also the group as an entity. The kind of influence changes in accordance with such variables as position, status, role, image, power, contagion, readiness, and so forth. A worker is part of the system and his influence which is brought about by his behavior or communication is but one factor in the process as every member is also influencing every other member as well as the group. The acts of the worker cannot be said to be the sole cause of any change or movement nor can any specific act be so identified. Moreover, the worker cannot consciously select a communication or an act to perform with any assurance that it will produce any one desired or preconceived result. The worker can only stimulate group interaction, help the members to become aware of what is happening, and control his own behavior. In a social system, a change in any component or process within that system will result in change in all of the components and processes. Although an accurate prediction of the results of any change is impossible, a worker must be consciously aware that changes in individual behavior or group climate will inevitably create changes in the system. Conversely, changes in the system will effect changes in the members. Variables changed by the organism also change the organism in a social system.

Since it is axiomatic that a group or open system is in constant transaction with the environment, it is not valid to assume that what happens in the group at any given time is the sole or even major influence on the group or the members. Consequently, the group's life cannot be analyzed or recorded by including only that which takes place in a group meeting. It has long been postulated that what one learns and internalizes in a therapeutic situation takes on its real meaning as the person uses it in a life situation. We also know from learning theory that new learnings must be reinforced if they are to become part of one's mode of adaptation.

These simple statements inform us that if group experiences are to be successful in enhancing social functioning, they must be buttressed, for example, by the institution in the case of corrections or treatment facilities, by the family in the case of the treatment of a member, or by the school or center, if those are applicable. They also tell us that group analysis and recording, to have meaning, must be broadened to include significant inputs and transactions with the impinging environment.

Social systems tend to be responsive to both internal and external stimuli and they correct their action through feedback. Uncountable numbers of stimuli come to a person and a group at any given time. There is, therefore, a wide variety of influences that assail the person and the group. Through an adaptive process, systems select from the feedback that to which they are ready to respond for self-regulation and self-direction.

Since it would be impossible for any system to respond to all of these stimuli, the members and the group develop an adaptive process for selecting and sifting the stimuli and defenses against some of them. These include mechanisms such as selective inattention, denial, disbelief, and resistance. Each person develops his own criteria for creditability or sensitivity and also a mode of adaptation to his situation. The person and also a group develop tendencies to respond in certain ways, limitations on response, and possible alternative sets. These give rise to habits for decision-making, for emotional reactions such as fear, and for patterns of behavior. Such variables as norms, expectations for role behaviors and the like, at best, can suggest only ranges of performance. Variables such as power, esteem, personal need-meeting and secondary gains often underlie how one selects or hears communication, and deep feelings can block cues being transmitted through feedback. Some of the most important variables which control the selection of stimuli and the accuracy of perception include past experiences, predispositions, characterological traits, personal goals, self-image, values, anxieties, norms, needs, and membership in a reference group.

The significance of these concepts lies in the quality and availability of information. It is of great importance for the groupworker to understand the nature of feedback loops and the dynamics of feedback control in order to understand behavior and, to be effective, how he fits into the group process. The effective groupworker feeds back information on what is happening, highlights information that is being ignored, and relates the consequences of their behaviors to the members so that they have the resources upon which to base self-corrective action. The members and the group as a whole can thereby see that some of their behaviors are dysfunctional responses to the incoming stimuli. By feedback the worker helps the group members become aware of this and thus stimulates within them the urge to become more responsible. The members are enabled to choose responses consciously instead of blindly.

The focus of the feedback is what the worker actually hears and observes. "Why" is not discussed. In a sense, "why" is irrelevant and an unnecessary impediment to a self-correction. The important factors have to do with "what" and "how," and by feedback to ask the members to come to grips with the situation and decide what would be in their best interests. In this endeavor, the worker cannot be said to be either permissive, nondirective, or dictatorial.

Social systems and, therefore, groups tend to develop cycles of events wherein their own output stimulates a repetition of their habitual behaviors. This is particularly obvious in family groups where, although the events may be distasteful to all and are dysfunctional, the groups seem helpless to break out of the cycle. Here, also, awareness through confrontation, the introduction of the worker into the system, and the establishment of a comparison of goals with the current consequencies are indicated.

Hierarchies of prestige and power based upon status and position limit the flow of feedback. They also limit the input of energy from the outside. Since systems tend to run down unless they can import as much energy as they use, it can be said that such hierarchies tend to encourage the gradual demise of the system. This phenomenon can be observed repeatedly in organizations.

All social systems function with tension and strain and consequently there always will be conflict. A worker must accept the fact that conflict is part of the group life. Stress, at first, seems to improve the performance of the group but continuing stress becomes destructive. Conflict can be useful if it can be an experience in growth and since growth does not occur in quiescence, tension may be a stimulator which can be strengthening for growth and change. Herein, the use of feedback can result in helping the members to rise to higher levels of interpersonal integration.

Systems tend to revert to a steady state, a state of dynamic homeostasis. Defining a group as a system has been criticized because it has been said that resolutions in a system return the system to equilibrium and that such a process is inimical to social change. It is true that restrictive solutions to tension can ease the stress by a return to a nonfunctional balance. If the groupworker is willing to accept dishonest compatibility in either a group or family, they may resort to dead-level equilibrium wherein all the members agree to make the best of an impossible situation. To be effective, the worker can neither retreat in the interest of peace and quiet, nor can he seize control and resort to interpretation and direction. Instead, the worker must probe for options, encourage freedom, and enable the members to make choices. Instead of settling for equilibrium, his approach is to facilitate spiraling, that is, dynamic homeostasis at a rising level from where the situation began. Thus, the use of conflict can result in innovation, creativity, and emergent solutions.

A system in equilibrium reacts to impingements by resisting, denying, defending, creating a new balance, by accommodation which can mean reorganization, or by dramatic change. All open systems are constantly subjected to a wide variety of strains and inputs from the environment and these inputs contribute to a continuous process which provides potential for structural reorganization. An important aspect of an adaptive system is that it has the capacity to change its structure, often in fundamental ways. It is also basic that an adaptive system can develop and change structure as a result of internal stimuli.

The Relevance of Systems Concepts

These observations underscore several important aspects for groupwork. The first is the importance of keeping the structure relatively loose so that rigid hierarchies are not established and, also, so that the system can remain adaptive. Secondly, the relationship of the group to its environment is a critical dimension of group movement. This ongoing relationship is fostered by the use of outside resources, program, involvement in councils and community endeavors, the introduction of visual aids, speakers, trips, and the like as well as the use of the worker as a liaison and resource. The match between the group and its impinging environment is an essential component of social groupwork. Social action by the group is one important medium for accomplishing these goals. Thirdly, the fact that adaptive systems do change structures is the basis in groupwork for a means of effecting change in the behavior of the members of groups by altering relationships. The group process and systemic interaction do influence status, position, role, power, communication, and so forth. This, of course, is one of the important ways by which group life can enhance the social functioning of the members.

In retrospect, we can see some important functions for a groupworker if the group is to be an adaptive system. He can facilitate a continuing introduction of various stimuli into the group which necessitate constant adjustment and coping. He can help to regulate the tension levels so that they will be optimum for the maintenance of the group and also be at a high level of need-meeting. He can facilitate communication within the group, between the group and its surroundings, and he can help to provide the linkage to a number of other systems. He can provide feedback. He can and must help the group to develop a viable decision-making process. For the group to be truly adaptive, it must be sensitive to changes in itself and in the environment; it must be willing and able to adjust values, norms, and goals; and it must have some way of perpetuating that which is nutritive and growth-inducing.

The basic problem in all of this is that groups tend to be blind. They must be helped to perceive their operations in the light of their purposes, goals, and futures. It is the function of the group-worker to help the group members become aware and to activate them to take responsibility for making choices. It is not the function of the worker, however, to tell the group how to achieve its goals. Even if he wants to, and I hope he does not, he will be constrained by the concept of *equifinality* which holds that a system can reach the same final state by a variety of means; there is no one way. He is also cautioned against any idea about simple causality in systems analysis. Simple causality for events is not useful as the interactions are too numerous, too complex, and depend upon reciprocal reactions.

I do not intend to beg the question or become clouded in semantics, but it must be noted that a person in a group functions as part of a social system and, as such, he is not an individual. He is related in a mutual, reciprocal, and interdependent way to everyone else in the group, and in it he relates and interacts in his unique way.[1] He cannot do anything else or be anything else. This is the essence of social functioning.

A social system is understood by examining sets of relationships. It is not understood by analysis or study of its members. The study of the individual members as discrete entities will not reveal the dynamics of a system. A system is characterized by the relationships between and among the components and their interactions. The focus of study is the interacts. Groupwork practice is not predicated on the influence of a groupworker on members; the group and the group process are the influences and it is the group that is the therapeutic medium. This statement that a system is a network of relationships and that a study examines relationships and interacts and not individuals supports the contention that the worker responds to what he hears and observes in the group situation and is concerned with the "what" and "how" of the situation. I contend, therefore, that extensive history-taking is not useful and that searching for causes or answers to "why" does not facilitate growth and change. Some aspects of the past are relevant insofar as feelings about it or memories of it are in the present but what happens, happens in the present and the members must resolve their problems with present solutions.

A social system is enclosed by a boundary within which are acts, statuses, sentiments, tensions, goals, roles, power, norms, sanctions, time, rank, and the like, but not individuals. Where one draws the boundary depends upon the variables which are under consideration. The usual method of determining where the boundary lies is to determine where there is a maximum interchange of selected variables. This is not a boundary determined by membership but by action. Once again, there are times when a group record, to have meaning, must reflect a wider boundary than membership or a group meeting. For example, sometimes the "invisible committees" are the crucial determinants of the interaction.

Systems analysis at best is a descriptive construct. It is a descriptive device which is useful for viewing a group but it cannot be thought of as a theory because it does not explain what happens. It draws pictures of the events. It cannot be called a model for the same reasons. However, even with these limitations, it is a very useful device. For instance, it provides a means for identifying the boundary that includes the variables which are significant for practice. This should make it possible also to identify influential subsystems and to define the important linkages over which inputs and outputs travel. Unless a group is viewed from this perspective, one can fail to perceive some of the most useful or critical variables in behavior.

The Usefulness of Systems Concepts

Systems analysis is useful because it permits the worker to locate the tensions and ascertain how they operate. Such identification can reveal major points of friction which may make the system nonfunctional or dysfunctional. The assessment of these major incongruents, distortions, misapprehensions, and the like is useful, for example, in family group counseling.

By charting a system one can find problems in structure, in process, or in the state of the components. This information can be fed back so that the group can correct or the worker can expose the group to stimuli that will help it to perceive its malfunction. The analysis also helps to relate functioning to goals, or to the absence of goals, the lack of agreement on goals, or to commitment to goals.

Systems analysis allows the group to ascertain the changes that

131

can be made with a minimum of upset or discomfort to achieve the maximum in the desired directions. It allows one to select the most feasible point of entry within the system or its subsystems, and sometimes in the suprasystem such as the agency or its procedures, for example. A careful analysis in systems terms can reveal the most rewarding point of leverage where a small amount of pressure might produce great changes.

An awareness of how systems operate alerts a worker to exercise care because a change in any one variable will result in a change in others. Although one cannot predict accurately what the eventual outcomes will be, one can make tentative predictions and assess the probabilities based upon the relationships of many of the variables in the system. For example, one often can predict that as certain members become more aggressive and assertive others will become sicker. By like token, a worker might be able to make some predictions about what might happen, by extrapolation, if nothing in the system were changed.

One of the more important values of a systems approach is that it helps considerably to ascertain what blocks movement and what promotes movement in a group. One can decide what maintains stability and how change occurs. Along these lines, it also helps to see what is usual or inherent in the particular group and what might be symptomatic of dysfunction. The systems approach is most useful for diagnosis.[2]

It can be gleaned from the writings of many systems theorists that there are four major functional imperatives of systems. These four give one a working basis for both diagnosis and treatment because the most common problems in group life, and especially in family group life, can be located in one or more of these areas. They are complementarity of roles, commonality of goals and values, motivation of the members for the survival of the system, and the meeting of the basic needs, whether real or perceived to be real, of the components.[3]

We will return to some of the ideas expressed in this chapter when we deal with groupwork method in Chapter 8 but now we are ready to analyze what occurs in the next phases of a group's development.

NOTES / READINGS

1. Don Jackson says in *General Systems Theory and Psychiatry*, edited by William Gray, Frederick J. Duhl, and Nicholas Drizzo (New York: Little Brown & Co., 1970), "We view symptoms, defense, character structure and personality, as terms describing the individual's typical interaction which occur

in response to a particular interpersonal context rather than as intrapsychic entities."

2. Alan F. Klein, *Social Work Through Group Process* (Albany, New York: School of Social Welfare, SUNY, 1970), pp. 137–147, and *The Application of Social Systems Theory to Social Work in Family Diagnosis and Treatment* (Albany, New York: School of Social Welfare, SUNY, 1969).

3. For a detailed analysis of social systems see Harry C. Bredemeier and Richard M. Stephenson, *The Analysis of Social Systems* (New York: Holt, Rinehart, & Winston, 1962).

5

✦✦✦✦✦✦✦✦✦

The Struggle to Be Free and
Have Equal Opportunity

In this chapter the second and third phases of group development
will be discussed. Once the members of a grouping begin to feel
comfortable with each other, and if some trust has been established,
the grouping as a whole will be ready to face the threat of the
authority of the worker. My observations that the members are
freed sufficiently from their fear of each other to become aware
of the particular power of the worker follows the theoretical formulation laid down by Garland, Jones, and Kolodny.[1] This is not primarily a question of transference but a matter of reality because,
in most instances, the worker indeed has power and can wield it
if he chooses. At the same time, a key concern is still the relative
power of the participants over each other.

Phase II—Resistance: The Struggle to Be Free

There are, then, two factors which facilitate movement into the
second phase of a group's development: trust of one another and
a feeling of some security about the social situation. The members
have some familiarity with the reactions of others, some knowledge
of the incipient social structure, and a vague idea of prevailing values
and developing norms. As a result, some people become more aggressive as they attempt to meet their needs and bid for favorable response. Some who are naturally passive remain passive. The theme
in the group is to resist authority and defy the worker by either
overt or devious means. This occurs because the members are willing

134

to test for limits and now that they have some allies they feel secure enough to seek to gain control of their situation and exercise will.

The battle of wills between child and parents which occurs in our society in the toddler years is resolved usually by clamping down firmly on the child's creative spirit. American educational institutions do not teach or encourage innovative thinking. Our industrial system rewards conformity and our political climate is repressive. We worship equilibrium and stability as being good, and to us socialization means inculcating the view of the establishment. Now, if the members find a democratic climate, stated in the contract and restated by the stance of the worker, which encourages them to think for themselves, free themselves of socially induced fears, and be what they yearn to be, this climate cries out to be tested. If the climate is autocratic, the members react as they usually do in repressive settings; they supress hostility to the worker and scapegoat members, they deviate in various ways to beat the system, they conform, or they act out. They become alienated and false or they may give up.

As the focus shifts from mistrust of peers to resistance to the worker, concomitantly a power structure is evolving and indigenous leaders are gaining control over some people and are preparing to challenge the worker. While some people are vying for leadership positions, these power struggles may result in scapegoating; when leaders emerge some people become followers, some become isolates, and some people fall by the wayside.

If the group is composed of people with emotional problems, there will be a free expression of anxiety, otherwise anxieties will be manifested in withdrawal or in increased aggressiveness. The thrust to cope with the worker is displaced onto each other. Some members are put down, cast into low-status positions which call for subordinate or subservient roles. Allies are found and lost, new ones are solicited; relationships are negotiated and clarified; members seek to resolve differences among themselves in order to present a united front.

Many writers assume that after these maneuvers subside, the majority of the members will have found ways to meet their needs in a satisfactory manner, and that they will have reached compromises about some of their desires and obligations. These authors assume that bond and commitment result. Unfortunately, this kind of reasoning rationalizes the patterns of our society: the strong reign. This model traditionally is carried over into many forms of treatment, placing the client or member under the control of authority—the worker, others, the agency—confirming the infirmity of the client and bridling his will. Many workers have trouble understanding or accepting this view of reality because they have been controlled and have incorporated and internalized social stratification so thoroughly that it is hard for them to conceive of freedom.

The attempt on the part of the members to develop a united front rarely is successful because the members are ambivalent about the power exerted over them by some and the roles into which they are cast, and they continue to jockey for position. The weak fall and the strong rise. It used to be considered good practice for the groupworker to form a coalition with those who become the leaders at this point.

The second phase overlaps and melds with the next phase. How the sequence occurs depends, in part, on the stance of the worker. However, major strivings continue as the members try to find places in which they can meet their needs in the emerging hierarchies; some of their solutions may be self-defeating or neurotic.

Phase III—Negotiation: To Find a Niche

There are vacillating reactions to what is occurring. The climate is hostile and filled with conflict. There continues to be discontent with some roles, new roles are tried and revised, and gradually patterns of relationship become more stabilized. There may be resignation to a pecking order and a retreat where the losers accept their usual fate and give up.

Four things have been occurring and it is important to know what they are so as not to be caught by surprise and not to take the events personally. *First,* jockeying for control and testing the tolerances of the group and the worker. *Second,* testing the worker's allegation that he will not repress or dominate them. *Third,* the members become anxious when they realize that the worker means it when he says they are free and that what happens in the group is up to them. Freedom is a frightening concept and while people yearn to be free, they are anxious and fearful of having to make their own decisions and live by them. It requires more energy, more investment, more ability, and greater maturity to think for oneself. If the decision proves to be a poor one, they have no one else to blame. So it is that groups want chairmen to run things, clients want workers to tell them what to do, and most students want to go to class and listen to lectures. While this is what they want, their spirits rebel and they feel infantilized, molded, demeaned, and angry. They want and accept an autocratic situation because they have learned to be passive under restraint. They have been trained to mouth democratic slogans but to fear democratic freedom. In a real sense, many people yearn to be restrained and to be threatened with punishment because they have always confused superego with external control. Now they are being asked to use self-control. *Fourth*, there is a beginning of mutuality. The members dimly perceive that "no man is an island" and their anxiety regarding freedom, self-adequacy, and isolation generates a felt need for the protection of the "tribe," an ancient need of the herd instinct. In reality, there is no group until this happens and, actually, no viable treatment milieu either. One can argue that the group experience up to this point has been growth-inducing and therapeutic for the members. There has been a great advance for many if they have been helped to reach the threshold of intimacy. The chances are, however, that the experience will not hold up unless the gain which has been achieved can be internalized, reinforced, and stabilized.

The action, then, has been either negotiation and success or capitulation and suppression. Usually, roles now become crystallized, structured, and rigid. The struggle to be free of domination subsides and the fight to be oneself has been won or lost. Either way, people now know who is who, what is what, and can interact with each other from agreed-upon positions, statuses, and roles. How this has turned out depends upon the presence and effectiveness of groupwork. If there is a worker who acts as an expert—the central figure, the doctor—the group process will be very different from what it is when there is one who is an enabler and a partner.

If the members are relieved of the struggle, they can move on to planning and, as we shall see in the next two sections, there is a renewal of a clarification of their purpose and a commitment to the group goal. The period is characterized by the establishment of direction and motivation. A unique group culture is discernible and the collection of people has become a group, ready to work on its concerns and tasks. The members can accept and trust each other and the worker, personal involvement can increase, there is a strengthening of cohesion, and a desire to achieve group goals.

It is toward the end of the third phase of group development that the question of what the members are really there for is raised even though purpose had been discussed before and a contract negotiated.

Purpose Becomes Meaningful

In the first weeks, much effort goes into the negotiation of a contract and into the enunciation of group purpose. It is assumed by some practitioners that the contract is agreed upon in the first or second meeting. The negotiations to enter into a contract are begun then and the broaching of purpose or group goal happens then. It is a great and ubiquitous mistake to assume that there is a contract or group goal much before the question of whether the worker is going to control the group is partially resolved.

Contracts are based upon good faith and, as I said before, in the first phase the members have no reason to believe that the worker is trustworthy or that his profession of his intentions is more than a trick. "What is his angle; what's in it for him?" lurks in their minds. Past experience has taught many that it is painful to hope or to commit oneself to any goal or person. The members may lack self-confidence, and a poor self-image is not conducive to a belief that the group or its members can succeed. Many people have been indoctrinated to believe in experts and in witch doctors who *could* cure them if they wanted to do so. Many have learned that the dominators do not want the people to be cured because either they do not care or they have something to gain by exploiting them. The members are ambivalent about dependency-independency. Each member wonders, since the other members have hangups themselves, how they can help him by anything as intangible as mutual aid. Each member is so involved with his own hurts and needs that he has no resources or time left to care about the others. Members transfer their hurt and their hostility toward authority figures or representatives of the established institutions to the worker, and can see no rewards for making the effort to change their behavior. There are many other reasons and feelings involved in the first phase, not the least of which is simply fear of other people and the worker. To assume that a collection of people and a worker are going to make a binding contract as poignant with meaning as a treatment contract in this emotional climate is fantasy.

I suggest that the members really do not hear the early discussion about contract, purpose, group goal, and expectations. They are much too occupied with feelings of fear and yearning, much too guarded to allow themselves to hope, and too frustrated and disappointed to "ever love again." Obviously, the more the members have been hurt, the more true this becomes. I submit, for example, that a group of so-called normal children in a settlement, in a center, or in a Y are beset with similar feelings but to a lesser degree. One could hypothesize that the deeper the hurt and the greater the negative experience with authority, the longer it will take for a group to reach successfully the point of readiness to become a treatment or growth group.

However, when people have been socialized into a pattern of conformity, or have had their wills broken, or have given up any conscious desire to be themselves and to find an identity, they may seem to go through these early stages quickly. Many a worker has been misled into believing that he has a treatment or growth group when, in fact, he has a collection of trained actors or zombies. The clues for recognizing the situation are to be found in continued and subtle dependency patterns wherein the members sense what the worker wants and give it to him, or hang back and seduce him into making suggestions with which they "enthusiastically" agree, or where the members are superficially going through the motions which usually are associated with intimacy. A more invidious event occurs when the members "sell out" by accepting the worker's version of reality as the price for his support and help.

If the members have begun to realize and accept each other, the group, the potential, and the integrity of the worker, then a contract can be entered into at this time and the group will be on the road to becoming a viable medium for enhancing social functioning. One can expect, at long last, such questions as "What are we here for anyway?" "What good is meeting like this and talking?" "This is no good, why don't we do something?" "We talk and talk but we never accomplish anything." "Why doesn't the worker tell us what we are here for?" In Eriksonian terms, if one can hope to do something, one can then will to do it. After this comes the realization and question, "To do what?" The group is ready to discuss and formulate a group goal related to its purpose.

The personal goals inherent in group formation and the group goals manifested in the early stage of development now can mature into enhancement or treatment goals. Often manifest or task goals are instrumental in creating or enabling the conditions in which treatment goals evolve. The long-range goal which may have been seen dimly in the first phases of the group's life now can become the immediate goal of the major phase of group development, the one in which enhancement and treatment are maximized. This goal is the development of conditions which facilitate the growth or habilitation of the members and in which the members can find themselves—intimacy and mutual aid. Such a goal evolves through interpersonal transaction and now motivates collective endeavor. The reasons why the enunciation of such a goal is vital in groupwork is explained in the next section.

The Emergence of a Group Goal

In Chapter 2 we noted that groups form around goals and they develop goals. We noted also in Chapter 4 that social systems are goal directed. However, when people come together in a group which is formed to enhance the social functioning of the members, a group goal may not be apparent to them and the members may not be motivated to develop a goal: Initiative or purpose does not evolve until hope and will have been established.

A group goal is something to work for; it gives meaning to working together. A group goal is essential because it focuses effort and directs the members out of themselves into the world of others. A group goal is a reason for anticipating meetings and wanting to attend them.

If there is a group goal, there is a reason to communicate with each other. In many families and in many other human relationships, there is no basis for communicating with others because they see little to be accomplished by this, but if there is a goal to be reached and people can talk about it, they can get to know each other. A shared goal is a basic prerequisite for intimacy, closeness, and human encounter and if there can be some movement toward a goal, there can be satisfaction, improved self-image, and a sense of mastery.

We have moved through several group phases. Some groups may spend more time than others on any one stage and some may reach these stages in different sequences. It is axiomatic that no group can be made to go faster than its members are able to go, and if it is pushed to an advanced stage before the previous one has been negotiated, it is almost always true that it will have to return to the stage that it slipped past before a maximum use of the group's potential is possible.

If groupwork has been effective, the members will be free to work on their problems, will be identified with treatment goals, will address themselves to interpersonal negotiation and to transaction with the environment, will view the worker as a partner and the agency as a helping resource. The stage is set for the phase of intimacy and mutuality and the task of achieving selfhood.

The excerpt of a record which follows illustrates the deleterious effects of domination when committed by a group member and permitted by a worker.

An Illustration of the Effects of Domination by a Group Member

AGE: Eleven and Twelve
SETTING: Settlement House
SESSION: Eighth

On Tuesday evening, February 11, the club presented the play *The Troubles of Camping Girls* for the staff group. Both the worker and the members agreed it was the best of the three performances. All the girls were less excited than before, less quarrelsome, and Mary was especially helpful in insisting upon order and quiet. The worker called for Louisa at 6:15 and was well received by her family, both the mother and father coming out to speak and smile affably. After the performance worker gave the girls a treat of ice cream bars (a great surprise which pleased them apparently, for they were all volubly appreciative and Lucia said, "Jees . . . it's swell t'git somep'n you didn't never expect"). The worker accompanied all the girls home, and they talked happily of plans for the near future. They have given up the idea of a skating party temporarily and Mary said they would like to give another spaghetti dinner and invite their mothers. The worker said we would see Miss A. about a date the first thing tomorrow (when the club meets), and all scattered to their respective homes.

The group straggled in very late—nearly 4:30. All were present but Louisa, and a new girl was presented to the worker by Lucia who said, "Miss Summers, this is Frances an' she's joinin'." The worker had seen Frances once at a skating party and spoke of remembering her. Frances is tall, slender, and fourteen, appreciably older in looks and actions than any of the Mysterious Maidens. The worker was astonished that she should have found favor with this exclusive group and watched for reactions from Mary. No explanation was forthcoming, however, till a little later Antoinette seemed to wake up to the fact that Frances was in our midst. "Git outa here, girl," she said to Frances, "this is our club." Lucia flared up, "She's *joined* our club, smarty!" and Mary added in a similarly peeved tone, "And just what do you expect to do about it, Antoinette?" Antoinette made a face, winked at the worker and said, "My God, what next?" but she gave Frances a friendly poke and no more was said.

All this went on in the hall. The worker asked Mary if the group would like to stop in Miss A.'s office and arrange a date for the dinner. She said languidly, "I suppose so," and we all went in. Lucia and Josephine talked excitedly to Miss A., telling her they were going to "make the swellest dinner for our mothers." The more they talked the cloudier grew Mary's expression. Finally she said, "Aw, our mothers can't come anyway. They gotta make dinner at home." Lucia looked distressed, turned to the worker and said, "But we want to show 'em how good we cook—don't we, Miss Summers?" Mary intervened. "We ain't gonna have it. We'll have a skatin' party." By now all were screaming their preferences. Miss A. hushed them up, saying she had to have cotton for her ears, and offered several alternatives: having the mothers come early, having a luncheon on some school holiday, etc. Mary downed everything. Miss A. tried to shift her attention by suggesting dates, and mentioned it would soon be Lent. Juliana burst out, "We can't eat no meat Wednesdays, either. That means no party." Miss A. asked why they didn't plan to wait until after Lent and maybe have something around Mother's Day or even a picnic later on. All were enthusiastic about this, even Lucia giving up her cherished plan with good grace.

141

Mary caught sight of Louisa across the street and rushed out to see her, followed by Antoinette, Josephine, Lucia and Juliana. Frances stayed behind and the worker had a moment to talk to her. She said she had been in the Fun Makers Club last year but didn't want to belong any more. She has no other affiliations in the house. The worker said, "Maybe you will find this club a little young," but Frances smiled and shook her head, saying, "I know 'em all good and Lucia wants me."

The others returned, breathless and angry. Mary was fairly exploding with wrath. "Louisa always thinks she has to go someplace—Club ain't good enough fer 'er. She can just git out!" Antoinette, round-eyed, said, "Oooooh! I'll tell!" Mary snapped, "*Tell* and see if I care!"

Once they were gathered around the table in the meeting room, Anna started a discussion of the skating party. From then on all was conversation (no action), so it will be recorded as such:

LUCIA: Well, let's git this party settled. When can we have it, Miss Summers?

WORKER: We will have to ask Mr. S. for a date.

MARY: We ain't havin' no skatin' party.

ALL: Hey! Aw gee! No fairs! Who said so!

WORKER: Girls, *please* . . . quietly! Sh! (*No attention paid.*)

LUCIA: (*distressed*) Mary, you said no spaghetti dinner, now no skatin' party. What's the matter with you?

JULIANA: Oh, she's an old ——— (*word in Italian*).

ANTOINETTE: Shut up!

JULIANA: Shut up yourself!

MARY: Shut up the *both* of you!

ANTOINETTE: Aw nuts!

MARY: You can git out of here, too!

(*Frances listened to all this, smiling back at Worker.*)

WORKER: This isn't getting us very far. . . . How about our party?

MARY: Thur ain't none.

ALL: (*Screaming incoherently and with deafening din!*)

FRANCES: I know what! We could bring sandwiches!

ALL BUT MARY: Sure. Swell!

MARY: Who do you think you are? I run this club.

WORKER: Maybe we could all think better if we stood up and stretched a while. Who has a game they like to play?

JOSEPHINE: Tommy Tiddler! (*Others called out but Worker did not catch what they said.*)

MARY: No! No! No!

WORKER: That's all right Mary . . . you don't have to play if you'd rather not.

ALL: (*subsiding*) We dowanna play neither.

MARY: Let's take some of our money and go to a show.

ALL: (*cheering*) Sure!

LUCIA: Hurray for the president! She has the best ideas!

WORKER: That *is* a good idea!

MARY: (*resting her head on her arms*) No! We ain't going to no show!

ALL: Aw, Mary . . . you don't want nothin'!

WORKER: You know what I think? We're all pretty tired and maybe we ought to plan later on when we feel more like it. Would you like to go down to East Victory, maybe, and look at the Valentine things?

LUCIA: Swell! Sure! (*All but Mary echoed.*)

MARY: Naw . . . I ain't allowed to walk. I'm sick.

JULIANA: How's come you jump around like that then?

MARY: Get outa here!

WORKER: Maybe we all should get outa here! We certainly aren't having any fun.

JOSEPHINE: I'll say.

MARY: I'm having fun!

WORKER: (*looking squarely at her and laughing heartily*) I'll just bet you are! (*The others laughed uncertainly, looking at Mary who grinned a little, too.*) But it's not my idea of fun or even of a club meeting. Are you sure you wouldn't enjoy a little walk to town?

ANTOINETTE: Please, Mary. (*The others looked expectant.*)

MARY: Aw, I ain't tired, even if the *teacher* said so. (*A challenging look at Worker.*)

WORKER: Well, I am and I guess that makes me cross. What do you think?

MARY: (*smiling again*) I don't feel like thinkin'! I don't feel like *anything*.

ALL: Me neither.

WORKER: (*smiling at Frances*) Cheer up, Frances . . . our meetings aren't always like this!

MARY: I say, let's go home.

WORKER: If you like. What about the rest of you?

MARY: (*quickly*) No! I'm going to stay till the building closes.

ALL: (*screaming and arguing again.*)

WORKER: (*severely*) The next person who yells *will* go home. I mean it. There's no reason why we can't talk like human beings. Talk all you want to and say what you please, but say it *quietly*.

LUCIA: Okay, Miss Summers; shut up, you kids.

MARY: My ears are bustin'! This is a stinky club.

JULIANA: It's a stinky house. I hate it.

ANTOINETTE: If Mr. Anderson (*former director*) was here it wouldn't be like this.

MARY: (*electrified*) Are you tellin' *me*. He was *swell*.

WORKER: Oh! Did you girls know Mr. Anderson?

MARY: Sure!

LUCIA: Wh . . . well . . .

WORKER: I thought he died long before you would have been old enough to come here.

MARY: (*sheepishly*) Well, he did. But my father knew him!

LUCIA: Ours, too! He was the right kind of a guy. You didn't see no stuff around here like you do now. You could do whatever you wanted in the house and he never said nothin'!

JOSEPHINE: I know, too. He was swell to my father. Not like Mrs. Anderson. Boy, do we hate her!

JULIANA: Yeah . . . I'll say . . . and Mr. Anderson used to let you play on the piano an' everything. An' they never put ya outa the house like they do now . . . big *men*, even, putting little girls outa the house.

ANTOINETTE: Yea, an' boy, what she did to my father! I ain't never gonna like B. H. no more after that. (*Her reference was to a situation in which Mr. Bordi believed he had been discriminated against by the house. The worker had heard of this before, in a staff meeting.*)

WORKER: But girls, you know that sometimes people don't do what's right when they come to B. H. and they have to be corrected or there wouldn't be nice things left for the rest of us to enjoy. No one is ever put out of the house if they play fair. You know that.

LUCIA: (*who has recently been "put out" by a staff member*) Aw! Anyone would go if you asked 'em nice, but no, they hafta take your arm an' drag ya! (*Voices again rose to a prolonged scream. Frances alone sat quietly.*)

MARY: It's a stinkin' place, an' that's that.

ANTOINETTE: You can believe what we say, Teacher . . . it's all true. Our folks hates B. H. and so do we.

WORKER: If you hate it so much, why do you come? (*There was a silence. Lucia grinned, and the others slowly smiled, too.*)

LUCIA: Oh, we don't really, I suppose . . .

MARY: We like club . . .

JOSEPHINE: We like *you, Teacher.*

MARY: Yes, we like you all right . . .

WORKER: If you could have things different here, what would you choose? . . . Just tell me a few things, and maybe we can find a way to do it.

JOSEPHINE: Meet in the Council Room!

WORKER: Another group has it on Wednesdays, but I'd be glad to ask if we might have a chance at it later.

ANTOINETTE: We want cookin' too!

MARY: Yes! We asked for it a way back, an' Miss A. never done nothin'!

WORKER: Have you asked her again?

JULIANA: No.

WORKER: She's pretty busy, you know, and she can't remember everything. I'll ask and see what can be done and tell you next time.

There followed a noisy recital of what happened at previous cooking classes; they had an "awful teacher"; they had to make "cold slop" (coleslaw); they never could choose what to make; they never "had a decent bite only a little dumb cupcake." The worker let this pass and said we would certainly have them talk over what they wanted with whatever worker they would have before starting a class.

Mary said (as if it were a brand-new thought!), "I guess we'd better plan that skating party!" In a trice it had been agreed to have pop, chewing gum, and no guests . . . Mary making most of the suggestions, the others agreeing exhaustedly as if in mutual cahoots to placate the president!

On the way out, Lucia whispered to the worker, "But can we bring sandwiches, too, if we want?" (This idea had been squelched by Mary.) The worker said, "Surely, why not?" and Lucia hastily hushed her, saying, "Don't leave her know about it!" The group left, with the worker promising to do what she could about a skating party date. "If you can't get next Wednesday we won't have it at all," was Mary's parting shot. The others looked distressed, but the worker laughed and said, "Ah, but we *will!* Wait and see!" and said she would get in touch with them later in the week.

This is an illustration of domination by an indigenous leader. Did the worker address herself to the problem? Was Mary helped or was she reinforced? Can the group members grow in such a situation? What might the worker do?

NOTES / READINGS

1. James Garland, Hubert Jones, and Ralph Kolodny, "A Model for Stages of Development in Social Work Groups," *Explorations in Group Work* (Boston: Boston University School of Social Work, 1965).

6

❖❖❖❖❖❖❖❖❖

Groupwork: The Method

Groupwork has been identified over the years as a field, a process, a scientific art, and as a method. In some lexicons, it was held that when a worker influenced the group process for social work ends it became social groupwork. More recently, especially following the "Social Work Curriculum Study" of the Council on Social Work Education in 1959, social groupwork has become recognized as a social work method. Of course, educational groupwork is an educational method and one could multiply the modifier in accordance with the field of endeavor and the objectives. Objectives do not lie within a method per se, but within the field wherein it is used.

Although careful distinctions were made in the Curriculum Study to differentiate method from technique, and both of them from skill, confusion still exists, not only in the use of these terms, but in their connotations for theory and practice. This book is primarily about groupwork as a method and these next chapters will discuss this methodology. A method is a procedure or process for obtaining an objective, that is, for reaching goals. Some people would prefer to say that groupwork is made up of many methods, but this really does not add anything useful to the concept. The word "method" readily encompasses "methods" as part of a procedure or process for attaining an objective. A difficulty arises when method is confused with technique. A technique is the *manner* in which a method is used. A technique has to do with a specific way in which a method is used effectively.

Techniques are not synonymous with method and hence I hold that techniques are not important to effective groupwork unless the worker is committed to and knowingly employs the method. The "refinement of techniques," said Spengler, is "the last gasp of a dying civilization." It is the stage at which everyone is concerned with techniques because they are unable to appreciate the ultimate goals and means of reaching them and because they are incapable of doing anything about them. Specific techniques are instrumental to method; they are useful but they are not prominent in my conception of groupwork. It is possible to perform acts that are techniques without employing groupwork as well as to use these same techniques and be doing groupwork. The techniques are not unique to our field; they are shared by all of the helping professions. The method informs how and when these techniques are to be selected, in what combinations, and with what intents. Social groupwork is a unique entity because it is a particular amalgam of philosophy, objectives, and techniques.

An example of method is the responsible, conscious use of self in a helping relationship; an example of technique is support, which is the manner in which the worker uses himself in the relationship; and an example of skill is encouragement, empathy, or the ability to help a member in such a way that he understands the worker's stance and intention and is able to participate in the relationship.

There are sixteen techniques enumerated in the National Association of Social Workers' statement.[1] A professor of social groupwork told me that his students compiled a list of several hundred techniques. These several hundred could be subsumed under the sixteen, and the sixteen might be condensed even further, but the method cannot be characterized by a listing of techniques. Committees of the National Association of Social Workers and the Council on Social Work Education have suggested that we need to identify what groupworkers do, act by act, before we can define groupwork and also before we can engage in respectable research. However, groupwork is not made up of acts per se—interventions or techniques—although, to be sure, these are part of practice.

It is seen by some as mysticism that what a worker is, what he believes, and how he does what he does rather than just what he does, characterizes a practice as social groupwork. However, the essence of interpersonal helping is the psychic interaction which takes place through relationship. On the other hand, some critics of the method read into this that all one need do to be an effective groupworker is to use appropriate techniques, to be supportive, to listen, and be a nice, accepting person. They seem to think that knowledge and skill play no part. It requires more knowledge and skill to be an effective groupworker as described in this book than it does to be a change agent, an intervener, or a manipulator. One reason is that the use of oneself as an instrument must be cultivated, another is that the worker must be sensitive to the messages of the group and the group members, a third is that the worker does not influence each member directly but must enable the group and the situation to do so, and still another is that the worker must be free and able to enter into a human encounter as a person.

Skill in the context of this discussion means having a knowledge of the means or method of accomplishing the task and the ability to use one's knowledge readily and effectively. Skill alone, meaning dexterity or proficiency, is not enough. One key difference between and among social workers is that some have learned dexterity without knowledge or commitment to a philosophy. While some may have a technical proficiency or have a developed or acquired ability to perform the acts, they may not be effective groupworkers within the context of this book.

Method has been discussed and illustrated throughout the preceding chapters because, in my opinion, the text comes to life and has more meaning when theory and method are explained together. The separation of theory from method is artificial because method is conceived of in this book as being inherent in the theory, the objectives, and the beliefs which constitute social groupwork. However, method will be isolated for the purpose of study and to help students learn to become groupworkers. From time to time, techniques will be included to illustrate the text.

The method which is described and explained in this and the next four chapters is recommended for groups in institutions, work with mothers in Aid to Dependent Children and Families, parents of emotionally disturbed children, retarded children, physically handicapped children, for groups of retardates, the emotionally disturbed, and the handicapped. It is applicable to child guidance clinics, schools, juvenile courts, child-welfare settings as well as rehabilitation centers and medical centers. It will be effective in public social services, in private family agencies, and it is suited to family group counseling. It is advocated for those traditional agencies such as settlements, community centers, Y's, religious groups, the B'nai B'rith, Young Judea, and so on. It applies to block and neighborhood clubs, enhancement groups in community-action programs, antipoverty groups, and, in general, in the underdeveloped areas in the community because these are the groups of people who need the kind of group experiences that will help them to develop ego strengths, social-action skills, self-respect, and will be compensatory for the deprivations to which they have been subjected by a punitive and ungiving society. The list is not exhaustive but is only illustrative.

In Chapter 14 I will deal with task groups such as committees, boards of trustees, and decision-making groups where the decision or group production takes precedence over the growth and development of the people involved.

The Groupworker's Stance

The groupworker, I have emphasized, is not the change agent; the group is the medium for change. The worker is part of the system and the way in which his behavior influences the system depends upon the many factors of structure, group stage, psychological predispositions, and the like. The groupworker operates from a stance and he must be clear in his own mind about his stance as well as comfortable with it. He must know his own function, his goals, what he believes, and who he is. To the extent possible, he should also know about his own predispositions, modes of adaptation, and be aware of his feelings and be able to express them appropriately. The worker is a poor example if he is unable or unwilling to express anger, hostility, anxiety, fear, as well as love and concern. Why should the members be expected to express their feelings if the worker cannot or will not express his? How can members experience an appropriate handling of feelings if the worker is unable or unwilling to handle his own human feelings? I am proposing that it is useful for the worker to be able to say, for example, "I am feeling quite anxious because of your attack on me," or "Such disregard for others makes me angry with you." Many children and adults are emotionally upset because they have been taught and have learned that it is unsafe to express feelings and, therefore, they have no outlet for them. The worker is reinforcing the prohibition if he cannot express or accept feelings. The members are not having an experience in learning how to handle feelings if they are restrained from expressing them.

When a worker in a group meeting is intent upon analyzing the process so as to make conscious interventions, the chances are excellent that he does not hear what is going on and that he is oblivious to the feelings and concerns of the group and the members. It is of the greatest importance that the worker be responsive to the entreaties of the members. To do this he must be free to listen and to hear the messages that are imbedded in their communications.

The worker must feel easy about his stance—he must agree with it philosophically, he must believe in it and have confidence in his ability to help the members achieve their goals. A variety of studies seem to confirm these factors as being indispensable in the helping endeavor.[2] It is essential that the worker know who and what he is and what he believes so that his behavior will flow naturally therefrom and, also, so that he will be free of conflict.

The worker reveals himself to the members through his meta-communication and no matter what he says or how he says it, his message will come through. If he feels punitive his statements will be punishing; if he thinks domination he will be dominating; if he feels superior he will convey superiority. If the worker is engaged in groupwork but does not believe in it, groupwork will not be effective as he practices it. On the other hand, if he is committed to meeting the needs of others, if he believes in the equality of members and worker, if he is convinced about self-determination, and if he is comfortable with freedom for himself and others, his stance will elicit responses commensurate with it. If he likes the members, they will know it but if he thinks of them as monsters, they will know this too, be they children or board members.

If the worker sees himself as a helping person and respects the members' right to their goals, his acts will flow from his stance and he will be responsive. Consequently, he must see his function as enabling the group process, as helping the members accomplish what they can within the limits of the well-being of each and all, and of freeing the group. He must view himself as a partner in the group enterprise.

A worker should not meet his needs at the expense of the members and the group. Little has been written about the meaning of the therapeutic experience for the therapist or of the group experience for the social worker. The experience must affect the worker if there is any validity to the thesis of this book. The worker can and should grow as a direct result of his involvement with the members. He is part of the system and he is a partner in the enterprise. If the group is engaged in mutual aid, the worker is included. The worker is environmental to each member as well as being within the boundary of the group. The way in which he handles himself affects some aspects of the environment of others and, by being responsive to them, he can provide resources that might be needed or used by them. The worker and his behavior are part of their reality.

As I have said before, the worker helps the members and the group transact with the impinging environments. He can be, and often is, a liaison and in that function he can explain and interpret the extrasystem; he can act as a communication bridge or, in some instances, as a linkage; for example, when he is the only point at which the two systems can transact in order to attempt to match. He does mediate and work on their behalf to stimulate social institutions which are supposed to serve them to do so properly and effectively. He acts also to help them negotiate the maze of procedures and regulations to obtain their entitlements. The worker is often instrumental in either securing hard services (housing, health care, employment, training, legal counsel, money, etc.) or accompanying the members to help them obtain these services. The worker engages them in social action, and participates himself within his professional association as well as in other avenues for influencing social policy. The important point is that he is *their* man. His function is unequivocally to help them achieve their goals, meet their needs, and cope with the system within the context of matching. He does mediate and negotiate for the members if they are unable to perform these functions on their own behalf. The old concept that the groupworker is a representative of the agency as he works with a group is no longer viable. We live in a new era and have a different conception of helping. We are helping the members to be and become, not helping the agency to mold them.

He is, of course, a role model but so are the members models for each other, depending upon their position, status, power, norms, and their ability to meet the needs of others. Should the worker become significant in the lives of the members, they may emulate him and should he become a "fink" in their eyes, they may reject his values. If he demonstrates that he is genuine and is their man, the probability is that some or all will learn about interpersonal relations and appropriate behavior from him. They may learn the meaning of closeness from experiencing it and also find that many of their fears are unconfirmed; they may experience honesty, learn how to express and deal with feelings, and learn about respect. If the worker is such a role model, one concludes that he has learned to trust others as well as himself, he has successfully negotiated autonomy so that he can be independent and allow independence with no need to control others; he must have achieved purpose through initiative, and be secure in his identity. Having hope within himself, he can hope that the members will grow and gain confidence through sensing his vision of what is possible.

The characteristics of a worker may be an important variable. Some groups at certain times may need more authority or control than others, just as the developmental phases in a group's life require different worker approaches. This is the concept of differential approach, but the worker's stance remains the same. A worker must be responsive to the group, and this means that the worker is flexible enough to respond to the needs of the members and the group within a range of acceptability. It is axiomatic that the worker responds differentially to each member depending upon the member's need. This is natural and normal for a social worker.

It is the major function of the groupworker to enable. The word "enable" can connote a lack of goal but it need not. If the worker can find out what people want to achieve, help them to recognize why they are not succeeding in achieving it, help them to eliminate the blocks and to develop skills, then he is enabling them to move toward their goals. The strength and the power lie within the people. The method in this book is predicated on the belief that strength lies in the members and in the group, and that social groupwork builds upon the strength of the members. It is my assumption that much of the power in the members and in the group is locked up and inhibited and that their strengths may be misdirected. The members and the group are enabled through effective groupwork by unlocking this power.

This brings us back to a recurring theme in this book, and the crucial core of social treatment; namely, that the function of the groupworker is to free the members. One could say "free them up" meaning, for example, free them from inhibitions; free them from old conflicts and the residues of old conflicts such as mistrust, shame, guilt, doubt, anxiety, fear, and so forth; free them from the effects of previous domination such as fighting against father and mother figures, transferences, and rebellion; and free them from current domination so that they can be themselves. It means to provide an opportunity to have a freedom of choice from among reasonable options with the support and encouragement of the worker to risk making choices. It means the explication and clarification of goals, the examination of the assumptions underlying these goals, the beliefs they hold, and the contradictions that have been compartmentalized. This is difficult for some workers because they are beset by anxiety lest the choices the group makes turn out to be "wrong." Unless the members can make some "wrong" choices, they will not learn the consequences of certain behavior.

The worker must be fully committed to freedom or the members will react to his uncertainty with the symptoms of anxiety or anger. It can be expected, in any event, that the members will test his sincerity and conviction. This predictable probing tries the best of workers and even the most skilled may be seduced into taking a position of authority. If this does happen, the members become convinced that the worker cannot be trusted; that it is a ploy, as usual; and that the worker and members are playing the old game, that is, both know that really there is no free choice but they act as though there were. The worker must not allow himself to be caught in this trap and he can prevent it by maintaining his self-control and feeding back to the members what is happening.

It is mandatory that the worker face the group members with the realization that they are free to make decisions which affect them in the group and that they cannot blame anyone else but themselves for failing to achieve the maximum within the situation. Unlike many adaptations of psychological theory, in this formulation the members have no recourse to blaming people in their past. They cannot excuse themselves because of their mothers or their fathers, or fate. They are being asked to take responsibility for themselves. They are being faced with that responsibility and are being helped to see that they will have no one to blame but themselves if they do nothing to change the situation.

The worker must be himself and not be role-playing. He must encounter the members as a human being who wants to help them and who is ready, willing, and able to perform a function (not a role) as himself. I am asking the worker to divest himself of his uniform, his insignia of position, and his obeisance to the establishment. If he cannot meet his members without these indicia of office, he really is not free to engage in an interpersonal relationship; if he cannot be himself how can he expect the members to interact as themselves? If he needs the protection, the guidelines, and the façade of a role, they will have to cling also to these defenses. To avoid a semantic misunderstanding, let me restate the position: I am asking the worker to perform the role that is appropriate to the function as himself and not as an actor role-playing a social worker. This might be illustrated by the case of a social worker who at five o'clock takes off his social work uniform and becomes a different person in his personal life, in interpersonal relations, attitudes, and way of life. What he is as a person will come through if he role-plays and he will stand revealed in his "emperor's clothes."

The worker has been described by Vinter as a means of influence,[3] an object of identification and drive.[4] The worker also encourages, lends hope, relates to feelings and is responsive; he is a person who becomes part of one, and who provides rewards or reinforcements. Vinter also speaks of the worker as a symbol.[3] He also confronts the members with the long-range consequences of their present behavior and decisions, and he clarifies treatment goals. Some writers regard him as an agent of legitimate norms and values. I have discussed this elsewhere in the book and rejected the concept except as it may apply to human values. If the worker acts as an agent of an establishment that still makes war, condones malnutrition, protects polluters, and legitimatizes racism, he really cannot exemplify humanistic values. The worker can use himself, however, as a symbol of human relationships and values that honor service, love, justice, and humanity.

Vinter sees the worker as a motivator-stimulator.[3] He is, in addition, one who provides feedback and confrontation and who helps in the formulation of goals. The worker also provides socio-recreational experiences, teaches role performance, prompts, and gives support. He is also a helper and a participant.

Saloshin lists the following functions of the worker: accepter, protector, supporter, authority, object of feeling, provider of climate, stimulator, source of information, feedback, mirror, cue giver, role taker, and manipulator of group factors.[5]

Both lists (Vinter's and Saloshin's) describe and clarify the meaning of the use of self. However, these categorizations tend toward the instrumental and would seem to imply acts. I prefer to view the worker in the context of the use of self—what the worker is more than what he does. The worker is a part of the environment of the person. He is responsive, feeling, empathetic, communicative; embodying nurturance for psychological hunger. His is the reciprocal self which becomes a matching environment for personal need-meeting. If the worker enacts these relationships, the group members can begin to make faltering attempts to include such human behaviors in their own interpersonal relationships.

The point is that the worker demonstrates concepts which are very difficult to put into words and even when verbalized can only initiate conscious and cognitive understanding. These include such concepts as the meaning of concern for another person and how it is manifested; the meaning of being oneself and of revealing oneself; the effective use of communication; how such feelings as anger, fear, and sexual interest are handled; the meaning of freedom within the limits of social constraints; how to love; and how to meet one's own needs without either exploiting others or thwarting others. Perhaps the most effective way of learning these things is by seeing, feeling, and touching them; by experiencing them and by acting them out. The groupworker is in a most visible and advantageous position to provide the demonstration.

The Groupworker in Phase I—The Development of Mutual Trust

Since anxiety is expected to be high when people meet for the first time, the reduction of threat is indicated. The first meetings should be pleasurable and satisfying. The worker must guard against exacerbating guilt by avoiding blame, judgment, or censure. In some way, the members must get something they want, be it information, the release of tension, friendliness, security, or the like. The worker should not use these first meetings for study (in the traditional sense) since that would serve his purpose and not theirs. He must also avoid the semblance of draining or excavating them. The worker should listen much more than he speaks in order to establish a pattern of communication among the members because it is the group interaction that is important.

The worker does not pressure for closeness; he allows social distance, realizing that the major feelings at this time are fear and anxiety. He feeds back into the group the observation that fear and anxiety are natural, and also that learning to trust each other and to trust him is what the group is working on. Since this is the major issue, the worker does not expect or encourage members to begin to reveal themselves this early. Where members do reveal themselves quickly, the worker wonders about the normality of such defenselessness and also about the accuracy of their revelations. He wonders whether there is an exaggerated bid for attention by this maneuver and whether the other group members encourage and allow a member to overventilate so as to protect themselves from having to interact. He is concerned that the member who reveals too much may be sorry and not return to the group, or if he returns he may withdraw from participating. Also, he wonders whether too open and too quick a revelation is not frightening to the other members in the group. A worker should prevent too much personal disclosure too soon.

On the other hand, some people have to tell something before they are ready to listen to others. This is especially true in committee and council meetings, but there the content is rarely personal or upsetting. People in treatment or growth groups usually have to get something "off their chests" and yet not so much as to increase anxiety and tension for themselves or for others; the guideline is moderation.

The worker must be able to hear what the members are concerned about, receive their messages, and be responsive. Shulman has been helpful and also explicit about how these concerns are educed.[6] He writes that in what he calls the "offering stage" the worker "tunes in" by studying the group and its members. Much of this can be done prior to the group's formation, through an analysis of age, sex, culture, and other face-sheet data. The worker "listens" at the meetings and by the hints, leakage, actions, assumption of roles, and symbolic communication of the members, he tries to get the meanings of their behavior. He also utilizes his knowledge of communication blockages which hide or distort meanings and he tries to elaborate upon the communications and interpret them while eliciting and inviting an expression of feelings. The main purposes of the worker in this stage of the endeavor are to look for and facilitate the emergence of affect and to help the group place its concerns on the agenda. It is very easy to do exactly the opposite by being too active, too studied, too program-directing, and too interrogating. It is more important for the worker to be sensitive—to listen and hear.

The worker initiates the establishment of a contract, and as part of this, facilitates the development of group goals. He does not expect or demand much at this early stage and, therefore, he avoids putting people on the spot or embarrassing them by having them introduce themselves and tell something about themselves. In the first place, anxious people spend so much energy sweating and thinking about what they are going to say that they hardly hear the others speaking; in the second place, this exercise allows people to begin to put themselves into habitual roles, statuses, and positions from which it is hard to escape later. Nor does the worker introduce them by telling who or what they are because, once again, ascribed statuses will be injected into the situation.

Beginning meetings are no place for competitive activities, for frustrating experiences, or for rigid limits. The climate should be trusting and trustworthy, protective and permissive, and should allow exploration. It should set the tone and establish the stance of the worker as supportive and enabling. The worker must show that he stands ready to support group action but that his acceptance and affection are not contingent upon the performance of the members.[7]

Many groupworkers from other disciplines like to begin working with a group by asking the members to start discussing problems and encouraging the members to tell about their feelings at once. It is unrealistic to expect anyone to be willing or want to unmask psychologically before strangers, or give credence to what will be said. Such procedures encourage distortions, fantasies, and the telling of stories in the hope of bartering for rewards. The worker who thinks he is getting at the basic concerns of these strangers may be deluding himself. At best, all he can hope to gain are some diagnostic clues about patterns of defense, distortion, or fantasy but he runs the risk of jeopardizing the whole enterprise by doing so.

The lesson the members must learn and have reinforced is that they do not have to use their usual or previous modes of behavior, to hallucinate, use distorted communication, or "act crazy" in this group in order to meet their needs, achieve their personal goals, and find themselves.

It has long been held that the prototype of group life is the primary group—the family; and that each member will enact in each group the patterns he learned in the family group. This premise stems from predeterministic theories and is no longer creditable nor is it useful. If it were true, group experience such as we advocate in groupwork or group therapy would have little chance of success.

The premise also is contradicted by the demonstrated effectiveness of learning theory.

There are, we do not doubt, fundamental learnings in the primary group that set patterns, predispositions, modes of adaptation, and in a sense program the behaviors of persons in future groups. However, the prototype for behavior in a group is set by one's recent experience in groups. This may or may not have reproduced or reinforced the primary group experience. The most recent groups in one's life tend to be peer groups and it is from peers that one needs validation. It is also one's peers who can provide or withhold that which one needs for growth and ego strength.

It is the function of the worker to avoid becoming the feared antagonist and thereby cloud the main issue, or becoming the central figure around whom the group coalesces because everyone fears him or hates him. Such a bond is destructive and malfunctional in that it blocks the real business of the group. It is the worker's function to facilitate, to enable the development of interpersonal trust as the first step in group formation. Until this is achieved to some extent, the group has not formed and there is no vehicle for treatment or growth.

If a group is forced into advanced stages before it is ready, the underlying feelings will remain and block the achievement of its goals. The group and the worker will have to return to earlier stages—in this instance, the first stage—and resolve the basic theme of trust before the group is ever to become a viable treatment or growth medium.

Treatment groups or growth groups cannot be short-term (say of six weeks' duration) because it is unrealistic to expect people to uncover themselves in so short a time. This does not mean that short-term groups have no validity. It means that one must select realistic treatment goals or purposes in the light of the limitation imposed by the negotiation of group phases.

Several record excerpts follow which illustrate the dynamics of a first group meeting and how a groupworker conducts himself. In this excerpt the worker discusses the purposes of the group.

An Illustration of a First Meeting in a Primary School Under the Auspices of a Youth Serving Agency

AGE: Latency
SETTING: Group Services Agency in a Host Setting
SESSION: First

The girls were asked by their teachers to come to a meeting in the auditorium after school. Some of the teachers explained to the girls that we were starting a new "club." Others did not know the purpose of the meeting.

The room was set up when the youngsters arrived with chairs around two tables pulled together. Place cards with the name of each girl were on the table in front of her chair. The place card idea served three basic purposes.

As the girls came into the room, I introduced myself and asked them their names. I told them if they looked around the table they would see their name on a card and should sit in the chair behind the place card. The girls seemed surprised and pleased with the place card idea. One youngster, M.P., stopped in front of the place card for M.G. and said I spelled her name wrong. She seemed visibly upset with this. However, when I pointed out her own place card to her, she smiled and ran around to her chair.

As the girls seated themselves at the table, I asked them if they would like to make a name tag like the one I was wearing. All responded positively. This procedure served to keep the early arrivals occupied while we were waiting for the rest of the girls. It also fostered some interaction among the youngsters in terms of passing out materials and so on. During this procedure we talked briefly about name tags being a help in getting to know others.

When most of the youngsters were finished with their tags, I started to explain to them why they were asked to meet with me today. I told them that we were starting a new group for girls in their grade, and that I was going to be the worker. I then asked if they knew what a group was like, or if any of them had brothers or sisters who belonged to clubs. Several of the youngsters raised their hands and one girl asked if it was like the Girl Scouts. I said that it was.

I then explained to the girls that we would be meeting at the school twice a week, if this was all right with their parents. We would be playing games, doing crafts, perhaps dancing and singing, and maybe even taking trips into the various parts of the community. I also pointed out that since we wanted to do things that they would enjoy, it will be their job to help me plan our meetings. I then asked the girls about the kind of things they liked to do. The girls' response to this question was enthusiastic and was accompanied by much talking and hand waving. Some of the suggestions of the girls were as follows: color, paint, play with clay, look at books, having plays, go fishing, dancing, singing, jumping, handball, tether ball, etc. I commented that it certainly seemed that they had many ideas for things to do, and that it would be fun to do them together. The girls responded positively to this with comments like: "Yes, it would be fun" or "I sure want to belong."

Pressure of time forced me to cut off this discussion and go on to explain to them about the letters that I was asking them to take home to their parents. I showed the girls a copy of the letter and told them that it was from the principal to explain to their mothers about the group that we were starting. I said that because I wanted to have a chance to talk to one or both of their parents to explain the plan and also to get their permission for the girls to belong that the letter asked their mother to indicate the time that she might be able to see me during the week. I told the girls that their mothers should fill out the bottom part of the letter and that they should bring it back to school tomorrow. I emphasized the fact that I would have to get all these slips back and see their parents before we could start. C. and S. both wondered if I would be able to see their parents because their mothers worked. I said that I would be available in the late afternoon and early evening and also on Saturdays and that I was quite sure we would be able to work out a time to get together. Both girls still seemed upset that I would not be able to see their mothers, so I told them not to worry about it and that we would definitely work out a time.

I then showed the girls the picture story showing Blue Birds in a variety of activities. This stimulated more interest in the possible things we might be doing in the group. C. and G. seemed particularly interested in the possibility of going on a picnic, and C. and E. were attracted to the idea of making puppets. I showed the girls that I had printed my name and telephone number on the front of the picture story so that, should their parents want to get in touch with me, they could telephone. At this point, M. commented that she did not have a telephone and seemed rather anxious that I would not be able to contact her mother for this reason. I assured her that it was not necessary to have a telephone. This was only if her mother wanted to get in touch with me for some special reason.

I also called the girls' attention to the fact that I had printed their addresses under their names on the front of the envelopes. I asked them to look at the addresses to make sure that they were correct so that I would be sure to know where to go when I went to see their mothers. I then passed out the envelopes to the girls and asked them to check the addresses, which they did. All seemed to think the addresses were correct except for C. and Y. Y., as it turned out, had her address confused with her telephone number and this was the reason she thought it was incorrect. C., who lives on the same street as Y., helped straighten her out on this point. I asked C. to stay a couple of minutes after the rest of the girls left to give me her correct address.

I then asked the girls if all of them had someone in their homes who spoke English. I explained that, since I did not speak Spanish and if their mothers could not speak English, it would be necessary for someone to be there to translate for us. This touched off a discussion among the youngsters concerning who did and who did not speak English in their families. The girls were able to discuss this point very comfortably, although the ability to speak English did seem to be a status symbol of sorts. One of the girls, I believe it was C., pointed out that no one in her family spoke English except herself. I said that if her mother made the appointment for the time that she was home, she would be able to translate for us. She seemed very pleased that I would have this kind of confidence in her, and some of the other girls also commented that they could translate for us. So far as I can determine from this rather disjointed discussion, there should be someone in each home who will be able to translate for me or else the parents speak English, with the possible exception of M.S. This child speaks almost no English herself, and consequently I was unable to really find out if anyone in the home could speak English. In addition, I am not at all sure that she understood much of what transpired at the meeting. I had hoped to try to get hold of her at the end of the meeting to check and see what she really did understand. However, she got away before I had the chance. Hopefully, her friend, N.R., who seemed somewhat protective of her, would be able to explain some of the meeting content.

After this I told the girls that although I would like to stay and talk with them longer, they should perhaps get home because their mothers might worry if they were late arriving home from school. I reminded them again of the importance of having their mothers return the appointment slips tomorrow morning. The girls seemed excited about the possibilities of beginning the group, and left the room talking animatedly to one another. As she was leaving, I reminded B.B. that she was to return to her classroom instead of going home.

It was my general impression of the meeting that the youngsters were responsive and excited about the idea of starting a group. I was amazed that they were so quiet and well behaved at the table. They did not seem squirmy at all, although the meeting lasted for almost half an hour. I did feel the time pressure was tremendous and wished that I had 15 or 20 minutes more to encourage discussion among the girls and answer their questions.

Did this worker reduce threat and forestall fear? How did she interpret the purpose of the group? Did she move too fast? Were the major objectives of a first meeting achieved?

This next excerpt illustrates how a worker interprets the group treatment and begins to establish relationships.

An Illustration of a First Meeting of a Children's Group in a Treatment Setting

AGE: Latency
SETTING: Child Guidance Center
SESSION: First

They wanted to know what we would be doing next week. I said each week we would be spending some time talking about anything the group wished to discuss—we could talk about things that were happening to them at home, school, or anything on their minds. But mainly, we would talk about our feelings, events that happened, or how we felt about each other—that this was a place where they could feel free and say anything they wished; it would be just among the six of us. Then they could play whatever they wished. I said there would be only two rules. Jo said, "I bet I know what they are!" I asked her what they were and she said we wouldn't be allowed to hurt each other or ourselves. I said that was exactly right. I said I planned to bring in some pumpkins next week and they could carve out jack-o'-lanterns, if they wished. This thrilled them as they have never carved one before. Frank said he would bring his hunting knife and Tim said he would borrow a scout knife. I said if they liked, we could make a kind of Halloween party out of it and maybe put on a puppet show. They thought this would be fun but asked how to do it. Tim described how he had done it in his previous visits with me.

They cleaned everything up voluntarily and put away the chairs. We sat around and talked about things they liked to do, each of them munching more freely on the popcorn. I noticed as the hour was coming to a close that Tim began stuffing himself on the popcorn as if he was afraid he wouldn't get enough before it was time to leave.

They hoped that other kids would be here next week. Tim said this had been "real fun." They seemed like a comfortable threesome and there was little striving for my attention; only Jo seemed overly concerned about my approbation.

My role today was primarily that of a catalyst to get things moving and then I retreated to the background, said little, and let the kids run the show according to their own inclinations. It was a good, uninhibited beginning and Frank seemed to feel as though he were really there in the role of helper. He voluntarily offered to undo paint jars, help assemble toys, etc. whenever the other two were having trouble. When Tim had to go to the john, he whispered to Frank, asking if there was a bathroom around. I heard but did not respond, waiting for Frank to answer. Frank turned to me and called across the room, "Is there a bathroom in the hall?" Jo told him where to go. They washed up their cups. I let them do everything for themselves.

Phase I—First Meeting

Making a Contract

For a group to form for growth and treatment, a contract is the first step; the worker initiates the negotiation in the first meeting. Although the term contract does not appear frequently in books about groupwork, it is very important that a contract be established. A contract is an agreement, usually both verbal and nonverbal, between the group members and the worker and among themselves about the purpose of the group endeavor and the way in which they will work together. If the members do not know for what they are there, it is less likely that they will be able to work together or appropriately. The contract mobilizes and focuses the group energies. For the group to move toward desired outcomes, the group members must be aware of what they are working on and how.

There are specifics that are to be agreed upon at the outset. These include such things as the time of meeting, the length of meetings, the number of sessions or weeks they will meet, the place, internal arrangements (if any) about refreshments, absences, coming on time, staying for the entire meeting, confidentiality of what is discussed, and the like. Some groups and workers discuss and agree on such matters as the members not socializing or calling each other between meetings or the members not calling the worker or seeking private sessions with him, or that anything one discusses with the worker can and should be brought up at a meeting. These may be called ground rules and what agreements are made about such points will depend upon the purpose of the group and the age of the members as well as the philosophy and style of the groupworker.

The contract sets forth the expectations members have for the worker (and the group experience) and what the worker expects of the members. Clarity about expectations avoids disappointment and frustration as well as provides guidelines. Knowing what one is expected to do also helps one to know what the limits are. These keep a focus and reduce anxiety. A well-conceived contract minimizes the need for much formal structure or rules, and it shifts responsibility for directing the group process from the worker to the group members where it belongs.

The contract establishes the fact that the goals for the group will be the group's goals and not goals imposed by the worker or the agency. Later, if the worker seeks to invoke the contract so as to focus or motivate, he does it on behalf of the group, that is, as an agent of the group and not as an authority figure or an outsider who is imposing his will. This concept is crucial. The treatment is not being done to them nor is its *modus operandi* a secret held by the worker. The contract is their contextual frame of reference and they are aware of what is happening.

Personal goals in a contract in groupwork usually are not tangible. The members agree that the purpose is growth, or an experience, or the freeing of creative potentials.

The contract is an agreement about the reciprocal roles of the worker, the member, and the sanctioning agency. Clarity about reciprocal-role expectation is important and in this aspect often nonverbal communication is most important. The worker conveys by his stance, his posture, his tone of voice, and his attitude what he is and how he will behave. He defines his conception of his position vis-à-vis the members and how he regards them. He shows whether he expects them to participate and take responsibility and whether he intends to allow them to do so.

First impressions have lasting value. If the worker sets a tone which indicates he perceives himself as an expert, an authority, and a conductor, it will be difficult later to change it or to offset it by his verbal invitations to participate. The members will not be able to hear what he says because his actions are so loud. How he sits, where he sits, how he gestures, the sternness of his face, are all nonverbal communications that interpret his view of the contract. Usually, the members come expecting the worker to act as an authority and to dominate. The worker must demonstrate that this is not so. He must demonstrate also the essence of trust, trustfulness, trustworthiness, and trusting.

Herein we can begin to see how a worker participates in the establishment of norms for the group and how he influences the structure without manipulating or directing. He behaves and conducts himself in such a manner as to set the reciprocal relationship of members to him. These become part of the contract. Within this beginning demonstration, the expectation that members are to participate is shown, that they are to reveal themselves is anticipated, that feelings are permissible and the revelation of them encouraged is reinforced, and that the group is a partnership enterprise based upon a person-to-person relationship is stressed.

These essentials are experienced by the way the worker sets the stage, and responds. Like all contracts, it is negotiated; it provides the framework, opportunities, and the limits of the human interactions that will follow. The contract is not immutable; the participants can change it by negotiation when appropriate and as the need arises.

The setting of a contract ensures the democratic rights of the members, emphasizes the egalitarian quality of the enterprise, sets the group up as a partnership and, hopefully, minimizes control and manipulation. It is also an essential in the establishment of morale since morale presupposes acceptance of group goals. The negotiation begins in the first meeting but usually the contract is not made all at once. Many meetings are needed to conclude it and, actually, it is an ongoing process; however, the main provisions of the contract are explored in the first meeting.

As we have seen, the main underlying theme is trust at the outset in any group. This includes trusting each other as well as the worker. Obviously, agreements are only as good as the people who enter into them and strangers are hesitant, and properly so, of entering into contracts with people whom they do not know. Many have built-in misapprehensions about authority figures and do not believe the worker. The beginning negotiations in the first meetings are tentative and exploratory but they are very important to the success of the whole enterprise.

Some who write about groupwork distinguish goal-oriented

groups from treatment and growth-oriented groups. This is a useful classification for some purposes but it obscures the fact that all groups have objectives just as any social system has goals. Once a growth-oriented group sets a contract based upon agreed-upon purposes, there is a goal. If there is no goal, no one knows what he is doing. In a treatment group, the contract is based upon goals such as "We are here to get well," or better yet, "We are here to help each other get well." A dichotomy between goal achievement and growth or treatment is false once there is an understanding that in any group wherein group methods are used the group, not the worker, is the growth or therapeutic agent and hence the group is engaged actively in problem-solving and goal achievement.

Purpose and contract are interrelated and they are related also to goals. The specifics of the method involved will vary according to the purpose, size, composition, and so on, but groupwork is groupwork as long as the group process and the group experience are the foci of the group and the worker. The contract is an agreement about purpose, means, and reciprocal-role expectations.

Relationship and Contract—Illustrative Dialogues

It goes without saying that relationship is the major indispensable conduit and agent in the growth endeavor. The bondage that may have arisen through social relationship can be released through social relationship. It should be easy to see that relationship between the worker and the group is an integral part of the contract. In social casework, the client comes to ask for help. In groupwork this happens, but more often the members are not asking for specific help and hence the steps in developing the relationship and contract may differ between the two; the essentials do not differ.

The relationship begins to evolve through psychic nonverbal interaction and also through statements. The interchange of messages (verbal and nonverbal) if they could be heard might sound something like this:

WORKER: I'm John Doakes. I'm your worker (or *teacher, therapist, leader, as the case may be*). I am here to help you accomplish what *you* want to accomplish (*within the agency purpose which the worker states*). I will try to help you as you define help and in ways that you prefer, and I will try to let you share in what I am doing. However, I am not the director or manager here. The group is the important part of this endeavor. It is the group that is the means through which a member grows.

GROUP: We hear you say you want to help us and we would like to believe you but we are uncertain and anxious. You will probably dominate us and cause us pain but we will try to be good children.

WORKER: I know that you have anxiety and fear. I stipulate that I will not hurt you, I will not be judgmental, nor will I reject you.

GROUP: You say that you will not judge us and that you will accept us but what will you ask of us in return?

WORKER: For me to be able to be of help, you will have to participate in the discussions, share your feelings and reveal yourselves, but you need not fear that I will abuse your confidence. You can rely on me.

GROUP: We want help and we want to share our feelings; we will try to believe that we can rely on you. We are willing to begin to work with you.

This interchange marks the beginning of a working relationship. Most of the messages in the dialogue are nonverbal and the group will proceed to test the soundness of the relationship. However, this is only part of the contract. The following will highlight illustratively the enactment of a contract. The group consists of six couples who are parents of emotionally disturbed children attending a day-care center. The service is not to treat the parents and hence this is not a therapy group.

WORKER: (*He has not taken the chair at the head of the table which the parents have avoided. Starting to pour coffee, he invites them to participate, to pass the cups, and the cream and sugar.*) Shall we begin? I am very pleased that you have all agreed to come. I have met most of you. My name is Joe Doakes. I'm a groupworker and I have met with groups like this before. This is Mr. and Mrs. L, Mr. and Mrs. H, Dr. and Mrs. O, Mr. and Mrs. Q, Mr. and Mrs. R, and Mrs. P. Unfortunately, Mrs. P's husband couldn't make it tonight. For a little while let's discuss why we are here. What do you think this group is all about?

MRS. O: Well, like you said. It's because we have troubled children and they need help.

MR. R: Yeah, I don't understand Ronnie and I might be able to learn something about his sickness.

MRS. L: It's terrible. We have been to six clinics. No one would take him or even tell us what's wrong. Dr. Luff said he's retarded.

WORKER: We want to understand more about our children.

MR. Q: Is it something that I have done wrong? I feel as though people think I am to blame.

WORKER: (*Addressing group*) What do you think about that?

MR. Q: I think I'm not a perfect father—but it must be something . . .

WORKER: Do you all have such feelings?

GROUP: (*Mixed chorus*) Yes.

WORKER: The staff doesn't think you or anyone is to blame. It is natural for you to have such feelings. Sure, you're anxious about being here but you are not here to be judged or blamed.

MRS. H: They always made me feel that I was wrong wherever I went with Shirl. I'm glad to hear you say that—but how does it happen?

WORKER: We think there are many things that just happen to come together by chance that result in a child having problems—sometimes they are chemical, sometimes they arise from peculiar circumstances beyond our control, but we do think that the relationships in the family can help your children improve or can hinder them. It's no one person but the interplay of everyone that helps to create a climate in which a child can grow.

MR. H: I'll buy that. I'd like to know more about it.

WORKER: Let's see now—our purposes are to learn more about our children, to relieve our anxieties, and to look more closely at our family patterns. Anything else?

DR. O: There is always an answer to a problem. You people make a business of studying children and families. Aren't you going to tell us what to do to help our children?

WORKER: Now Dr. O, I'm no expert on what *you* should do. Besides, I believe that no one is helped just because someone else tells him what to do. We believe here that people do best when they can find their own answers and also we have learned from experience that the best way for this to happen is in a group like this. This is a group where everyone helps the other members.

MR. R: Sounds good, but if everyone here has a sick kid, how does anyone know how to help the other if he can't help himself?

MRS. Q: It's like he said. You know, you can see an answer to your neighbor's problem but you are blind to your own. Talking it over with someone else is good, I always say. Sometimes just by talking you get some ideas. Anyway, it makes me feel better.

WORKER: So we can add to our reasons—to talk it over, to express our feelings making us feel better, and to help the others look at their problems more objectively. To do these things, you will have to talk at the meetings and, of course, you will have to come regularly. It is better if we can come on time because time is so short anyway with a group of this size. We want everyone to have a chance to say what he wants to and to get all the help he can. (*Pause*) Is Tuesday night convenient for everyone? (*Group members nod.*)

WORKER: Then it is every Tuesday evening from 7:30 to 9:00. I have a schedule of holidays and the summer vacation here and I'll pass them out so you can see when we do not meet. We go on until June 28 when camp begins but we'll tell you about camp later.

MRS. L: I'd like to know whether he's retarded or not. Sometimes he seems so smart and then he's off again.

WORKER: We will talk about these things when you want to, but may I make a comment here? Our focus in this group is on us—by that I mean, how do we manage our children, discipline them, set routines, talk to them, and things like that—and how do we feel about it and how do we all get along in the family. The children are being treated in the Center and the staff there knows how to help the children. You are free and are encouraged to make appointments with the day-care staff—Dr. Shep, the psychiatrist; and Dr. Olean, the psychologist—in fact, they will call you for appointments from time to time. In this group, I'm here to help the parents work together on their problems. What do you think?

MRS. L: Are you trying to say that us parents need a psychiatrist? Are you a psychiatrist?

WORKER: No, I'm not a doctor and I don't think you need a doctor. Your children are getting competent help here and you can seek the answers to such questions as how your child is doing from the staff. Living twenty-four hours a day with a troubled child isn't easy. I don't have to tell you that. I admire you for how well you do under this kind of stress every day . . .

MR. R: . . . and night.

WORKER: And night. The group is a place where you can talk about these stresses and find ways of handling them, and also find ways of making family living a little more pleasant under the circumstances.

MRS. L: I see.

WORKERS: That's why we will be kind to each other here. We have just a few agreements about this. I will never hurt you knowingly—and if I do I expect you to tell me. I will not let you injure another member in the group nor will I let you injure me. All of us should try not to hurt each other. Within these simple agreements we should feel free to say anything we wish, to share our feelings, and to offer suggestions. This is called a mutual-aid group—agreed?

GROUP: (*Nods around the room.*)

WORKER: From time to time as we get new children into the Center, we may add parents to the group. I will always let you know beforehand. Is that okay?

GROUP: (*Nods around the room.*)

WORKER: Oh, and what goes on here is just among us. We don't discuss it outside. It's just among us.

DR. O: Why do we both have to come each week? It is pretty hard for me to make it.

WORKER: (*Looks around the room.*)

MR. Q: It isn't easy for me either, but if it will help Rick, it's my duty to come.

MRS. Q: Your duty? You *want* to come!

MRS. O: It's like we were saying. If it has something to do with the family and how it lives, I guess we both have to be here.

WORKER: That's the point. Both parents are involved in each other and the children. There's another point. We on the staff are convinced that really we cannot help your children get better if you don't come. You see, as they begin to change with treatment there will have to be changes in your behavior also—both of you—and changes in family routines. You have to anticipate that. (*Parents now begin to talk about their own situation until the meeting closes.*)

167

In this excerpt, one sees the elements of a contract begun. The worker invites the members to include their understandings and he does the same. Of course, every now and again in future meetings some of these same things will be repeated.

The Groupworker in Phases II and III—The Struggle to Be Free and Have Equal Opportunity

It is the function of the worker, particularly in these phases of a group's development, to demonstrate explicitly that he does not intend to coerce or repress. It is not enough for him to say this, he must enact it. It is up to him to set the climate and he does this by stating his intentions and by telling the group that *it* is the arbiter, the decision maker, and the treatment. He does it also by his body language, that is, how he stands and sits, the expression on his face, the tone of his voice, and his avoidance of commanding or rejecting gestures. He does this by placing responsibility on the group and referring decision-making and self-discipline to it. He rewards initiative and creativity with praise and approval. He does not reinforce conformity, control, or regression to dependency. The worker shows in these early stages that he will encourage group process, intimacy, and self-revelation. He chooses not to sit at the head of the table, not to sit in the one comfortable chair, not to be the first served with coffee, not to be the center of discussion, and not to be the one who answers the questions. However, he is not passive; he is very active. His activity, first of all, lies in how he conducts himself and then, in the feeding back to the group what they are feeling, how they are behaving, by pointing out the conflicts and power struggles that are taking place. In this way he assures the group that no one has to act in this group as they may feel they need to act elsewhere, that they need not fear him, and they can find guinine friendship if they want it.

The worker reaffirms the basic purpose of mutual aid and he reintroduces his function as a helping one. It is useless just to say he will help; he must do something to show that he will help. In some groups this may mean suggesting a pleasurable experience through program. Where program is not indicated, he can help by listening, by supporting, by empathizing, and in some instances by making suggestions.

In treatment groups, the worker is advised to relate what is happening in the group to similar events in the daily lives of the members. He may gently point out how they get into trouble by flying off the handle, or how they look for hidden slights that are not intended, or how they do not convey what they mean, or how they hide.

The effective groupworker is more than an object of identification or a role model. The group's encounter with the worker is an experience in human relations. This encounter results in some part of him becoming part of each member which extends beyond the time span of their relationship and permeates their lives. It has been said that this provides a new or different experience with an authority figure. Granted, but above all it should be a positive experience with a human being. Although I have contended throughout that the group is the helping agent, it is obvious that the worker is present and is a component in the system. The worker does occupy a position, he has an ascribed and an earned status, and there is an expectation for his role performance. All of the attributes of these indicia have an influence on the group and the members. In addition to his position-status-role, he also has a personality which is epitomized by how he presents himself. With these attributes, the important question is how does a worker use himself? He accepts the members and the group, he does not sit in judgment, nor does he manipulate or exploit them. He may limit them, and he may guide them but he does not control them; he enables freedom and the positive establishment of will.

The worker must search his soul and purge himself of any need to control if he is to be of help to the members, and he must accept their hostility for refusing to allow them to become dependent upon him in this period. A supervisor, peer group, or consultant can be useful in helping to prevent the worker from falling into a trap. A groupworker must be concerned with such questions as *whether or not he is imposing when he lends a vision.* He is not if his vision is that the members can fulfill their wishes. *When they find him to be genuine do they identify with his goals even if he does not voice them?* Yes, they do. This is inevitable and a fact of human encounter. Interaction always results in people becoming part of each other. For this reason, it is important that the worker be genuine and not merely be playing a role, using tricks, or playing the therapy game. The members will identify with what he is, not with what he seems to be; therefore, what he believes has more influence than what he does. *Does the agency purpose and its structure color the group goal?* Yes, it does and, therefore, it is important for the agency to function as a therapeutic milieu.

The members will resist the worker, will resist his offer to help, and will test whether he can be trusted. He must be patient, responsive, restrained, and demonstrate who he is and what is his function. This is illustrated in the following excerpt.

An Illustration of Helping a Group with Its Feelings about Authority

The twenty members of this group have defied training-school rules, have refused to work, and have assaulted guards and other inmates. The leader, Biff, is a rebellious hoodlum. He has warned the members to remain silent. The members sit stiffly and Biff glares at the worker. The worker crosses his legs, sits relaxed in his chair and looks interestedly from one prisoner to another.

WORKER: Can anyone tell me the purpose of this group? (*No reply.*)

WORKER: What are you men interested in doing? (*No reply. Members look at Biff who smirks at worker.*)

WORKER: (*Looks back at Biff*) You don't have anything to say?

BIFF: (*Spits. Responds with a four-letter word. Members laugh.*)

WORKER: (*To the first man, a young inmate*) What do you want to do?

FIRST MAN: Get out! (*Men guffaw.*)

WORKER: Right. That's what we all want to do. (*Biff looks contemptuous, spits, and curses.*)

WORKER: Okay. Can anyone tell me how to get out of this place?

FIRST MAN: Escape.

WORKER: (*Laughs*) Sure. That's one way. Is there any other way?

SECOND MAN: Die. (*Some laugh.*)

THIRD MAN: Pull your full bit.

FOURTH MAN: Probation.

WORKER: Die. How long would that take? How old are you?

SECOND MAN: Eighteen. (*Laughter.*)

WORKER: Serve your time? That's a long time. Probation? How many of you want parole? (*Everyone but Biff raises hand.*)

WORKER: Okay. How do you get parole?

SECOND MAN: Politics.

THIRD MAN: Good behavior.

FOURTH MAN: The rules are tough. You can't keep out of trouble. The guards provoke you.

WORKER: Well. Do you think it is worth talking about?

THIRD MAN: It can't do no harm.

Second Meeting

WORKER: (*Recaps last meeting.*) Who has a problem he'd like to discuss? (*Looks at Biff.*) No? Well then, I have one. Why doesn't Biff like me? You heard what he called me. Why does he hate me?

FOURTH MAN: (*Mutters.*)

WORKER: What's that?

FOURTH MAN: He don't hate you. I mean he don't give a damn whether you live or die.

WORKER: This guy's right, Biff doesn't hate me, he hates what I stand for. What does he hate?

SECOND MAN: This goddam jail.

WORKER: Right again. The jail, the guards, the fuzz, the state. Biff hates all authority. He's always burned up. (*The members agree.*)

BIFF: What the hell. Why are youse all on me 'cause I said one word?

WORKER: Then why the hell did you say it?

BIFF: You wouldn't know if I told you.

WORKER: Okay for now. We'll take it up next time.

Third Meeting

WORKER: (*Recaps. Members complain about probation system, guards, food.*) Sometimes when you hate one thing you take it out on another. How do we get these hates anyway?

SECOND MAN: Some guys have a rough time as kids. Ya know, like they don't get along with the old man.

WORKER: Is that what happened to you?

SECOND MAN: I ain't talkin' about me. I hear other guys talk.

BIFF: He means me—Ya wanta know? Well my old man kicked me around like a piece of shit. I'd be scared to go home, or to fall asleep when he was drunk. He'd belt me. He beat my mother till she died. I was eight . . . I wanted to kill him.

SECOND MAN: Your old man was a fart.

THIRD MAN: So what happened?

BIFF: I run away, that's what—so that's how I got arrested.

WORKER: How did you make out?

BIFF: I'm here ain't I—get off my back.

Phase III—To Find a Niche

In this phase, characterized by conflict and skirmishes as members probe for openings and advantages, the worker must be calm and perceptive. Many writers see this period as a necessary concomitant to the formation of group structure. Some suggest that the worker should limit the conflict, facilitate the formation of the relationships, and enable the structure to evolve. In my view, this is true up to a point, but if the worker allows things to develop as they are wont to do, the structure will be a replica of the environments of the members outside of the group; all of the old scripts will be enacted. It is the function of the groupworker through groupwork to free people and hence he must help them to experience freedom and thereby to thrust toward the fulfillment of their potentials.

I have described in the section on the use of structure how a worker refuses to sanction autocratic members, how he gives status and recognition to those who are denied them, supports helpful contributions and ignores others, and teaches people to perform so that what they do is for the benefit of the entire group. He also consistently refuses to allow people to become dependent upon him.

It is especially important for the worker to pay close attention to what is being reinforced in any group. He must seek to reinforce egalitarianism, to extinguish power hierarchies and domination, and to give support to mutuality and intimacy. A major aspect of the method in this phase is feedback so that members can be aware of their conflicts and putdowns, compare these behaviors with the contract and with their desire for help, and become empathetic to the needs and hurts of others. A second important part of the method is a relationship within which the worker demonstrates how one behaves toward others and especially how people in positions credited with authority should act. The problems of the group are group problems and must be dealt with by it. The worker must make it virtually impossible for the members to project onto him; therefore, he must not threaten, confront, challenge, or punish. I said in Chapter 5 that four things will occur. *First*, jockeying for control and testing. This means a testing for standards and sanctions, both of the group per se, and also of certain members who bid for dominance and seek to command the top of the hill. The worker must avoid direct collision with would-be indigenous leaders and refer the situation to the group to be handled by it. Although the worker puts forward his preference for an egalitarian group, it is not his place to do battle with any member of the group. However, it is wise to postpone elections and hold out against hasty decisions about formalizing structure. Treatment groups do better without officers and the worker can explain the concept of shared leadership and participating democracy to the members.

The *second* thing to occur will be a testing of the worker's allegation that he will not repress or dominate them. This period is a trying time for any worker and if he gets angry, loses patience, and does clamp down, the jig is up. The group will have proven to themselves that the worker is not to be trusted, is deceitful and controlling like many of the other leaders they have known. This does not mean that a worker does not limit as, for example, in the case of a group of children, but that he limits in the name of the group, the group contract, and the consequences. In other words, he limits to help the group members accomplish their purposes and not to punish or discipline them.

At one time in the history of groupwork, it was the custom for a worker to begin with tight limits and gradually to relax them as the group became more able to control itself. It was said that if he began by being easy, he would never be able to "handle" the group later. A worker does not have the privilege of handling a group; he is most effective by handling and controlling himself in the service of the group members. The preference now is for the group to be afforded every opportunity to be free and given the responsibility for controlling itself to the limit of its ability or maturity to do so, and at that point the worker then limits on its behalf.

The worker must expect to be tested. The limits, such as they are, must be firm, for if the members find "rubber walls" they will probe and push endlessly. They seem to need to provoke in order to become ready to trust him. A few members may also attack and defy the worker in a direct confrontation. This should be dealt with as a group problem and the worker must use patience and restraint.

If the worker is able to weather this confrontation and prove himself, he will find ways to demonstrate security and assure the members that they are safe. Security is enhanced through routines, meeting regularly on time, at the same time, and in the same room. The worker should not be absent, nor should there be major changes at this stage such as the introduction of new members, workers, rules, and the like. The worker must also enact the contract by protecting members from attack or punishment. The worker should accept and encourage freedom of self-expression and be unshockable.

Third, the freedom promised by the worker results in heightened anxiety and ambivalence about taking responsibility. The resulting anxiety may produce either flight or renewed fighting. In activity groups this is a good time to introduce programs that can channel these feelings by providing experiences in mastering media. In such a setting, crafts have been used successfully.

Fourth, the group begins to develop mutuality and the beginning of intimacy. The balance of this chapter and the next three discuss method once the group is ready for intimacy.

Since it takes this long—the group must negotiate three difficult phases—I believe that twenty weeks is perhaps the minimum time for a treatment or significant growth group. One of the important functions of the worker toward the end of the third phase is to deal with questions of direction and purpose. He enters into dialogues on this subject and endeavors to renegotiate and reaffirm the contract. It is important that group goals be developed in workable units and in operational terms. While there will be long-term goals that are equated with the purpose of the group, the worker must help the members develop also a sequence of proximate or short-term goals which can be accomplished and cumulatively, step by step, lead to the fulfillment of the major objectives. The beginning goals must be feasible and give every promise of success so as to motivate renewed effort, give credence to hopes, and give a sense of pride in "our" group and what "we" can accomplish if "we" work together. This is the kingpin in establishing the viability of mutual aid.

That the goals must be operational means that they must not be vague, global, or philosophical, but be based on concrete eventualities that can be observed and evaluated. Examples might be, "There will be fewer fights in the group meetings," "The group will help John control his temper outbursts," or "We will plan and carry out an overnight hike." It is unlikely that there will be much meaningful process or interaction unless there are goals. A group of people must know what it is working on or toward if it is to expend and direct its energy in a meaningful manner.

It is not enough to formulate goals and express them. The group and the members must also be or become committed to the goals. This is a most important aspect of groupwork. Through discussion and agreement, the group must invest. Groups or people do not invest in superimposed goals and hence the goals must be drawn directly from the group. Neither do goals of one clique or majority motivate much input from a reluctant or compromised minority. Time must be spent in negotiating, in finding common ground, in relating personal needs and goals to the broader group goal, in exploring "what one hopes for," and in identifying various consequences. Adequate time and support must be afforded the minority to voice objections and reservations. A man convinced against his will is of the same opinion still.

The worker and the group must uncover deeper desires than those that are obvious and bring into the open the fears that underlie resistances and apathy. It is important for each member of the group to make a public commitment, not as a ritual or blood oath, but in the course of the discussion. Goals evolve, goals change, and goals develop as the group and the members grow. This factor should be observed and honored by the worker and also fed back for group awareness. Goals that are improbable or impossible to achieve should be confronted. For example, when a group of parents of very sick children set themselves a goal of helping their children reach the stage where they can attend public school, the worker must introduce realities to avoid shattering frustration and distrust as well as grinding disappointment.

A question arises about the ability of all groups to come up with viable goals and to state them in operational terms. Encouraging free choice, self-determination, and self-expression does not mean that the worker offers nothing. He encourages and invites the group to express all of their opinions and ideas and when he thinks that it has no more to give, he offers tentative suggestions. He may say, "Have you thought of this alternative?" "Do you think this might help?" or "Do you think this might work?" He provides resources as long as he believes that by so doing he will not block the group from thinking and working and as long as he has no need to defend his suggestions. The worker verbalizes and restates what the group has been saying or meaning so that it can put the thoughts into usable forms.

When a group has worked its way through these phases, it will be possible for the members to be involved in mutual aid and to interact with each other as people, revealing themselves, their fears and yearning, asking for help and accepting it, and taking responsibility for themselves and others.

NOTES / READINGS

1. National Association of Social Workers, "Working Definition of Social Work Practice," *Social Work*, Vol. III, No. 2 (April, 1958), p. 7. The techniques listed are:
   1. Support.
   2. Clarification.
   3. Information-giving.
   4. Interpretation.
   5. Development of insight.
   6. Differentiation of the social worker from the individual or group.
   7. Identification with agency function.
   8. Creation and use of structure.
   9. Use of activities and projects.
   10. Provision of positive experiences.
   11. Teaching.
   12. Stimulation of group interaction.
   13. Limit-setting.
   14. Utilization of available social resources.
   15. Effecting change in immediate environmental forces operating upon individual and group.
   16. Synthesis.
2. Charles B. Truax, "Significant Developments in Psychotherapy Research" in *Progress in Clinical Psychology*, edited by Abt and Riess (New York: Grune & Stratton, Inc., 1964).
3. Robert D. Vinter, "The Essential Components of Social Group Work Practice" in *Readings in Group Work Practice*, edited by Robert D. Vinter (Ann Arbor: Campus Publishers, 1967).
4. See Fritz Redl, "Group Emotion and Leadership," *Psychiatry*, Vol. V, No. 4 (November, 1942).
5. Henrietta Saloshin, "Development of an Instrument for the Analysis of the Social Group Work Method in Therapeutic Settings" (Unpublished Ph.D. dissertation, University of Minnesota, March, 1954).
6. Lawrence Shulman, "The Anatomy of the Helping Act," paper at the National Conference of Social Work, New York, June, 1969.
7. James Garland, Hubert Jones, and Ralph Kolodny, "A Model for Stages of Development in Social Work Groups," *Explorations in Group Work* (Boston: Boston University School of Social Work, 1965).

175

7

❖❖❖❖❖❖❖❖❖

Components of Groupwork

What follows in this chapter is a classification and explanation of the components of the method. Some of the modes were used by the groupworker in the first three phases of group development. All of them are integral to groupwork and are instrumental in accomplishing the ultimate objectives of a social groupworker. They are, therefore, the components which are used in the establishment of a therapeutic environment, in facilitating a readiness for treatment, and in the growth and treatment phase itself. We will build on this as I demonstrate how the components are used with a variety of targets.

Composition Inheres in Method

The composing and forming of a group have been discussed earlier in the book. The way to compose lies in determining the significant variables in relation to purpose and arranging scales which can be used to balance the group in favor of desired outcomes; predicting role behaviors and avoiding ego-alien combinations; providing for homogeneity of problems and heterogeneity of coping patterns; and including enough stimulation to avoid static homogeneity.

Intake

Intake into the group is part of grouping; it inheres in groupwork. A separate chapter will be devoted to intake into the agency. The group intake process consists of securing information which

176

will help the worker determine whether the person is appropriate for a group and for a particular group, and to help that person accept the service and move into a group.

The worker begins by reading all the information available in agency intake records, using collateral resources, and by observation, if this is possible. He looks for those variables that are related to the principles of group composition and are crucial to the purpose of the group. It is highly recommended that the groupworker see and talk with the prospective member himself. In this interview he endeavors to assess the social functioning of the person in an interaction and to gain some knowledge about his modes of adaptation, role behaviors, habits, self-image, and readiness to enter a group. The worker interprets the group treatment as an offer of service and helps the person understand what group treatment is, what to expect, and why it is being offered. For example:

"Mr. Tuttle, the staff and I think that a group will be of help to you. In our experience, we have found that discussions with other persons, such as yourself, open doors to new and satisfying solutions to problems. I think you will enjoy the group and will be comfortable in it. You will not be embarrassed in any way and you will have a chance to talk over your concerns and get help. Would you like to try it? You will not be forced to stay if you do not want to."

"What do you do there?"

"It is a small group of people who meet with me once a week for an hour and a half. We talk about how to solve our problems. We share our experiences and we give each other support and encouragement."

It is better for the worker to do this himself and not rely upon a referring caseworker, intake worker, physician or other staff member. Not only does it ensure accuracy, but it also begins to establish a relationship with the worker and an easier entry into a group of people who are strangers. It is preferable also for the worker to do this himself because one of the functions and skills of a groupworker is to compose the group, and his firsthand contact with prospective members is most important in his decision about the member's appropriateness for the group. As was stressed earlier, this beginning rests upon clarity of purpose.

Group Formation Inheres in Method

Group formation rests upon establishing some modicum of group goal, a beginning relationship of the members to the helping person and to each other, commitment to a contract, enabling communication, fostering success and satisfaction in goal achievement even if this is minor and peripheral, developing hedonic tone—enjoyment—minimizing competition, making resources available and equally accessible, minimizing threat, and facilitating the establishment of trust. A group really does not form because of common interest, goal, shared values, or even symbiotic attractions alone. Bond does not develop fully until the members reach a stage of intimacy and this means that closeness, independence, and purpose have been enabled. These have been discussed in an earlier chapter.

Basic method principles rest upon (1) providing nurturance, (2) making resources available, (3) maintaining freedom, and (4) encouraging group decision-making. Nurturance means that the worker meets needs, is responsive, accepting, trustworthy, trusting, and offers unconditional affection. Making resources available means that the worker himself is available when needed and not only provides resources but sees to it that they are available equally to everyone in accordance with their need. Resources in this context are those things that human beings can use in order to grow and prosper. Freedom means the absence of exploitation, domination, and control. Group decision-making means that there are options and alternatives, known consequences, and that the group is encouraged to decide how it will achieve its own tasks or resolve its own hangups.

Therefore, a collection of people becomes a viable group for social enhancement when there is substantial agreement on goal or purpose, satisfaction with how it is working toward it, and mutual trust. Stated in other terms, it occurs when closeness has been approximated, control resolved, and there has been a clarification of and a commitment to purpose.

In practice, there has been reliance in the past on certain techniques and instrumentalities for achieving this stage. I refer to such things as group names and similar symbols, room arrangements, social mixers, and the like. The commitment to a group goal and satisfaction in working together transcends symbols. The room arrangement can and does facilitate social climate and communication but primarily it is a tool to achieve and reflect closeness. Where and how the worker sits and his tone of voice and body language are techniques that reflect the dimension of control. Food is both a symbol and a facility. It relaxes because of its oral, need-meeting connotations, it symbolizes communion and friendship (to break bread together), it occupies one's hands and hence relieves embarrassment, and it is enjoyable. The use of food in groupwork is an important implement in method.

Space is a variable to be considered and used. If the room is too small it causes jostling and tempers become aroused. Crowding produces anxiety when closeness is an issue; it enforces body contact which can exacerbate fear and anger; it can cause withdrawal and also acting out. If the room is too large, it encourages running, social distance, fragmentation, and "wool-gathering." If the room contains interesting equipment such as laboratory apparatus, sewing machines, typewriters, and similar distractions, these seduce the members to touch and play with those objects.

If the room is cold (below 62 degrees) or too warm (above 78 degrees) the group will expend energy on its feeling of discomfort and be less able to concentrate on its real problems. The same applies to uncomfortable chairs. However, if the chairs are too soft and the room too comfortable, people tend to relax and think of the meeting as a social one instead of as serious business. These environmental variables can be arranged by the groupworker and later the group, and this is part of method.

Up to this point in our discussion the group has been getting ready for its major purpose. The members have begun to trust each other, they have progressed in their struggles to resolve control, they have developed a form of egalitarian structure, they have agreed upon a goal, and they have some motivation and commitment to it.

The worker has performed his functions in the preparation. He has clarified purpose, composed and formed the group, negotiated a contract, helped it through the first three phases, and enabled the group to formulate a goal. We now turn to clarify the aspects of method that have brought us this far and are the essence of groupwork in enhancement and treatment.

It will be noted that in the implementation of the components of method certain techniques reoccur. Once again, this is because the number of techniques are limited, they are not the crucial aspects of the method, and each technique can effect multiple results depending upon how it is used.

The Use of the Contract

The contract, both as it is being negotiated and when it has been agreed upon, provides leverage and sanction for the worker to guide and to confront the group. The worker reminds the members that he is asking them to work on achieving *their* objectives. It is through this medium that he is absolved of manipulation and can address himself to two foci: to keep the group aware of what it is presently working on compared to what it wants to accomplish, and to keep it working. The contract sets several expectations to be faced which include revealing oneself, mutual aid, and working on one's concerns. The more one reveals oneself, the more vulnerable one becomes to change, and the increasing ability to reveal oneself results in the greater likelihood of a change in behavior, validation and being valued by others, and of the development of intimacy.

The worker can ask what the discussion or a particular comment has to do with the group goal; he can wonder aloud why the group backs away; he can remind it of its contract and hence his expectations; and he can couple responsibility for outcomes with the group's willingness to accept responsibility for itself. Along with choice and options must go responsibility so that group members are faced with the obligation which is associated with freedom; namely, that each man is responsible to himself and for himself, and that he cannot escape by blaming others. This is an important discovery which can be facilitated through a change of script or "game," role-playing, other program, experience, and feedback.

The Use of Choice

All social systems such as groups enforce certain imperatives and one is informed in some books that the way a person behaves is so determined. This is a fallacy which stems from translating general systems concepts to human beings in social systems. Every person—although guided by his position, status, role, past experiences and predispositions, value orientations, and by his self-image, aspirations, and other variables—selects those stimuli to which he will respond from the many that crisscross from different directions and bear upon him. It can be said that a person is conditioned or that he has habitual modes, perhaps learned, or that he is capable of selecting only certain influences due to his training, or selective inattention, or misinformation, or the like. Social groupworkers are involved in freeing people from these old patterns and helping them to find their way out of their repetitive cycles. The methodology when translated into theory is complex and consists of many different facets, but it is less difficult in practice.

1. The worker and the group must provide options. There can be no choice if there are no alternatives. For there to be freedom, responsibility, and a mastery of the environment, there must be exercise in making choices.

2. The worker and the group will point out that there are choices and what these choices are.

3. The worker will not make the choice nor will the group make the choice for any member, but they will press for a choice to be made.

4. The worker and the group will point out repetitive patterns that result in defeat.

5. The worker will teach the procedures for making choices.

6. The worker and the group will begin to correlate choices with consequences.

7. Rewards or reinforcements will be provided for making choices that are adaptive.

It becomes possible then, in an atmosphere of trust, free of domination and committed to mutual aid, for alternative courses of behavior to be tried and for consequences to be tested. One of the greatest assets in working within the group process is that one can test what probable consequences might accrue from certain actions for reaching specified goals. The action can be altered and new behaviors learned as a result of this experience in an environment which is reasonably safe, and with a worker who can be relied upon and trusted to protect the learners from hurting themselves, hurting each other, or hurting him.

The modes are the affording of awareness, providing support, resisting dependency, provision of experience, reward, and the use of a feedback control system. The members become aware of *what* the situation is, that is, *what* they do *actually* and also *what* they *can* do. They can do something other than what they usually do, if they so choose. They become aware of *what* the consequences of different alternatives are and that they are responsible for what happens. They are restricted from projecting blame, finding excuses, or absolving themselves from making their own selections. They learn that if they wish to make other choices, the worker and the group will help them. No one will make choices for them and hence they cannot easily retreat to infancy nor regress to dependency. When they make other than habitual choices they are rewarded by the results of their new behaviors which afford satisfaction and favorable responses.

Awareness allows the members and the group to understand what they do and how they do it; i.e., it helps them to learn how these behaviors affect others and cause certain responses, and how the interactions become locked into cycles that perpetuate maladaptive scripts, that is, cycles that produce unwanted consequences. If they can become aware, they can become ready to consider options for how to behave and respond differently. The usual techniques include confrontation, suggestion, clarification, the introduction of knowledge which the group does not have, reflection, and lending the vision of the worker and others as to what might be or could be (hope). Implicit in this is the worker's belief that the members can improve.

The method being discussed here does not rest upon insight. The effective motivators lie in knowing what the reality is and the question posed by the group is "What are we going to do about it?" The sequence goes from what they desired to do, to what they are doing, to what keeps them from doing what they wish, to what is possible and feasible, to what they can do to change so as to more nearly approximate behavior that will approach their goals and enhance their environment which, of course, always includes other people.

The method involves the feedback control system. It is postulated that most people do not know how they behave or how they affect others. They do not know what options are available, what the consequences are of behaviors, or what they could do about any of this if they wished. While I do not discount emotional blockages, I do hold that a combination of awareness, motivation and hope for change, support, and learning enforced through rewards will allow many people to self-correct and most people to make adjustments. The methodology, therefore, is the use of feedback, the teaching of perception and sensitivity to cues, and the demonstration that change is not only possible but also advantageous.

The Use of Problem-Solving in the Here-and-Now

If we combine several of the modes which have been discussed above, we can conceptualize method as the use of problem-solving in the here-and-now. The premise is that people can find solutions to their problems of living and to their hangups if they can identify them, are committed to seeking a more satisfying and fulfilling adaptation to life, and are helped to be themselves. This is accomplished, in part, by enabling the members to make conscious choices about their behavior, to select and practice more functional coping patterns, and to exert themselves to modify their impinging environment. The group is helped to explore what the members do not like about their situation, how they cope with or try to solve this problem, and what obstacles, as they see them, keep them from achieving their goals. This process is readily usable with children as well as adults.

The method is appropriate for treatment and correction. Modes based upon providing learning experiences, reinforcement, teaching, exploration of values, goal explication and the like are recommended for growth and development. However, in both types of groups, the worker helps the group to become aware of "games," scripts, façades, and maladaptive modes of adaptation. Samples of this kind of behavior. that have been observed and heard in the group sessions are examined. The focus is on what the members are doing, how they are acting and feeling in the here-and-now of the relationships within the group. The messages lie within all of the communications in the group, which include body language and other nonverbal cues.

The study process is based upon investigating the interactions within the group, and between it and its surroundings. It is a study of systems relationships. Since these relationships occur within the group, extensive history-taking is neither necessary nor useful. The study is less about individuals and more about interpersonal relationships. Clearly, the study is of social functioning and not of intrapsychic dynamics. That which occurred in the past or outside of the group is relevant as it is manifested in interaction within the group; however, the question of why is avoided, as I have said before. The answer to the question "why" is unreliable because most people do not know why they do what they do or feel as they do, and it is debatable whether the worker knows either, but even more important, because "why" is often used as an excuse and can be a way of avoiding doing something to improve the situation. It becomes a justification.

What the worker does is to ask the members to face up to their situations and their behavior in the group and to decide whether their behavior is in their own best interests. The worker in the use of group method is active though not directive.

The following excerpt illustrates problem-solving *in* a group, not by a group; the latter is discussed in Chapter 14. The form of recording is interesting and it will profit the student to examine it carefully.

An Illustration of Problem-Solving in a Group

AGE: Latency
SETTING: Children's Behavior Clinic
SESSION: Sixth

The purpose of the group is to help the children resolve their problems.

During the last part of the previous session, Tommy had wanted to play dodge ball but none of the other members would join in the game with him, continuing to work on their individual projects instead. The worker had promised Tommy that at the beginning of this meeting he could try to get the group members interested in playing since there had been other activities already planned when he had wanted to play during the previous meeting.

Group Interaction	*Worker Interaction*	*Interpretation*
Group members entered the room noisily. Tommy got out the ball and asked the group to play dodge ball with him as he bounced it about the room.	Worker remained in background and verbalized Tommy's request to group.	Gave group members freedom to decide for themselves. Reinforced Tommy's request thus showing approval of game for group.
Sandy immediately said no and began to work with his pot holder. Brad seemed to hesitate, almost joining Tommy but then deciding to remain seated. Jeff listened to Tommy but worked diligently on wallet project showing no indication of being willing to play. Tommy disappointedly grumbled about how no one ever did what he wanted to do as he pretended to be playing basketball by throwing the ball above the high cupboards.	Worker verbalized Tommy's disappointment to the group.	Support for Tommy and an effort to help group members realize needs of others in the group besides themselves.
No response from other members to worker.	Worker waited for a few minutes and then said to Tommy in front of group that he knew he was disappointed but no one seemed to feel ready to play the game with him yet. Worker suggested that maybe Tommy could find something else the group would like to do together.	Letting tension build up for a few minutes to see if any member would respond to Tommy's expressed disappointment. Breaking tension by supporting and redirecting Tommy. Giving verbal recognition to group members of their real fears in not wanting to play dodge ball and supporting and directing interaction among members on a more comfortable level. Giving Tommy opportunity for continuing efforts as leader.
While Tommy continued with ball expressing his disappointment, Sandy	Worker joked with Sandy about the "surprise ride" the tire gave him and	Provides emotional relief, redirecting Sandy's energies from anxiety

184

Group Interaction	Worker Interaction	Interpretation
began swinging on tire hanging in center of room. Suddenly tire slipped from its hold in ceiling causing Sandy to fall off. He appeared dazed at first and then laughed anxiously with other members.	asked if he knew how to fix it.	developed by situation to constructive problem-solving of situation.
Sandy insisted he knew how to fix it and elaborately did so with the help of the other members by twisting on tire to tighten it. Other members pushed Sandy to make tire twist.	Worker agreed verbally that Sandy did know how to fix the tire.	Reinforcement of Sandy's achievement and ability to handle situation.
Game developed on tire between Sandy and Tommy. Tommy tried to throw ball through tire while Sandy kept the tire in motion. Game became quite aggressive with Sandy often remaining on the tire and occasionally being hit.	Worker came over to Sandy and tried to help him swing the tire more effectively without always ending up on the tire and getting hit.	Help Sandy participate aggressively in game without getting hurt thus trying to prevent reinforcing his fear of aggression as disastrous danger.
Sandy became very upset with worker's intervention, screaming at him to leave them alone. Became so upset that he quit game and crawled up onto window seat.	Worker went to him apologizing for upsetting him and interpreted his intervention as a new idea suggested to him and Sandy for their game.	Trying to show Sandy that he was not doubting his ability nor rejecting him, but only trying to be helpful.
Sandy continued to sulk in window seat.	Worker went back to individual project of Sandy's he was trying to fix so Sandy could continue it. After a pause, worker began to talk to Sandy about the pot holder which he had had trouble with and which was now ready for him to continue, that there had really been nothing wrong with it.	Refrain from reinforcing Sandy's feelings of being extremely upset but to let him work through them himself. Interacting with Sandy on positives. Redirecting Sandy back into the activities of the group meeting. Enabling Sandy to return by emphasizing his successes.

Group Interaction	Worker Interaction	Interpretation
Tommy put away ball. He asked worker if they could play one of the table games.	Worker asked Tommy what game he would like to play and said he would play with him. Worker wondered if Tommy would like to ask the other members to play.	Discouraging Tommy's request for leader's authority. Reinforcing Tommy's idea of the table game by agreeing to play. Redirecting Tommy into the group leader role Tommy had desired.
Tommy asked members. Brad enthusiastically agreed and helped Tommy set up the game. Jeff did not respond to Tommy's invitation verbally but continued working on his ceramics project he had just started at the table.	Worker participated in group as equal to other players. Occasionally went to Jeff to see if he needed help with his project and encouraged him to play game with group while project dried.	Continuing efforts to give Tommy opportunity to direct group into game and for group interaction to occur spontaneously. Supported Jeff to help him remain with the group at the table and tried to encourage him to participate with group nonthreateningly by also recognizing Jeff's need for security through his compulsive needs in working with project as means of defense against threatening group situation.
Much interaction between Brad and Tommy as Tommy teased Brad for mistakenly taking worker's turn in his excitement to get ahead in the game.	Worker continued interacting as an equal, refraining from any direct leadership.	Enable further interaction to occur between Brad and Tommy.
Jeff seemingly becoming very anxious at table, wanting to ask worker for help but feeling unable to do so. He anxiously moved from his chair around the room and then back to his chair.	Worker did not seem to be aware of Jeff's anxiety.	Anxiety increased.
In the meantime, Sandy becoming active again, swinging on tire. He tried to get worker's attention by calling to	Worker continued game with group, listening to and giving recognition to Sandy's overtures but not reinforcing them.	Showing Sandy that there were no hard feelings about earlier conflict. Trying to help Sandy express himself but not

COMPONENTS OF GROUPWORK

Group Interaction	Worker Interaction	Interpretation
him and showing off on the tire.	Encouraged Sandy to come join them in the game.	playing into Sandy's showing off with reinforcement. Trying to give him opportunity to gain attention.
Sandy continues to show off. Expressing feelings about hating teacher in school to worker while continuing to play up to the worker.	Worker asks Sandy questions about these feelings on an objective level.	Encouraging Sandy to project his feelings of anger against worker onto a situation outside of the group to enable Sandy to find a comfortable and socially acceptable outlet for his feelings which will not threaten him more in the group situation.
Sandy continues interacting with worker in this manner but begins asking for greater attention as he shows off even more on the tire.	Worker ignores Sandy's elaborate showing off and suggests that he start the popcorn for the group's snack.	Nonreinforcement of infantile behavior and redirection of member to group interaction, discouraging direct interaction with worker to continue.
Sandy began making the popcorn. Jeff began acting out his anger at the worker by swinging on the tire.	Worker continued game with Brad and Tommy and interacted occasionally with Sandy in response to Sandy's continued verbal overtures.	Worker seemed to sense something occurring between him and Jeff as he anxiously seemed to look over at Jeff frequently. He did not seem to know how to interact with Jeff at this point. Counter-transference here as worker seems to feel more comfortable continuing with Sandy and seems angry at Jeff for uncomfortable feeling present between them.
Sandy ignored popcorn as he went from one individual project to another and yelled to worker that he had better get popcorn before he lets it burn as he did last week.	Worker ignores Sandy's ridicule of him. Asked if someone would get the plates for the popcorn as worker continued playing game.	Setting limits for Sandy and giving him opportunity to constructively come back into the group.

187

Group Interaction	*Worker Interaction*	*Interpretation*
When no one got plates, Jeff quietly took them from the cupboard and inconspicuously placed them beside worker.	Worker did not seem to see Jeff's actions. Worker talking to Sandy about not getting out juice today because he thought they might go to machines in other part of building for soda today. Posing idea to them for decision.	Worker seems to be unconsciously ignoring Jeff. Giving group members opportunity to experience new social situations within a framework of expected behavior.
Sandy ignored plates as he requested everyone to grab for his own out of the pan.	Worker continues relating his expectations of group as they go for soda.	Jeff seems to feel rejected by worker and group evidenced by his walking ambivalently around the room.
Group members leave room following worker. Jeff runs back, fills plate with popcorn and takes it with him.		Afraid it would not be there when he returned.

The trip for soda was a success considering it was the first time they tried this together. All of the members and the worker again gathered around the table as they ate their refreshments. Sandy took a plate for his popcorn but nothing was said about it. As the group verbally interacted, Jeff removed himself from the table after taking more popcorn for himself. He explored boxes of toys, walked about the room and occasionally returned to the table. He appeared very ambivalent about being at the table with the others.

The group made candles from paraffin. The worker took the responsibility in melting candles and the final process was quickly accomplished.

All group members surrounding worker except Jeff, while worker prepared material. Jeff continued showing ambivalence. At one point he walked up behind worker with toy gun hidden behind his back.	Worker answering many questions of group.	Initiating interaction as central figure. Jeff becoming quite aggressive in displaying his anger against worker.

Jeff begins acting out with toys. Sandy also plays with some of the toys but does not interact directly with Jeff until the two begin swinging wildly on the tire, both expressing much of their pent-up anger and anxiety about the group process.

188

Group Interaction	Worker Interaction	Interpretation
Sandy suddenly falls off the tire when Jeff pushes it. This appeared to be an accident with both very surprised. However, Sandy becomes very upset and accuses Jeff of pushing him off deliberately.	Worker assures Sandy that Jeff did not mean to and asks Jeff to apologize to Sandy.	Interpreting situation and giving direction for boys to be able to work out their feelings about the situation.
Jeff softly says he is sorry to Sandy.	Tommy takes role of worker and says, "Now Sandy, it is your turn to say you are sorry to Jeff for accusing him of doing it on purpose."	Recognizing Jeff's feelings and gives support.

Sandy is finally persuaded by Tommy without worker's intervention to apologize to Jeff. Worker refrained from intervening in order to let group members have an opportunity to handle situation. Group continues with worker to finish candles. Jeff also is a part of group interaction at this point.

Boys gathering things up getting ready to leave.	Worker asks Jeff to show group ceramics box he had completed.	Giving Jeff an opportunity to be positively recognized by other members and facilitating interaction between group and Jeff on positive grounds in order to tone down previous emotionally charged interaction.

Group, including Sandy, asks Jeff many questions about how he made the box and showed interest in trying to do one themselves during the next meeting.

Enabling Solutions That Support Wishes and Alleviate Fears

Many people have learned throughout their childhood that when they have acted in accordance with their own wishes and needs they have been punished or, at least, that the ways in which they have sought to satisfy them have resulted in pain. When a group or its members resolve tensions or reduce stress caused by a problem by defending themselves against their fears and back away from learning new ways of coping, this does not solve the problem and

189

hence it is a restricting solution. It restricts the group members from dealing with the problem itself and only deals with their feeling about it or the consequences that members think might result from acting as they might wish to act. This kind of resolution does not permit them to be themselves. The function of the worker is to assist them to find and act upon enabling solutions which free the members to fulfill their wishes within the bounds of social requirements.

The methodologies are to face the group with its restrictive solutions, to support their trying out and testing new solutions, to provide experiences through role-playing or program that call for new behavior, to help members test reality and find out that new behavior will not result in the eventualities which they fear, to create a group that gives members courage to test new solutions, and to give the worker's support, encouragement, and hope in an accepting and nonjudgmental atmosphere. When the members succeed in these strivings, rewards reinforce their continued effort.

Freeing People to Be and to Become

This phrase, to be and to become, I have explained means to be oneself and to reach the limit of one's potential. A very large component of groupwork is the freeing of the person to find his "self." Instead of being themselves, many people are poor reflections or projections of others. This is perhaps one of the gravest concomitants of unhappiness, of thwarted growth, of neurotic hangups, of acting out, and of poor self-esteem.

Since one of the major objectives of social groupwork, as delineated in this book, is the finding of oneself, the methodology to be used is the removal of domination, manipulation, exploitation, and external personal controls. This means the elimination of control and domination by the worker, the agency, indigenous power figures, and the group.

I renounce the concept found in some groupwork books which holds that the group pressure is salutary or that the press for conformity is the essence of socialization. Such concepts merely substitute one form of autocracy for another and require that the member give up his "self" at the price he must pay to belong. Conformity is inimical to creativity and self-actualization. I hold instead that our groups should be systems of mutual aid predicated upon equality. In such a group, one is honored for what he contributes to the need-meeting and well-being of the others rather than because he conforms. These postulates, while they may sound like philosophy, are in fact methodological.

The Use of Milieu

The importance of growth and potentiality is a key premise in these pages. The thrust for life and growth is innate, and there is a ground plan which must be followed if an organism is to develop with positive health. Positive health is much more than the absence of disease; it is the maximization of well-being and the efficient use of all energy and resources to be and to become all that is possible. We are concerned with three aspects of growth: (1) providing the climate and nutrients that are essential to support growth, (2) preventing insults and blocks to growth, and (3) restoring growth if it has been retarded or stopped.

In the natural scheme of things, no one grows flowers; flowers grow. The gardener facilitates growth by providing for light or shade, soil, water, fertilizer, temperature, and sometimes transplanting. Should the plant be attacked by fungus or insects, he may spray to defeat the invaders. The groupworker also functions by making a milieu available in which people can grow, by providing for a healthful climate that allows and encourages growth, by restricting injurious conditions, and by defeating noxious elements that thwart growth by attacking or living off the person.

The groupworker seeks, by enabling, to make the group an environment in which people can grow. He enables closeness by fostering trust; he is trustworthy and trusting. He maintains security through the provision of routines of the same meeting time and place and consistency of social climate, and he offers the protection of a retreat in which the usual sanctions are absent. The worker removes the domination and control of the authority figure and replaces it with mutual aid, equality, and concern for others. He seeks to eliminate those factors which generate dependency, mistrust, shame, self-doubt and guilt. He seeks to interfere with extrasystem inputs which attack the egos of the members and he helps them to develop their initiative to overcome the external insults through appropriate social action. On occasion, he joins them in repulsing the injustices and exploitations of those who would live off them or over them.

Social Action

The environment provides or denies the opportunities for need-meeting and the available options. It controls the destiny of a person except, as we have said, for the choosing one does within options. However, all available options may be depriving or, at best, poor fare. Social action is essential as the individual must be able to make the environment more suited to his needs and the needs of others. The environment is a tool, an instrument, or a facility which must be fashioned to serve people.

Prevention

Prevention is an integral part of groupwork. Prevention means not only the provision of need-meeting nutrients, the elimination of endangering elements, the making available of growth-inducing experiences, the training of personal skills, and the like, but it also means inhibiting deterioration processes and keeping things from getting worse.

The Use of Positive Experiences

All that happens within the group is an experience which becomes part of the members. Groupwork involves the provision of experiences which support growth, teach, correct, and reinforce. The growth potential or therapeutic potential of the group rests upon several methodological modes. The group process must reinforce positives and extinguish negatives. The procedural steps for this are spelled out by Gambrill, Thomas, and Carter.[1] The worker must not follow the same script that the members have played over the years or allow himself to play their "games." He must be careful to avoid playing any of his own "games" as well. Part of the technique is to feed back and confront the group with the script and ask for an exploration of the consequences in relation to the goals. An analysis of what the worker does and what the group does to reinforce and reward maladaptive behaviors, attitudes, and feelings is crucial. The group meeting is a stage upon which each member is a participant-observer and as such it is an ongoing experience that is susceptible of immediate replay and also proximate redoing. The worker may engage the members in both a feedback which is a replay and a redoing through role-playing or through allowing the group event to be reviewed and new coping patterns tried.

The fact that the group experience takes place in the lives of the members and before their eyes opens the way for life-space analysis, that is, the group can examine and discuss what it has done or what any member has done within the context of events that are real and firsthand. The immediacy of the events and the fact that they are "for real" makes it possible for positive learning to take place. I do not imply that experience is necessarily a good teacher, but that the combination of factors such as knowing and being motivated to work for certain outcomes, awareness, support, and experience make for a meaningful learning milieu, especially when one adds the assessment of consequences and the satisfactions that accrue from accomplishment. Such experiences allow for the taking of risks if the climate of freedom has been established and if the provision of mutual aid has been maintained. The experiences take on great meaning if the groupworker demonstrates how to be a human being.

The group experience is a "slice of life." The members are "playing for real and for keeps" with a real worker; the group experience is reality.

The Use of Self-Expression

How one feels is emotion regardless of why it is felt. It includes affect in interpersonal relations and also group themes such as fear, mistrust, and anger. When feelings are not expressed openly, the self is being concealed and modification of dysfunctional behavior is restricted. The restriction or internalization of feeling can result in serious neurotic suffering and the hiding of it can produce physical symptoms. The meaning of catharsis is to express oneself and unburden the pent-up or carefully guarded feelings. Intimacy or closeness is seriously limited when people are not free to communicate feelings. Group norms determine which sentiments can be expressed and how they are to be expressed. An inability to express sentiment or to manage one's feelings to relieve tension in a socially acceptable manner also can be destructive to society. In group life, the handling of feeling is a necessary process to prevent sentiments from obstructing goal-directed activity and also to release the motivating forces for achieving group goals.

If members are to express themselves, feeling must be made legitimate. For the people in the group, inappropriate tension-management mechanisms block spontaneity and enjoyment, and seriously distort communication. A major importance of social groupwork lies in the communication of affect to promote mutual aid rather than in the fulfillment of a charge.[2] Cooperation, solidarity, commitment to group ends, and willingness to invest oneself in others can result when tension is managed appropriately and feelings are expressed freely. Here, the most important aspect of method lies in the worker's use of self.

The effective groupworker cannot be objective in the old sense of the word, nor impassive. He must share and express his feelings; he cannot avoid conflict or deep emotion, either consciously as a technique, or out of his own discomfort. He invites, accepts, and reinforces the expression of sentiments. He operates on the level of feelings instead of intellectualizations; he is willing to show his sentiments; he demonstrates as well as says that feelings are natural, normal, and universal; he creates a climate that is free of sanctions; he introduces program that releases feelings, such as fingerpainting, psychodrama, and puppetry; and he reflects the feeling messages as well as being responsive to them.

In the excerpt that follows, the group process helps the young patients to cope with anxiety about their physical disabilities through expressing their feelings.

An Illustration of the Effectiveness of Expressing Feelings

AGE: Seven to Ten
SETTING: Medical Hospital

The following excerpt from a record is presented here to illustrate in microcosm some of the objectives and techniques of the social groupworker. This group is used to prevent and treat excessive regression, denial, repression, dependency, guilt and hostility; to provide opportunities for the expression of aggression, for mastery and achievement, for sublimation through activity, for positive, normal social peer relationships and for protective, supportive relationship with a helping adult; to encourage expression of fears and concerns about the current situation in order to permit worker's handling through support, explanation, reassurance, and clarification. This group is made up of three boys from a surgical ward totaling ten who, through individual intake interviews, are found to be in need of, and ready for, a treatment group.

The following are very brief thumbnail sketches condensed from the extensive records:

Bobby, age seven. His leg injured in an auto accident, Bobby demonstrates in individual play his unconscious fear of loss of limb through identification with brother who recently did lose leg in a train accident. Bobby comes from a troubled family, has had no visitors, and is seductive with female worker.

Charlie, age eight. His physical disability has kept him in and out of casts most of his life. As with Bobby, his family is broken. He talks about his two brothers who died recently. He is so annoying to nurses with his demands for attention that he is punished by being restricted to bed. He handles this by throwing himself off the bed and splitting his new cast.

Tommy, age ten. A fall from a bridge resulted in a complicated break. He is frightened and depressed, but otherwise seems to have no serious disturbances in relationships. Family situation is good.

Excerpt

When we sat down in the group together, Bobby and Tommy at first were not involved as group members except by their physical presence, but for very different reasons. Tommy was new and afraid and could not quite trust the function of the group. Bobby was interested in getting individual attention from me and not in working with the other boys. Charlie on the other hand was trying to get the group going by offering play material to everyone and he tried to be supportive to the worker. The significant part of the group meeting came when the conversation started after fifteen minutes of individual exchange with the worker and silences.

Bobby was playing with the train; he said that he had seen a whole bunch of men with their legs cut off. He said that when your leg got broken they cut it off. His brother Frankie has had his cut off. I remarked that yes, Frankie had had his leg amputated. The doctor had to do it because it was very badly injured. The doctor helped his brother to get well by doing this. I assured him and the other two boys that their arms and legs would not be cut off. Bobby commented on his cast and how it itches and hurts. The other two boys did not respond to what Bobby had said. They just sat there. Then Bobby said that if you broke your neck, they cut off your neck and you couldn't see. Tommy and Charlie at this point laughed nervously and said that he was silly, and that, of course, they didn't do that. They fixed it. Then I said something about the fact that all the hurts were being fixed. Tommy really responded to this remark. This was one of the first times he really got involved. Tommy talked about how he had been in the hospital before, and that this was his second time, and that his sister was always coming here for cuts and bruises. He told of a cousin of a cousin who had had "dramatic" fever among other things and had been in the hospital for six months and that they had made him very fat, demonstrating a bloated belly. After further exchange between the children, I again reassured them that this would not happen to them. Tommy said that it was scary when you come for an operation because you didn't know what to expect. He said that they were going to do something to his cast that afternoon. I asked Charlie if he would tell Tommy something about cast changing. Charlie told about it happening to him lots of times. Tommy asked him how long he had been here, and Charlie seemed a little distressed. Tommy said, "Two months?" Charlie said, "Two or three months . . ." Charlie then talked about operations when they put you to sleep. They all agreed that they didn't like the smell of ether and it was scary. The group then went on to dart shooting.

Although the three children were so different from each other, they had common fears, problems, and experiences. They also had the common experience of treatment for physical disability; life on a surgical ward with its unique atmosphere, culture, and its imposed limitations on their activities; their common fear of mutilation and castration; and their fear of the unknown hospital procedures. The children used the group to express their fears and concerns. The worker used techniques of reassurance, support, and clarification to help them. At the end of the meeting, they chose to use darts as an expression of aggression and also as an exercise of control as they attempted to combat feelings of helplessness through mastery and achievement in a masculine activity.

The Use of Values

It has long been the premise of groupwork that it teaches values although social workers contend that they believe in self-determination and, therefore, value judgments do not enter into their practice. Social workers should not make value judgments. However, social groupwork literature has stated explicitly that it transmits values. This is inherent in socialization, of course.

The group has been characterized as a microcosm of the culture; the members bring the outside culture into the group or socializing institution of society; it is a form of social control and, as such, it represents societal values or at least the so-called dominant values of society. The agency which sponsors the group and pays the worker represents the dominant values of its sponsors and has as a function the transmission of these values even in the most pristine of social agencies. To deny it is a hypocrisy in itself and fails to take into account the intent of its board of directors or the legislative body.

In groupwork, the worker has been said by some writers to be a carrier of values, a symbol representing societal norms and values. Moreover, norms and values guide his role behavior, his assessments and diagnoses, and his method. One cannot deny that the groupworker is a carrier of values and that the more significant he becomes to the members, the more likely it becomes that they will adopt some of his values. Certainly, if we hold that he becomes part of the members, his values will be included in the incorporation and, if he provides an experience, his personal enactments will expose his values. However, the important aspect of his method, aside from his stance, lies in helping the members *find their own values*.

Today, it is not viable to contend that value change based upon the transmission of established values is the desired objective of our practice or that value change is a prerequisite to behavioral change. Values are based upon fundamental assumptions and beliefs and are related to individual goals. It is possible that values which are held by groupworkers today may become out-of-date, especially if they are sympathetic to the many aspects of life that stress competition, survival of the fittest, obedience, and conformity. There is reason to believe that the norms for group life which are considered appropriate and proper in groupwork literature are not suited to the world of the future.

The values that seem to be evolving for the future and are conducive to human survival are:

1. From considerations of quantity toward considerations of quality.

2. From the concept of independence toward a concept of interdependence.

3. From the satisfaction of private material gains toward meeting public needs.

4. From the primacy of technical efficiency toward considerations of social justice and equality.

5. From the dictates of organizational convenience toward the self-development of the group member.

6. From authoritarianism toward participation.

7. From the preservation of the system's status quo and routine toward the promotion and acceptance of change.

The people who read this book, in all probability, will be professionally active in the year 2000 and the children who are in today's groups will then be in the prime of their lives. The values the worker may be transmitting now are already old hat. We just must realize that our own life experience in growing up did not prepare us to set values for tomorrow. We have no idea what the world will be like. It is to be hoped that the values and norms that have permitted the continuance of war, condoned pollution, allowed exploitation and racism, and called the domination and control of others normal will be superseded by norms that are based upon human values.

However, having said this, we can help people to think through values, to develop their own values that are relevant to reality. This process is accomplished by searching out and challenging basic assumptions and testing their appropriateness to reality, by seeking the alternatives and expanding the options, and by testing the various consequences of different actions. In such a confrontation, goals are important but goals must be matched by assumptions. It is part of the learning process for the groupworker to press for the assumptions that underlie the goals. Goals, values, and assumptions are related on feedback loops. In addition, there are human values that inhere in our social work profession. These have to do with the value of the person, his dignity, his freedom from domination by others, and his right to maximize his own potential. A primary value today is one which will enable human society to survive. In social work and education, these values are not to be transmitted like a message over a telephone line. They are to be demonstrated in the relationship of worker and members, teacher and students.

197

Members of a group can learn how to relate to each other in a meaningful encounter in a group if the group climate allows them to relate and if they are encouraged to do so by the worker. This is facilitated if both the worker and the members can be themselves and if the worker demonstrates by his behavior how people relate to each other as human beings. From a method point of view, the alteration of norms and values changes behaviors and the maintenance of such patterns perpetuates behaviors. One questions whether value change is an end in itself or in groupwork practice is a means of changing behavior.

In the following excerpt the worker permits the group to find values and to explore their own basic assumptions.

An Illustration of the Learning of Values

AGE: Nine
SETTING: Youth Center
SESSION: Sixth

The Mods were coming home with their worker from a very enjoyable hike in the woods and as they approached the fringe of a cluster of houses, they filed past a house where three small Negro girls were playing on the sidewalk. One little girl, about six years old, dropped a dime on the walk and all of the boys scrambled after it, shouting and pushing each other.

Jake, a quiet but sturdy boy, came up from the scramble with a dime in his fist. With no hesitation, he quietly went to the little girl who looked anxious and on the verge of tears and handed the coin to her. She accepted it without a word, turned and ran into her house.

The boys walked on in silence for a time until Len spoke up in an angry tone.

"Why did you give it to her? We should have kept it. Finders keepers."

"It was her dime," Jake answered without looking at Len.

"Yeah? You didn't have to give to her," Len went on. He was disgusted. "She lost it."

"It was her dime so I gave it to her," Jake said in a matter-of-fact tone.

None of the other boys said anything. Jake stuffed his hands in his pockets and looked down as he walked.

"It's unfair," he burst out. "It's unfair to be mean to them just because they're black. My mother says they're just the same as us. Dark skin don't mean nothin'."

There was no response from anyone. After the group returned to the House and were sitting down having bottles of soda pop, Len suddenly burst out, "Justa same, you shoulda kept the dime."

Jake said nothing but just glared. Tony asked Len if he were a Protestant. Len replied that he was not.

"If you was a Protestant you coulda kept the money 'cause if you kept it that's stealing and stealing is a sin. It's okay for Protestants to do sins," Tony said seriously.

The worker asked whether all the boys agreed with Tony about Protestants. Jimmy was silent but he looked troubled. The boys had not really thought about Protestants and sins before but nonetheless, they had to support Tony. They loudly chorused that Protestants were sinners. Jimmy was a Protestant and Billy was half Protestant but they said nothing.

"I am a Protestant," the worker said softly. "Did you know that?" There was an awed silence. Such a possibility had never occurred to them. Jimmy edged closer to the worker. Tony looked puzzled.

"I guess maybe it's all right to be a Protestant, huh? You don't steal do you?" The worker assured him that he wouldn't steal.

"Do you think it is all right to take someone else's money?" the worker asked, directing his question to the group.

"No, like it's their property and all that, unless they are your enemies," Tony replied quickly.

At this Jake almost lost patience. He shouted, "What's the difference anyway? It's still their property. It isn't yours and if it isn't yours, it's stealing. Anyway, that black girl didn't do anything to you."

Len was impressed. He turned to the worker. "Are them niggers the same as us—you know, the same as anybody else?"

Jimmy said solemnly, "You shouldn't call them niggers. They don't like it anymore than you like to be called a mick, or you a wop," the last directed to Tony.

Jake said, "My mother says it's worse 'cause everyone picks on them 'cause they're black."

The worker said Jake was right. Black people are as honest as white people and they are not different except for their color.

Billy said, "There's a kid in our room that I wanted to ask to join our club but I was afraid to 'cause he's black but sometimes him and me play together. He's a good guy and a real good hitter. You know, I thought you guys would throw me out if I brought him."

Len said, "It don't make no difference. Didn't you hear Reg? Black's the same as us."

Here is an incident which centers mostly around the question of values. All of the members of the group except Jimmy had a Roman Catholic background and had been nurtured in that kind of religious culture and set of values. Jake's mother, besides being careful to convey this family culture to her children, had conveyed other valuable social values regarding the acceptance of difference and had created within her son feelings as well as information. Tony's family, which is Italian, had imbued in him a feeling of righteousness about being Catholic and the feeling that only Catholics were free from sin. Len who was as fervent as the others, however, had little of the feeling of the other two and was willing to condone and practice nonacceptance of Negroes and taking the dime. He was a more deprived child. Billy, who had one Catholic parent and one non-Catholic parent, had no convictions either way. Being a very sensitive child and receiving information and feelings from the others, his own feelings were affected. Jimmy, the only Protestant lad, became anxious whenever this subject arose because he was a minority in the group.

In this situation, the worker, who knows the boys well, had general goals for them. When the incident with the Negro girl arose, the immediate goal became one of general acceptance of the differences of others. Before the worker had had to do anything, however, Jake took over the situation on the basis of his own feelings and home environment. This had a tremendous effect on the other members, causing them to think a little about their attitudes toward blacks, which was valuable. Many times, in an effort to move in and take advantage of a situation in order to begin an educational process (in this case, the acceptance of blacks), a worker tends to perform this task when the group members could do the job with much greater effect. The fact that Jake's mother was the person who had influenced him in his feelings, and the fact that it was a feeling, had considerable effect on the others so that they thought about it a great deal. This sensitivity to the tone of the group helped the worker to decide to allow the attitudes and values of some of the group members to affect the values of all the members. Withdrawing himself from the process and assuming a stance which permitted a member to carry the goal-affecting material involved skill in perception, a conviction of the necessity to use the situation, and skill in timing and pacing the variety of involvements so that the results would be useful. This was a positive use of freedom.

In the session back at the House there was no reference made to this incident at first and another discussion arose over the dime that Jake had returned to the little girl. The whole question of stealing had been anxiously solved by Tony's home teachings regarding "sin" and the relative value differences between Catholic and Protestant living. Forgetting that Jimmy could not share the comfort of their Catholic teaching, the group was willing to accept Tony's explanation—even Len who had been most anxious to take the dime in the first place. They were feeling quite virtuous because Jake had done the "good" thing and Tony had explained it from the Catholic point of view as he understood it. This made Jimmy the only potential thief in the group. He was quick to feel this and was the only one to feel it. The worker had two choices. One was to ask them if they felt that Jimmy would be more inclined to steal than they, since he was a Protestant, and risk increasing Jimmy's anxiety; the other was to declare himself a Protestant and rely on himself, both as a symbol and as an adult whom they liked. The worker chose the latter because he felt that it was necessary, not only to afford protection for Jimmy's feelings but for the continued acceptance of Jimmy as the only non-Catholic member of the group.

Unlike the incident regarding the dime where the worker withheld his comments in favor of the comment from a member, here he asserted himself so that his opinion would support values to which all members could respond because of their own feelings for the worker as a significant adult. After the assertion, however, it was not enough to allow the situation to rest on the fact that he too was a Protestant. It was then necessary, once the boys had accepted the fact that all people could be honest, irrespective of their religious teachings, for them to discover the general value of accepting the differences in others which, regardless of their backgrounds, would be held in common by all. This supported Jimmy as well as strengthened the others. Before the end of the session, it was also necessary, despite Jimmy's statement of his feelings about using the word "nigger," for the worker to assert himself in support of Jake, reinforcing the point for everyone, and to convey new information to the group members.

Certain conditions were necessary in these situations before anything of value could take place. First, it was important to note the tone of the group. There was a feeling of acceptance and trust here and a real relationship between the boys and the worker. Without this, much of what occurred might not have been so helpful. The worker was in control of his own participation in the group process and was able to increase or decrease his influence in the process when he felt it appropriate. It was necessary for him to time his participation with accuracy and to make it congruous with the texture and tone of the group climate. There was a lesson here to be learned by the members and the worker had to work out the most effective way of allowing the educational content to evolve so that it had meaning.

NOTES / READINGS

1. Eileen D. Gambrill, Edwin J. Thomas, and Robert D. Carter, "Procedure for Socio-Behavioral Practice in Open Settings," *Social Work*, Vol. XVI, No. 1 (January, 1971), pp. 51–62.

2. Task, charge, and task oriented refers to committees, boards, councils and similar socio-groups. These are not to be confused with terms such as group goal or ego tasks.

8

❖❖❖❖❖❖❖❖

Ways and Means

Through Group Structure

Behavior is related to the place one has in the group structure and hence behavior may be modified by change in one's location. The place one occupies is also a factor in self-image, in the meeting of one's needs, in attitudes and values, in the ability to risk, and ultimately, in identity. The formation of the group structure and alterations in it are important aspects of method. Another dimension of this is helping members to function appropriately in different locations within the structure.

The worker helps a group to develop a structure which is appropriate to its purpose, to the age and experience of the members, and is conducive to the growth of the members. A universal principle is that there should be only as much structure as is needed by the group to function. This means that the usual suggestion for officers, constitution and bylaws, parliamentary procedure, and the like is neither useful nor appropriate. This imposition of the trappings of legal organizations and parliaments upon small groups hampers the development of appropriate structure that would facilitate interpersonal interaction, it blocks true democratic process, it prevents some members from meeting their needs, and it creates legalistic processes instead of human ones. The business of most small groups can be conducted more effectively without the symbols of governmental structure. Parliamentary procedure polarizes the group members instead of unifying them; it encourages competition rather than participatory democracy.

My preference is to minimize formal structure for treatment groups. Treatment groups function best without officers and also

202

without hierarchies of status, power, and position. The method is not only *not* to encourage such structure but also to discourage it. The ultimate goal is to develop a climate of equality within which each member can have access to the resources which he needs for his growth and habilitation.

As part of method, the worker does not sanction or use the group's attempts to develop hierarchies, that is, he does not recognize budding power leaders, he treats incipient low-status members with the same respect as any other member, and he gives status differently from what the group might give at the outset. Some of his expectations about the egalitarian nature of the group are expressed in the negotiations of the contract. It is important that his own behavior does not afford him special privilege or unwarranted status. Also, he acts as though there were no vertical structure. His second technique is to feed back what is happening in the group to the group and thereby guide the members to see the consequences of its structuring for the group and the members.

Predicated upon the purpose and the contract, status is given for the contribution a member makes to the group goal. It is not given for blocking, nor for selfish or unsocial behavior. The group can learn to do this by verbal encouragement, example, and the skillful use of rewards. The assumption of leadership in the group is encouraged, but the concept of shared leadership is verbalized and taught. Moreover, people who have leadership potentials and display them are taught how to use leadership for the benefit of the group and the members.

The effective groupworker uses his knowledge of group structure to prevent structure from endangering members or retarding the enhancement of social functioning. He seeks to effect a matching of the members' need dispositions with the social environment (which in this instance is the group), for the benefit of both the members and the group.

As I explained earlier in this book, people seek to structure their environment so as to stabilize relationships. People who lack social competence demand structure and use it to avoid interpersonal encounter. The worker helps the group to see this, he endeavors to prevent the members from escaping into structure as a defense against closeness, and he seeks to help the group to form itself so as not to duplicate and perpetuate the endangering social environments from which the members have come and which fostered their hangups.

In working with treatment groups, the worker endeavors to block the development of hierarchies and prevent roles being assigned that are deleterious to the occupants. He seeks to foster a structure which is horizontal and one that allows maximum freedom and variety in interpersonal relationships and role performance. The treatment group is a protected setting and, as such, the milieu is designed to be therapeutic. However, in other types of groups, it is inevitable that structure will develop. The worker must then help the group to develop the structure which will be most useful to it. This is done by suggestion, by the teaching of role skills, by confronting them with their behaviors, by shared leadership, by helping with decision-making, and by the use of a wide variety of programming. In groups which do not use activities, this can be done through the use of a group observer who reports to the group what it is doing; through role-playing to learn and experience different patterns; through the use of the tape recorder or video tape and playback; through life-space interviews in which the group members immediately review critical situations that occur in the group; and through what might be called reality discussions.

As usual, the commitment to a group goal and a well-defined contract help the worker to ask the group to compare its structural arrangements with the consequences of them and ascertain whether they are effective. In a climate of trust, the members also can discuss how they feel about their positions, statuses, roles, and the group's pressures. The worker does not bring about the changes; he enables the group to effect changes.

The low-status member is helped to rise in status by developing skill and confidence, and gaining favorable response; the clown is helped to gain acceptance and attention by making valued contributions; the blocker is helped to become a supporter by gaining awareness and finding other roles that meet his needs and hence the group's; the exploiter is not rewarded for exploiting and, therefore, his behavior is extinguished; the isolate is interacted with rather than ignored, and so on. These are examples of the kinds of means that can be employed; awareness, support, and learning are the basic ways through which effective groupwork is accomplished.

The following excerpt illustrates the dynamic consequences of structure for behavior and a groupworker's skillful use of this knowledge.

An Illustration of the Use of Group Structure

AGE: Ten to Eleven
SETTING: Settlement House
SESSION: Eighth

The following club session takes place in a lower-middle-class neighborhood of a big city. The agency's purpose for the group is growth of the members, socialization, and the acquisition of social competence.

204

The group is coeducational and multi-ethnic. The program consists primarily of activities. The worker is female and a member of the full-time staff.

"Listen!" said Reva, choking on her words. "Either he gets out of this club or I do."

"You . . . You get out!" Joan said, giggling.

"Yes, you get out!" the others shrieked. "We don't want you, we want Charlie."

Reva regarded them dumbly. Her face was frozen in pain. She tried to say something, choked on her words and turned away. The children watched her guiltily.

"Well . . . she's always saying things," said Marge, as if to justify herself.

"Yeah!" Jeannie said.

"She calls everybody names," someone added.

"She's dumb," another chirped.

"I'm not saying anything," said Joan, changing tack.

Slowly the children returned to their artwork. Reva stood near me.

"He hates me," she said. "He never liked me. Never! He always starts it. He poked me with a stick—hard. Did you see?"

I said that I saw. I said I knew that Charlie had been starting things with Reva lately. I wondered, I said, how this had started. At some time, I asked, had she started to provoke Charlie too? Reva denied this vigorously. I said that I would talk to Charlie to see if we could work this out somehow. Later, I talked to Charlie. I said that I had seen what happened and I wondered what the trouble was.

"I dunno," said Charlie. "She gets me mad."

"When?" I asked.

"I dunno, she just does."

"You don't like Reva, do you, Charlie?"

"Nope. Sometimes I don't care, but sometimes she gets me mad, I dunno why."

I said, "Well, nobody expects everyone to like everyone else, but you do start things with her, don't you?"

"Yeah, I do," he said honestly.

Then, later, when I left the room for a few minutes, apparently more trouble started. When I returned, Reva had her hat and coat on and she was quietly getting ready to leave. She came to me.

"Can I see you in private for a minute?" she asked. We walked out into the hall together.

"Please," she begged, "can't you make him get out? If he stays I'm not coming anymore."

I said that I could not ask Charlie to leave. It was not my club; it belonged to the members. Perhaps there were other ways to work it out. I asked what Reva thought. She began to cry.

"He doesn't like me and he won't let anyone else like me." She sobbed loudly. "Even Joan, who used to be my friend, doesn't like me anymore."

I said, "You want people to like you, don't you?"

205

"Yes," she sobbed.

I said that I liked her very. much and I wanted her to be happy in the club and I would like to help her. I said that maybe we could talk it over and see what we could do. I asked her whether she would like to come to talk with me in my office sometime.

"Could I?" she asked.

I told her that I would write her a letter and make an appointment. She smiled weakly and said good-by.

I returned to the room and all the children looked at me questioningly. I asked them if they would please come around the table so that we could talk. I said that I knew Reva did not get along with the rest of the group, but I didn't know too much about it. Would they tell me their ideas so that I could understand it better.

"She doesn't like us. That's the whole trouble," Jeannie said.

"I know," I said.

"She is always calling people names," Charlie said, "and she curses. She don't curse when you can hear, but you should hear her when you're not around."

"I don't like her," said Marge.

"Me either," said Leroy.

"Me either," someone else echoed.

I said, "So I guess that no one in the club likes Reva."

"It's 'cause she don't like anybody," Marge said.

"That's the whole trouble," said Charlie earnestly. "She don't like anybody."

"Does she know we don't like her?" asked Joan uncomfortably. At this everyone exchanged embarrassed glances. I nodded.

"Yes, she does—I wonder how it feels to know that no one likes you."

There was grave silence.

"She never tries to make people like her," Charlie said.

"I know," I said. "She doesn't know how to get people to like her. She wants you to like her but she doesn't know how to get you to like her."

"But," said Marge, "if she wants people to like her, why doesn't she try to be nice?"

"She never learned how, you dope," Charlie said. "I don't care if some people don't like me, but she does."

I agreed that people were different. There was a long and thoughtful pause.

"Maybe," suggested Joan, "if we just didn't pay any attention to her for a while, she'd try to be nicer."

"No," said Charlie. "I don't think so. That would make it worse. If she knows nobody likes her anyway, that would make it worse."

"That's a good point, Charlie," I said.

"Well then," said Joan, "maybe if we were nice to her and tried to be friends, she'd think we liked her and she'd try to act nice."

"That's certainly something to think about," I agreed.

"Well, I guess she isn't mean all the time," said Leroy.

"She is good in clay," said Jeannie.

"She has some good ideas," said Joan.

"Yeah, she gets some good ideas," said Marge.

"She's good in nature. At camp she's the one who caught the bugs, and caterpillars, and the snake," someone added.

"Then I say we should stop being mean to Reva, and all try to be nice," said Joan.

There was a murmur of assent.

I said, "I think it is just great the way you people have thought this out. It may help or it may not, but it is worth a try."

The children all looked pleased with themselves.

The situation was one of conflict in which one member was a scapegoat. The probability is that Reva contributed to her being cast in that role because it fitted her self-image and her experience. She knew how to play that role. It is also probable that the group had a position of isolate available, either because of the multi-ethnic nature of the group or the pressures from the impinging environment, such as the agency, school, or neighborhood, or because it served to enhance the self-images of others in the group. It prevented Reva from meeting her needs.

Reva was the isolate. Charlie held the position of indigenous leader ("We want Charlie" . . . "He won't let anyone else like me" . . . "I don't care if some people don't like me," etc.)

At the outset Joan ordered Reva to get out. Shortly thereafter she changed her tack. We learn that Joan used to be Reva's friend. As long as Charlie, the leader, did not like Reva, it was not safe for Joan to like her. Charlie had high status. If Joan wished to maintain security and have status she felt that she would have to conform to the norms set by Charlie, which were to scapegoat, to provoke, and to dislike Reva.

I would hypothesize that Joan might have been unchosen sociometrically herself, and if she chose Reva, the dyad would have been isolated. Instead, she aspired to cultivate Charlie. If Joan were a leader or sought to be a leader, she would not have had to abandon Reva nor would she have been the first to tell her to get out.

At the beginning, the members got on the bandwagon and all agreed that Reva should go. Here contagion set in. It was not safe for anyone to take Reva's part. All could release hostility as the result of Charlie's poking Reva and the group consensus that Reva get out. Marge, Jeannie, and Leroy were the followers; we see how readily they followed the leads and changed to conform.

The worker knew that if she confronted Charlie directly he would have had to defend himself and the group members would have had to support Charlie against the worker in order to preserve the status quo. The worker believed that if Reva remained in the room during the discussion, Charlie would have had to justify himself. He could not back down or he would have lost face. Consequently, the worker let Reva leave when she did.

The worker's stance then was to be accepting, nonjudgmental, and nonimposing. She demonstrated that in her opinion the group belonged to the members and they had the responsibility to solve their own group problems. By so doing, she raised their status, gave them respect, and held out the hope that they could handle the problem. She also demonstrated that they could trust her as she trusted them.

Her strategy was to feed back the situation to them ("So I guess no one in the club likes Reva" . . . "I wonder how it feels to know that no one likes you"), and to provide some resources that might not be available to them. ("She doesn't know how to get people to like her. She wants you to like her but she doesn't know how to get you to like her.")

In the worker's willingness to let the group struggle with the problem, Charlie lost no status and consequently he was able to maintain his leadership. Not having to fight for status or to keep his position, Charlie could rise to the occasion and allow Joan to make a few suggestions. In order not to challenge Charlie's position, Joan's first suggestion was mild. Charlie replied by opening the door to a more positive proposal and the worker gave the support of her status to Charlie. Now Joan was freed of her fear and could suggest that the group members be nice to Reva and try to be her friend. Joan was her friend before and now it appeared to be safe to act as her friend again.

As soon as Charlie made it possible for the members to befriend Reva, one could see the effect of contagion once more as everyone joined in with the suggestion that they be nice to Reva. In order to salve their guilt about their behavior, each found justification for liking Reva.

The worker returned the group to reality to avoid disappointment by saying, "It may help or it may not, but it is worth a try."

All of the elements of group structure are in this short report and demonstrate the influence of position, status, role, and power. Also, one sees that there are many messages in the communications that confirm and enforce the structural relationships. In this instance the worker uses her knowledge of the structure to help the children resolve the conflict and to make the group a better environment for Reva. At the same time, Charlie learned a little about how to use his leadership constructively.

Through Group Process

The group and the group process are the effective media for growth and change in the members and in the group's environment. The groupworker is part of the group system and the group process but he does not direct the process nor change people or behavior. The worker influences the process within the limits of his position, status, role and function to the extent that these interact with the psychological dispositions of the members.

Group process encompasses everything that happens in a group. For our purposes, we will discuss communication, validation and reality-testing, the management and communication of feelings, boundary maintenance, control, and decision-making. The ways in which members achieve status, and how roles are assigned and performed are also processes. These have been dealt with elsewhere. Goal-setting and the movement toward goals, which also are processes, appear elsewhere in the book.

Communication

The inability to communicate and distortion in the sending or receiving of messages frequently are contributing causes of maladaptive behavior. An effective groupworker seeks to help members improve communication. This can be done in a variety of ways, and I will give some to illustrate the method.

Members are helped by the group and the worker to become aware of how they communicate through feedback, that is, to be conscious of their facial expressions, body posture, tone of voice, and the words they use. They can be helped to detect the semantic differentials and the subtleties in the decoding of messages. For example, they are asked whether what they have said, either verbally or nonverbally, is what they mean and, if not, what they do mean. They can be asked to repeat what they have heard, that is, how they filter and select meanings in the messages, and the group will check the accuracy of what they repeat. This also provides for reality-testing. The hearer can be requested to restate in his own words what the speaker says, and the speaker can be asked if that is what he means.

The groupworker can act as a bridge by either repeating what is said or interpreting it. He may call attention to the fact that no one responds or answers the speaker. For example, "Peggy looks upset today. Has anyone thought to ask her what is the matter?" or "I wonder if anyone heard what Joan said a moment ago. What was she asking us for?" or the worker interprets: "Joel wants to be liked but he doesn't know how to ask you to be his friend. He did not mean to hurt you when he hit you. It is the only way he knows how to tell you that he wants to have something to do with you." In order to avoid the restriction of information and its being available only to leaders or an ingroup, the worker disseminates it or requests that knowledge be disseminated widely throughout the group.

The worker reflects double-bind messages. He asks them what the speaker wants the hearers to do with his message. He reflects how the manner in which a message is given seeks to reinforce status levels or confirms disrespect; how some ways of saying things can castrate, eviscerate, or cut down a hearer; how repeatedly interrupting another tells everyone who is important; how constant failure to finish a sentence leaves hearers in a quandary; and how distorted speech can be a ploy or a defense. The worker uses such techniques as asking, "What is the message?" By his example, members also begin to ask that question. He explains how no one can not-communicate because silence and withdrawal or failure to participate tell their own stories.

Explicitly permitting and encouraging self-expression and interpersonal interaction, the worker addresses his communication primarily to the group and less to individual members. He refrains from talking much so as to allow and facilitate the members' interaction. If communications are directed to him when they should be directed to another member or the group, he indicates this verbally or through gestures. A worker can ask, "What did he hope to accomplish by that remark? Did it accomplish what he wanted it to? How else might he have expressed it?" He teaches the group how to discover and correct its own distortions and those of the members. He confronts the group with its "games" and scripts. He instructs through demonstration, practice, role-playing, suggestion, and direct feedback.

The worker responds to the messages sent by the members and the group. A group theme can be the conveying of fear, anxiety, or insecurity, or can be pride in its progress. The worker does not respond to these themes on an intellectual level, but rather, he responds to what is being requested and to what they are intended to convey. He tests to find out whether he is coming close to understanding the messages and whether they understand his. Much that has been illustrated here dwells upon negatives since these are more usually the blockers but the worker also helps people to communicate the positives, some of which embarrass people both in the giving and the receiving. They must learn how to give praise, to express love, and how to build the egos of others. They must learn also how to receive gifts graciously and be able to reciprocate.

Validation and Reality-Testing

It is through such reciprocal response that people become validated. Validation is the confirmation of one's authenticity. Failure to be validated relegates one to a state of nothingness or to the status of a thing. Some children grow up within families that refer to them as "it" and treat them as nonpersons. Some people experience a condition of nonexistence or unreality. One can be validated and validate others through interacting with them and attesting to the fact that they do exist. The group isolate or the person who is not chosen in a sociometric sense is invalidated by virtue of his position. The scapegoat is validated, but as a distasteful thing to be ejected. Validation is the confirmation of self in the eyes or assessment of others and it is the basis of self-image.

The process of validation takes place within several areas. The *first* occurs in an explication of group beliefs and a matching of one's own beliefs with those of others. This process is inherent in the acquisition of identity. Beliefs are shared, compared, acted upon, and explored in the group sessions. The *second* facet occurs through favorable response and this usually is coupled with learning to know and to meet social expectations. It includes learning social competence and developing sensitivity and empathy. Some educators do not believe that empathy can be taught existentially. It can be learned through group experience and hence it can be taught. Perhaps the major means of learning to effect favorable response is to develop a code for cues; this is learned through communication, feedback, and the worker's help in analyzing one's own wishes and behaviors. Programmatically, story-reading, dramatics, and role-playing are excellent for this teaching. If activity program is not possible, group discussion and enactment are the vehicles to use. The *third* facet occurs through a positive demonstration that one exists. One exists because one feels, believes, knows, and acts. These are attested to because the environment registers the impact of one's being in the manner of a radar blip. Herein, the group and the worker render one of their greatest services. However, in addition to all of the other aspects that inhere in this discussion, accomplishment is the most positive of influences. If one can demonstrate mastery of the environment and of self, one can begin to "be" in relation to the social world.

The worker, by enabling interaction and by including each member sets the stage for experiences in being, being touched, and touching in a psychic sense. By teaching social skills, by dedication to the concept of change, by reinforcing responsibility for self and others, by permitting freedom to act, and by supporting risk-taking, he makes it possible for the members to deal with and create new environments which emanate positive validations.

Beyond being validated, people must also validate their environments. This concept means to confirm reality which involves the ego-developing process of reality-testing. Reality-testing requires a reaching out along with the capacity to risk as well as having effective perceptors and in this context, the freedom to test within the group takes on immense significance. The lurking and frightening dangers of a hostile society are made less incapacitating in the group by brightly lighting the "corners," by disarming the fears, and by strengthening one's repertoire of coping skills.

The methodological aspects rest upon the creation of trust within the group; the use of confrontation which compares the perception of others with one's own definition of reality; the support to relinquish one's distortions which may have been comforting in the past but may not be needed in the protected environment of the group; the provision for experiences in risking which result in satisfaction instead of anticipated pain; and the acceptance of the group members by the worker along with his nonjudgmental or nonpunishing attitude. It is within this context that such concepts as seeking out the common ground between the goals of the person and the demands of society, identifying the blocks that prevent one from moving toward one's goals, and viewing the options that are available take on meaning.

Validation is not an automatic process. Inaccurate beliefs regarding the environment or one's relation to it may be self-defeating. Beliefs that lie in the unconscious or are carryovers from the past may result in behavior that seems to others to be irrational. Beliefs that violate a norm may result in punishment, ostracism, and guilt. Such knowledge, based upon one's belief system, can inhibit rational social functioning. Persons, therefore, need to learn how to chart the environment; that is, to test the reality of the group's structure and where they fit in, what niches they occupy, and what relationships they have to the others. They must be able to accurately perceive the expectations, the mores and customs, and the direct relationships between action and consequences.

One learns how to chart the group and hence the social environment through experience and the corrections that are suggested by one's peers and guides. The worker helps to focus and clarify the reality of the environment while enabling the members to risk testing it. He allows them to correct for distortion and to see and hear by looking and listening. The worker must be careful lest he impose his version of reality on the members and he must caution the group members to avoid accepting the group's image of reality without question. He must also warn against validating reality by consensus. His forte is to facilitate continuous testing. It is by such assaying and comparing that belief, feeling, and action can become consistent, and a true matching of personal need-meeting and the environment can be achieved.

Controlling

A group, or any social system, needs social-control processes if it is to exist. This truism poses one of the dilemmas of our time and is a knotty problem for social groupwork. When social systems are discussed, people often translate controlling as a process into the capacity to control others. This represents, of course, a value. Controlling others is injurious; the value upon which it rests is no longer in keeping with the morality of the times.

In traditional discussions of controlling as a group process, one thinks immediately of power. The usual view of group structure embodies the component of power. To offset the unpalatable connotation of power in social groupwork, the concept of authority has been introduced and it is defined as the right to control, held by the members and conferred by them upon a person or persons. To sweeten the discussion, it is alleged that this established authority resides in a position-status-role combination and not in the person as such. Though believed by many, this is mythology. There are several other ways, however, of viewing power; as, for example, when the member is so conditioned or motivated that he obeys even when another does not ask or expect him to do so, or where the member is controlled through a bargain which rests upon having one's needs met as the price for obedience. Processes for control which are more subtle take place in group life. Some of these are the skillful use of manipulation, the development of social obligations through trading upon past favors, the use of a superior knowledge of the system, and the specter of power through implied threat even though the power does not exist. There are also personal factors such as transference, symbiotic relationships, a need to be controlled, wealth, reputation, and self-image. All of these factors operate in the decision-making process.

The ultimate in social functioning lies in self-control and the aim of social groupwork is to free the member to become autonomous and to develop the ego strength to be able to control himself. Self-control does not develop within strongly applied external controls. Social control, to be therapeutic, must be coupled with mutuality. Some practitioners make the mistake of believing that the members have been freed from autocratic control if the worker does not control but allows the power to control to rest in the hands of one of the members, a clique, or the majority. I have explained earlier that this is not an acceptable solution to the problem of domination. There is an implication in the writings of some authors that the aim is to foster group domination or group control over the members. We can see this phenomenon in groups which demand rigid conformity to group mores and punish members who deviate. For a worker to allow or encourage this is a renunciation of the basic conditions that are necessary for ego growth. Social control is a matter of negotiation, agreement, and mutuality between and among the members, free from exploitation, the use of naked power, or guile. It rests in an egalitarian structure wherein the members negotiate the equations of group good and personal need-meeting. This is the method. It allows people to grow and take responsibility for themselves and others.

Boundary Maintenance

Boundary maintenance is a process through which a group preserves its identity and maintains its characteristic patterns. It can be viewed from a variety of perspectives. The most obvious aspect of boundary maintenance is control over who is admitted and who belongs. In many groups, this is determined by the members or, more specifically, by those members who constitute the majority; or by those who influence decisions through position, status, or power. In treatment groups, the membership is determined by the groupworker or other staff personnel.

The boundary of a social system is drawn by reference to the locus of the maximum interactions among the constituents. The staff may decide who is in the group, but the group decides, in the last analysis, where the boundaries are drawn. An example may be seen in a family group-therapy program where the therapist sees the conjugal family group but does not include the wife's mother because either she does not reside in the household or he does not perceive of her as a member of the immediate family. If, as a matter of fact, the wife's interactions with her mother are many in number and great in influence, the mother is within the boundary as drawn by the family group.

The reverse is true in many groups where maximum interactions occur among some of the members but exclude others. The real boundary of the group is, therefore, drawn around a subgroup. The boundaries are set by such variables as congruence of values, reciprocity of role relationships, status levels, sociometric acceptances and rejections, and social competencies. A groupworker must assess the boundary accurately if he is to know with what group he is working, and part of his method is to include and effect the inclusion of everyone who should be in the group, meaning those who are essential to the purpose of the group and helpful to the members. We have seen that this result can be achieved in many ways. Groups bond around the worker as an object of affect, around interests and mutual goals, congruent values, psychological reciprocities and the like, and these are the variables which the worker seeks to modify through member-to-member and member-to-group negotiation, through feedback, commitment to treatment goals, mutual aid, and other techniques.

The concept of cohesion is directly related to boundary. Cohesion results when the group is more attractive to the members than the lures outside the group. It is doubtful that a group can have much positive impact on members who lie outside the boundary or who are peripheral. The worker should be endeavoring to facilitate cohesion and the key lies in how attractive the group is or becomes.

A startling corollary lies in the lesson one can learn from observing the result of excluding some youth from the accepted circle in the high school culture. These young people tend to reject the values and social imperatives of the school and develop their own deviant culture. They draw a boundary around their own ingroup which becomes an outgroup to the social body. This is, perhaps, an example of what happens when people are excluded from the family boundary, that is, are not in the networks of affect and communication, or are excluded from the peer group or the ingroup in school. Is this the real meaning of alienation? Do these rejected isolates set up a deviant subculture which society labels as sick, emotionally disturbed, or schizoid? One can predict that subgroups which are outside the group boundary will deviate. In overly simplistic terms, the worker must draw a circle that includes them and enables the interactions to become maximized throughout the total group. The three networks involved in this endeavor are communication, affectional relations, and group structure. The underlying facilitating factors have been discussed; namely, the establishment of contract, goal, trust, freedom and the creation of a climate conducive to adaptation and integration. In this chapter so far, we have indicated that a group is supported by processes such as communication of feelings, the use of resources for expressive and integrative purposes, tension management, boundary maintenance, and socialization. A groupworker may facilitate change in the system itself, in the structure of the system, in the processes within the system, or in the actors. Inevitably, change in any will influence change in all. Different ways of change lead to different consequences in the personality processes.

Decision-Making

Decision-making is usually regarded as a cognitive process. As such, it is more appropriately discussed when considering the task-oriented group, or the traditional group in a center, settlement, or community-action program. Overt decision-making, which connotes voting or verbalizing a formal process of group agreement, is less applicable to treatment groups. It is my conviction and experience that formal decision-making procedures are not helpful for growth and developmental groups, and I have explained why in a previous chapter. In this section, we will explore some of the ramifications of decision-making that are both cognitive and affective. The basic differences lie in how one conceptualizes the process, that is, whether human relations are an end or a means to and end. The subject is introduced here because decision-making is a group process. Its initiation into action articulates with power and it is this attribute which must concern us.

Groups are involved in complex psychic interactions which include many aspects of systems processes. The psychological person is essentially an organization that is developed and maintained through continual, ongoing, symbolic interchange with other people. Esteem and prestige, authority and power, expertise and leadership, ego strength and competence underlie group decisions and these, in turn, channel actions, attitudes, collective behavior, and system change. Social systems theorists helped us to see that physical systems differ from social systems which involve psychological and communicative processes. The group is a psychological and social organization. The interrelationship of psychological and social processes which operate through communication creates an entity which we call a group.

The group as a social system operates by virtue of the fact that its components are people, and as such they have options, make choices, and experience variety. It is the free choice to act on differential options that determines group movement and directions, group processes, and, therefore, group decisions. Whether the member is free to make choices and is self-determining, or whether he is viewed as predetermined and programmed by virtue of what he is and the rigidities of the structure of the group is not the issue. He does have choices, although they are always within predetermined limits. Our purpose is to help him to elaborate and expand the options and free the capacity to make realistic choices.

Norms and role expectations can prescribe only ranges of accepted behaviors. Behavior can be altered within ranges so as to be less self-defeating and less injurious to others, hence more gratifying and socially constructive. When decisions are being made, the process is composed of the interaction of needs, motives, goals, and so on of each individual member intersecting, overlapping, meeting, and opposing the paths of other members, and the behaviors are the attempts of each to meet his needs and reach personal goals while going through the maze. (See Figures 1 and 2.) The pathways are not laid out like air corridors and, consequently, movement can be in any direction. The choice of direction depends upon the individual pilot, the condition of his vehicle, the forces in the field, the structure of the environment, the alternatives available, and the goals sought.

The subjective individual with his valences, his predispositions, his perceptions, his goals, and needs enacts his preferences within the context of his position and status in the group, his reference group, his role prescription, the pressures upon him, and the rewards as he perceives them. Decision-making is not quite the rational and cognitive process that some would like to believe it is. The influence of group structure and pressure on the individual personality is crucial.

Decisions in treatment groups and growth-oriented groups are based, primarily, upon psychic interactions. The influences are mediated through communications that convey power and threat, status levels and reward, and safety or risk that can raise anxiety levels to intolerable heights or allow one to relax. The same dynamics are at play in a task group but are hidden by the rules of the intellectual game. The overt appeal in a task group is based upon its merits and logic but these appeals are less evident in the psychological group.

There are few overt group decisions to be made in a treatment group, although one technique which some therapists use is to ask the group to make a public commitment about some kind of behavioral change. "Shall we agree that strapping your baby to the training seat and making him stay there until he 'goes' is what we are not going to do anymore?" More usual group decisions are preconscious and are agreements about the group culture, group feeling, or group theme. These agreements are not made verbally.

TYPES OF FORCES AT WORK ON AN INDIVIDUAL (PSYCHOLOGICAL)

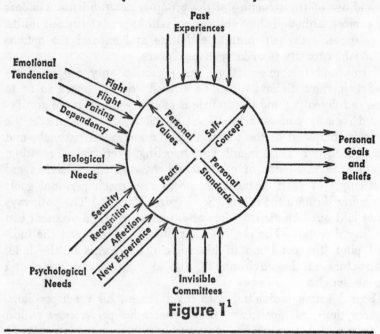

Figure 1[1]

NEED DISPOSITIONS

PHYSICAL SECURITY

SEXUAL SATISFACTION

EXPRESSION OF LOVE

SECURING OF LOVE

EXPRESSION OF SPONTANEITY

ORIENTATION TO ONE'S PLACE IN
   SOCIETY AND PLACE OF OTHERS

SECURING AND MAINTAINING MEMBERSHIP
   IN A DEFINITE HUMAN GROUP

SENSE OF BELONGING TO A MORAL ORDER
   AND BEING RIGHT IN WHAT ONE DOES; i.e.,
   BEING IN A SYSTEM OF VALUES

Figure 2

Some examples are: decisions that the members do not trust each other, will not reveal themselves, are afraid or, on the positive side, will help each other, will talk about their problems, will try to change their behavior.

These group decisions are the result of contagion, psychic interaction which plays upon personal characteristics, suggestibility, lack of self-confidence, and fantasy. The factors may be realistic or they may be imagined and distorted. The method that a groupworker uses consists of providing a climate in which decisions can be based upon goals rather than fears, reducing the hierarchical levels in the structure, facilitating communication, demonstrating reality through experience, giving support, introducing information that is needed, providing resources, and relating decisions to probable consequences. It is essential that the worker help the group to see that there are alternatives and that it is free to make decisions. Of course, to do this, he must free it of his control and he must not be seduced into making decisions for the members.

Since the groupworker is not inanimate, he cannot avoid communicating and, at times, imposing his preferences on the members. In the process of discussing their needs in the presence of the worker, the members are influenced, often profoundly, and may end up wanting some of the things the worker thinks they should want. The worker must explicitly advise the members that they are free and that his acceptance and love are not conditional on the selection of his preferences. The major method lies in helping the members to become aware of the forces at work and how decisions are being made. The members can decide whether they like or approve of the dynamics, want to change them, or prefer the consequences. Alternative routes to decision-making are explored and perhaps tried. Blockages are exposed, games and power plays are made visible, repetitive detours disclosed, and new channels are opened.

The reader is reminded that, in all groups, decisions are made as a result of many factors and that these are neither obvious nor overt.[2] Every member participates in the group along with his "invisible committees." These include the images of status people such as parents, the symbols of social control such as religious leaders, one's professional or occupational identification, various vested interests, and other referents. One may feel that one owes obsequiousness to such outside groups and, therefore, participates in decision-making with these interests in mind. One may also seek to be accepted or rewarded by these referents by acting upon their supposed wishes.

We are aware of the influence of sociometric subgroups and that people side with or seek to please "friends" in the group or, at least, seek favor. Other dynamics which have been discussed elsewhere have relevance in application here and will be reviewed to illustrate the points. People who occupy high positions have knowledge and expertise ascribed to them and, therefore, are to be heeded when one is asked to participate in a decision. One hears people in high positions more readily than those in low, and one realizes that leaders can withhold favors in retribution. Information upon which decisions are to be made often is monopolized by those at the center, can be withheld from those on the fringe, and can be slanted in passing it down. Half-truths are often transmitted or heard. People in low positions are often more fearful and less willing to take risks.

When several people of high status take a stand, usually it either sways others or intimidates them. High-status members support the stands of other high-status members but rarely support suggestions made by lower-status members. Low-status people perceive that they must conform to norms or patterns that are supposedly central to the group culture if they wish to be permitted to belong. People in high positions and status suggest actions which are in their own interest. As a group assigns roles or as members gravitate to roles, the followers are differentiated from leaders. Followers are expected to follow the leaders in decision-making. Leaders are more contagious than others and they trigger decisions and actions in others. They may not control consciously, but they do influence others. The more confident a person is and the more secure he feels, the more he inspires others to perceive him as knowing the best thing to do. Once this attribute is acknowledged, he has more influence even in matters in which he has no demonstrable competence.

All of these factors conspire to work against logic and systematic problem-solving. There are two major things that can be done by an effective groupworker. He can teach the group how to function as a group and teach the members how to be group members; this is group training. He can teach the group and its members how to analyze group dynamics and, thereby, how to be alert and aware of the influences on group decision-making. The mechanics of these methods are well established for the task-oriented group by the National Education Association which conducts institutes at Bethel, Maine, and elsewhere. The dynamics of the method for treatment groups has been elaborated by writers such as Dr. Eric Berne and others.[3]

The Decision-Making Procedure

Let us assume that group decision-making is a logical and systematic process and that one can disregard all of the hidden factors for the moment. There are procedures which can help a group arrive at decisions that are preferable to haphazard floundering. One is suggested below.

The group is helped to clarify the issue about which a decision is to be made, that is, the issue is to be stated in such a way that everyone understands the problem or question. It is necessary in this step to determine whether there is one question or several and, if several, which must be decided first and sequentially in order to determine the main question. For example: "Shall we allocate one hundred dollars from the treasury to be given to the Red Cross to purchase amenities for prisoners of war in Viet Nam?" The questions are: (1) allocate money? (2) if yes, how much? (3) to give to whom? (4) for what purchase? (5) for whom? (6) where? As the question now reads, if I disapprove of any one of the subissues, I may decide in the negative. A good chairman will not ask for a group decision on the question unless he is sure that all of the parts are, in fact, one question. He will divide it and seek decisions on each part in some order. If he does not, a worker might help the group to see the many questions and restate the questions to be decided upon in such a way that the group can work on it.

A good working agenda should be so constructed that the question to be decided upon is well stated. When the question is clear, the worker should help the chairman ascertain whether everyone knows and understands what the issue is and also what relevance it has. The next step is to ask what solutions are available, that is, what alternatives are seen by the members; and these are then listed. It often happens that the members can see a limited number of possible solutions. After probing for others, the worker may introduce still others in the following manner: "Have you thought of this as a possibility?" "Do you think that this might work?" "How would you react to this?" "Do you think this is feasible?" "Why isn't this a possibility?" "I have heard that some groups are doing the following." "I have reason to believe that this is working in some instances." If the group sparks to any of the worker's additions, these are added to the list of alternatives.

The group is asked to look at each possible solution and list the advantages, disadvantages, and probable consequences. When the same advantage is evident for all of the alternatives, it is eliminated, and the same is done for disadvantages or consequences. During this step, it may become obvious that there is not enough information available or that resource material is lacking. The worker may inject it or ask members to check it out. In this step, costs are estimated and it is determined whether the group can or is willing to afford that solution in money, time, or involvement, and

221

also whether there is enough commitment to it to predict success. Each member must be aware of what he is committing himself and the group to if he supports the decision, as well as the consequences of failure.

Most groups would vote at this point. If the question is not very important, voting is a viable way of recording a decision. If the matter is important other means are preferable. Sometimes it is useful to have a straw vote to gain awareness of the situation and what seems to be indicated to achieve consensus. The ultimate aim is to seek consensus based upon the development of emergent, creative versions of solutions to which all can subscribe or at least not oppose. An essential aspect of this is to endeavor to have the real reasons for opposition and support expressed. If there is trust, this is possible; if not, the decision-making will be a table game with hidden cards. It is very difficult to gain consensus or to effect a viable solution so long as members refuse to express themselves. Sometimes the worker will express the messages that he thinks he hears. The tactics the worker employs will vary and he will function differently in a treatment situation than in a committee.

We must remember that majority rule is still rule, and in many groups the minority is always obliged to accede to decisions and demands which are distasteful to them. Compromise, which many workers seek, is not a preferable solution because generally no one is satisfied and hostility and anger remain latent. Consensus for the sake of consensus is not preferred either. Consensus is desirable when it represents a true solution and a true solution is an enabling one.

When an agreed-upon decision is reached, the group should be helped to know what it decided and the consequences should be clear. It should be explicit also that the validity of the decision will be evaluated at a later date. It is vital at this point that the chairman or worker set up the steps, assignments, or timetable for action and accountability, if this is appropriate.

This procedure can be learned by groups and can help to facilitate efficiency and to effect more viable decisions more quickly.

NOTES / READINGS

1. Malcolm and Hulda Knowles, *Introduction to Group Dynamics* (New York: Association Press, 1959), p. 38.

2. Barry E. Collins and Harold Guetzkow, *A Social Psychology of Group Processes for Decision-Making* (New York: John Wiley & Sons, Inc., 1964).

3. Dr. Eric Berne, *Games People Play* (New York: Grove Press, 1964).

9

❖❖❖❖❖❖❖❖❖

Groupwork Through the Utilization of Program

There are five main implements in groupwork for effecting change and growth. These are the use of group structure, the use of group process, the use of self, the utilization of program, and agency function. The first three have been discussed in some detail in earlier chapters and we come now to the fourth. I will approach this from several angles and in several contexts. First, we must reconcile the concept of the use of program by a worker with the important aspects of freedom of decision and choice by the group members. Then I will relate this concept to the structural concepts developed earlier in the text, and will make reference to differences in degree between treatment settings and the traditional group services.

Principles of Program Utilization

Program in groupwork is a modality both in treatment groups and in the self-determining club in a center. In both instances, program and activities are opportunities for experiences, and in both there should be choices available to the members. In treatment groups, the choices are circumscribed prescriptively by the worker to ensure that, although options are available, the experiences will be therapeutic, noninjurious to any of the members, and will minimize the opportunity for control by some members for their own benefit over others to *their* detriment. In nonclinical settings, the range of choice will be broader but even here it is incumbent upon the worker to limit the choices to those that will be beneficial and

223

growth-inducing. Not all program is constructive. Some can be inappropriate generally and some can be destructive to certain individuals. I am not using the terms program and activities interchangeably. Program consists of everything the group members do; activities refers to such things as crafts, dramatics, games, and the like.

The members have the final authority to decide whether or not to participate in any program. It is manipulative when the worker uses his position and status to coerce the members to engage in any activity in order to fulfill his own desires, his convenience, his needs, or those of the agency.

The worker and the members are equals, as I have said before. This means that no one in a group should hold a position, function, or status in order to command. Also, although they are equals, there are differences among them which are based upon function; some people have specialized knowledge, resources, and skill. The groupworker, by virtue of his function, is with the group to enable it and the members to achieve their goals and to find self-realization. He has training in means, that is, he knows something about people, about the values of different activities, and about procedures for reaching personal goals. The effective groupworker is an expert in program utilization for the achievement of these ends. One of his competencies lies in his knowledge of the qualities of program which foster positive growth as well as those which are dangerous to certain individuals and to group life. These properties and aspects will be discussed and illustrated. Consequently, in the initial contract and also later in the group's development, roles and functions in the group are negotiated; and the groupworker, by agreement with the members in the group, assumes functions which include that of being a resource person for program. I hold, therefore, that a suggestion which a worker makes about program is a resource, not a tool.

When people join an agency or become clients knowing what the agency purposes are, theoretically at least, they join agreeing to or approving of them as they apply to themselves. If the agency does not reveal its purpose to the applicant, it may be guilty of manipulation in its use of program. If it has revealed its purposes through intake and, later, through the groupworker, an understanding has been reached and the worker has a mandate which is provided voluntarily and by free choice by the group. However, even where the group is not a voluntary one, such as in an institution, the group members can know why they are in the group, can know the function of the worker, and can negotiate whether or not they will involve themselves in the enterprise. As long as the function of the groupworker is to carry out a mandate on behalf of the members, there is no contradiction between the concept of program utilization and freedom. Inherent in method is the effort of the worker to help the members become aware of the compatibilities between the common good and the personal goals of each member. It is also part of his function to help them to match better both the impinging environment and the basic needs of members.

Program should be based upon group choices and decisions within available options along with an understanding of the consequences inherent in the various options. The effective worker really proffers program options rather than prescribes a program. As we shall soon learn, the way a program is carried out is often more important than the program medium itself. As the group members develop trust and resolve problems of autonomy, and as they reveal their needs, fears, and goals, the effective groupworker proffers suggestions for program in a spirit of partnership; that is, he works with them to achieve their goals. The members bring their goals forward and the worker helps them, openly and aboveboard, so that they know what choices there are, what the outcomes are likely to be, and what they are doing. He feeds back to them what they are doing, and he faces them with what they do and its relationship, if any, with what they say they want to accomplish. They are able to use the program for these ends, modify it, or innovate program if they so choose.

Let us look first at an example of program utilization that involves group structure. A person enters a group situation with a particular self-image and his own uniquely individual needs. The group places the person in a specific position with a status and a role expectation having a concomitant behavior pattern that interacts with and perhaps affects the person's concept of self. In other words, he enters with distinctive personality needs, and he becomes part of a structure which has a definite hierarchy of positions and certain expectations for role performance. To these, we add a piece of program such as a game.

The game may provide a set of positions, each with status and role expectations, and a set of basic controls and limits. The game, therefore, may be a means for developing new roles for the individual, it may solidify old role patterns, it may enhance his status or reduce it, and so on. Whether some of these results will accrue will depend, in part, on the skill the person possesses or can acquire and on the prescriptive pattern of the game. Low prescriptiveness means that there is a wide range for individual performance with little role definition as, for example, in a low-organization game that does not require the player to perform in a specific way or with a certain style. However, even low-organization games do call for quickness and some coordination. In low-prescriptive activities, one can expect that the existing role hierarchy of the group will be perpetuated in the game. High prescriptiveness denotes specific role expectations and definite skills for game positions. Games which are highly prescriptive develop role hierarchies of their own which can differ from the usual role hierarchy of the group. Baseball is such a game and I will use it for illustration.

The game of baseball is made up of nine positions, each of which has a prescription for how the player can and should act. Each must perform as part of an organized whole and contribute to the team effort. Each must cooperate with all others. One is a good player if he can perform the role prescription for his position with skill and by so doing help the team to win. While each position is essential to the team and cannot be eliminated, some positions require more skill and are considered more important than others, some provide more opportunity for visible excellence, and some involve more risk. The winning or losing of a game is credited to the pitcher. He must perform continuously with a high degree of skill but basemen and fielders do not have to act unless the ball has been hit by an opponent. Even among these positions, some are considered more important than others and have higher statuses. The occupants of the positions may be perceived by their peers as having different statuses in their game positions than they have in the structure of the group.

It should be remembered that members will want to play games in which they excel and the dominant subgroup members will seek to influence the choice of activities so as to maintain or enhance their own statuses. Since role and status in a game inhere in the capacity of a person to perform his specialized function, a group member with low status who can pitch well may enjoy a change in status if the group has an interest in or a commitment to playing baseball. In this way, an activity which has status can affect the patterned set of relationships that exist within a group. We must remember, however, the low-status members often will play below their ability so as not to threaten those with high status, or perhaps because their low status puts them off their potential form. A temporary group role such as the one of pitcher carries a risk and some individuals may be unable psychologically to take the risk of carrying such a high-status role. If placed in it, they may withdraw or go to pieces.

There are two principles involved here. The game may provide an opportunity through which new positions, statuses, and roles may be afforded members, and their self-images may be enhanced and their needs met. A worker must be aware of and sensitive to the potentials for enhancement as well as to the dynamics which may inhibit people from achieving.

There are factors within games which can produce either cooperative or noncooperative behavior. Baseball and football are examples of games that require cooperation, yet they impose threats to individuals. A tug-of-war does not develop the same role demands as softball nor ask the same degree of skill, yet it does demand group cooperation in which reward goes to the entire group rather than to individuals. A game such as King of the Hill is based upon competition among the players and has a tendency to produce antagonisms within the group. As such, it is group-deteriorating rather than group-enhancing.

Group structure is influenced also by the quantity and quality of interaction; for example, the communication system is affected by activities and there is an effect on the number of interactions and who interacts with whom. Members who are constructing individual models need not talk with each other, but the development of a dramatic skit demands verbal interchanges. Structural attributes also provide for inherent, depersonalized controls of behavior which can be accepted by a group with less of an emotional reaction than those associated with controls that are set by adult authority. As one example of a program activity, the development of a game structure from less control to more through elaborating the rules can be a means of helping a group develop a set of social controls that will extend beyond the game.

Activities have mechanisms within them for the release of hostility or for its buildup, for the production of anxiety or its resolution, for the support of the ego or its deterioration; and they can provide for inherent rewards or frustrations. Activities also can be a means of working through developmental problems. An example of this is the adolescent seeking for identity and trying to understand his relationship to the opposite sex through dancing and social games. Competitive sports can be a way of releasing hostility and also of developing a masculine role image. Activities are useful to work through symbolic preconscious and unconscious problems as, for example, the properties of certain games such as chess where a player may commit regicide by checkmating the king as a symbol of patricide in the oedipal conflict. Program activities are related to societal expectations and values such as: we are competitive in our North American culture, but there are other cultures wherein people see a different focus or objective in their lives. With such group factors as a frame of reference, let us turn to an examination of some of the relevant literature.

227

Wilson and Ryland provide prescriptions for program media.[1] They point out that pencil and crayon tend to encourage tight movement. They are inflexible and demanding because the lines that can be made with them are relatively fine when compared with large paintbrushes and fluid colors. Watercolors are free and expansive and they are also harder to control because they run and splash. However, they encourage broad strokes and wide movement. Such free-flowing media may frighten anxious and insecure people and on the other hand may offer too little limits for the undisciplined. There have been studies made which indicate that many middle-class children are less able to enjoy finger painting than lower-class children. Because finger paint is less precise than water or oil, one might conclude that lower-class children are less constricted than those of the middle class and, also, one might suggest that the anal quality of the finger paint medium is less acceptable to them. Clay is receptive, malleable, and does not resist. It tends to remain as the molder fashions it, but it too has anal connotations. As such, it is a useful medium for "dirty" play, allowing children with anal fixations some release, but it may terrify them as well. By contrast, wood is not flexible; it is demanding, and it calls for precision. Model-building, such as of airplanes, is even more so as it calls for small movement, adherence to rigid plans, and provides little creativity or freedom. It appeals to compulsive and perfectionistic people who like blueprints to provide them with limits. Some people find this kind of activity supporting and comforting.

Wilson and Ryland also help us to see that there is a sequence of development from games with low organization to those with greater structure. Proceeding from circle games through relay types on to team games, a person may pass from activities which require few rules and roles to games which are complex. In the transition through the sequence, one can learn to internalize social controls, learn self-discipline and cooperation, and establish a basis for role differentiation, as well as acquire skills and an improved self-image. A similar developmental sequence can be seen as beginning with activities involving cutting, tearing, and taking apart, such as the preparation for making papier-mâché which allows for the release of destructive tendenices, through to media that involve putting together, building, and constructing which channel one's energies into production or industry.

Sutton-Smith has elaborated on the relationship between games and status.[2] Games provide play-status values and they also contain prescriptions for control. Roles which carry high status, such as the role of a pitcher in baseball or the quarterback in football, provide the player with control over the game as well as over the other players. Other positions in the game do not usually provide much influence over the game or teammates and are, therefore, of lower status. We see again that roles which provide control give that role player access to need-meeting rewards while denying them to others. It is the prescription in the game itself which governs the allocation of roles and also the skill content of these roles. When the control system is strong, the subjective desires of the individual player will have little influence and, as the popular saying goes, he will have to "play the game." Although Sutton-Smith discusses only games, crafts, and dramatics in his articles, the principles which he illustrates apply as well to other types of program media.

There are no roles pre-established in informal dramatics as there is no script. The players proceed to devise their own play and to establish the parts. As a consequence, informal dramatics are one of the most corruptible of all programs and the most susceptible to the influence of peer status and its potential for domination. A high-status person who dominates the group can decide to be the king or the teacher and thereby assign all of the play roles to the others. In informal dramatics, a low-status person may be subjected to exploitation and control and can be patronized easily by stronger ones. Some of the lessons which the low-status person may learn through this experience are how to lord it over younger or weaker people and how to accept minor and subordinate roles. Such experiences are not positive and afford these people little support or protection. The written play is more highly structured and within it the high-status people are confined at least to the role prescriptions of the play. Formal dramatics are more likely to bring more security or gratification to the low-status person; hence it is incorrect to assume that informal dramatics, in and of themselves, are better program media in social groupwork than formal dramatics.

In games which require skill, the acquisition of skill permits anyone to gain status up to a point, but where there are role prescriptions for skill and style or form, low-status members have little chance to improve status and image if they lack the competence or motivation to develop activity skills.

Gump developed some of these ideas more fully.[3] He pointed out that in some games the person who is "It" has great power while in other games "It" lacks power and must protect himself simultaneously from all of the players. The lower the power of the "It" role, the greater will be the skill or competence required of the person who is "It." In his study, Gump illustrates some of the impact of these ingredients of program activities. He tells of Frank who is a boy with moderate skill in games but who is distrustful, withdrawn, and unpopular. Frank at first refused to play in the game of Tail-Snatch where "It" calls the signals and thereby has an advantage. Finally he came into the game but was reluctant and uncertain. With each new success in his "It" role he became more confident and vigorous in his play. Soon he began to laugh. However, when he played Cat he had no success. The mouse continued to taunt him and the group protected the mouse. Frank became frantic and in a temper he quit. In Cat, "It" lacks power and requires more agility. However, timid and unassertive children usually do not take high-powered roles effectively and comfortably even though they can play non-"It" roles with enthusiasm. If a game allows a low-status child to become and remain "It," the role becomes a scapegoat role and as such it can be used to duplicate and perpetuate his rejected position.

In "The 'It' Role in Children's Games," Gump concludes that high-powered "It" roles lead to less failure for "It" and, therefore, to fewer negative reactions by the group toward "It" and to a better feeling by "It" about himself.[4] If an unskilled player can be helped to carry a high-powered "It" role in a game, the experience will facilitate his achieving success more frequently and having fewer negative experiences in the future.

Gump, Schrogger, and Redl discovered that activity settings—the physical provisions and the pattern of constituent performances that are part of the milieu—are coercive to behavior.[5] As an illustration, they say that the amount of interaction is greater in a free swim than in a craft activity, but mutual helping is higher in crafts. Asserting, blocking, and attacking are greater in swimming. The use of the body in swimming is loose and impulsive and more fantasy tinged than in crafts. Gump and his colleagues say, "When props and performances are so organized that valued actions are delayed or are in short supply, the activity setting is likely to produce competitiveness."

With relatively normal children, a crucial ingredient for growth is the amount of participation inherent in the action of the game. Activities which are most successful for our purposes enable expression and allow the continuous involvement of all of the participants. In music, for example, inactivity for long periods of time triggers mischief, complaining, and aggression in many children.

Vinter attempted to bring many of these ideas into one framework, apply them, and add some insights of his own. He developed a formulation, predicated upon selected dimensions, which might facilitate predictions with reference to probable respondent behaviors.[6] The dimensions he chose are: (1) the prescriptiveness of the pattern of the activity, (2) the institutionalized controls which govern the participant activity, (3) the provision for physical movement, (4) the competence required for performance, (5) the provision for participant interactiveness, and (6) the types of rewards available, their abundance or scarcity, and the manner of their distribution. The formulation provides a set of variables and correlations which can be used to compare and classify activities—different activities might be alike in regard to several variables which are deemed significant in a treatment plan, while similar activities might prove to result in behaviors that are dissimilar if one varies such dimensions as controls, rewards, and rules, or allows the participants to move around rather than remain in one place. Such information is very helpful to a groupworker when recommending program, especially in reconciling the interests of the members with activities the worker would suggest based upon desired outcomes. It is feasible often to use the program which the members prefer and by altering some of the dimensions, render the activity therapeutic.

Vinter goes further in his studies. He provides some specific characteristics for each dimension. For example: (1) high fatigue and satiation are likely to result from high prescriptiveness; (2) if control is exercised by one or a few persons, there will be dependence on the controllers and greater interaction with them; (3) fatigue is more associated with less body movement; (4) rewards go with task performance rather than interpersonal satisfactions when there is high minimum competence; (5) cooperativeness, high sentiment, and friendly relations result from high facilitating interaction; competitiveness, rivalry, and hostility result from high hindering interaction; and (6) participants are attracted more by a greater range and variety of rewards, but scarcity of rewards leads to competitiveness, rivalry, and unequal distribution of power. To test these general predictions, Vinter applied them to crafts and swimming, demonstrating that a groupworker could use the formulation to assess program activities and be in a good position to suggest them with greater precision and prediction for approaching treatment goals. For those who are not involved with treatment, "dimension variance and respondent behavior" can point out the relation of interest span to the likelihood of fatigue, or the increase in hostility and aggression, or the calming effect of a program activity, for example. If one were to apply Vinter's insights to the general thesis of this book, one would take note, for instance, that the more broadly and evenly rewards are distributed, the greater the likelihood of cohesiveness, trust, cooperation, and responsibility—scarcity of rewards leads to a maldistribution of power—or that cooperativeness, high sentiment and friendly relations are related to high facilitation of interactiveness; or formal controls reduce innovation in roles.

Shulman has attempted to break away from the traditional

models discussed above.[7] He does not like the word "program" because he thinks it creates a dichotomy between doing and talking. I do not think that this was ever a dichotomy in social groupwork although conceding that it may be in other therapies. Social groupworkers for many years have considered that program includes everything that takes place in the group. Shulman thinks that relationships among people can be described best with a "mixed transactional model"; people express feelings, ideas, support, interest and concern through a variety of mediums. He holds that all of these mediums be included when considering the means by which transactions are negotiated and consummated. From this position he deduces that one need "not ascribe social work purposes to specific forms of activity" (I do not think I do), "but rather identify how group members use a particular *medium of exchange* to meet their common needs."

Shulman objects to the idea that a worker assesses group member needs and "prescribes" to meet them. He prefers that the members determine their needs of the moment and the mediums for dealing with them. In this context, the worker is a catalyst and a resource. He writes, "Information about possible group activities—mediums of exchange—is one form of informational input that a worker can openly make available when it is relevant to the group's current tasks." It seems to me that the worker might select the information he will put in about possible group activities more appropriately if he were grounded in the attributes of program and how they are likely to affect behavior; this is his professional responsibility. It is granted that program is not a tool; it should not be used by a worker to manipulate; but neither should members be permitted to use it to hurt, destroy, or control others or to support pathology.

We have been examining the most significant contributions appearing in our literature about program activities. In the following pages I shall develop a more comprehensive point of view about program utilization in groupwork. Discussion is not included as an activity because discussion is part of method, that is, discussion is to groupwork what interviewing is to casework. Discussion is used in all program as it is a primary channel for relationship, important in decision-making, and the basis for communication. It is verbal, nonverbal, and motoric, and through it program is effected.

Wilson and Ryland introduced the concept that program media have inherent values. This idea is useful and is a noteworthy contribution to the practice of social groupwork. It is useful also to conceive that program has prescriptive patterns, control, physical involvement, aspects of competence, patterns of interaction, and rewards. These various concepts are applicable to the analysis of any type of program activity as one may begin with the inherent quality of the media and then analyze the activity with these added dimensions.

Since the characteristics of any activity can be ascertained through this process, a worker and a group can select an activity that has the qualification which they desire. Many types of activities have the same characteristics as others to different degrees, and hence group members can base their choice of program on their interests and their goals. The same can be said about working toward differential treatment goals.

However, it is not adequate to analyze program by the nature of the media alone, such as painting is self-expressive; or from the structure alone, such as informal dramatics allow for peer status to dominate; or from only the controls that inhere in it. One must approach the study by viewing the nature of the program medium and its prescriptiveness in the light of the experiences that it affords. The crucial aspect for assessing its impact upon the group and its members is the utilization of program with regard to all of its characteristics. The key is the nature of the experience and what it reinforces or perpetuates. For instance, if one wishes to use a release activity to help to relax members after a day in school, one should not select a game like dodge ball because it heightens tension. Body-contact games are not release activities and active games of this kind do not drain tension or reduce conflict and hostility. Creative dramatics and puppetry, on the other hand, do allow acting-out that can relax one.

Much depends also on how a worker presents a program. He can present it verbally or by nonverbal invitation. Too often, it is presented verbally to young people. One can put out rhythm-band instruments, put on a soft but rhythmic record, preferably not a march, and let the music and the power of suggestion go to work. On the other hand, if you do not want the group to use the instruments, do not have them out where they are available and can be seen. One should teach the positive use of self-control and not have to resort to discipline to correct the members after misbehavior occurs. The discipline and controls, therefore, should be built into the activity.

It is difficult to utilize any one piece of program to meet the needs and interests of all the members at any one time. Specific programming is used for specified goals which should be clear and precise, but it must not be contraindicated for any member of the group. Composition of the group should be done with the feasibility of program utilization in mind. The objectives of program should be conceived in operational terms, such as to help A make friends with B and C, or to allow A to gain enough success to be able to begin to risk. Consequently if A must learn to play a game because of the values of his reference group and to acquire a role that will give him status in that group, it would be ineffectual to make him a scorekeeper or an umpire.

There are two foci that govern program selection simultaneously: the professional goals which are based upon needs, diagnosis, or developmental task, and the goals of the member. The therapeutic setting often neglects one, and the traditional setting the other. Program also should be viewed in relation to growth needs. To do this, one may use a Freudian, Rankian, or other psychological frame of reference. I am going to use Erikson for illustrative purposes because his concept of the developmental tasks is a practical guide for most practitioners. His approach is geared to understanding the primary growth and socialization needs of the individual at various stages of development. Program selection can be made to support the task achievement at each stage. I have adopted Erikson's stages and altered his ranges slightly in order to make them most useful.

The first stage in the earliest years necessitates the development of a sense of trust. The sense of trust is the cornerstone for the establishment of a strong ego and it must be strengthened throughout one's lifetime. Trust engenders hope and is the key to motivation and the ability to risk. Trust is built through security and can be buttressed by rules, routines, repetition, and programming that moves from what is known and familiar to what is new. It calls for fairness from the worker, consistency, and the observance of game regulations. Program must provide a trustworthy environment, structural security, and a real hope that one can achieve.

Closely following upon trust is the need to develop autonomy. Autonomy is fostered when activities provide for independence, creativity, and a chance for adventure. Program which is not adult dominated is helpful, and those activities that allow for group decision-making strengthen the will to develop initiative, to seek for purpose or goal, and to be self-motivating.

By eight or nine years of age, the development of trust and autonomy remain as tasks, industry is added, and one programs to develop the ability to do and to make things with others. All forms of crafts are excellent at this age. Standards for workmanship are introduced and one is expected to finish what one begins. The school-age child needs and wants skill and hence looks to adults to offer instruction. Program is used also to elaborate purpose for the participants and this is reinforced through the development of social goals. There is no better type of program to encompass these dimensions than a project.

The task of developing an identity begins early but from six on it intensifies. Role identity such as maleness and femaleness, adulthood, and the like can be developed through stories, dramatics, role-playing, emulation of role models and exploration of the world of peers. Value orientation is also important through discussion with confirming adults. The task of learning intimacy or relationship competence begins in earnest around twelve. This implies expanding interpersonal reciprocity through group program and shared activity. One should de-emphasize competition and try to develop psyche-groups which are based upon mutual need-meeting and which can lead naturally to the development of creativity as opposed to stagnation. With a judicious worker, a person continues to develop his sense of will and begins to learn to exercise self-control through rules that are clear and free of domination.

Much of what has been said seems to apply to children rather than adults, but this is not really so. These methods of analyzing activities apply to adult program as well. For example: Adult classes may be prescriptive and restrict group interaction; but when a groupworker wishes to develop relationships, his use of himself and the deployment of his tools, plus an invitation that the members teach each other, can result in group interpersonal relationships. Bridge and Mah-Jongg are prescriptive and competitive games wherein role and status depend upon one's skill and a rigid adherence to rules. Basically neither is a social game.

Music can have a multiplicity of uses, especially in such activities as choral work. Square dancing is group-mixing and provides movement. At the same time, it is prescriptive but does not prescribe position or status. It requires some skill but less than does dancing the merengue, for example. It is highly conducive to interaction and requires active participation all of the time.

To summarize, program utilization means selecting activities that will accomplish what the group wants and needs to achieve. All of the characteristics of an activity can be ascertained by applying the principles that we have been discussing. Many types of activities have the same general characteristics to different degrees and hence program can be selected to meet the interests of the members. The way the worker and the group use program is the basis of groupwork.

To view program from the nature of media alone, or prescriptive structure alone, or from inherent controls alone would not suffice for groupwork. The effective groupworker views the nature of the media and the prescription as one would an instrument. The real key is the way in which program with its particular characteristics is used. The worker uses himself as well as program.

The inherent values are not only in the media. If one adds the admonition not to get any paint on the floor, or if there is fear of getting it on one's clothing, one changes the nature of the program media. Further examples are: the number of colors which are available; the kind, size, and shape of the containers available; who mixes the paint, the worker or members; whether one can move about the room; whether there is freedom to talk and the room is organized so that one can talk to others; whether the easel is prescriptively nonsocial; the size of the paper and the brush; and the consistency of the paint.

The key lies in the use of the activity. How any activity is used determines the effectiveness of the program and, as always, these factors also are conditioned by the structure of the impinging environment in which the program takes place.

The following excerpt illustrates how a worker uses program in the early stages of group development. The group meets in a primary school after classes.

An Illustration of the Use of Program

AGE: Early Latency
SETTING: National Youth-Serving Agency
SESSION: Second

After this, we all went to the playground and started a circle pad game. I moved into the circle next to B., and she and I demonstrated how the game was to be played. The girls seemed very excited about it and responded well. It started to rain just as we had really begun to play and the girls were beginning to get the idea of the game. I told the girls we would have to go inside and asked N.R. to go back to the auditorium and get the other girls. I reminded her to come right back.

The rest of us then went to our meeting room, took off our coats and sat down at the table. We were soon joined by N. and the other girls. While we were at the table, I explained to everyone that this would be the room in which we would be meeting. I reminded them that at our next meeting they should come directly to this room and not to the auditorium. I then asked the girls if they remembered the name tags we had made at the last meeting. They said that they did, and we talked about how the name tags would help us get to know one another. The girls admitted they did not know one another. All of us then got up from the table and went over to the clear space in the room. I had made name tags for the girls in the shape of birds which would fly through the air like a paper airplane. I threw one of the tags in the air and asked one of the girls to go get it. She then tried to figure out to whom the name tag belonged with the help of the rest of the girls. During the procedure most of the girls, as would be expected, clamored for turns to go get the name tags. M., M., and N. were relatively quiet and did not tease to have a turn. M.R. was particularly quiet and seemed to stand off to the side quite a bit. I spoke to her and asked her if she had had a turn and she said no. After she had had her turn she seemed to enter into the game a bit more. During this time B. wanted to help each of the girls retrieve the name tag. I reminded her that she had had a turn and should allow the rest of the girls to have theirs. She still did a great deal of running out when the name tags were thrown, but did not interfere with anyone else getting them. C. was the only one of the girls who asked for help from me in pinning on her name tag. The rest of the youngsters were able to manage for themselves or got help from some of the other girls. This indicates again that C. needs to get attention from adults. This procedure seemed to foster a good deal of interaction between the girls in terms of figuring out which name tag belonged to whom, although each of them perhaps learned the names of the other girls in the group but were not particularly interested in each other's identity at this point.

After the name tag game, we all returned to our chairs. I asked the girls if they had ever been on a "lion hunt," and they replied very excitedly that they had not. I said that if they wanted to we could go on one today. C., who was sitting on my left, started to get out of her chair. I explained to her that we were going to go on a "lion hunt," just pretend, which had been presupposed by the other girls. I told the girls they were to say and do everything I did. As they began the game, they quickly caught on and copied all my sentences correct to the final intonation. They also caught on to all my actions and found "walking through the mud" and "crossing the bridge" particularly funny. All of the girls participated excitedly in this game, even M.G. whose English is not too good at this point. They seemed to be able easily to throw themselves into this pretend game with wide-eyed enthusiasm. C.A., an efficient, serious member, seemed to be able to let go in this game and she was giggling and enjoying it right along with the others.

After the game was over, we talked about how it was possible to tell many kinds of stories in this way and to make actions and different sounds in doing many things. B. "crossed the bridge" for us again and M.R. and S. showed us how to "walk through the mud." Other original ideas, however, were forthcoming.

I then reminded the girls that in our first meeting, several of them said that they would like to dance and sing. I said that today I thought we might do a combination of both, a kind of singing dance which many of them had done before. I asked how many of the girls knew the "Hokey Pokey" and about half of them raised their hands saying that they had done it in their physical education class in the auditorium. I then suggested that we get into a big circle in a clear space in the room. During the move from the table to the clear space, there was a good deal of commotion and B. and C. ended up on the floor. After we were in the circle, I told the girls that because the floor in the room was very slippery they would have to be very careful and not run. I said that we did not want anyone in the group to get hurt and they knew they could get hurt falling on a slippery floor. As we went through the words of the song, it became apparent that all the girls had done the dance before. However, some of them were not sure of the words. I pointed out how the words went together with what you did and told you what to do. I said that even if they did not know the words too well, they could catch on by listening to what the other girls were saying and watching their motions. As we did the dance none of the girls had any difficulty with the motions. However, M.G., C. and S. seemed to have some difficulty with the words. All the girls participated actively in the game and did not get in one another's way. Even B., who was having a good deal of difficulty keeping off the floor and keeping her hands off others at points during the meeting, did not have any problems while we were doing the "Hokey Pokey." She sang loudly and did all the motions with enthusiasm, but did not feel the need to interfere with the others or to show off particularly.

After the dance was over, we all returned to the table to make calendars. I explained to the girls that, as they already knew, the group would be meeting two days every week after school. I said that while their mothers and the teachers could remind them about the meeting for a while, they would want to learn what days the meeting would be so they would know without anyone telling them. I showed them the calendar and explained that we would use this to help remember when the meeting was to be. After the calendars, crayons and pencils had been passed out, I asked if anyone knew what day it was today. M.R. said that it was the 12th and everyone agreed that it was. I wondered if any of the girls knew the days of the week in order. Y. said that she did and began to name them, with some help from C. and M. I then wondered if anyone knew which one of the days it was today. No one did, so I explained that it was Thursday. I then made a picture of a calendar for the girls to see and we found today and wrote in the 12th. We then wrote in the other numbers of the month on the calendars. C., who had seemed to be so slow previously, quickly caught on to this procedure and had her numbers filled in before any of the other girls. N., S., M.G., and M. seemed to have some difficulty with this procedure. While we were working on this, C., M.R., and a couple of the other girls wanted to know if they could color pictures and put them on their calendars. I said they could with either crayon or pencil, and also they could write their names on the calendars as well. When most of the girls had finished putting the numbers on the calendars, we located all the Mondays and Thursdays and put circles around these numbers to indicate that they were the dates we would be meeting. I showed the girls they could make a cross through each day as it occurred and when it got to the next circle they would know that this was the day the group was meeting. In spite of all this explanation and procedure, I felt that the girls did not really understand the idea of the calendar. As we were doing this, C. asked if we would be meeting tomorrow. I said not tomorrow and we went through the next day and the next day. I explained to the girls that the very next day would be Friday, then they could have two days when they would not come to school. The next day would be Monday, the first day they came to school, and this was the day they would be meeting. They seemed to understand this much better than they did the calendar procedure.

As C. had finished her calendar before the other girls, she noticed a sample that I had made. She asked me if she could print my name on it for me and draw a few pictures. I said that she could and told her how to spell my name. She did this and I thanked her for it.

When we were finished with the calendars, I asked the girls if they would like to play a game over in the clear area of the room. They responded enthusiastically, and this time after the frustrating experience with the calendars, the move from the table to the clear area was real chaos. There was much slipping and sliding on the waxed floor and a couple of the girls fell down. I reminded them several times again not to try to run on the floor. B. was particularly rowdy at this point and had managed to excite C. and D. The three of them were running about the room and ran over to the cabinet in which some large wooden blocks were stored. They started to get out the blocks and I went over to them and explained that the blocks were for the use of small children and that we could not play with them today. They responded to this and joined the other girls. However, I again had to put my hand on B. to get her to stand up and join the other girls. During this time, M.G. and E. had gone to the blackboard and said that they would like to draw on it. I explained that we did not have enough chalk for everyone to draw at this time. We would try to use the blackboard the next time.

We then got organized into two groups, and I asked the girls if they had played the "lemonade" game. About half of them knew something about it, but nobody seemed to be really clear as to what words were said and so on. I explained the words to the girls and had them say them after me. I also explained the rest of the game, about how they acted out something and the other team would try to guess what it was. I said that since we were inside today and couldn't run on the floor, we would not be able to chase the other team, but at least we would have a chance to learn the first part of the game and to act out some things. I said that next week if it didn't rain and we could play outside we could really play the game after we knew how. With some help from me to get organized, the side that was to act out something decided to try to sweep the floors. This had been C.'s suggestion. The girls acted it out and the other team was able to guess what it was. I then went over to the other group and helped to get them organized so that they could decide what they wanted to do. C. suggested that they could wash their faces and this was agreed to by the rest of the girls, so that they acted this out and it was guessed by the other team. While this group was trying to decide what they were going to do, B. and C. seemed to instigate the other team to sneak up close to them so that they could hear what they were planning. I told the girls that they would have to go back to the other side of the room and that it was not fair to hear what the other girls were planning. This did not do much good. They kept trying to sneak up. I finally told them that the other team had not done this to them and they should be as fair as the others had been. This seemed to work and they did not sneak up any more.

After this, the two teams acted out washing dishes and hanging up clothes. Both still needed some help from me in the organizing of themselves to decide what they wanted to do. By this time, most of the girls had acted out things in the game and everything went along reasonably smoothly.

As it was about 3:30 and the meeting was scheduled to be over at 3:30, I got all the girls together in a circle to say our good-byes. Before we did this, I asked the girls if they had any suggestions as to the things they wanted to do the next week. C. said that she would like to paint or to draw and most of the other girls enthusiastically agreed with this. C. said that she would like to dance and one of the other girls mentioned singing. I said that it seemed possible to do all these things at our next meeting. M.G. reminded me about drawing on the blackboard and I said that I would try to get some chalk for this for one of our meetings. While we were doing this, B. kept jumping up and down pulling D. with her. I told her that she would not be able to do this because someone might hurt herself and that she would have to stand up with the other girls. This did not help much, so I again had to stand next to her to calm her down.

As I was interested in starting a traditional way of ending our meeting, I had the girls in a circle and explained to them how we could each make a wish and pass it along the circle by squeezing the hand of the girl next to us. I said that each of us would think about one wish and not tell it to anyone else, but that we could say good night to each other by squeezing each other's hand. The girls did not really understand what this was all about, and it was a poor choice on my part because the youngsters were really too "antsy" to settle down to this kind of procedure. It rather disintegrated into a contest in seeing who could squeeze each other's hand the hardest. Consequently, I quietly ended this friendship circle and told the girls that it was time to go home. We all went back to the table to get our things and I asked them to bring the pencils and crayons to me which they did without any problem. I reminded the girls again not to run on their way out the door because of the slippery floor. This did some good, but they were doing quite a bit of running and pushing as they left.

On their way out of the meeting, N. and C. came over to me and said good night and thanked me for having a nice time. I told them that they were very welcome and that I would see them at the next meeting. I walked everybody to the door and told them good night, and reminded them that the next Monday, the first day they went to school next week, we would all meet together here, not in the auditorium.

The Place of Mass Activities in the Use of Program

Almost every group services agency using groupwork method sponsors and provides for mass activity as part of its ongoing program. Games rooms, dances, parties, and socials are regular and accepted media in most settings. The groupworker on the agency staff usually is responsible for one or more such activities as part of the work load; he either plans, supervises, or actually runs the program. Despite the fact that a fair percentage of every staff person's time is spent in this way, very little has been written on how it is done or why. It would appear, in searching the literature, that the mass program is not recognized generally as a mode in groupwork method and is, therefore, not considered worthy of concern. The groupwork process has been defined and conceived so narrowly by some writers that unless groups of people fall into specialized and stylized configurations, they are not recognized as groups and consequently are not subject to groupwork method. Such a view is much too confining and unrealistic in the light of actual experience.

People need experience in both small and large groups. They must learn how to move from one to the other and to behave appropriately in each. The small, intimate, face-to-face group provides for intense interaction, with small social distances, while the large group allows for greater mobility, variety, and anonymity. People spend a certain proportion of their time in close and intimate relationships and grow, develop, and change within them, but a large percentage of life is spent in much less personal relationships, on the job, in the social world, and elsewhere. To be a well-adjusted person, then, one needs the practice and experience of feeling comfortable in large and impersonal settings.

While a mass of people cannot be regarded as a group, they can and often do take on group characteristics. People within a mass program do interact with each other and the groupworker; there is the phenomenon of contagion; there is group tone or morale; and often there is an implied group goal. It is obvious that the frequency and intensity of interaction are far weaker than in a small group, and also that the guidance of the worker is diluted, but groupwork method and principles do apply to the mass program to a large degree. The groupworker does not cease to be a groupworker because he is on duty at a party. Of greater consequence is the importance of viewing the mass program as an integrated part of agency function and closely aligned with the group program so that there is continuity of experience between the two. A member enjoying both experiences should find consistency of approach, goal, and method so that no conflict is raised. The agency should never seem to operate as a split personality.

A mass entity is made up of subgroups: affiliated units which may be triads, dyads, or isolates, just as the small group is usually composed of these same elements. It, too, is usually composed of social groups which are related to each other through an intergroup process. Within this complex social organism, the group worker must find his function and develop his skill and methodology.

The kind of skills that are required by leaders of organizational meetings such as large political units, large PTA meetings, NASW chapter programs and the like are analogous to those needed by groupworkers.

The values of the mass program are many:

1. It provides for a larger milieu and a more social relationship.

2. It is recreational—all the concomitant values of recreation and those of specific activities are implied.

3. It is a way of becoming related to the agency and getting to know it, that is, oriented.

4. It brings groups together.

5. There is groupwork value in the process of planning for the activity.

6. It develops social skills.

7. It brings people of diversified viewpoints and backgrounds together.

8. It provides experiences which offset heterosexual self-consciousness.

9. One may recruit for small groups through it.

There have been several references made in this book which emphasize the need to direct effort toward the fulfillment of personal goals and the development of values. This is especially true in the area of the mass program. While the importance of such programs has been recognized, too often the objectives are not realized because workers do not use the media purposefully. There will be a discussion of the teen canteen later, but for the sake of illustration here, it might be noted that groupworkers have insisted that one of the prime values of the teen canteen and teen dances was that small club and interest groups were formed from them. Analysis of many such programs reveals that this is not achieved often and that the number of groups that actually evolve from canteens is far too small to justify it as a value. This does not mean that it cannot happen or that the potential is not there, but it points up the fact that such results do not occur by themselves and that there is a need for skilled groupwork method to be applied to the task of group formation.

The reader will find that the explanations in this chapter are given in detail. This has been done because so little has appeared in our literature in this area to help and guide the practitioner, and also because the proper handling of small details ensures the success of mass-activity planning. The objectives set forth in previous chapters are often unfulfilled because workers do not pay enough attention to the minutiae of routine or because they do not know how to function in this context. The hallmark that distinguishes groupwork method in mass programming is its meticulous adherence to standards designed to promote growth.

The Games Room[8]

The agency games room is well established as an activity. It has great value for the total program and is a very useful mode for the groupworker. In most agencies, the person assigned to the games room is young or inexperienced and untrained—and yet this is one of the most difficult posts in the agency. Why have a trained groupworker when there is no group? Such fallacious reasoning must be corrected. The games room unit is not a group but it is a vital spot for the use of skilled groupwork personnel.

For many people, the games room is their first contact with the program. New to the building, without friends, and with a sense of insecurity and anticipated rejection, they wander into the most obviously enjoyable, unthreatening place. This new experience will or will not start them off on the right track, depending upon what happens to them there. At this point, questions of their needs and interests arise; they must be helped to find friends; they want to know what else is going on in the program although they may have been told by the registrar; they need support and freedom to choose; they want to become involved in games with others; they want to test out the worker as a symbol of the agency and authority; they want to probe and explore the limits and learn the routines or the "ropes." The games room may be the open door to the program; and either gingerly or boisterously, they come through that door seeking adventure.

243

The games room often is the refuge for the isolate, the unwanted, the antisocial, and the person who has no readiness for group relationships. It is the place where people, hungry for affection, attach themselves to the worker, and do not want to venture beyond that point. It is the haven for the person with a short interest span, a sense of inadequacy in crafts and cultural activities, and often a low level of ability in general. This does not imply that all people who use a games room are of this type, but rather that such people gravitate to a free, impersonal, and undemanding program.

The games room is a catch-all for people who are waiting for their scheduled activity to begin or for those who have been to a club meeting or interest group that is finished. It is the place where they go when nothing else is available or when they just do not feel like going to their regular activity. It is the place where they can go when they are angry, despondent, lonely, rejected, discouraged, or exuberant. If these are some of the consumers of the games room fare, along with all the other members, and if they are to find what they seek, it is clear that there is a need for a worker who is highly skilled and resourceful. Whether or not they use the games room depends upon how satisfying this program is to them.

The Worker in the Games Room

The more obvious function of the worker is to provide for such facilities as room setting, temperature, ventilation, light, and games. At the outset, the games room should be located in an accessible place where most people pass or congregate. The fact that it is available should be declared by adequate signs which are easy to read, and to offset anticipated rejection, they should invite participation. Where possible, it is helpful if the layout of the room avoids the overcrowding of equipment so that as people move about, accidental jostling is minimized, for this encourages fights. Equipment that demands group play rather than isolate play is preferable. Some of the latter should be available, however. If there are rules or routines, these can be set forth clearly on a poster, done in colors, with illustrations such as stick figures.

The worker is responsible for setting the atmosphere and for being aware that a games room is a place in which to have fun. In the first instance, he is a friendly, smiling person and an obliging one. The worker who shows by his facial expression and voice as well as by the way he drags his lazy body across the floor that a request for help is a nuisance cannot hope to run a successful games room. The worker greets people as they come in or as he spots them, but his sensitivity to them tells him how forward he can be. The person who is shy and frightened will not respond to a direct, forthright, and enthusiastic greeting, but will have to feel warmth, acceptance, and a nonthreatening approach first. He will have to be helped to know that assistance is available and be left to gain a bit of confidence; if the worker is overly attentive, he may withdraw. In setting the atmosphere, the worker tries to learn as many names as possible and see to it that everyone knows his name. In addition to names, he tries to learn something of the interests and backgrounds of his members. People respond to being recognized by name and open up to workers who remember something about them. A greeting that is personalized goes a long way toward establishing relationship.

He slowly moves about the room, showing interest in the activities that are taking place by making a suggestion, praising a play, passing a jocular comment, and keeps the atmosphere easy by lessening tension when it appears to be developing. As he moves about, he never concentrates on any one person or activity but continues to be aware of all that is going on in the room. He observes the behavior of everyone, tries to remember and mentally place each person, and begins to read their behavior in relationship to their needs, interests, and likely grouping. In order to do this effectively, as well as systematically, the keeping of records is recommended.

Now and then he stops and chats with one or two who seem to be aimlessly playing or doing nothing. Perhaps he may talk about something of general interest and draw them out, or he may invite them to play a game with him, instructing and encouraging them in it. Shortly thereafter, another person may come along and watch or seem to be drifting about. The worker then will ask the new person please to take his place in the game as he must leave to do something else. He has organized a game and included several isolates, and he leaves them to do it again, moving from group to group, organizing new games but not staying in any one place very long.

It is important that the worker see himself as a groupworker, not as a supervisor, overseer, or policeman. It is true that part of his job is to keep order, to see that the room runs smoothly, and to impose limits, but these things are incidental to his main function. Because of this, the participants can be helped not to regard him as a monitor. He sees that the table tennis is not monopolized, that wild running is curtailed, and he acts as a judge or referee. As he moves about the room he unobtrusively rearranges chairs, asks members to pick things off the floor, and encourages the return of games not being used so that the room presents a reasonably attractive appearance right up to closing time. He discourages the misuse and mishandling of equipment. These are administrative matters and must be taken care of, but the worker is more than a games room administrator.

He is accepting of all who come to him, utilizing all his understanding of people and groups. When he functions in this way, people then begin to talk to him, telling him of their desires and fears, their dreams, and their anxieties. Soon they are telling him of school problems, home difficulties, recreational interests, and other personal matters. When this happens, the worker is in a better position to help these people become related to groups and activities that will meet their needs. He shares his information with other staff members, those who work with these members, or who can seek out these members and encourage them to enter other activities.

The support of the worker gives the games room habitués the confidence to venture into other areas, and having enjoyed a satisfying experience in the games program, they are now ready for a more intensive relationship. A capable worker exercises skill to prevent the development of a personal attachment to him, utilizing program and grouping to avoid it. As he observes subgroups, isolates with similar interests, and possible group formations, his function is to enable grouping. After getting a small group to play together for a time he may then ask, "Say, you all know each other now and you have fun together—wouldn't it be more fun to have a group?" Perhaps he suggests to the individuals that a club is possible and that a room and a club worker are available, or maybe he learns that six or eight of them like the same things and have developed an interest bond. For example, several may have revealed that they collect stamps. He asks them to bring their stamps to the games room and after getting them together, he suggests trading stamps and, finally, a stamp club. Perhaps he encourages the model-plane builders to work in the games room and thereby develops the interest of others which eventuates in a crafts group. Girls may be encouraged to bring dolls and engage in a clothes-sewing activity or just to develop mutual friendships which can result in a group. The worker enables, encourages, and provides the opportunity for the relationships, and then he brings group formation to fruition. The same process may be cited for team formation.

As the games-room program evolves, the worker remains conscious of the need to develop responsibility. More and more, people are asked to give out games and see that they are returned, take attendance, straighten and clean up the room. Although it is a mass activity, a sense of belonging and a "we feeling" evolve. Committees of helpers and planners are useful and come into being as they are needed. The beginning of self-discipline and self-government show that people have grown to the point where group experiences are meaningful.

At some time in every games room session, it is advisable to encourage a group game involving everyone for a short time. As the worker promotes such an activity, he relates people to each other, gives them an opportunity to experience a group activity, mixes friendships, and diversifies acquaintances. The social values of the game and the socialization of the members accrue to the entire group. The people also are helped to learn to function at parties and in other agency activities that may come later. The games room takes on a groupwork orientation as everyone is encouraged to be part of a large, loosely knit group, anonymously, unthreateningly, and with good fun. At the same time, the games-room setting remains open so that new people can join in easily and the flow of intake and orientation can continue. A sensitive worker is cautious about using games that involve individual competition or about asking people to risk themselves before they are ready. Many people who come to a games room are not ready for so personal a risk. Gradually, as the worker sees them develop, he moves into games that are organized more highly. This caution also applies to the use of tournaments as a part of the games-room program. Tournaments have their place and are more effective when related to the needs of the people, keeping in mind those who need instruction and encouragement before they are ready to compete.

Group singsongs, a games-room carnival, demonstrations and exhibitions showing what other activity groups are doing, auction sales and other similar activities build groups. If the games-room program is to work in conjunction with the group program, then clearly its job is to prepare people for group life and supplement the groupwork activities.

As the games-room program evolves and people play together, there is ongoing interaction. Conflicts, harmonies, planning, cooperation, and hostility develop as they do within any club or small group. Status, recognition, a sense of belonging and adequacy, and an opportunity for adventure are provided in a games room by the program and by a groupworker who is aware that his job is helping people develop. Where children who use the games room are too young for one to expect clubs to evolve, the experiences they have there ready them for a satisfying group life later on.

Lounge Programs

Many agencies provide lounges and lounge programs for teenagers and young adults. Much that has been said about the games room applies to the lounge.

The lounge has not fulfilled its promise in most instances where a study has been made. Again, there would appear to be a high correlation between the availability of skilled groupwork guidance and the successfulness of lounges. Here too, people who find difficulty relating to others come seeking satisfaction and relationships— people who do not know really what they want to do and are looking for an answer, and those who want to do nothing but just find acceptance, come to the lounge regularly. Generally, those who have found friends and have their own interests drop in occasionally and for short periods of time, but to the others the lounge becomes their group. If their needs are as described and if they are seeking answers to such problems, the lounge program can be used to help them. This is not radically different from the criteria for the small group and, therefore, group methods are useful.

The lounge program seems to be most effective when operated by a committee which is intelligently chosen by the lounge members. As the program allows for people dropping in and out, an election becomes more difficult; but given sufficient buildup as an activity in and of itself, enough interest can be generated to bring out a substantial vote. The election procedure can be a valuable lesson in democracy. The committee is not the sole justification for the groupwork program in connection with a lounge or canteen. There are some practitioners who believe that the committee is the only place where group methods apply in a lounge program, but I believe that it is only one of many places.

The lounge is to be seen as a program, devised to meet the needs and interests of the members and as a source for groupings. If the lounge has no program, it is not a valid activity within an agency committed to groupwork method. There may be a place for a lounge as a room where one strolls in to play a game, have a dance, sit around, and leave at will, but it is doubtful whether such an activity can be justified in a groupwork setting. It would be difficult to relate such a program to the function of the agency or to argue that it really meets any but the most superficial of needs. This is a generalization, for in a residence building of an agency such a lounge may be viewed as a sitting room for the residents and, as such, would be very acceptable. In a recreation agency, however, such a lounge becomes a hangout for the members and serves a far more useful purpose if there is skilled guidance. Many agencies that have tried lounges without any staff help have not found them to be successful.

The worker's function in a lounge program is that of an enabler and a resource person. Teenagers need more help than young adults. The most desirable approach to teen lounges is to keep them informal and seemingly unorganized with a minimum of routine and pattern, yet at the same time to provide meaningful activity which is planned and developed by the members. Games are available as well as records for dancing and listening. The use of the games and the other facilities depends upon the worker's activity in a large measure. He moves around the lounge, invites people to play, makes the equipment conspicuous and available, and encourages others to listen, dance, or talk. Stimulating conversation and discussion is an important part of his job. He sits down with one or more and talks about matters of interest, introduces a controversial question, a newspaper or magazine article, or a TV announcement. A discussion can develop by drawing out the members in this way. This method proves more successful than announcing a discussion topic for a given evening. As the group begins heatedly to argue a point, others sitting around may be attracted and join in. After some examination of the topic, it may become opportune to suggest that a speaker be invited or a film shown, to give them more information on the subject.

The worker, if he is able, teaches a new dance step, introduces and teaches a new game, or helps with the finer points of other games. He talks with the members individually and learns about their interests and needs, and, as in the case of the games room, he constantly endeavors to form new groups and channel people into existing groups. A large part of his time is spent in developing friendships, enabling members to relate to others and using program to develop confidence, especially in social and heterosexual relationships. For this group and in this setting, the help with interpersonal relations is paramount. When people are helped in this area, they often become ready for a satisfying group experience. An alert and informed worker gives great assistance to the intergroup relationships as group members use the lounge.

With teenagers and young adults, and especially with those who do not belong to clubs, the lounge provides a place for the exploration of their interests in vocational choice, sex education, current events, boy-and-girl relationships, and premarital courses. It may be pointed out that the YMCA So-ed (social-educational) program has been successful in the past with young-adult groups, in part because it is predicated upon such interests. However, the additional essentials in lounge work are the close relationship of the worker with all the people involved, the intercommunication within the lounge, and his fostering of small groups. Added to interest fulfillment, then, is the interpersonal enabling and meeting of needs. Here also are numerous opportunities for status, recognition, achievement, and so on. Where the lounge is managed by a committee, the worker helps the committee to involve as many other people as possible in the planning. One effective method for doing this is to invite anyone who is interested to attend the committee meetings. People other than committee members can be involved in the planning process as well as the execution of the programs.

In order to relate the lounge to other activities in the agency and to stimulate interest, a demonstration of each of the interest groups (such as crafts, dramatics, and dancing) may be successful. In this type of program, the committee asks the groups and instructors to come to the lounge for one evening to show what they do and how they do it. In this way, the lounge people are exposed to all of the agency programs without going to them. This can be followed by an evening where the lounge members try their hand at the activities themselves. Some lounge workers provide simple craft materials and encourage subgroups to work in the lounge in order to stimulate hobbies and interest. Where the lounge program requires entertainment and skits and subgroups work to put these on, one sees another example of activity-subgrouping. A lounge group may cook and serve a supper, plan trips and theater parties, or watch TV forum programs and discuss them. The closer the relationships and the more the members do together, the nearer they come to a group experience and to a readiness for grouping. Bond is important in this process. Where the lounge is run or sponsored by a council, one can see the effectiveness of intergroup bond and the possibilities of groups working together.

It is possible to overdo program in a lounge. The program evolves slowly and as the members are ready for it. It does not evolve full grown at the outset. At the same time, one can provide ample opportunity for quiet play, informal dancing, chatting, and withdrawing from groupings to be alone. It is the worker's job to sense their readiness for program and to judge the timing and the proportion of program to free activity. This type of programming provides for personality growth, stimulates interests and broadens horizons, and helps to fulfill the purposes of the lounge. There is neither time nor money to waste with meaingless busy-work in agency program. The application of sound groupwork method to lounge programs ensures against such a possibility.

The Junior Social

Junior parties are fun and they have an important place in an agency program. This type of activity has many values that prepare young people for good group experiences a few years later. The games and programs used at the party have their specific values. These have been discussed earlier.

The party serves to bring a number of children together in a wholesome atmosphere for recreational purposes. Within that atmosphere, it is possible for them to learn some of the social graces which are indispensable for getting along in social situations. They learn how to behave so that everyone has an enjoyable time, how to observe rules, and the general lessons of cooperation. It is in this setting that the agency prepares members for teen and young-adult activities, for children who learn how to function in a mass activity carry that skill into the planning and carrying out of their adolescent programs. Many of the problems of teen dances could be prevented through good training and experience at the junior level. For these reasons, junior parties should be well run. Chasing, milling, screaming, and generally bad behavior at parties are poor learning situations and defeat the purposes of the agency.

Every activity conducted in an agency should be in keeping with its function and objectives. Anything short of this formula cannot be acceptable to the groupworker, and where it is applied to the junior party, it means that they are run to help people adjust, get along, share, learn to work with each other and the opposite sex, work through their problems, and grow. With these as the more obvious objectives, it requires skill to run a party for children, and the skills of the groupworker are appropriate to the task. A well-run agency sees all of its program as an integrated unit, each section meshing with the others in order to fulfill the general purposes. The party is as much a part of total program as any other activity and, while it may not be regarded as groupwork, it is so entwined with all other branches of the program that it cannot be seen apart from the groupwork program. In addition, the worker must be as aware of the basic human needs of children in the party setting as he would be in any other group. There are many opportunities for drawing in the shy and isolated child, for providing recognition, as well as for subduing the overly aggressive and active child.

Children's parties require staff planning and preparation, and the worker's function in junior program of this type is to plan, conduct, and supervise. There is little readiness on the part of this age group to do more than advise and express opinions on their likes and dislikes, and to assist in the mechanical aspects of the preparation, such as making favors, helping with decorating and with refreshments. The planning of the program is a technical matter requiring a conscious choice of games, careful timing, and skillful logistics. The key to success is that everyone have a good time, and for this to happen the worker must help them, carefully and expertly, to conduct the party. Parties must be planned well in advance if they are to be worthy of a place in agency program.

The practice of last-minute preparation, playing it by ear, dashing in and scurrying for equipment or supplies is indefensible. Parties, in the context discussed here, are media for personality growth and being child centered, they require thought. They cannot be conducted in a haphazard and stereotyped manner and if there is not time to prepare them properly, they should not be attempted. One of the first steps in the plan after a theme is chosen is the drafting of the invitation. It should be sprightly and attractive but very simple, with emphasis on time, place, and price. Children do not read wordy invitations and prefer cards with eye-catching illustrations, basic information, and plenty of space around the words. The invitation can be colored or cut out and pasted by the children themselves. If sent too far in advance, smaller children forget. In addition to the invitations, a poster or two in a conspicuous place in the agency act as reminders. It is well to remember that the invitations are as much to advise the parents of the event, time, and price as the child, and some mechanism to get the information to the parents is required. Mailed cards seem the easiest and best method, but another might be to ask the children to take the invitations home to their parents.

When a party is in prospect, children have a tendency to arrive very early and the staff must plan for this inevitability. If the children wait outside the door for a long period, push and shove and get into conflict situations, they will bring a temper and tone to the party that will make it more difficult to handle. Suggested alternatives are to open the games room for the early arrivals, provide a reading room, or post a staff member on duty where they are waiting. A good party always begins and ends on time and at the time stated in the children's invitation.

When the doors open, provision can be made to avoid a mad rush and scramble. If this event is to be part of training for living and the beginning of learning how to conduct oneself at a party, the staff starts right at the outset to be ready to deal with the usual trouble spots. Adequate staffing, quiet direction, and repeated instruction seem to set the pattern and tone. It is not being suggested that the party be run on a police basis, regimented and ordered, but that the staff be accepting and cheerful, and that children be allowed great leeway and freedom. However, rowdiness and unnecessary commotion must be avoided and limited, with explanations as to why it is preferable for them to cooperate with each other. The intent is not to create unnatural children or to inhibit them, but to develop respect for people, positive attitudes toward social living, and a foundation for mature behavior. These are the responsibilities of social workers, recreationists, and educators, and the opportunities for such teaching are abundant within the agency.

Much confusion can be avoided if some attention is given to traffic patterns. Where do the children go to check their clothing and, when returning from the checkroom, must they cross the checkroom line or intercept others coming in to get to the party? How are the tickets purchased and is there a bottleneck at this point? Are directions clear as to where they go and what they do? Long waits, idleness, and uncertainty generate tensions that lead to hostility, aggression, and overt mischief. When the children enter the party room there should be something to do, a game that can be played while people straggle in and that can be interrupted at any time. Pencil and paper games, wall exhibits or games, and similar types of things serve this purpose. A staff person must be on hand to instruct and direct as well as to prevent aimless running.

Each staff person on duty should know exactly what he is to do and when. It is advisable for all staff to have been involved in the planning, but this is not always possible. In the planning, the groupworker in charge defines the jobs to be done, the points to be covered, and the timing, and then staff persons are selected for each duty. A children's party and in fact any mass activity must be adequately staffed to do a quality job. The number of people needed will depend upon the tasks to be done, the size of the group, and the type of facilities. Exact requirements are determined by an analysis of the places to be covered at any given time. It is recommended that every staff person have a schedule of the party program and requirements from the time the children come in until they leave, and that each contain cues for particular jobs. This is essential for people who have not been at the planning sessions. Groupworkers should use staff to their fullest potential, and they in turn must know what is expected of them at every stage of the proceedings. Where volunteers are used, this is an often neglected aspect and yet a most necessary one. The foregoing implies that one person is responsible for the running of the party and that the others look to him for direction.

Having all the staff posted and instructed, the equipment ready, easily accessible, and set out in order of use, a volunteer or assistant can stand by to bring it forward when needed and to keep it from becoming disarranged. It will avoid time lapses in the program if every detail is anticipated. The momentary pause in a party program encourages restlessness, shouting, and general difficulty with young people and, therefore, every aid to a smoothly paced party is important.

The choice and sequence of the program items reveal the skill and understanding of the worker. At the outset, a game may be devised to permit movement about the room, the mixing of people, and new arrivals to participate. The room, however, should be set up in preparation for the second game, and if chairs are arranged so that the young people can see and hear the worker when they are seated, this facilitates the giving of instructions and the evening begins successfully. For example, when the children arrive they can be given paper and pencil and asked to identify pictures on the walls. This keeps them walking about, focusing on the wall rather than the large center area, and it uses up time while waiting for others to come in. When they are given the pencil and paper they are told what to do and, also, that when they are finished they are to sit down and await the next instruction so that when the group is assembled and most have completed the game, a large percentage are already seated. The worker who has distributed the pencils by now is moving about quietly telling those still standing to find seats. The party is ready to begin. It has been started with a minimum of shouting and commotion, and the preceding activity has placed the group for the following one. When one plays billiards, the skill is in placing the cue ball in a position where it is ready for the next shot. The expression used is that "english" is put on the ball in order to move it into position. A group worker uses "english" on the group so that each game places the participants for the next event.

Whistles are things of the past for children's parties. They are appropriate for large areas where the voice is difficult to hear or where groups are widely scattered or where safety demands an immediate response. Whistles are useful in the gym, on a hike, and at the waterfront, but they are out of place in a social setting. Pounding on a piano is just another form of whistle-blowing. Children should learn to know to be quiet when the worker stands up to make an announcement, because in later life they are not going to hear whistles blown before a speech, entertainment, or an announcement. It is obvious that one should be quiet and attentive when someone stands up and asks for their attention. There are many tricks suggested and described in recreation books to begin this learning, such as asking each child when he sees a worker raise her hand to raise his own and be quiet. These are only tricks and techniques and are to be regarded as such. Social learning should strive to become free of such devices as soon as the children are ready to accept self-discipline.

The first games played may well be active games to release energy and channel exuberance. While it is suggested that all the pre-party arrangements avoid boisterousness, now the program consciously can drain off the excitement, give outlet for the need to run, shout, and be aggressive. Each game ends with group formations that make it possible to announce the next one. If the chairs are not to be used again or are to be moved, staff people can move them swiftly and orderly while the children are playing in another part of the room. When the children are asked to do this the chairs are likely to get piled into heaps and the party atmosphere has to be built up all over again. As a general rule, games are concluded at the peak of enjoyment, with the groups anxious for more, rather than after boredom has begun to set in.

The groupworker is now in the role of motivating and directing the program. As is usually the case, the atmosphere depends upon him. He must be enthusiastic, smiling and gay, and very friendly. Fifty or more children can get out of hand quickly if the direction is not firm and if rudeness is not discouraged. Instructions are given in a clear voice, but only as loudly as the size of the room and the group demand. The worker need not shout to be heard above their voices but should speak only loudly enough to be heard in the rear of the group. When the people in the back cannot hear, they react to the frustration by causing trouble. The assisting staff can aid in maintaining a degree of quiet by placing themselves in positions where they can direct attention to the worker. When staff themselves stand around in pairs talking during an announcement, they are not helping the worker or teaching good manners by their example. Expressions like "I'm waiting for you to get quiet—I have all night and you are just wasting your own time," are not effective, reveal impatience rather than acceptance, and do not impress children. Merely standing and waiting do not gain quiet either once the noise gains momentum. A calling down is neither in keeping with the party atmosphere nor good practice. It is preferable to make the announcement in a quiet voice, move into an activity by demonstrating something or starting a new game. If something interesting is going on children usually will become attentive.

Instructions are given in clear and brief terms, with emphasis on all the fun to be derived. The group must be told the rules in understandable language and also told what constitutes winning. If the game is new, a demonstration is advisable. Status and recognition can be given by one's choice of demonstrators, leaders, and helpers. The game will be enjoyable only if all know how to play and consequently it is desirable to have the description and demonstration short enough to hold their attention yet complete enough to be clear. As the game proceeds, the staff can correct and instruct as the occasion demands.

Active games can be followed by quiet games to change the tempo and maintain interest. The names of games and the games themselves can be altered to fit into the general pattern or theme of the party. Younger children and less experienced ones require games with very few rules and a minimum of organization. As the season goes along, they may become ready for more complicated games or rules. Care must be taken not to choose games that are too difficult or not suited to the age group or its level of maturity. The experience of moving from simple games to more complex ones is, in and of itself, a maturing influence. Care must be taken to provide for children who are unable to keep up with the others in pencil and paper games or to understand more complicated routines.

Play-party games and simple folk dances are acceptable if properly motivated. An example of this type of motivation is illustrated by running a western party and asking all the children to come in western costumes, even if it involves nothing more elaborate than adding a handkerchief around the neck. Games are tailored to fit into the theme. In the middle of the party the worker asks if anyone knows what kind of dances cowboys and cowgirls attend and several children volunteer "barn dances" and "square dances." The worker says no cowboy and cowgirl party can be complete without at least one square dance and soon has sets formed doing simple figures. It is useful to do some advance folk-dance training with one group before the party night as a primer.

Active games and quiet games are alternated with each ending by placing the group in position for the next. As the time for refreshments nears, the quiet games predominate so as to calm the atmosphere in preparation for eating. The activity immediately preceding the serving of refreshments may be the singing of one or several songs. An active game immediately before refreshments encourages crowding, snatching, and jostling. Where songs are to be used, the last song should be a quiet one for the same reasons. As in the case of the games, no time should elapse between songs. It is helpful if the accompanist is ready and knows the songs and keys. It is poor planning to require a conference between worker and accompanist between each song or to have to stop frequently to raise or lower the key. More songs should be prepared than are needed in case of an emergency. More games should be on the list than are needed and, as the worker watches the time, some can be dropped if there are too many. At any given time it may seem advisable to use more active games or the group may need more quiet activity. A full program can be cut and arranged as one goes along, but a skimpy one is difficult to expand if it should become necessary.

The programming described illustrates the principle that it is desirable for children's parties to be participator parties and not spectator parties. Youngsters do not benefit much from watching entertainment, and well-meaning board people and contributors should be discouraged from putting on a party "for" rather than "with" the children.

No party is a party without refreshments. The worker watches the time and gives the staff responsible for the refreshments a signal when it is time to prepare and serve the food so that the program and the refreshments will be synchronized. Food should be wholesome, simple, easy to manage, and attractively served. One should be careful to avoid food that can be thrown easily or that is not acceptable to the children. The plan for the refreshments and the service can result in very good or very poor learning. The announcement of the refreshments is designed to avoid a free-for-all, the setting is suitable for eating, provision is made for the disposal of waste, and arrangements are made to avoid unauthorized second portions. A suggestion: Have the children remain seated and serve them or have a smaller room adjacent to the party room set up with tables and have perhaps twenty children at a time come in to eat. If the latter is done, the units can be selected by giving the children different-colored tickets with the "greens" going in first, the "blues" next, and so on; or by an alphabetical sequence; or by having the last game played in teams and then going in one team at a time. Whatever the plan, those who are not eating must be occupied and those who are finished must know where to go and what to do. The refreshments room should be well supervised to promote quiet and pleasant surroundings and encourage social talk. The children should be encouraged to clean up after themselves.

In some agencies, older juniors are interested in experimenting with social dancing. A workable plan is to permit those who wish to dance to do so while the others eat, and then by reversing the procedure, the younger ones can have a game while those who have been dancing eat. The very last game can facilitate the ending of the party by using "english" which gets the group moving and the children can be directed outside. In anticipation of this, the staff posts itself at important locations to direct the movement of traffic, cover the checkroom, and send the happy children home with a cheerful "good night, see you tomorrow" kind of atmosphere.

Teenage Parties

Parties for teenagers place the groupworker in a different role from the one played in children's parties. As would be expected, the leadership that the worker is called upon to give to children's programs gives way to a more enabling kind of assistance. The teen social, like club and interest activities, is a program mode and a medium for growth and development. It is one more opportunity to experiment with a social setting, boy and girl relationships, social activities, and to find appropriate roles. In most teen groups, status depends upon popularity, social skill, and an ability to dance and to get along with the opposite sex. The teenager seeks adulthood, and his emotional being strives to understand himself and his feelings while he tries to conform to a peer society. His adult self and his childish self dominate him alternately and his acceptance of adult guidance fluctuates accordingly. His horseplay and her giggling, his swagger and her coyness, their studied untidiness and hero worship are all signs of adolescent insecurity and the need for support.

Because the teenager has the body of an adult, workers are prone to expect him to act like an adult who is fully capable of taking care of himself and others. Experience soon shows that he is not as capable as was supposed and yet that he resents adult help. He does not want to be treated as a child nor does he want to assume the full responsibility of adulthood. If he is warned that one of his plans will not work he curtly rejects the advice, but if he is not warned and he runs into difficulty, he loudly proclaims that no one cared enough to tell him and that it was all the adult's fault for not warning him.

The teen dance or social, as part of an agency program, can be designed to help the teenager resolve these conflicts and meet the needs of his growing up. His frantic dancing is just part of his need to release his troublesome energy. For the adolescent, heterosexual program is vital to supplement one-sex clubs, and the worker who fails to take into account the teen need for heterosexual experience and development misses one of the most important aspects of teen programming.

Teenage parties and socials are handled best through planning committees; with such committees the function of the worker is that of the enabler. It is the function of the worker in this setting to assist the adolescent to accept and carry out responsibility and thereby receive recognition and status for achievement. The committee allocates and assigns tasks to its members which they may or may not fully carry out. They may regress to childish dependency or lose interest at a critical moment. Progress toward maturity is not direct, but fluctuates widely from responsible behavior to undependability. The groupworker does not permit important jobs to remain undone because a member fails to do them. He follows up by checking on the members, by anticipating and calling the chairman to encourage him to check on the members, by reminding people of the things they have to do, and by getting others to fill in when tasks are unfinished. An example of anticipating is to be found in the situation surrounding "cleanup." The worker, knowing who are on the cleanup committee, sees that they do not slip out without helping so that he does not find himself alone in the kitchen. Occasionally, the worker may have to do some of the chores himself in order to see that they are accomplished.

There is a transition stage in the worker's role from children's to adults' parties. In the children's program he is the direct mover. However, he cannot suddenly withdraw and expect that as soon as the children become teenagers they are ready to do everything for themselves. It is true that he has been helping the juniors to take on more responsibility as they become older, but there is no magical change in them because they are a year or two older. The transition in the worker's role is a gradual one and as he withdraws he finds it necessary to support the committee members, check up on them, and see that the jobs get done. This is important because, while it might be sound training to allow committee members to see the consequences of their failure to carry their responsibility, the ultimate result would be a poor affair for the total membership and, consequently, frustration and negative learning would result. Teenagers are in open rebellion against adults and authority, and are not sufficiently mature to understand that it is their own committee which is failing. Their hostility becomes directed against the staff and agency when their affairs are failures and nothing is gained in the process. It is far better learning for them to experience successful events, perceive the advantages of democracy, of participation, planning, and committee structure than to cope with inadequate committee members at this stage of their development. Moreover, it is better for the committee members to learn through positive experiences and success rather than to be placed in a negative and status-losing position and feel imposed upon. Democracy is learned through program and experience and it must work in order to prove itself.

When members fail to do their jobs, this is handled and discussed in the committee meetings. The obvious results of forgetting to order the ice or the refreshments, or failing to report for door duty are thrashed out in committee where the members are able to speak freely, bring pressure to bear upon irresponsible members, and discipline themselves. It is one thing for a member to lose status in his committee because of a misdeed and thereby be helped through this experience to do better the next time, and it is another for the entire committee to feel that the failure of the party rests on their collective shoulders and to see the result as a disintegrating teenage group. There are times when the worker can risk allowing

259

something to remain undone as an object lesson, but when he does so he must be quite certain that the learning will be positive and that little damage will be done. As time goes on, he expects committee members to have learned and to be more responsible. As this happens, he exerts less pressure on them, but he still stands by to pick up the loose ends when it becomes necessary. He hopes that the chairman will learn to do the checking, the prodding, and the calling and assume his role as leader.

Within the committee meeting and in the execution of plans, the worker helps to point out the places where subcommittees are needed, where caution must be exercised, and where there is a job that must be done. He is a resource because he knows how parties are run most successfully, what the needs and interests of the members are, where things can be procured, and he can foresee difficulties. While his role in the children's party was to run it, here his function is to see that it is run.

It is also his job to help the committee plan meaningful programs that can serve as media for fulfilling agency function. Here also, the program is not valid if it is not part of agency function and integrated into the total groupwork program. The needs of teenagers generally, and these teenagers specifically, must be met while endeavoring to reach other social work goals. Is not enjoyment a goal in itself and hence if the dance provides enjoyment, has it not served a purpose? This is true as far as it goes, but all recreation is not automatically good, and the recreation provided by a social agency is not valid unless it has social value. The recreation movement long has recognized that recreation has values over and above enjoyment. Poorly conducted recreation can and often does produce negative values. It follows that it is the type of program in addition to the fun itself that is useful in helping teenagers grow and it should be used consciously for personal improvement.

The trends in programming are to include the open-house type of activity in which opportunity is given for freedom of choice, the emphasis being on cooperative rather than competitive activity in order to improve social attitudes, as well as creative and cultural activity instead of only physical games, and the opportunity for rhythmic expression as, for example, through folk dancing.

Parties and dances for this age group lend themselves admirably to the use of themes. The theme gives the affair atmosphere, adds spice and interest, prevents the program from becoming stereotyped throughout the season, and provides a vehicle for decoration and program. The theme dresses the invitation and makes the social more than just another dance. It also takes away from the monotony of using the same room regularly. The theme need not be adhered to strictly throughout the night, but it does help to hold the entire program together. Suggestions for themes and ideas can be found in any good program book.

In children's parties, the program must be full and move quickly while, generally speaking, teenagers want to dance and do not want an elaborate program. However, not all young teenagers know how to dance nor are they secure enough to mix easily and some are afraid to introduce themselves to each other in order to dance. This would seem to point up the need to use program to help young people get together and feel free enough to dance. It also illustrates that program can be withdrawn or reduced after its desired effect has been achieved. Programs that mix people at the beginning of the social serve this purpose. Programs that involve people early in the evening in group games where the individual boy and girl contact is minimized also are helpful. When the social atmosphere relaxes and warms up, these are no longer necessary, but so long as the boys and girls remain a room apart, the program must try to bring them together. The simple fact is that they want to dance but some are unable to do so without help and support.

Workers often find that their efforts to get adolescents on the floor to participate in programs fail, and they are left with the same cold lineup. In the first place, the junior programs suggested earlier would have prepared the group for the teen socials; but one cannot go back with them to re-create these early experiences. The worker works with his committee to help the group participate. The committee members show the way by participating and encouraging the others to join in. The worker is accepting, reassuring, and definite. He acts as though he expects everyone to participate because it is so enjoyable. He does not apologize for the program but points out that their committee planned it for their enjoyment and invites them to a good time. If only a small number volunteer, he runs the program with these few who are having such an obviously hilarious time that the others become tempted to try. He does not berate or embarrass them, because he understands that their failure to respond may be the result of insecurity, and bullying will not help them—only encouragement and acceptance will.

Sometimes the room lighting aggravates the problem. If the room is too brightly lighted, many people will hesitate to risk themselves. A dimmer, not darkened, room is more conducive to mixing. Spot dances, prize dances, broom dances, and special events often will do the trick. Elimination dances do exactly the opposite of what the worker is trying to achieve. Snowball dances, where one couple starts to dance, breaks and each selects a new partner until everyone is on the floor, serve to get people dancing and, therefore, are recommended.

Good party programming includes an atmosphere of friendliness, plenty of action with an opportunity for wholesome fun, diversity of program to meet different interests and changing moods, spontaneity and flexibility to adjust to the group, something new to avoid monotony or a stereotyped program, change of pace with time to socialize, a theme to coordinate the party, and a good ending that is not anticlimactic.

Interesting decoration, in keeping with the theme or season of the year, helps to break down strangeness and sets a festive atmosphere. The worker helps the committee plan and execute clever and creative decorations. The traditional, unimaginative, and easily strung crepe-paper streamers should be relegated to the closet once and for all, to be replaced with a mural, a hand-decorated cutout, and expressive built-up settings. This is program at its best, related to the ongoing agency program, allowing for self-expression, and developing creative personalities. The decoration is not left to the committee to do alone. Many of the total group can be involved in various subcommittees; the more people become involved in the planning and preparation, the more they gain from the experience and thus have a stake in the party.

At the social itself, the worker has a vitalizing job to do. He is the one who creates the atmosphere of gaiety, warmth, and sociability. He greets people, chats with them, and exudes the spirit of the party. If the attendance is poor the worker does not look glum and tell those who have come that the affair is a flop. On the contrary, he is more energetic and cheerful, telling people that there is lots of room to dance and that they will all have a wonderful time, so that those who have come will enjoy themselves, stay to the end, and advertise the dances that will follow. The worker moves about constantly to check on the way things are going and to be available wherever the need might arise. He visits the door to see how tickets and change are being handled, has a word with the checkroom boy, looks in on the kitchen, and visits the lobby. At the dance he will circulate and be easy and friendly. His job is not to lean against the wall with arms folded looking like a chaperon, glowering at everyone, but to smile and enjoy himself, and at the same time always being attentive to everything that is going on. He assists members to learn how to make announcements and to act as masters of ceremonies, and comes before the group to lead games or call dances at the request of the committee which should be announced by the teenager in charge at the time.

He sits down with a few who are seated and talks with them, moves on to a group in the corner who are getting restless and jokes with them to relieve their tension and discomfort, asks their cooperation, gives them a job to do, or warns them if that seems

262

to be necessary. He dances and enjoys himself, selecting girls who are not popular but in such a way that it does not become obvious that he is dancing only with the wallflowers. While he is dancing, his eye will continue to take in the entire room. A woman worker dances also, helping the shy boys to improve their steps and the cocky ones to calm down. The worker changes his partners so as to mix couples by switching partners on the floor, or by taking his last dancing partner over to a group where they chat for a while and he then unobtrusively takes one of the other girls as a partner. He does not embarrass either the girl or the boy by introducing them and pushing them into a dance. Teenagers resent that kind of treatment.

Perhaps he may clown just a little if there is a feeling of tension in order to get people laughing, or he may encourage some spontaneous fun as one couple, perhaps without meaning to, puts on an exhibition of fancy dancing. He teaches by example, such as never leaving a girl standing in the middle of the floor at the end of a dance but bringing her back to where she was before their dance. A woman can accomplish the same results by smilingly asking for that kind of treatment. He moves about, breaking up a stag group, bringing several people together, dancing and mixing, relieving tension, and anticipating difficulty, but always in an unhurried, friendly, and accepting manner. He talks about agency and neighborhood interests, club programs, a new recording, future plans, personal matters, so as to be part of their group, developing interest, poise, confidence, enjoyment, loyalty and good feeling.

The worker also has to be a limiter. While his committee can help to promote decorum and the observance of rules, they are young and callow and often ruffle feelings rather than help. As he moves about, the worker must see that house rules are observed and that the party is a medium for learning acceptable habits. His admonitions are courteous and cooperative, but firm. If there is a rule against smoking he gives them the reason and asks for their cooperation. If he is defied or ignored, he must act quietly and quickly but not in anger or to punish. It is a fact that one cannot smoke and stay in the room and the choice is up to the member, either to put the cigarette out or smoke it outside. "We are all here to have a good time and I don't want to have to ask you to leave—why not smoke it in the smoking room and then come back?" The provision of a place to smoke is an excellent idea since it is always preferable to be able to suggest an alternative rather than to have to forbid or deny. Bold-faced refusal to comply obviously requires ejection. Scenes can sometimes be avoided by asking the resister's friends to deal with him. Where they are all members of the agency, there is a rapport from which to work. The question of outsiders will be discussed later, but if outsiders come with members, they are the members' responsibility and it is up to them to deal with infractions of the rules.

As a limiter, the worker and staff patrol other areas in the building to avoid unacceptable behavior. The washrooms must be checked regularly to curb gambling, fighting, and drinking. In some schools, recently, it was found that community-center members were keeping bottles of liquor and pot in their gym lockers to use on dance nights. All areas of possible difficulty must be kept under surveillance. In order to discourage drinking outside, some agencies will not allow members to come back to the social once they leave the building. The worker is the obvious person to intervene in the event of a fight. To anticipate and prevent it is preferable to stopping it, but this is not always possible. A calm approach, reasoning with them, appealing to them not to fight in the agency, asking their friends to separate them and cool them off, or removing the one with the low boiling point are methods of dealing with the problem.

Where outside groups attend the social and create a disturbance, they should be asked to leave, but in a relaxed and easy fashion and not in a manner likely to cause more difficulty. "These girls are too young for you. Why don't you leave them alone?" "There is a dance at such and such a place where you will have a better time." "Fellows, we are here to help everyone have fun—why break it up? If you want to enjoy yourselves, stay and dance, but if you are not interested in that why not move on?" Throwing them out adds to their antisocial feeling about the affair, while offering them agency services can sometimes offset their initial hostility. On rare occasions it may be necessary to close the affair completely or to call for help.

It is the worker's job to see that the music is adequate by supervising either the person playing the records or the orchestra. No matter who has hired the orchestra, its conduct and selections are the concern of the worker if he senses that they are the cause of tension or discontent. Most agencies find that records and equipment last much longer if only authorized people are permitted to use them. Long intervals between sets or records and long intermissions in teen socials are, generally, sources of difficulty and should be avoided if possible.

The decision of the "last dance," the enforcement of the closing time, the provision for staff supervision in the lobby and at the checkroom, the supervision of the cleanup, the removal of the decorations, and safeguarding the funds are all part of the worker's responsibility. Lest he forget, he is reminded to thank his helpers and congratulate his committee when and if appropriate. If admittance to the social is by ticket, attendance-taking is easy, but if it is free to all members, some accurate method of counting is the worker's responsibility and he avoids guessing, exaggerating, or depending upon the committee's estimates.

When the evening is over, it is useful for the worker to make a few notes of things he wishes to discuss at the next committee meeting. There are other matters that are not actually a part of the teen social that should be discussed here. For young teenagers who are uncomfortable or unsophisticated at their first socials, and for others who are not interested in dancing all evening, the addition of a games room solves many problems. It gives the young person a chance to retreat and still be part of the activity or a chance to find friends or engage in a game with boys and girls before attempting to dance. It gives the girls a place to be when sitting on the sidelines becomes obvious, and it removes people from the dance floor who are disruptive because of insecurity. It provides an activity for those who have come early and reduces the spectators when the floor becomes crowded. The games room is most useful when it is in an adjacent room rather than when it is in the same room as the dancing. Also, it can be used as the smoking room and the place where refreshments are served; refreshments eaten in the dance room make it untidy and are difficult to manage.

Often boys do not know how to dance, and this simple fact makes the program unattractive to them and unsatisfactory to the girls. Most boys will resist learning to dance at a social. Only the more aggressive ones or those who have a special girl friend will attempt it. This indicates the need to teach boys to dance before these affairs can be a success. Dancing instruction can be introduced into the group program, using skilled teachers and the assistance of girls' clubs and volunteers, or it can be done by means of a dancing class. The experience of many agencies shows that dancing classes are more successful and reach the shy boys when the classes are unpublicized and not shown on the agency schedules but are whispered around. Girls are eager for help in how to be attractive, how to behave, and for instruction in glamor and etiquette as their preparation for dances and parties.

Special events and extra programs can be introduced into teen socials as a result of committee planning and worker stimulation. These serve to heighten interest and provide variety. Included in this area are: entertainment by members or outsiders, exhibition dancing, quiz shows, dramatic skits by the members or the drama club, craft exhibitions, costume affairs such as a Gay Nineties party, cabarets, barn dances, fashion shows, and the like. Able committee work improves the socials and promotes social education and human development.

The Young-Adult Dance

The worker has a more difficult time defining his function with young adults even though he has much less to do at their dances than with either of the two younger groups. These group members are adults. What do they expect or need of him? The worker first has to determine whether they are adults or at least whether they have reached that degree of maturity where they can be regarded as responsible. If the group is actually adult, the worker's function differs from what it was with adolescents, but if they are still adolescent he conducts himself in accordance with the level at which he finds them and the amount of experience they have had in running their own affairs.

Young-adult programs usually are planned by a committee, or less frequently by a council. It is the worker's function to work with the planning group, with and through the chairman. The worker is not directly responsible for seeing that the affair is run. The chairman is the person who sees that everything necessary is managed and accomplished. The worker is an enabler who helps the chairman learn how to carry his responsibility and he is a resource person who can instruct, show, and explain, but does not do the job. It is up to the committee to plan and run the dance with his help. He is there to give help if it is asked for or obviously is required, to interpret the committee's function and to interpret agency policy.

When working with adult committees, the worker may find that he has to call his chairman frequently to remind him that certain things must be done or to ask if they have been done. Also, he calls many of the members to keep in touch with what they are doing or need. Adults generally do not spend much time around the agency and, therefore, are kept in communication through the telephone. Wherever possible, the worker suggests that the chairman do the calling, but many people who act as chairmen may have other commitments as well as full-time employment and need help from the worker. For this reason, and not because adults cannot take responsibility, the worker often finds that he must act as the administrator of details. The term administrator implies that he coordinates, reminds, allocates, delegates, and checks. However, when tasks are left undone, the worker does not do the job for them. Responsibility lies with the committee which is accountable to the membership, usually through an executive committee. Adults should be able to place responsibility where it belongs and deal with the committees appropriately. It is part of the executive committee's function to hold the dance committee chairman responsible for carrying out his assignment, and the total membership looks to its officers for action.

The worker sees the activity as social, as a place to continue heterosexual adjustments, and if he is realistic, as a marital meeting ground. Girls come to meet boys, and boys come to meet girls. This latter point, however, raises serious problems if the committee does not require couples to attend, as in many instances the girls may greatly outnumber the boys or vice versa, thereby reducing the enjoyment for all. For this reason, it is important for the program to be attractive enough to draw the members to it. Dances that serve only as a place for boys to select girls whom they then take away from the dance are not in keeping with the objectives of the activity. Diversity of program to appeal to the serious as well as the less intellectual is, therefore, advisable. Reference already has been made to the So-ed type program as an example of successful young-adult programming.

It is to be hoped that young-adult mass program will, in fact, result in interest-group formation. The agency can serve this age group best in this way and still retain its contact and service. Interest groups can be formed through the use of interest-finder questionnaires, the setting up of groups and announcing the times and places of meeting, or the selection of committees to develop certain groups. An effective and quick device is to ask for a demonstration of interest in certain selected hobbies right at the dance. Those who are interested go to designated corners of the room during intermission and groups are formed right then and there.

At the dance itself, the worker is not as active as he would be at a teen dance. He dances and socializes, talks to many people, stimulates and encourages, and acts as a resource person to the officers. Where things are not running smoothly, he calls the attention of the responsible officials to this fact and offers suggestions if this seems advisable. He is the agency representative as far as rules and house facilities are concerned, and a helping person as far as the young adults are concerned. The progression from being the director of the children's party through to being the enabler and facilitator in teen parties should reach its culmination with adults, leaving the worker as only a resource person who offers little supervision. It is hoped that the adults will be able to handle their own limiting and will need little help from the worker.

The program at the dance is somewhat more sophisticated than that for teenagers, but essentially it is the same. Games, specialty dances, folk dancing, entertainment, theme dances, and mixers are all standbys. Adults may come to such programs feeling that the affairs are cold, that they do not know anyone, that there is an imposing stag line or wallflower line, and as a result, that they cannot dance, do not like to dance, and are social failures. They should leave feeling that the dances are friendly, they have had fun, they can dance, they have met some people, have had an interesting discussion, were interested in a group, and felt wanted.[9]

The Worker's Function in Mass Activities with Different Age Groups

It is to be stressed again that there is no sharp line between these age groups. Growth occurs along a continuing scale and hence the role of the worker must be suited to the level of the group with which he is working at any given time.

The Worker's Function with Each Age Group

Children	Adolescents	Adults
Plans and directs.	Plans with a committee.	The committee plans.
Runs the affair.	Sees that affair is run.	Advises if needed.
Handles traffic, supervises cloakroom and general conduct.	Checks details and calls committees' attention to jobs to be done. Enables them to take responsibility.	Works with chairman. Jobs are their responsibility.
Sees that all have fun. Motivates and runs program. Supervises staff.	Helps all to have fun. Motivates—is resource for program with member acting as master of ceremonies.	Administrator of details. Enables. Offers little motivation. Offers little supervision.
Sets limits.	Helps organization run smoothly. Limits. Encourages meaningful activity at the social as a medium for growth.	Limits less. Concern with what will grow out of the mass activity, i.e., activities.

Senior Citizens

In recent years, interest has grown in the area of program for people over sixty-five. Clubs and recreational programs have been springing up all over the country in existing agencies as well as separate "golden age" clubs. There is a considerable body of opinion maintaining that recreation programs for the aged should not be separated or segregated from regular recreation agencies. It is argued that old people are made to feel unwanted and lonely by segregating them in separate agencies, and that they are happier when they are included and made to feel that they still belong to the rest of society.

The development and handling of program for this age group is not very different from that of adults in general. The aged do not want to feel or be treated differently; they do not like to be patronized or made to feel enfeebled. However, there are a few items to be considered. Old people like active games, dancing, and party activities, but the older they are the less able they are to participate in a very active program for long. They enjoy cards, crafts, dramatics, amateur theatricals, discussion groups, singsongs, and entertainment.

All activity and its handling should be related directly to their physical ability; as, for example, announcements are clear so that they can hear, an awareness that they may have poor vision when activities requiring eyesight are planned, a slower tempo for dances and games, and a provision made for ample "breathers." Parties for the aged require programming as generally they do not like to dance for an entire evening.

Studies indicate that most workers in this field recognize that old people can plan and execute their own parties through committees and, in fact, need to feel able to handle their own affairs. However, in practice, most agencies reporting reveal that parties are staff planned and run. Time and opportunity should be allowed for members to choose informally programs of interest to them. They can discuss programs to be planned for the next month, volunteer to sit on a committee, decide about the name of the club, how money can be raised and how it should be spent. Gradually, this type of opportunity develops into a decision to have simple business meetings and hold elections. From the principles outlined for the other age groups, the groupworker selects the function that he will be required to assume in parties for the aged.

Requisites for Mass Program

If mass program is to be regarded as an integral part of agency program, consistent with the social-agency function and directly related to the purposes and objectives of the service, some thought must be given to who attends. It has been argued in these pages that all program within the agency is valid only insofar as it fulfills the agency's purpose, and as a social agency, the purpose must be consistent with the broad philosophy of the field. Agencies and workers, committed to social groupwork method, are concerned with personality development and social values. Welfare councils and community chests are interested in implementing the desire of the community to render a social service and allocate funds to that end.

If mass activity within the social agency is to foster the values claimed for it, certain conditions are essential. These are:

1. The attendance must be regular and continuous. If people attend sporadically there can be little progress or progression of experience and learning, and the process toward social learning is thwarted.

2. The attendance must be consistent. If the group changes constantly, the planning committee cannot plan to meet the interests or the needs of the group, nor can any sense of belonging be achieved, nor is the committee truly a committee of the group.

3. The mass program must be related to the ongoing agency program. The mass program supplements the small-group program by offering different experiences consistent with the aims of the program in general.

4. The groupworker establishes a relationship with the members and uses himself as a helping person.

5. The people who come are aware of agency function.

It is doubtful if any worthwhile social purposes can be achieved through dances where the people who attend are not members of the agency or, if they are members, join solely to attend the dances and do not attend other agency programs. It is doubtful that social agencies can justify the use of their funds, facilities, and staff, measured either in purpose or results, for nonparticipating members. The values of the mass activity alone, without the relationship to the workers, the acceptance of agency function, and the influence of other agency groups are not sufficient to justify the effort.

Where dances are attended by large groups of nonmembers, they are not related to the staff and are not being reached by them. In the event of unacceptable behavior, they have no reason to accede to the worker's demands or to accept his limits. In most instances, they are influenced only by the atmosphere of the dance, the tone of decorum, and the examples of the others, and if the preponderance of outsiders creates a boisterous atmosphere, little is gained. By like token, new members are not touched by agency policy and are not influenced by what the agency stands for through the medium of a dance. The mass program can be an effective program modality only as it supplements the balance of agency program.

The sponsorship of dances for recreational purposes for the general public is a function of the tax-supported agency and should be left to it. There is no implication in these words that public-supported dances are inferior, but rather that there is a difference in purpose and function. Public dances serve an important role in a community but social-agency dances are designed to serve an equally important role directly related to its specific constituency and function. It is not the function of the social agency to conduct public dances.

Where member clubs wish to run dances within the agency as fund-raising events or for other purposes, that is their privilege. These clubs are using the experience of planning and running a dance for their social growth, but such is not the case when the agency sponsors an open dance. It can be argued that such dances are useful to attract members who later join other activities. If this were true and consciously promoted, it might be valid. A detailed study made of the attendance at a weekly dance held in one large agency over a year revealed that of an enrolled group of 300 young adults, only 35 actually participated in other aspects of the program, fewer than 100 attended more than 10 per cent of the dances, and the 35 mentioned before were the only consistent and regular attenders, even though the dances averaged an attendance of 150 per week. Although this may not be typical of many agencies, it means that the agency was serving 35 people through this activity with an outlay far in excess of what it would cost to service a club of 35 people.

It is suggested that if agencies choose to use the mass program for recruiting, adequate safeguards and procedures be employed to carry out the plan effectively, and that it be made known that they are not in the business of running public dance halls. Possible methods of doing this are to allow people to attend a limited number of times as guests of members who are responsible for them, to issue temporary membership cards, to have prospective participants interviewed by a committee of members before being admitted, or to have a follow-up committee recruit participants for committee work or interest groups.

Another serious problem to be considered is that of the "rounder" or person who attends a dance in a different agency every night. It should be obvious that this is not a broadening experience, that no genuine personal development results, and that community funds are not being well spent. The encouraging of young adults to travel all over the city in pursuit of dances possibly may serve a useful function by enabling them to cross the boundaries of ingrown neighborhoods, but it does not develop sound neighborhood service. The practice of going to an adjacent town or neighborhood is often a prelude to promiscuous sex practice. Most agencies are set up to serve defined geographical areas and are budgeted for members they serve. If a person attends dances in four agencies he is counted four separate times. Multiply that process by a few thousand people and the central budgeting of a community can be affected in significant terms. The remedy for such practices is better interagency cooperation and clearance. This needs further study by agencies.

It is suggested that the matter of mass activities and their use is not consistent with agency policy in many instances and that many agencies maintain them as open affairs to support their budget demands because they swell the attendance figures. As long as boards and chests are more impressed by numbers than by the type and quality of service, such practices will continue. The groupworker is more interested in the people served than the numbers served and is committed to a high-quality program. It remains for him to interpret the groupwork program in those terms.[10]

NOTES / READINGS

1. Gertrude Wilson and Gladys Ryland, *Social Group Work* (Boston: Houghton Mifflin, 1948).

2. Brian Sutton-Smith, "Peer Status and Play Status," a report of research conducted under an N.I.M.H. Grant, No. M-550, Wayne State University Library.

3. Paul Gump, "The Ingredients of Games and Their Impact on Players," Wayne State University School of Social Work, 1955. (Mimeographed.)

4. Paul Gump and Brian Sutton-Smith, "The 'It' Role in Children's Games," *The Group* (February, 1955).

5. Gump, Schrogger, and Redl, "The Camp Milieu and Its Immediate Effects," *Journal of Social Issues*, Vol. XIII, No. 1 (1957).

6. Robert V. Vinter, "Program Activities: An Analysis of Their Effects on Participant Behavior" in *Readings in Group Work Practice* (Ann Arbor: Campus Publishers, 1967), pp. 95–109.

7. Lawrence Shulman, " 'Program' in Group Work: Another Look" in William Schwartz and Serapio R. Zalba, *The Practice of Group Work* (New York: Columbia University Press, 1971), pp. 221–239.

8. This section applies also to a day room in a hospital or a games room in a senior citizens' center or similar programs.

9. Also see:
James K. Whittaker, "Program Activities" in Trieschman, Whittaker, and Brendtro, *The Other 23 Hours* (Chicago: Aldine Publishing Co., 1969).

Paul Gump and Brian Sutton-Smith, "Therapeutic Play Techniques" in Nicholas J. Long, William C. Morse and Ruth G. Newman, eds., *Conflict in the Classroom* (Belmont, Calif.: Wadsworth, 1965).

Fritz Redl and David Wineman, *The Aggressive Child* (Glencoe, Ill.: Free Press, 1957), pp. 318–394.

10. For background references, see:
Robert Waelder, "Psychoanalytic Theory of Play," *Psychoanalytic Quarterly*, Vol. 2, No. 2 (April, 1933), pp. 208–224.

Lili Peller, "Libidinal Phases, Ego Development and Play," *The Psychoanalytical Study of the Child*, Vol. IX (New York: International Universities Press, 1954), pp. 178–198.

S. R. Slavson, *Recreation and the Total Personality* (New York: Association Press, 1946).

10

❖❖❖❖❖❖❖❖❖

The Use of the Agency

The phrase "use of the agency" has several connotations. It conveys the ideas that are associated with the influence of the setting on practice. These include the structure of the agency, its social climate, the congruent or dissonant messages that it sends, the willingness of the agency to permit a particular kind of practice, the compatibility of the other services in the agency with the group services, and whether the agency policy and operation evidence belief in and support of social groupwork. The phrase is also associated with that school of thought which places great importance on "function" as an integral part of practice. While I recognize the value of all of these meanings, they are not the focal point of the discussion in this chapter.

Working with Agency Policy and Function

We are concerned here with the use of the agency as part of the method which is available to the groupworker when he is working with a group. The use of the agency is of the same order of things as the previous four categories of method which we have been discussing; namely, the use of group structure, the use of group process, the use of self, and the use of program. Its most significant use lies in the policy and function of the agency, both as they limit behavior and as they enable it. The policy and function of the agency should be known in general by the members since they are what the agency symbolizes in the community, what its reputation is based on and, presumably, why the members come to the agency for service. Function as used here includes purpose, sanction, and mandate. Policy and function should be interpreted to the applicants for service in the intake interviews. It is not realistic to assume that all of the policies and functions of an agency can be conveyed to an applicant or members, that they are ready to hear them, or that they understand and accept them when they are discussed. The policy has to be introduced again into the group deliberations when it is appropriate and pertinent. Two illustrations will help to make this clear.

A group of young adults in a YWCA are discussing a service project and they have agreed to raise money to help an agency that is rendering a social service to families of autistic children.

SARA: In this town and for our friends, the best way to raise money is to put on a big dance with a good band and with a name performer, believe me.

MARIE: She's right, ya know. Besides, then we can have a good time also.

JOAN: It's the best idea. We could swing it and maybe raise a thousand dollars.

WORKER: A dance such as you are talking about takes a lot of hard work and organization.

JONATHAN: Hard work doesn't bother me. We can get help, ya know, from a lot of people, sell tickets at work, and do a real job of publicity. I have some contacts with the newspapers.

MARIE: The work doesn't bother me either. What scares me is handling it. If it's a good bash, all kinds of people may come. You can't keep people out and before you know it you have trouble; drinking, fights and . . .

DICK: Okay, okay, let's set it for a Friday night. There's a big brawl at the Afro-American Club on Fridays, ya know, and those people will go there. If we charge a few dollars more for our tickets, the blacks will go to their own club.

MARIE: Great! We'll have it on a Friday. That solves the problem.

WORKER: Not entirely. Aside from the question of assuming that black people cause trouble or that excluding them in this way eliminates the problem of how to control behavior at a public dance, the YWCA has a policy of inclusiveness which I thought we all believed in. Exclusion by this device is still exclusion and I don't think we have that choice.

DICK: But we can't risk having the dance ruined.

SARA: Then I guess the question we ought to talk about is how to set up proper controls at the dance to avoid any trouble.

WORKER: Right. After we solve those problems in relation to the money-raising event, maybe we can talk about the meaning to us of Christian brotherhood.

Obviously, the group has not dealt with its attitudes or its racism, but that topic will take time and energy and this is not the teachable moment. The worker has faced the group with its bias and paved the way for further exploration while not increasing their resistance. The policy of the agency has been used to limit the action.

In the second illustration, a group of parents of emotionally disturbed children are meeting in a day-care center. Each couple have brought their child to the agency with the object of having that child cured. The parents view the sick child as the patient. In both intake and in interpreting the group session to the participants, the agency policy and function have been interpreted but, as the meetings go on week by week, the parents seek answers from the worker, focus the discussions on the children, and resist talking about themselves. The worker can invoke agency policy and function. Using this means does limit, but it also enables the group to get on with its proper business.

WORKER: I wonder if I might refocus our discussion. It may be helpful. This center is here to serve families that have children with problems. This means that we are here in this group to talk about our families; the whole family and not just the children. It is our policy to treat children directly which we do in day care, but of equal importance is helping you to bring about changes within your families. Now, if we are going to be able to help the children, the center is convinced that there must be some change in family life.

MR. OLMSTEAD: I see your point, but whenever Mrs. Link asks you how her family should change, you throw the question back at us or you just look blank.

WORKER: The staff is not here to tell you what to do. We do not believe that it would help you if we did anyway. Help, in this center, means helping you to find answers that are suited to your family and its situation. I am here because this agency wants to help you, and telling you what you should do is not what we think will help.

MRS. COATES: Every once in a while he has given a suggestion about what to do and I notice no one pays any attention to it anyway. I guess we are all looking for an easy way out.

The Use of Agency Resources

The agency provides resources in personnel, in material things such as facilities, and in procedures. Some people find it difficult to see procedures as an instrument that affords aid but procedures can provide security, can reinforce the giving of and acceptance of responsibility for what happens to a person, can help one to focus, and can energize a person to do something about his problem. The use of crisis-intervention procedures provides such help. Some will take exception to referring to crisis intervention as procedure, but that is what it is. When a worker uses it in group service, he is assembling resources to surround the person with a surfeit of nutrients at the critical moment of need and when there is a readiness to make use of them.

When an agency provides a rumpus room equipped with soft walls and floors, sandbags, punching balls, and places to hide for the use of the worker for children, the provision for such a facility is an expression of its policy and treatment philosophy. How the worker uses it conveys nonverbally the kind of behavior which is permissible and expected of them.

The provision of a staff-team approach in an agency is another manifestation of agency policy. The same applies to coleadership, the provision of tape recording and playback equipment, or the presence of one-way glass in the doors. How and if the worker uses them implies his use of the agency. Social workers tend to be uncomfortable with the presentation of patients or clients to an audience but the practice is normal and usual in psychiatric treatment settings and is sanctioned by agency policy. By like token, the presentation of a group for training purposes or study, when prepared for and executed properly, can be a meaningful experience for the members. The same applies to the introduction of clients into a classroom in a school.

Where an agency provides none of these facilities or resources, or a worker does not avail himself of what is provided, this also is a use of the agency because we must assume that the decision has been a conscious one.

The Management of Problem Behavior

Whenever working with groups is discussed by staff workers or students, inevitably the question of problem behavior is raised. This is true especially if the groups are composed of children or adolescents, but also it seems to apply to groups that include old people. The philosophical premise in this book is that individual problem behavior is the group's problem and that it should be referred to the group for solution. Also, it is premised that the management of behavior lies within the actor and that the ultimate goal is self-control.

I have suggested throughout that the actor must be helped to know what is expected, to gain competence in his performance, to resolve antisocial and self-defeating resistances, and to overcome emotional blocks. I indicated the use by the worker and others of awareness, support, and learning through such devices as reinforcement and reward, feedback, reference to consequences, large doses of need-meeting nutrients, and demonstration. There is the salutary influence of group sanctions but there are also dangers such as group provocations, group assignment to a deviant role, and contagion.

It is a viable principle to rely upon the group for the management of problem behavior *after* the group has reached the stage of mutual aid or intimacy. One must be wary of group discipline before that time because it can be destructive and provide an opportunity for some members to hurt, exploit, control, and punish, as well as project. However, the worker must also look closely at himself. He may be the instigator of problem behavior, that is, group members may be enacting his secret desires, or he may be rationalizing a need to punish in the name of discipline. Many sins are committed against members and patients as a consequence of such dynamics in the name of their own good, or treatment.

With these cautions and an explication of the beliefs of the author in mind, one must be realistic about practice. For some or for many people in groups, external behavioral controls and guides are necessary, reassuring, and growth-inducing. Many groupworkers work with people who do not have the ego strength to apply self-restraints or to engage in cooperative group rules. Many members are unable to comprehend the concept of social good or to trust others. Some think that they have nothing to lose and hence can only perceive hedonistic self-indulgence while others think they have too much to lose to entrust what little they have to a group of peers.

If the worker permits problem behavior, the implication is one of not caring. Some youngsters go so far as to blame the worker with "You let me do it," meaning that by not stopping them he has condoned it. Delinquency or deviance can produce guilt which is relieved by acting out so as to be punished, or it can produce a breakthrough of defenses and open the way for an emotional collapse. One can always anticipate with the people in our groups that unlimited misbehavior creates its own anxieties and generates fear of reprisal. These events create repetitive cycles. For the actor, with the exception of the person with no conscience, misbehavior that is permitted exacts a psychic price and as often as not can produce a physical insult as well. Theoreticians hypothesize that self-control develops through the internalization of social controls. If no social controls exist, that is, if the worker is permissive, the actor has nothing or no one to incorporate. If a worker loves his members, he will limit them.

This section does not aspire to be a manual on the management of behavior problems. There is no recipe or set of instructions for how to do it. Here again, the most important determinant is the worker's stance based upon his beliefs about people and who he thinks he is. A second determinant lies in his understanding of what constitutes problem behavior. Conformity and pleasing the worker may be pathological (as is the revealing of oneself too early in a group of strangers). Revolt and rebellion may be healthy ego functioning. The behavior of residents of a ghetto may seem to a middle-class graduate student to be immoral, but much of such behavior may be rational, appropriate when examined in the light of the social system in which it occurs, and a means of survival.

Technique and Style

The exploration of ways and means is offered only as a guide for the reader, who is encouraged to develop his own style. These means are subordinate to and are to be informed by those mentioned in the preceding sections. The worker may use the techniques suggested below, but the way in which he uses them should be in keeping with the basic themes in this book.

A usual approach to the management of problem behavior is an appeal to the intellect or reason. One argues that one kind of behavior is better than another, or is more reasonable, more pragmatic, or more normal. Appeals to reason are sometimes made through suggestion, sometimes through empathy, and sometimes to one's pride. One form of this appeal is persuasion. This includes reference to self-interest or to being rewarded for behavioral change. Traditional groupworkers like to state or imply that acting differently is more fun, will make one more popular, or will gain the acceptance of the worker. This kind of appeal comes close to barter in which one trades on basic human needs such as self-esteem or recognition. I believe that a member's needs should be met because he is a person and because we are concerned, and not through a bargain which implies conditional love. In the long run, it leads to a more healthful resolution. An entreaty based upon moral grounds may work, but these grounds must seem relevant to the member if he is to be impressed. On the assumption that the members want to please the worker, and this will depend upon relationship, it is possible to request behavioral change for the worker's sake, to enhance the worker, to make life easier for the staff, or not to disappoint the worker. A more viable means lies in promoting mutuality and in developing a concern for others. The implication is that the members have all been victims of punishment, domination, exploitation, and rejection; and, knowing how it feels, it might be suggested that in the group at least they could be nice to each other.

This could be a first step within the intimate group that would enlarge in concentric circles to include greater spheres of interpersonal relations. It is also an approach that can be a stepping-off point in family group therapy.

Standard works on the handling of problem behavior suggest tactics such as the use of humor, that is, joking or kidding someone out of an action; of substituting a diversion; the showing of displeasure; of appealing to friendship, such as "I like you, but"; offering a postponement, such as "You don't have to do it now, but"; the suggestion of an alternate behavior or of appealing to shame.

There are times and situations wherein subtle approaches are ignored or taken as a sign of weakness. There are members who have been trained not to respond to suggestion or persuasion. There are people who must test the limits and, if they are elastic or inconsistent, will be driven to act out. Many people who come to us for service are chronic provokers and derive secondary gains from being perverse. Many of the techniques which groupworkers traditionally employ tend to reinforce such behaviors, especially if the worker's stance is a questionable one. To be effective, a groupworker should be understanding of misbehavior and not be irritated by it. The occurrence of misbehavior should be anticipated. If deviant behavior annoys a worker, it can be assumed that he wants to work only with client-members who have no problems. Some social work educators have the same attitude about students who have difficulty learning.

This discussion has been leading up to the fact that there are times and places where a groupworker must resort to his position and exert authority or power. How he uses this and why are the crucial questions. Techniques associated with this use of authority include invoking rules, commanding and directing, taking a firm stand, reverting to one's position, such as "I am the cottage parent and what I say goes," or in softer terms, "I want you to stop that." All power influence rests upon threat, implied or real. It is axiomatic that a worker never threatens unless he intends to and can carry out the threat. It is far better for consequences to flow from the circumstances rather than from the worker personally. However, once a threat has been made and the person defies it, the consequences must follow and there is no room for either discussion or delay.

There are aspects of this use of authority which include environmental manipulation, such as removing seductive equipment from the room, ejecting a stimulator, ejecting the one who is misbehaving, removing the jelly beans that are being thrown around, stopping the activity such as a game or film, turning on more lights, and the like. We have stated before that the worker does not "handle" the behavior; he handles himself. This is a cardinal principle. By this we mean how he controls himself but also it can mean such things as touching the misbehaving member, putting one's arm around his shoulder, or, in an extreme case, embracing him so as to physically restrain him when he is having a tantrum or is flailing about while the worker verbally interprets his act as an attempt to help, not punish.

Physical force or restraint is absolutely the last measure and it can be rationalized only as a means of protecting others, the actor, or the worker from injury and, on rare occasions, protecting property. Physical force may never be condoned to punish, hurt, or discipline. This entire discussion is about the management of problem behavior, not about punishment or discipline. Punishment has no place in groupwork and this includes punishment by the group or by any member, in addition to the groupworker.

There is a difference between punishment and the removal of rewards which sanction desirable behavior. Punishment implies a purpose to hurt; learning theory informs us that punishment usually does not extinguish the undesirable behavior and often reinforces it. The management of problem behavior calls for systematic extinguishing by careful use and withholding of rewards. The intent is not to hurt but to teach.

A considerable amount of problem behavior is a response to the social setting. This includes the group as an environment, but even more, the agency as a milieu. The most desirable management of misbehavior is its prevention by careful elimination of its causes and especially those that can be attributed to the agency policy or its implementation in practice. It should be understood clearly, in the context of this book and *Social Work Through Group Process*, that the impinging environment of our society is also a major contributor to personal misbehavior, and hence that social action to alter these noxious influences is essential and is an inherent part of social groupwork.

Above all, there is reason to believe that when people are treated as human beings they learn to act as human beings.

An Illustration of Contagion

AGE: Teenagers
SETTING: Jewish Community Center
SESSION: Twelfth

At the suggestion of the group, I arranged for transportation to take the girls swimming at another branch of the Center. They are adolescent girls and in planning the activity, expressed a desire to invite a boys' group. Since there was some conflict among them as to what group of boys to invite, the final decision was "why not invite a boys' group that they did not know." The reasoning behind this seemed to be that they could increase social contacts and widen acquaintances.

I contacted one of the male leaders of a boys' group, familiarized him with the plan and made all the necessary arrangements. Before giving a final answer, he spoke with his group and the boys were all in favor of the plan. The night the groups were to go swimming, the girls' group, without any previous knowledge on my part, invited eight girls from another group at the Center to accompany them. This brought the total number of girls to 16. However, with all of the naïvete of a novice, I anticipated no problems—after all they were all adolescents and seemingly quite mature. With the boys' group of 13, there were 29 kids, and two leaders.

Both the male leader and I were feeling that we deserved a pat on the back for group controls exhibited on the bus and at the pool. The bus programming went well with good participation. The "ice-breakers" of boy-meets-girl seemed effective, considering in particular the crowded bus and the awkward seating arrangements.

On the way home, about a mile away from the branch where they had just gone swimming, one of the girls who was a guest of my group stood up on the seat and flung a scarf at one of the boys. This incident started a chain reaction which ended up in the most bizarre behavior that one might ever have anticipated. The moment the one girl succeeded in getting the reaction she might well have expected, that of "retaliation," nearly the entire girls' group stood up on the bus and started throwing things.

At first, pleading, which later graduated into real firmness by the other worker and myself, went over like a wet Kleenex. The boys by this time had also joined the act and began tugging at some of the girls' hair, shouting obscene language to the motorists, jumping over seats occupied by some of the kids, etc. The bus driver stopped the bus amidst this, but it seemed next to impossible to reason with the kids in terms of danger or threats to remain there indefinitely if they did not calm themselves.

I attempted to approach a few of them individually, but suffice it to say that a narrow bus aisle crowded with excited teenagers was no place to seek a truce. Finally I was able to approach the president of my group after the excitement waned slightly and I said that they would be expelled from the agency if this did not stop at once, and also, each of their parents would be contacted. I don't know whether it was this threat, whether it was the person to whom I spoke, or whether they were sufficiently exhausted—or perhaps a combination of all three— that restored order sufficiently to continue.

Although the initial action was taken by one of the guests, and I'm not sure which of two girls it was, the complete loss of group control was prompted so instantaneously that it was overwhelming to me, particularly when my experience was so limited. It was impossible to remove any of the kids because we were on a bus; yet on the other hand, it seemed impossible to control them because the excitement had infected every one of them, and whatever technique of control might have been possible in an ordinary situation in an agency building, it could not be applied in the bus.

Could these problems have been anticipated and prevented? What preparation is required for this type of event? Once the trouble erupted what might the workers have done?

NOTES / READINGS

Walter Lifton, *Groups: Facilitating Individual Growth and Societal Change* (New York: John Wiley & Co., 1972).

Helen U. Phillips, *Essentials of Social Group Work Skill* (New York: Association Press, 1957), pp. 51–92.

Norman Polansky, Ronald Lippitt, Fritz Redl, "An Investigation of Behavioral Contagion in Groups," *Human Relations*, Vol. III (1950), pp. 319–348.

Fritz Redl and David Wineman, *The Aggressive Child* (Glencoe, Ill.: The Free Press, 1957).

George V. Sheviakov and Fritz Redl, *Discipline for Today's Children and Youth* (Washington, D.C.: Association for Supervision and Curriculum Development, National Education Association, 1944).

Jessie Taft, "The Relation of Function to Process in Social Casework," *Journal of Social Work Process*, Vol. 1, No. 6 (November, 1937).

Neal Timms, *Social Casework* (London: Routledge and Kegan Paul, Ltd., 1964).

Harleigh Trecker, *Social Group Work: Principles and Practice* (New York: Association Press, 1972).

Rudolf Wittenberg, *Adolescence and Discipline* (New York: Association Press, 1959).

11

❖❖❖❖❖❖❖❖❖

The Termination of the Group

We have discussed pregroup fundamentals, formation, and the beginning and middle stages of groups of various kinds. Emphasis has been placed on the group as a means of growth and treatment during the middle period once mutual aid has been established, and now we come to the last stage of the group, the terminus.

The termination of a group may come about for many reasons. It may be the end of the agreed-upon or stipulated duration; it may be that the members have completed the task or achieved as much as they think they can or are willing to work for; or the end may be dictated by circumstances beyond the control of the group, such as the departure of the worker or a discontinuance of the program. The intensity of the relationships and degree of intimacy, the interdependence achieved, the dependence on or involvement with the worker, and the prospects for the future are some of the variables which will affect the emotional and behavioral response of the members, but regardless of the degree of reaction or the kind of group, certain factors will be present. I will discuss these briefly first and then consider what the worker does.

Termination of a group, as in most human relationships, and especially where the participants have gone through a lot together and have developed a sense of closeness and mutuality, is fraught with sadness. It is akin to losing someone dear and feeling grief, or to feeling that one is being abandoned. It leaves one with the dread of loneliness and of having to "go it alone." It reactivates the fear of risk and the anticipation of inadequacy and hence failure. Mingled with these anxieties, if the group has been a help, are feelings of hope, of power to succeed, and of the adventure of facing a new day. The task group has less of the personal, emotional content

283

but there are still feelings of sadness and loss coupled with a sense of accomplishment. However, where the task group terminates, having failed to accomplish much, there are emotions of inadequacy and anger as well as frustration.

Thinking of the composite sentiments, it is inevitable that the members will deny that the group is ending and that they are about to lose their friends and the relationships which they have experienced. There will be a resistance to planning for the future, an unwillingness to face the facts, and a retreat to business as usual. If one does not recognize the inevitable, maybe it will go away. The impending doom permeates the group and settles in as a theme, even when denied and ignored. The result, as with any strong group sentiment, intensifies closeness as members instinctively cling to each other, as do lovers at dockside who are about to be separated. The pervading spirit grips the worker also.

Grief carries anger with it and also incredulity. "Why us, what did we do to deserve it?" The anger is aimed at the groupworker and projects onto the agency and other likely scapegoats. The resentment is real and it intensifies dependency. Some of it can spill over onto one's self and can trigger depression. Pessimism mingles with optimism, fear mingles with courage, but more often what appears to be courage is not courage but a reaction to anger.

One can expect that anxiety, fear, and anger will result in regressed behavior. Old symptoms reappear, seemingly resolved conflicts re-emerge, group disorganization takes on the aspects of the way the group was in the early stages of its life. Learned behavior becomes unlearned and people seem to become unglued. These events can be explained in two ways: the regression is an unconscious reaction to the fear and anger; and there is a semiconscious attempt to announce that they are not well, that they need the group and the worker, and that how can they be abandoned when they are still so needy. Masked and overt anger are revealed in friction and sometimes in expressions of self-pity.

Occasionally, the group will decide to continue outside of the agency auspice and without the worker. However, this rarely succeeds and the group tends to disintegrate after a meeting or two. Sometimes the members plan and carry out a party to veil their hurt and to forestall that sinking feeling. At the party, if there is one, and at meetings, there is a recollection of past events, a retelling of things that have happened, a remembering of how they used to behave and how they used to feel, and a pervading nostalgia. Partly because it is true, partly to bolster resolve, and partly to feel successful accomplishment, members usually tell how they are going to act in the future.

The worker encourages the group to evaluate its experience, chart its course, and assess where it is now. He permits the testimony of individuals. He does this because he knows that a public declaration buttresses one's decision to carry out implied promises, and also because he believes that it is important for groups and members to confirm that they have achieved positive results. He does it also because he needs to feel useful and recognized; it is his reward. Adult groups tend to be positive in these evaluative sessions. Mild neurotics also profess to having been helped. However, acting-out teenagers, institutionalized delinquents, and hostile young adults often will deny that they have changed or will change, they punish the worker who is leaving them, and they provoke by missing meetings, quitting, or being obnoxious. Experienced workers know that members of such groups on occasion will commit crimes, revert to drug abuse or violence about the time that a group is ending, or will elope from the institution.

Where the group is terminating at a time when the members are ready for the change, members will leave with optimism and will find other groups or activities, other friends or partners, and perhaps establish happy reunions. These people welcome the opportunity to have new, fruitful experiences. Where the group terminates before the members are ready, the event may be tragic in its hidden meanings; that is, there can be renewed feelings of failure, terror at being back where they started, anxiety about struggling to find themselves and being stopped just short of achievement, and reactivated feelings of rejection and abandonment, reinforcing the belief that they are born losers. All of the sentiments I have been describing throughout this chapter must be assessed and dealt with by the group and the worker. This requires understanding and careful planning. No group should just end, nor should the worker just leave.

Garland, Jones and Kolodny write that the actions and emotional states in this phase of group life follow no patterns or progressions. They report that these reactions can occur in flashes and in clusters, that they all can occur in a brief space of time, in one meeting, in any sequence, and that group members can fluctuate rapidly between rationality and emotionalism. In my experience, whatever the overt actions, all of the emotions I have described are present, and whether or not they break through to the surface, they must be dealt with. Neglecting to do so can result only in retarding the stabilization of change, in negative reactions to proffered group experiences in the future, and in leaving vestiges of unfinished business that will be discomforting long after the group is gone.

The Groupworker and Termination

The groupworker often has many of the same feelings that the group members have about terminating the group. He cannot hide them nor should he try because if he does, his behavior will aggravate the situation and he will be either too soft or too cold in his responses. The worker must be honest but keep his focus on the needs of the members instead of his own. It is up to the worker to initiate discussions and prepare the group for the severance. Generally, this should begin a month in advance. Often when he broaches it the group will change the subject but the worker must bring it back to face the facts.

The situation poses a dilemma for the worker because it is up to the group to deal with its feelings and to talk about the ending, but it will deny them and hence the worker is forced to be direct. Even if he uses feedback and asks the group to look at its behavior, he is likely to have the subject changed or to have it treated lightly. The groupworker feeds back, he interprets, and he verbalizes these feelings. He universalizes, he empathizes, and, if necessary, he speaks of the consequences of repressing the feelings of grief. Grief must be externalized, it must be talked about, and in some instances acted out in art, music, drama, or be related to a previous experience with the loss of something that was valued. To accomplish this ventilation, the worker may have to query, to speak of loss, and to interpret some of the things that are being said obliquely.

In like manner, it is important to bring feelings of abandonment into the open, to allow anger to be expressed against the worker, the agency, or the direct cause of the feelings, and to reduce the projection of that anger onto each other. The method is to draw the anger, accept it as normal and allow it to be discussed. By talking it out, the group realizes that it is not being abandoned. The worker should offer to be available if needed and to provide resources to which the members can be referred if they need specialized help. In the past, writers have contended that the worker should cut his relationship cleanly and abruptly to avoid lingering dependency and to prevent interference with whatever subsequent relationships the members might make. I am not in agreement with this viewpoint. The worker should be conscious of the dangers noted and minimize their possible occurrence; but the paradigm of groupwork that has been presented in this book requires a more natural, human response than an abrupt end. The group experiences do not finish with the dissolution of the group, nor can one hold that with the termination of the group the function of the groupworker ends. The influence of these experiences, the memories, and a relationship with the worker continue, but the kind and quality of the relationship changes. The change which is to occur should be prepared for and should be made explicit and clarified for the group members. In effect, a new contract is made.

The formulation of a new contract, the empathetic climate of the transition, the provision of resources, plans for what the members will do, and the availability of the worker for appropriate functions go a long way to relieve the threat of loneliness and to minimize the fear and risk of having to go it alone. The worker must offer reassurance and it is to that end that the group members discuss the progress they have made and the confidence they have acquired.

The support comes from the group; the confirmation of progress and change comes from the group, but the impetus and concurrence is infused from the worker. The depth of feeling and fear causes the group to look to a nurturing parent surrogate to release and emancipate it. The group had become a mutual-aid enterprise wherein the peers relied on peers and the worker sedulously avoided acting as a parent and was a partner instead, and now the group becomes dependent on the worker in the crisis of dissolution. This may seem to be a contradiction; however, it is a normal regressive reaction to fear. Since all the members sense the fear in each other and huddle together in defense, the regression fosters a more infantile state. Once the worker reassures, conducts himself with confidence, and attests to the ability of the members to go out on their own, the peer-group support takes over again.

The crucial aspect here is the stance of the worker, for he must be free and willing to let go. If the worker is hung up and cannot or will not let go, an unhealthy dependency ensues and the grief and anger cannot be resolved. If the worker harbors doubts or believes that he has failed, the group will be caught up in his feelings but will not understand his misgivings.

Through all of this ambivalence and turmoil, the worker must continue to help the members become aware of what they are doing and why, and to realize that the way they feel is permissible and normal. They not only must know but also accept their feelings. The worker helps them to see that the enactment of old symptoms and conflicts is not a sign of relapse or continuing malfunction, but a reaction to stress. He must confront denial and resistance vigorously. These very direct acts by the worker are inherent in a crisis intervention and pave the way for the group to regain stability, recoup from regression, and find strength to cope.

There can be optimism and hope in the face of the passing of a phase and the loss inherent in it if faith in the future and belief in themselves and their capacities were born and nurtured in the group through mutual respect and trust. The experience of growth and warmth helps one to look forward and to anticipate new and satisfying experiences and to be optimistic about growing up. As in the life cycle of a person, the successful negotiation of a stage passes one on to the next stage with hopefulness, and motivates one to look forward to the additional responsibility and challenge of increased maturity. If the tasks and conflicts are resolved in an atmosphere of caring, and if the rewards for maturing are provided, then one gladly leaves childhood with pleasant memories and the ability to grasp opportunities along with added knowledge, skills, and confidence that one has the power to succeed. The adolescent moves forward asking himself whether he can make it, whether he will ever be a competent adult, and whether he compares favorably with his peers. Can he be loved and is he lovable so that he can move to the ultimate human experience of caring? So too, the group becomes ready to move on with the same questions. If the group experience has, in fact, been one of mutual respect, human concern, and caring, the answers come easily.

If the groupworker has enacted his function with maturity and has been a symbol of caring, he will be an ever-present role model for them. If the groupworker has not dominated, controlled, or been the prime mover, the members will have acquired the habit of self-determination and of handling themselves and their problems. Moving out from the worker does not become complicated by a dependency upon him, and one need not be looking continually for clues or approval in his face before making decisions. Members can leave with self-respect, a respect for others, and a social commitment because they have found some aspects of self that allow them to function with autonomy and because mutuality has developed. All mature humans are both independent and dependent. Although the members have become dependent on each other and the group, the group experience also has been strengthening and makes it possible for them to go on to other interpersonal relations with less fear of rejection or anxiety about closeness. This is the essence of the thrust for living which takes its natural course unless something intervenes to block the growth process or to cause insult to the organism. The true meaning of the group experience is to support natural life processes and unblock the results of former injuries.

Admittedly, this is an ideal group ending, but it is the ideal toward which we labor. To aim for less is to settle for mediocrity; it is not necessary to compromise; success is within reach. Group experiences can never be erased; to have made a friend remains part of oneself; the group is an experience in becoming a part of others, and they a part of oneself. To have shared the group with a groupworker such as I have described is something that never ends because it exists in the here-and-now of one's memory and is an ever-present part of one's ego. This is a major significance of groupwork.

An Illustration of Termination

AGE: Young Adult
SESSION: Seventeenth and Terminating Meeting

About this time Marge arrived and I suggested that we should now sit together and really do some evaluation of the group experience. I asked first what they thought the group experience had meant to them. Fern, as in the first meetings, took the lead and said that the group had apparently helped all of them to gain a great deal of self-confidence. She said that though she had not been there all of the time, she felt that at least she now was able to interpret her illness to others and she herself did not feel as badly about it. She said, for instance, that the first time that she had the seizure, we had discussed in the group how to approach the girls, and she had been able to do this. Actually, there was not great feeling, but a simple acceptance of the facts by her shopmates. Certainly she was quite frightened and thought that probably her work would be stopped, but she understood that there was reality because she certainly caused a lot of difficulty. She also said that in looking at the other members of the group she felt that they had gained a great deal in self-confidence.

Ted spoke up and said that the self-confidence shows in the relationship with other people. He said many of their acquaintances have commented on how very different Lucy is. She is much more relaxed and seems to be more friendly with people. He said they have several neighbors at the house, and all of them had commented on how much nicer Lucy is in her relations with them. It was kind of amusing to observe Lucy during this because she was a little embarrassed and quite flushed. To make it a little easier, I kidded her and said it was nice to have such compliments from her husband. She nodded and said that she really felt that somehow it was easier to talk with people. I said that I also thought that this was one of the major aims of the group and though I was absolutely sure that we hadn't finished this, and that each one of them would have to continue working on their own security, that we did hope that we had improved this. I said that it would be helpful if we looked at some parts of the plans to achieve self-confidence, for if we did, maybe I could mention some aspects that I thought the group should accomplish, or had accomplished at least partially.

I started out by saying that I hope they understand their sickness better. There was a great consensus of opinion and several said that they realized that their sickness was not a mental sickness, but a real one, and that it was partially physical, and partially emotional, and

289

they would have to work on both aspects of it. Fern said at this point that the most important thing was to learn that the sickness is a reality; that one knows that one does have seizures, and one cannot just do away with them, and that there are limitations which the sickness imposes on them. She said she had a friend who was crippled by infantile paralysis at an early age, and she has also learned from him what he had to learn; to accept himself with all the limitations that it imposed on him. Marge joined here and said that the point was that they should still like themselves, that she had for a while almost hated herself and wouldn't have wanted to continue to live. The group has helped her to see that she was actually as good as everybody else, even if there were limitations. Ed added that one has to know that actually there are many more people in this world who have difficulties, even if one cannot see them.

To summarize this discussion: they had learned to begin to accept themselves with their sickness as a reality and would have to continue to learn. I added that the limitations imposed on them might not be static, as medicine was trying to learn more and more about this kind of sickness and I added, smilingly, that there might even be a possibility that they might go swimming some day.

I then said that the next point on which we apparently had to work in this group was their relationship to the family. I said that at their age everybody had to deal with his feelings about wanting to be independent of the family. With many people this is even started much earlier. Their difficulty is that their specific illness had increased their dependency on the family. They had expressed a great deal of resentment toward this in the beginning of the group, and it would be interesting to see where they thought they were at this point. The group members decided that on this question they wanted to go around and each one wanted to see where they stood. Lucy said that she felt that she still has to learn a great deal about her feelings, about her family, that it isn't all clear but that somehow, just especially in the last two weeks she has learned to accept the relationship as one that isn't quite as hurting as it had been. Ted added that it would be good to stay away from them. I said at this point that it would be all right, but one can do that only if one feels actually free to stay away. Lucy said that what she sees is that she has started her own family now and this is to become the most important problem in her life.

Marge said that she certainly had come a long way toward independence and that she felt she could never have done it without the group discussions. She said that her mother was not living with her anymore, and that certainly this was difficult. Recently the landlady had said to her that it wasn't right that she had sent her mother away and for a moment she really had felt very guilty. But then she told herself that really she had not sent her mother away, and that she had to stand on her own feet. She wanted to be clear though, that we understood that it wasn't very easy even now.

Joe said that actually he hadn't had as much difficulty with his

290

family as the other members of the group, but that he saw in the course of the group that he was just sliding over things and didn't really try to understand them. After he understood a little better, he too wanted to become an independent human being. He felt that he could be more on his own and it had helped in being more secure in his learning. So he felt that he is in a better relationship with his family, but still with some of the difficulties that he had previously.

Ray was somewhat more hesitant than the others in seeing much progress clearly. Obviously, he was still quite dependent upon his mother. We discussed, for instance, whether he still let her prepare his medicine, etc. and he said that he was trying to be quite independent about it, but he still took quite a good deal from her in this respect. He felt very strongly that he should have a summer job so that he could get away from home and also so he would feel more certain that he could really hold a job.

Fern said that she had gained in spite of the fact that she hadn't been coming regularly. She said that her younger sister had asked to live with her and if one knew about their relationship this was terrific progress. I asked her whether that would be really helpful or if life would be very difficult in staying with the younger sister. Fern said, no, that she felt that actually it would be very good, that it was better than to live with a stranger and she also felt it did something for general family relationships. We discussed that difficulties would arise and that she should be prepared for this reality. She said that she doesn't see her older sister with whom she had the greatest difficulties. She feels that that is helpful because again, it doesn't hurt as badly anymore. She thinks that her feelings had been especially hurt previously because she felt so very close to the children of her older sister. Right now, she thinks that she has overcome that and has made friends elsewhere and that would help her in her relationship with her family.

Ed said that he still feels quite dependent and especially quite guilty toward his family. He thinks he should help his father but certainly that would be impossible in the kind of job he has to do, because it is working on high places and with electricity. He had sincerely hoped for a summertime job because it would take him away from home. I had to tell him at this point that probably nothing would come out of it, at least not at this specific time, because the vocational counselor had to go out to the lake with the youngsters. Ed didn't take this calmly and said that he would then look for something else. He was thinking that he could work on a construction job and then said, "But Miss Jones said this was not good." I discussed with the group what it means if one always says that somebody else said it isn't good. I interpreted this point more intensively than I had done before; actually what Ed was doing here, instead of putting the responsibility on his parents, was putting it on another person. The question is, does Ed himself feel that he can work on this construction job? In discussing it, it became clear that he himself didn't like the idea that he might get the job only because the men wanted to do a favor for his father.

It was clear though that Ed still needed some help in getting a summer job and also more of a feeling that he could become independent. With him it is related very much to his own feelings of insecurity and also to the reality of the situation of his not being decided on what job, or what vocation to choose.

After the rounds were made in the group and each one had spoken, I said that the third area that this group was supposed to help with was in relation to a job. At this time we didn't go all around in great detail but we mentioned what help had been given. Fern said that she had been very happy on the job but certainly, rethinking now, she knew that she would not want to go back to a job in the same organization. She questioned whether the job was perhaps too strenuous for her. I said that I could not judge but one has to think of whether the strain did not lie in the job but in other problems that were working on her during this time.

Fern also mentioned that recently Don had called her and that he sounded so much better than at the beginning of the group. She made this connection because she said that she felt Don was helped a great deal by being able to take a job. I told the group that Don was not exactly in the job he was trained for but he felt it was helpful to stand on his own two feet. Joe joined in here and said that it had helped him, especially in the last five weeks when we had made him talk in the group, and that he was able to do well in school, that he sees what he is accomplishing and he thinks that his course will be finished in June. At that point he thinks the best thing will be to take a job and see again whether he can stand on his own two feet. Later, he can consider whether he wants to go back to study. I felt that though Joe hadn't made the best adjustment this was an amazing step forward compared with what it had been about six weeks ago. Marge certainly felt completely at ease about this since her job is completely secure, she has a camp job for the summer and will start as a counselor at the Home in the fall. Ted told the others that he thought once in a while one does have to take something that is not the ideal and maybe one never finds the complete ideal; that one has to take the responsibility for one's family and start working, and later see whether one can move to something else. In general, we discussed that perhaps nobody ever finds the complete and most wonderful kind of vocation he has ever thought of, but that we can try to approximate it as closely as possible.

I then said that the fourth area that this group had been discussing was social relationships and wondered whether they felt they had made an improvement. It was clear that Lucy felt that this was her major improvement during this time. Ted mentioned that it was helpful to see that one can trust other people and he thought that everyone in the group should know that sometimes church groups have very interesting young adult programs which they could join. I supported him and said that it was something he and Lucy could think about, or, for instance, groups in the settlement houses. They talked about the fact that when they came they were so very frightened, for instance, about dating, and that most of them had not had much experience with it and felt very handicapped. Now, at least they were willing to risk themselves a little more.

NOTES / READINGS

James A. Garland, Hubert E. Jones, Ralph L. Kolodny, "A Model for Stages of Development in Social Work Groups" in *Explorations in Group Work*, ed. Saul Bernstein (Boston University School of Social Work, 1965), pp. 41–46.

Erich Lindemann, "Symptomatology and Management of Acute Grief," *American Journal of Psychiatry*, Vol. 101 (September, 1944).

Elizabeth Kübler-Ross, *On Death and Dying* (New York: The Macmillan Co., 1969).

Donald Morton, "The Role of the Social Worker in the Termination of Service to Groups" (unpublished M.S.W. thesis, School of Social Work, University of Southern California, 1964).

Helen Northen, *Social Work with Groups* (New York: Columbia University Press, 1969), pp. 222–237.

Sheldon K. Schiff, "Termination of Therapy," *Archives of General Psychiatry*, Vol. VI (1962), pp. 77–82.

Juan Ramon Valle, "The Role of the Social Group Worker within the Process of Planned Termination" (unpublished M.S.W. thesis, School of Social Work, University of Southern California, 1964).

12

❖❖❖❖❖❖❖❖❖

Six Additional Modalities

I am opposed to any monolithic approach to theory and am convinced that there is no one way to practice groupwork or to help people. There are many roads to Mecca. Until such time as there is empirical proof which has been demonstrated through careful research that one school of thought is superior to another, I hold the position that there is much to recommend several different orientations. Since this is a text for students, it is desirable to discuss briefly six supplementary modalities to the major one presented in this book.

The Mediating Model

One of the most creative theoretical orientations for social groupwork has been developed by Schwartz. He suggests that the function of the groupworker is "to mediate the process through which the individual and his society reach out for each other through a mutual need for self-fulfillment."[1] Schwartz sees this being accomplished through five implementing tasks which he enumerates. They are: (1) to search out the common ground between the member's perception of his need and the social demand with which he is faced, (2) to detect and challenge the obstacles that obscure this common ground, (3) to contribute otherwise unavailable and potentially useful data, (4) to reveal and project the worker's own feeling for the member and his problem, and (5) to define the limits and requirements of the situation in which the member-worker relationship is set.[2]

In this model, Schwartz suggests that the worker set forth the concern that the agency has for the group and then proceed to develop a contract which will guide the worker and the group in what they will do together, thereby freeing the members to contribute to a group enterprise and work for a common group purpose. The worker also is free to contribute facts, information, value concepts, and the like where appropriate to help the group achieve its purpose. The worker "tunes in" on what is happening in the group and, if the members are not working on the task, he challenges the obstacles which are blocking their efforts. He relies on the group to provide mutual aid. The worker is a role model, he "lends a vision" and he helps the group to identify its themes. The worker also helps the group terminate when its work is done, and make a transition to new experiences.

Tropp discusses this method in the following terms:

Today, in the arena of social group work theory, there are two polar views, and various people take stands at stages in between. There is Robert Vinter, at one end, who sees the group as the means by which the worker can meet individual treatment goals—carefully studied, diagnosed, and prescribed for each individual in the group—by unashamedly manipulating the group and its members to achieve these highly particularistic and differentiated goals. In 1959 Vinter honestly faced a dilemma that he was unable to resolve: If the natural forces of group life are the most potent means for effecting individual change in the group, how can the worker justify becoming deeply involved in controlling and fragmenting the group process? . . .[3]

At the other pole is William Schwartz, who has developed the concept of the group as a system of mutual aid and who sees the group and its living experiences as the crucial focus for the worker.[4] He sees the worker and the members as engaged in a common enterprise, that of carrying out the group's purpose. He sees the individual members as growing essentially through their group-oriented efforts. Now, Schwartz's position, vis-à-vis Vinter's, holds within it something far more important than a technical difference. It is a philosophical difference—the value orientation—that is strikingly at issue. To Schwartz, the group is not a mélange of wholes and parts to be arranged, taken apart, put back together, and generally manipulated by a social worker in accordance with his own goals for different individuals; to him, the group is an organic whole that develops a life of its own and an integrity of its own, which the worker had better respect if he is to be useful."[5]

Schwartz has disagreed with those who hold that each act of the worker can be consciously performed based on an analysis of the process at a given moment or upon diagnoses of individuals.[6] His emphasis is in developing the tasks on sets, that is, broad categories of actions. One also gathers from his writing that understanding the group member is not based upon the usual notions of psychological functioning, but upon comprehending his behavior within systems. This seems to imply that behavior can be assessed as appropriate or inappropriate, that is, functional or nonfunctional within the system and also within the value orientation of the system instead of upon some internal set of psychic norms. He is concerned with what the member does more than with what he is.

One senses in Schwartz's work some of Parson's thinking, some of Szasz's, and a little existentialism. The central assumption rests upon an interdependence between the individual and society. The design fits very comfortably into the social philosophy of the times; namely, reduction of authoritarian control, egalitarianism or partnership of the worker and member, equality of peers in a mutual-aid endeavor, and the importance of using systems concepts to analyze social phenomena. The Schwartz formulation, while designed for social groupwork, is applicable to social work generally.[7]

Transactional Analysis

In the last few years, transactional analysis has become popular in some circles as a theoretical frame of reference as well as a group practice. It rests primarily upon the work of Berne.[8] A basic assumption of transactional analysis is that all people are composites of three ego states, a Parent, an Adult, and a Child. The state that dominates a person gives the behavioral impetus to how he stimulates interpersonal transactions and how he responds to others. The focal point in the group treatment is to ensure that adults transact with one another as adults. Transactional analysis is a practice theory of social intercourse which is based on the partial transformation of the hunger for stimuli in infancy into the hunger for recognition in adulthood.

In the theoretical formulation, the Parent state is characterized as a coherent system of feelings which are related to being a parent, such as a feeling or nurturing, of being angry or critical, or of replicating parental influences and acting as one's parents would have liked one to act. The Adult state is characterized by an autonomous set of feelings, attitudes, and behavior patterns which are adapted to current reality. The Child state is composed of a set of feelings, attitudes, and behavior patterns which are relics of one's own childhood, some of which are natural childish behaviors and some of which were learned or adopted under parental influence.

Berne writes that basic methodologies should be stated simply, learned easily, and be accessible, hence the vocabulary of the method contains basically only five words: Parent, Adult, Child, Game, and Script. A Game is a set of repetitive social maneuvers which appear to combine both defensive and gratifying functions. It is an ongoing series of complementary, ulterior transactions which progress to a well-defined and predictable outcome. The goals of Games are ulterior motives and payoffs.[9] A Script is an unconscious life plan.

The goals of this form of group treatment are a reorganization of the member's personality, remission of symptoms, increased socialization and capacity for intimacy, increased control of feelings and overt behavior, and the abandonment of stereotyped relationship patterns. The worker in this approach is the "expert." He chooses the treatment and he plays any one of the three roles, Parent, Adult, or Child, as he deems appropriate at any given time. He sets a contract which follows the briefing of each member in an individual interview. He sets up the first group meeting and makes the decisions about physical layout, seating arrangements, and time elements. The worker must be aware of the habit patterns that are at work in the group and in spite of restricting habits, be responsible for moving the group toward growth. He clarifies for the members what games they are playing, always being on the lookout for the determinants, underlying symptoms, and responses. Because of the changing determinants, it is the worker's responsibility periodically to show the way toward clarification of the contract.

In this modality, the worker must remain a human being. He is said to be a keen observer, a thoughtful listener, a tireless collector of data, a curious investigator, a disciplined clinician, a meticulous technician, a conscientious professional, and an independent thinker. He utilizes techniques such as interrogation, specification, confrontation, explanation, illustration, confirmation, interpretation, and crystallization. These are employed within several methodological categories, depending upon the worker's attitude or ego state. These are supportive treatment, admonitions, analytic interpretations, and activity therapy. It would seem that the method itself is a mixture of psychoanalytical interpretation of behavior within an existential framework.

The worker clarifies communication, detects and rectifies transactions, and identifies the group dynamics. Some typical aspects of the method will help to make it operationally clear. No language limits are imposed but physical violence is prohibited. Once people come into the group session they are expected to remain for the entire session, and confidentiality is emphasized. The sequence of events is based upon analysis, synthesis, and modification of behavior in the here-and-now. Early sessions are characterized by greeting rituals and pastimes. A ritual is a stereotyped series of complementary transactions programmed by external forces; pastimes are a series of semiritualistic, simple, complementary transactions that revolve around a single subject wherein the primary objective is to structure an interval of time. These form a basis of acquaintance and friendship, confirm roles and stabilize positions. Rituals and pastimes help members to find out who the others are, to reinforce each other through "positive strokes," and to examine each other for ways of structuring time and relationships. The more gratifying forms of social contact are games and intimacy and, therefore, after it has engaged in rituals and pastimes, the group moves in its treatment sequence to structural analysis so as to identify the ego states of the members. The goal is to establish reality-testing of the ego states and to free them from contamination by archaic and foreign elements. After this is accomplished, the members are able to proceed to transactional analysis. When there are high levels of tension or anxiety, groups revert to pastimes and rituals. Groups use pastimes also as restrictive solutions to avoid discussion of painful subjects. In some instances where the members are socially quite incompetent, the first meetings might be characterized by withdrawal with fantasies and autistic behavior, but usually this is not common in groups which groupworkers conduct.

Subsequently, the group moves to an analysis of game-playing. The worker predominates in this phase as he identifies the games being played, offers diagnostic interpretations, and facilitates new forms of behavior. In the subsequent phase, there is movement toward intimacy based upon trust, revelation of self, and sometimes physical communication such as patting and touching. There are informal controls, usually instigated by the worker, to keep these from going too far.

As part of the approach, it is necessary for the worker to have a clear contract with each group member about the behavior changes which are sought for him. The worker must have a treatment plan. The members gain satisfaction from new forms of behavior and from seeing the effect of this upon others. Change is effected and stabilized through awareness and reinforcement, both of which occur through feedback from the worker and the group. As social work becomes more and more committed to the use of group methods to offset isolation, alienation, and the dehumanizing effects of society, group treatment of the kind described here is being adopted as one means of helping people achieve intimacy. The evidence which is accumulating seems to indicate that group treatment is the strategy of choice for many people who experience difficulty in interpersonal relations and that it facilitates enduring changes in their human interaction.

There is a philosophical difference between the theory and practice of transactional analysis and the form of groupwork developed in this book, but that difference does not extend to the basic methodological orientation. I see much merit in the method, but hold that the primary function of the worker should be to teach the members how to identify their rituals and pastimes, how to become aware of the games that they play customarily, and how to rewrite their scripts. There seems to be a fundamental contradiction in the worker being an "expert" and making the important decisions, and an existential view of the worker as a human being in the encounter. This might be resolved if one could cast the worker as an enabler rather than as a change agent, and the group as the major influence in the achievement of intimacy.

A Problem-Focused Social-Function Approach

One of the better examples of groupwork with people who have problems is represented in the writings of Cholden.[10] Although Cholden was a psychiatrist whose specialization was blind people, the method which he described is neither psychiatric nor confined to blindness. It is a viable approach to helping people who have problems to cope with them, and enhance their social functioning. He wrote:

It might best be explained as one client recently explained the group session to a newcomer. He said, "We just talk about different things that disturb us and try to understand them." The sessions usually open with my question, "What are we going to talk about today?" The responses vary from, "Let's talk about why sighted people are so stupid and always make me uncomfortable on buses," to "How would you raise children so they wouldn't be afraid of things hurting them?"

In general, the leader's role is that of picking up the predominant feeling or its lack; noticing when the group seems especially aroused about a subject, and wondering about the cause; attempting to bring the more withdrawn members into the discussion; and attempting to separate himself from an authoritarian or teaching role. Intermittently, the group will use the leader as an authority and occasionally the requested information is offered, if it is not felt that it will block further movement by the group. However, the leader's role is viewed primarily as directed toward facilitating and stimulating emotional communication among the members.

This brief statement neatly summarizes an effective system for working with a group.

A Modality for Work with Acting-Out Adolescents

There have been many demonstration projects in the past decade using groupwork with acting-out adolescents.[11] The term "acting-out" is used popularly to mean aggressing against authority, being violent, or being delinquent in response to anger or a desire to hurt or punish. Used more accurately, it means a partial alleviation of tension by responding to a current situation as if it were the situation which originally caused the feeling, such as anger. In some way, the present situation is connected by association with a forgotten experience and it is used as an occasion to release the repressed feelings by acting them out against someone or something in the present. Many groupworkers sincerely believe that groupwork is the most effective means of reaching alienated youth, and so it has been a disappointment to find that traditional groupwork has been assessed by Mobilization for Youth as less than effectual.[12] The major reason put forth for this is the influence of the social environment of the group members and of the groups themselves. It is a premise in the MFY project that the groups and the sponsoring agencies would create and constitute a new and different culture for the members from that of the neighborhood, and would become a referent for a new set of values. MFY reluctantly admits that it did not have the skill to carry on effective social action to bring about the necessary changes in the impinging environment.

This highlights the contention in this book that social action is inherent in groupwork; it is a *sine qua non*. It also confirms my underlying theme that one must function in all of the pertinent systems so as to effect a matching of them. Any attempt to seek to make individuals change to adapt to dysfunctional communities must result in failure. The MFY experience also casts doubt on the traditional reliance on work with natural groups for reasons which have been stated earlier. It also emphasizes the hazards that accompany the usual formation of group structure in such groups. Polsky's *Cottage Six* reveals in bold relief how groupings structure themselves into replicas of deviant subcultures and perpetuate delinquency.[13]

There is growing evidence and reason to believe that psycho-analytically based treatment approaches are unsuccessful with acting-out adolescents and young adults and that insight and interpretation do not work. Experience seems to point to the importance of three modes; namely, problem-solving in the here-and-now, the experience in the group, and behavior modification. This last will be discussed in the next section. These modalities rest upon a theoretical premise based on a feedback-control-system approach. One example of the method can be found in the Hyde Park Youth Project in Chicago.[14] The techniques are cognitive and the assumption is that delinquency is role behavior used as a solution to broad social problems. The groupworker makes extensive use of life-space interviewing in the environment.

A fundamental principle is that the worker gives support, encouragement, and hope, and that there are rewards for positive, new behaviors. Secondly, the worker sets an example which he makes explicit, and he helps the group through the use of program to have new and satisfying experiences which reinforce humanistic values and also restructure the impinging environment. It is indispensable in this approach for the group to be involved actively in social-change efforts. Righteous indignation must be expressed against the causes of injustice instead of in random revenge against society or in the internalization of anger. Verbal therapies are anachronistic when they operate on the premise that if one expresses one's feelings in a group the anger is liberated.

The repertoire of techniques include the following:

The worker appeals to self-interest. It should be apparent to experienced workers that when a person is deprived, has been exploited, and hurts he has too few reserve resources to be able to think of service to others, the good of the community, or how others feel. The important mobilization of energy is to do something to benefit himself, to solve his own problems, and to become aware of his self-defeating behavior and how foolish it is. Ego growth must be buttressed by experiences in mastering the environment on his own behalf before he can become an altruist.

The worker helps the members to ferret out underlying values and wrestle with conflicts among beliefs held by the worker, the group, and the members as they relate to goals and consequences. These young people are pragmatists before they are idealists, and both aspects of the value question must be explicated. The worker must be very astute and alert to avoid reinforcing the basic assumptions which underlie delinquent behavior by his own actions or by what he condones.

The worker stimulates positive identifications and this necessitates that he function as a significant person in the lives of the members. Obviously, he cannot do this unless he spends considerable time with his members and is available to them. An important technique lies in presenting alternatives and problem-solving in rational and logical terms. To offset impulsiveness, the worker employs delaying tactics which give time for the members to think and reason together. The worker in these situations mediates in the group among the points of view in conflict and also is a mediator for the group with societal institutions.

Luther concludes:

The attempt to use group programs as socializing mechanisms generally proved unsuccessful. The value of the purposeful use of group activities and group structure as a prevention or cure for delinquency is open to question. While such methods and processes can harness peer support and can make possible a relationship between members and groupworker, most of the problems of delinquents and the delinquent-prone are not amenable to solutions solely within the confines of a group. MFY's experience shows that the single most effective and socially useful way of helping a delinquent youth was to provide him with immediate and concrete assistance with his personal problems. Manipulating group processes can be useful in marshaling peer-group support for members seeking and using help offered.[15]

I subscribe to the methodology that would place such youth into groups that are formed for providing the help that is required and are conducted to make available concrete assistance with personal problems within a nutritious milieu. In any event, whether ghetto youth are in natural groups or in specially composed groups, it is essential that hard services be provided concurrently with group counseling or groupwork. Hard services include financial assistance, employment service and vocational counseling, tutoring, health and dental service, work with families, sex education, and mediation with law-enforcement agents.

In the record below, the worker endeavors to engage the members in problem-solving in the here-and-now, to look at themselves and their usual ways of coping, to relate behavior to consequences, and to marshal peer-group support for change.

An Illustration of Work with Acting-Out Adolescents

AGE: Teens
SETTING: Juvenile Court Probation Department
SESSION: Fourth

WORKER: Where do we start today?

MIKE: His fight, remember we were talking about his fight.

WORKER: What did you want to tell us about your fight?

GARY: I don't know.

MIKE: You brought it up last week, remember?

DANNY: Tell what happened.

GARY: We were having a fight. See, this kid came up to me—Bob came up to me and said this kid was saying stuff about me. He got sort of pushy and we started fighting and stuff.

MIKE: Then what happened?

GARY: I got knocked out.

BILL: Did you get hurt?

MIKE: He lost his teeth, that's all. What did the cops say?

GARY: What do you mean, what did they say? Stenson said I got into a lot of fights down there. Charlie Fromson stuck up for me and said it was the first fight I got into. That's all he said; then I had to go down in front of the mayor next morning. He said I would be sent to George Junior and all that stuff.

MIKE: I think that's what they all say.

BILL: You mean he said you were going to be sent to George Junior?

MIKE: What did you do? Did you have to go to Court or what?

WORKER: What was it about, this fight that you wanted to talk about? I mean what was the incident about?

DANNY: I think he wanted to express that not all adults pick on you. Like Charlie Fromson stuck up for him.

WORKER: Don't you think he has some other feelings about the fight?

MIKE: Well . . .

GARY: I should have found out for sure if that kid said anything about me, but still I don't know whether he did or not.

MIKE: Well, when the fight started I was there. I saw them. He came up and goes like that (*indicating shove*).

BILL: The kid grabbed him first.

MIKE: Then he went up to the kid and said, "I hear you can take it," and went like that there. I always do it in a joking way and that kid hit him and he fell down.

GARY: Flew up.

BILL: Flew up; then fell down.

MIKE: I mean, I don't think it was his fault.

WORKER: Do you believe that Gary wanted to talk about this fight to bring out the fact that Fromson stuck up for him, or knew about it and stuck up for him; or did Gary want to bring out the fact that he was involved in a situation which resulted in his being brought into Court, and that he doesn't really think that he was in the wrong or at fault in any way. What's he really trying to say?

DANNY: The cops are down there fighting each other and that, and adults always pick on us, and he was giving an example of an adult that didn't pick on him.

WORKER: Were there other things he wanted to bring up?

GARY: I don't want to bring anything up.

WORKER: How do you feel about what happened to you?

GARY: I feel sort of bad because I lost, and I lost my teeth and I got in trouble over it.

BILL: He wouldn't have felt too bad if he hadn't lost his teeth and the fight.

WORKER: What about the trouble over it?

GARY: I'm sort of worried about going to Court.

WORKER: When you look over this situation, what really happened?

MIKE: How did it start?

WORKER: How did it happen?

GARY: Bill Boyd came up to me and told me that redheaded kid was saying stuff about me. So, I went over there and asked what he was saying about me and we started pushing each other around and just "pow"; that's all that happened.

DANNY: Boyd is always trying to start trouble.

303

MIKE: I was going to say that.

BILL: What about the other kid?

MIKE: When somebody is picking on him, he doesn't like that too good. I think he would have stayed out of trouble if he would have first found out if that kid said them things instead of flying off the handle.

BILL: The kid hit him first. He didn't fly off the bat, the kid did.

DANNY: I just wouldn't have said anything about it. I pass things off like that all the time. If somebody wants to say something about me, I don't care, let them say it.

BILL: I think it's nicer to have them say it to your face.

DANNY: If they have enough guts.

BILL: Well, they shouldn't say it behind your back because sooner or later you're going to hear about it anyway . . .

DANNY: I suppose so.

BILL: What happened to the kid? Did he have to go to Court too?

GARY: No.

MIKE: Why not?

DANNY: He wasn't on probation.

MIKE: It was really that kid's fault, though.

GARY: He went in front of the mayor, that's all. We were just sitting in that office and the kid says to me he was going to say he started it, so I figured I was supposed to say so too. I went out of the room and the mayor talked to him and let him go. Then the mayor asked me if I started it, and that that kid told him he didn't so that left just me. Nice kid!

DANNY: Why admit something if you didn't do it?

GARY: It would have kept us both out of trouble.

MIKE: They would have known one of you started it.

GARY: How could they get it out of us?

MIKE: You shouldn't trust strangers like that. If he was willing to be blamed and you knew him pretty good and he said something like that . . .

BILL: If he was a friend.

MIKE: But, I mean a kid like that, if you get in a fight he is bound to snitch. He probably said that because he knew that he was going in first and then he could pin all the blame on you; and when you went in you just said "yeah" and that guy was a liar, that's what started all the trouble.

WORKER: When we look at things that happen to us, when we are involved, do you think that we see all the details of how this occurred?

MIKE: Sometimes, I think.

WORKER: Do you think Gary has seen all the details in what occurred?

GARY: Yes.

BILL: Yeah, more than we should.

GARY: Yeah, just don't trust anybody when they tell you something. Don't believe them.

DANNY: Do you know any reason why he was saying something about it?

GARY: He just wanted to see somebody get in a fight. I don't know whether that kid said it or not.

DANNY: That kid didn't have any reason to say anything about you. It made it look like you were looking for a fight. You should have asked if he said anything about you.

WORKER: From what's been said it appears to me that you feel that Gary was the one who was sort of made an example of in a situation. He was really a victim of circumstances because he didn't start the fight but got sent to Court because he was on probation.

MIKE: That's it.

WORKER: How do you feel about it, Gary?

GARY: Well, it's just that when you are on probation and you get in a fight or something like that, Winehart—he's a detective, just figures, well, he's probably the one that started it because we got a paper that says you been in a lot of fights. That's what sort of burnt me up.

WORKER: Was it really the other kid's fault that he hit you?

GARY: Both of us. I should have found out for sure whether he said it or not. I grabbed him first, so he probably had a right to defend himself.

BILL: He grabbed you too.

MIKE: When I seen you, he went up like this here, and I seen that kid—pow!

WORKER: In other words, Gary laid a hand on him first.

GARY: Yes. And from what you said when you were at my house, that means I started the fight, right? That's what you said.

BILL: You said he hit you first.

GARY: But I laid my hand on him first.

WORKER: Was there more to it than that?

GARY: What do you mean, was there more to it than that?

WORKER: Besides laying your hands on him. Was there any indication that you were going to assault him?

GARY: I didn't hit him. I grabbed him and went to push him away with my hand and *pow*, that's all there was to it.

WORKER: Could you show us?

GARY: Could I show you what?

WORKER: What happened.

GARY: The kid is not here right now.

MIKE: I'm just as good as that kid. I'll do it.

GARY: Yeah, I'll show you.

(Portion omitted)

WORKER: Why do you fellows believe that Gary wanted to talk about this?

DANNY: Because maybe he felt guilty about it and he didn't know for sure how you felt about it.

MIKE: He wanted to find out what your opinion was, and in case

305

it happens the next time maybe he'll find out what to do and what not to do.

WORKER: What do you think he felt guilty about?

GARY: I don't know, I felt in a way I sort of started the fight and I really don't feel guilty about anything.

MIKE: I think both of you started the fight.

GARY: In the first place, after he hit me I told him that was enough. You know we wouldn't have got caught if it wasn't for anything like that. He put on a big show; he jumped around the place.

MIKE: He hit you and you fell on the floor; then you went after him and hit him.

WORKER: How do you think that talking about this is going to help Gary?

GARY: I don't know. I already know what I should have done. We are not talking about anything that's going to help us and that's what we're here for.

MIKE: The only thing we've talked about is your fight.

GARY: My fight?

MIKE: Well, in case it happens to us, we'll know what to do.

BILL: If you get mad, you aren't going to think about it.

WORKER: Gary's comment that we aren't talking about things that are going to help us, can you say more about that?

GARY: It's not helping us any.

WORKER: Could I ask what we can talk about that's going to help us?

BILL: I don't know.

DANNY: I think we talked about that before and we just come up with the same thing.

GARY: It seems like every time we always end up talking about the teachers and the cops.

BILL: What are we going to talk about that's going to help us?

GARY: You mean stuff that nobody knows is in our minds? Is that helping you?

DANNY: Well, everybody gets their own ideas.

BILL: What is there to talk about that's going to help you?

GARY: I don't know.

DANNY: Do you feel that the cops are all wrong or . . .

GARY: No, I don't; I never said it.

MIKE: Well, you said some of them are.

DANNY: If we talk about why they do things, it will clear things up.

GARY: Yes, but is it helping us?

DANNY: Yes, it's clearing up your ideas. You get a better idea of why they do things.

WORKER: Is what Danny mentioned about talking about other people and not about ourselves, is that what you are doing here?

GARY: We are talking about other people more than we do ourselves. We are just talking about the teachers or the cops or some other people—some other adult or something like that.

WORKER: What did you think about what Danny said?

GARY: What did he say?

WORKER: Would you want to explain it further?

DANNY: Well, we all got our ideas about people and why we think they do things; like Charlie Fromson stuck up for Gary and Winehart tried to put him down. We tell why we think he stuck up for him and we talk about Winehart and why he did it.

WORKER: But before, you mentioned something about your own feelings and why we do the things we do; or were you talking about these other people in order to avoid talking about yourself?

DANNY: Well, I don't think anybody likes to cut theirselves up but I'm willing to admit my mistakes.

WORKER: It's not easy sometimes to talk about the things you have done yourself that you feel are in poor judgment. Sometimes it is difficult to talk about your own attitudes if you think they are different from other people's.

DANNY: I'm not ashamed or scared to contribute my ideas and things like that because I think everybody has their own ideas.

GARY: I haven't done anything since I went to Court that's on my mind to tell you.

DANNY: You said, "What are we doing in the community that these people have an outlook on us?" I don't see we are really old enough, but I mean all we can do now is just live and I guess help out and make it a better community. I mean we can participate in things and that, and that's about all we can do.

BILL: Help clean up, paint things up, like that? They make fun of the way we dress and comb our hair.

MIKE: No, they don't.

BILL: Yes, they do.

DANNY: Not all of them; they just aren't used to seeing guys like that.

MIKE: I mean there is some people that go too far.

GARY: Some people look good in some kinds of clothes and we don't; they expect us to wear those baggy old things they wear.

MIKE: I mean, I can see why some of them run down the teenagers, especially like that Wall kid whose hair is like a girl's.

BILL: So, that's the way he wants to wear it. What's wrong about that?

MIKE: I mean, it's okay with me; but some grownups see stuff like that and they think the rest of us are going to get the idea. I mean, they think that all of the kids are like that—that they are going to have their hair long, trying to get close to the prehistoric days.

WORKER: How do you fellows feel that the people in the community look at you?

GARY: Bums.

BILL: They think of us—because you wear long hair you can't afford a haircut.

DANNY: Well, some of them think it's just ridiculous because you don't look right.

307

BILL: If it's long, maybe that's the way you want to keep it. Why should they care; they're not wearing it?

(*The discussion continues and Gary tells that he resents the age limits for using a poolhall and that one can never please adults. Mike concludes that "you can't please anybody except yourself."*)

WORKER: All the things that you fellows are saying are sort of avoiding the point of how you really feel about yourselves. This has been brought up several times: how do you feel you fit in the community? Several of you have brought it up and we have made an effort to talk about it but it seems you are avoiding talking about yourselves. Why is this?

GARY: Maybe some of us don't want to talk about what we did wrong—don't feel it's anybody's business.

DANNY: When you say we avoid talking about ourselves, I mean, what do you mean "talk about ourselves"? I mean, do you want us to talk about our mistakes or how we feel about things or what, when you say talk about ourselves?

WORKER: What do you think you could talk about that would help you? When you are in a situation as some of those brought up, have things developed in a way that you hoped they would?

DANNY: I thought that's what we were talking about. When a situation comes up and things about what we do and what we didn't do. Is that what you mean about talking about ourselves?

WORKER: Yes, examining what you have done; how you reacted. Danny mentioned that the things we talked about aren't the things that were going to help us and we said we were going to talk about the things that would help us today. . . . I don't want to put you on the spot, you know, but could we ask you what you mean?

DANNY: We ought to do things that are going to help us to stay out of trouble until we get to an age where you can fit yourself into society, like, you can't just go out at sixteen years old and start up a business or be a manager of something. I mean, you are just a teenager now so you just have to live a teenager's life.

MIKE: What you are getting at is you want us to tell what we have done in our past years that we have done wrong and try to clear it out of the way.

WORKER: If that's what you want to bring up; but what Danny mentioned was that we aren't talking about things that are going to help us and I wonder if he would tell us what he really means by that.

DANNY: Things that are going to help us is stuff that is going to occupy our time so we can't be running around the streets. If we can find something to keep us busy—if we participate in a sport.

(The close of the session)

GARY: Like the other day, that kid with his girl, and we was sitting in The Greek's and this college kid came in with this girl and us guys glanced over and looked at her. He started swearing to beat hell.

"What are you guys looking at?" and he said worse words than that. And do you know who was kicked out? They kicked us guys out just because we turned around and looked at her, we just glanced at her and that college kid—I don't know who he thought he was. We ran his ass out the front door.

MIKE: What about the girl?

GARY: He ran way ahead of her.

WORKER: Well, it's about time for us to stop for today. . . . Do you feel that at that time we should maybe set down sort of clearly what we are going to do at these meetings in order that we may get some benefit from it?

GARY: Really, I don't know what we can do to get any benefit out of it. What are you going to say? Like next week, I don't think I'll be able to come.

WORKER: That's Christmas and New Year's. What do you want to do about it?

MIKE: Skip it because we are on vacation. "Brain Boy" over there will be working. He took my job. He'll be working and I think I'll be working too.

WORKER: The next meeting we'll have, what date will that be? The first Wednesday of the year . . .

GARY: January 5.

WORKER: Fifth of January. Okay. That sounds fine.

The essential elements were present which could have made this a meaningful experience for these boys who are on probation. The student is invited to analyze the record to determine what was lacking and what the worker might have done to capitalize on the positives in the group process. The record is included because what transpired is typical.

Sociobehavioral Practice[16]

Since this is a textbook primarily about method, I will not review the theoretical basis of reinforcement theory or operant conditioning. I will focus on a summary of the work which is cited. In it, the authors present the procedures for sociobehavioral practice in twelve steps which follow the general principles for behavioral modification.

The first step is to inventory the range of presenting problems of which the member is aware and the worker discerns. The next step is to select priorities and to decide which problem should be tackled first. This is engaged in by members and the worker or the group and the worker, and forms the basis for a contract. The negotiation for a contract agreement continues with the objective of gaining the members' or group's commitment to invest themselves in the treatment process, to cooperate by providing information, and by working. The fourth step is important and often missed by groupworkers. It calls for operationalizing the treatment goal by specifying the behaviors that are undesirable and which are to be changed, and to what they are to be changed. Obviously, diagnostic labels or vague and ambiguous terms, generalizations, or inferences are not useful in this procedure. Step five calls for quantifying the problem behaviors. Scales such as "very often, often, frequently, seldom, and never" must be made operational. For example, how often does the member do what he wants to change? The sixth step is crucial in any regimen of behavioral modification and it calls for an identification of the stimuli that precede and follow the problem behavior and seem to control its happening, when it happens, and how. This may be said to be a diagnostic step. Step seven seeks to assess the resources in the environment which may be useful in the behavioral modification. The eighth step is to set the treatment goals with specificity. Behaviors to be changed must be stated as to frequency, duration, intensity, quality, and context so that a plan can be made in the following step. That plan includes the role of the worker and the techniques to be employed. The plan now can be implemented, the effectiveness assessed and, where appropriate, modified. As in all change procedures, the last step is to stabilize the change. I do not propose to go into the techniques or to explicate the method as there are excellent books on the subject.[17]

I believe that the use of the sociobehavior techniques in groupwork is efficacious and for many members it is a preferable strategy. The group is an ideal medium for its use as it and the members are excellent instrumentalities for feedback and for reinforcement, and can provide the variety needed to educe new behaviors, i.e., shaping a milieu for extinguishing undesirable behavior.

Methods for Work with Groupings That Are Not Groups

Many readers of this book may work in hospitals, clinics, institutions, and similar settings with groupings of people who have very limited capacities to develop interpersonal relationships. Others may work with groupings of people who are not able to control themselves or invest themselves in a group and submit to group norms or expectations. Such workers face frustration and often criticize themselves for failing to be able to utilize groupwork methods, and they compare their groupings with groups about which they read in the literature. It is to these workers that I now address myself.

Many groupings that are formed in settings such as child guidance clinics or institutions for children with problems are not groups and may not become groups during the duration of their treatment. Various forms of group treatment can be used with success, but a worker should not expect to be able to use all of the principles of social groupwork or to develop a group that compares favorably with those that reach the intimacy stage in group therapy.

Some groupings achieve a *modus operandi* and function, but do not negotiate the task of basic trust, and consequently, the members do not reveal themselves. Their behaviors are filled with suspicion and their modes are superficial or provocative. Some groupings never reach a level where mutual aid is possible and one cannot hope to be able to use a method in which the group is the main therapeutic agent. There are some operating principles for working with such collectivities.

1. People who are together over a period of time become a social system. The relationship concepts that apply to social systems such as position, status, role, communication, norming, and so on apply to these groupings. They can be modified and this can influence behavior.

2. As in systems in general, feedback can be an effective medium. The method is to stimulate awareness and the major mode, feedback, which the worker must use. The worker observes and reports back on the behavior of the members. The feedback is universalized, that is, usually it is said to the group and not to individuals. The worker does not expect the members to respond verbally. He does not ask them to speculate on deep causes of behavior. He does not feed back to confront, embarrass, punish, or disapprove. His intention is to help everyone to be aware of the behavior.

The worker relates behavior to personal needs, desires, and goals, and does not interpret behavior in the classical meaning of the term. Part of his methodology is to teach the members to observe and compare behavior and to help them control themselves, learn new ways to meet needs, and see that their old habit patterns are nonfunctional. These methods usually are not applied in formal, verbal meetings, but the grouping is fed the observations while engaged in program activities either as a group or when the members are scattered about the room engrossed in their own pursuits.

These methods apply also in the physical therapy session, in the lounge or day room, in occupational therapy and similar places; for example:

WORKER: What is Joe doing?
A PATIENT: Wiping his nose.

WORKER: Joe is wiping his hand on his pants.

ANOTHER PATIENT: Wiping snot on his pants.

WORKER: Why would anybody do that?

FIRST PATIENT: Got no rag.

WORKER: Joe is wiping his hand on his pants because he has no handkerchief. Where could he get a handkerchief?

THIRD PATIENT: The nurse.

WORKER: If you want a handkerchief you ask a nurse. (*Joe rises and shuffles off to the nurses' station.*)

3. In groupings, all of the principles of reinforcement apply; however, the worker is the more important reinforcer. The worker reinforces through meeting needs and extinguishes through the withholding of rewards.

4. The group sessions are both a milieu and an experience. The worker structures the experience and sets the climate.[18]

5. People with weak superegos and self-controls learn by internalizing the prohibitions of good or loving parents. Members of groupings cannot develop or incorporate parent figures or internal limits if none exist; therefore, the worker must be the surrogate to incorporate, and provide the external limits if superegos are to develop.

6. The worker must demonstrate and, by so doing, teach what a human relationship is and also how people behave, i.e., how they act toward others and themselves. The worker not only enacts these scripts but also verbalizes them.

7. In groupings that are not groups, the worker must be active; he is the therapeutic agent but he does not dominate, exploit, or manipulate. His focus is not on himself and he is not motivated so as to behave to meet his own needs, but his focus is on doing and saying what will help the members. However, he is the central figure. Everything that he does is designed to help the members form a group, to learn to relate sufficiently to others so as to be able to become a group.

This discussion should not be confused with the first stage of any group—the stage of pregroup affiliation where people are jockeying about to find a basis for trust. In this section, I am talking about people who are unable to relate or who have little capacity for self-control. These are people who have been too hurt or too deprived to see anything to be gained by relating to anyone, or who anticipate no rewards in meeting any social expectations. They definitely can be helped through a group experience, but they are not ready for groupwork based upon the mutual-aid group as the treatment medium; hence the method differs from the general model which is presented in this book.

NOTES / READINGS

1. William Schwartz, "The Social Worker in the Group," *Social Welfare Forum* (New York: Columbia University Press, 1961).

2. William Schwartz, "Toward a Strategy of Group Work Practice," *Social Service Review*, Vol. XXXVI, No. 3 (September, 1962), p. 277.

3. Robert D. Vinter, "Small-Group Theory and Research: Implications for Group Work Practice Theory and Research" in *Social Science Theory and Social Work Research*, Leonard S. Kogan, ed. (New York: National Association of Social Workers, 1960), pp. 123–34.

4. William Schwartz, "The Social Worker in the Group" in *New Perspectives on Services to Groups: Theory, Organization, Practice* (New York: National Association of Social Workers [for National Conference on Social Welfare], 1961), pp. 7–17.

5. Emanuel Tropp, "The Group: In Life and in Social Work" in *Social Casework* (New York: Family Service Association of America, May, 1968), pp. 267–274.

6. In *The Practice of Group Work*, edited by William Schwartz and Serapio R. Zalba (New York: Columbia University Press, 1971), Schwartz seems to have moderated this position. Credence is given to the acts of the worker.

7. Records which illustrate this method can be found in Lawrence Shulman, *Casebook in Social Work with Groups* (New York: Council on Social Work Education, 1968).

8. Eric Berne, *Principles of Group Treatment* (New York: Oxford Press, 1966).

9. Eric Berne, *Games People Play* (New York: Grove Press, 1964).

10. Louis S. Cholden, *A Psychiatrist Works with Blindness* (New York: American Foundation for the Blind, 1967), p. 39.

11. See: Saul Bernstein, *Youth in the Streets* (New York: Association Press, 1964).

12. Betty Luther, "Group Service Programs and Their Effect on Delinquents" in *Individual and Group Services in the Mobilization for Youth Experience*, edited by Harold H. Weissman (New York: Association Press, 1969), p. 134.

13. Howard W. Polsky, *Cottage Six* (New York: Russell Sage, 1962).

14. Ralph Fertig, Fritz Mosher, and John Gandy, "Report on the Hyde Park Youth Project," Chicago, May, 1957. (Mimeographed.)

15. Luther, "Group Service Programs."

16. We acknowledge a debt to Professor Edwin J. Thomas and also to Eileen D. Gambill, Edwin J. Thomas, and Robert D. Carter, "Procedure for Sociobehavioral Practice in Open Settings," *Social Work*, Vol. XVI, No. 1 (January, 1971), pp. 51–62.

17. Albert Bandura, *Principles of Behavior Modification* (New York: Holt, Rinehart & Winston, 1969).

Edwin J. Thomas, ed., *The Socio-Behavioral Approach and Applications to Social Work* (New York: Council on Social Work Education, 1967).

18. Sallie Churchill, "Pre-Structuring Group Content," *Social Work* (July, 1959), pp. 52–59.

13

❖❖❖❖❖❖❖❖

The Agency Intake Process

Up to now, we have been talking primarily about the use of groups for the purposes of promoting the growth of the members and to facilitate improved social functioning. In the preceding chapters, group methods within the group itself have been described. These methods apply to groups in social work settings, in treatment settings wherein social work is a guest in a host agency, and also to the traditional group-services agency.

The group-services agency is usually a multiservice setting and there are aspects of its functions which differ from other social agencies. There are additional dimensions also which, although they are not strictly speaking social groupwork, are vital to the groupwork program. We turn now to a discussion of some of these important areas. There will be no attempt to include all of the multiple functions of a group service, but rather to deal with those which have not been given much attention in the literature recently.

The Intake Process

There are major differences between a treatment setting and a traditional group-services agency. When a person comes to or is brought to a treatment facility, a request is made to alleviate symptoms which have manifested themselves; the applicant at a group-services agency usually applies for recreation or club activities and does not ask to be given treatment or to have his behavior changed. In a casework service or a treatment agency utilizing group services, intake is regarded as an integral part of the treatment process. Skilled workers are employed to fulfill this function and no client who comes to the agency meets another member of the professional staff until he has been seen at intake. The intake process is not regarded as registration and it is not handled by a clerk. Intake, as part of the process of helping, has not been used in the same fashion by the group-services agency. Sporadic attempts have been made to do so, a few agencies do use it conscientiously and others make the gesture but, by and large, the intake process has not been developed as part of the service. This is unfortunate because the purpose of the agency should be stated clearly at intake and the negotiation of the contract begun there. We have seen in the previous discussion of composition and grouping that the determinants of who goes into which group should be ascertained before the group is formed. This information is obtainable through intake.

Earlier, we discussed the intake of persons into the group: here we are discussing intake into the service. Every person has the right to be treated as an individual and to be respected as a person when he seeks social services. His introduction into the agency begins when he first encounters it while waiting to receive the personal attention of a member of the staff. He brings universal needs into the agency with him, and he also brings the dominant needs which are unique to him, that is, he brings his total life experience which is different from that of anyone else. If his special needs and interests are to be met through the resources of the agency, they must be assessed consciously and systematically. The intake process itself must be responsive to this person and the worker must "tune in" and listen.

The stance of the agency immediately becomes apparent to him, whether personal or impersonal, person-centered or self-centered, responsive or impinging, giving or taking, flexible or rigid, free or controlling, trustworthy or to be approached with caution. This entry point is the beginning of the establishment of trust and the development of relationship; and because it is so crucial, intake should be done by a highly skilled staff member.

In the group-services agency the introduction of members into the program is predicated upon interest. At the outset this is generally an overt or expressed interest. Often people really do not know what they want; their horizons are limited and they want only what they know about. Their selection of activities may be inappropriate or not responsive to their need if it is based upon superficial criteria for choice. Sometimes people would like to try something new with which they may not be familiar, but new things are risky and provoke anxiety. They challenge one's safety, expose one to the possibilities of failure, and they may threaten one's most important life supports or needs. In order to be able to venture, the applicant must be able to talk about the possibilities, explore options, obtain support, and test the trustworthiness of the environment.

Interest cannot be considered without reference to basic and often unconscious need. A feeling of inadequacy about a particular activity, for example, can be coupled with doubts about one's masculinity or femininity, and a fear of being stripped, shamed, or ridiculed. Interests reveal personality characteristics or learned fears and hence disclose need priorities for reassurance and support. The selection or rejection of a particular activity provides useful knowledge about the person and such knowledge forms the basis for grouping and for the utilization of program media. One usually thinks of intake as being conducted through interview and as a verbal interchange, but it is also appropriate for intake in group services to go beyond this and to be carried on consciously by observation and study in the lounge, games room, or the short-term group formed for just such a purpose.

Many applicants for service have not thought out why they want to become members or what they really want from the agency or association. A need for friends or to belong undoubtedly may lie beneath the desire to join a group, a craft class, a team, or other activity. The desire to learn to dance may be rooted in the need for association with the opposite sex. It is axiomatic that if a person's real interest or reason for asking for service is not met, he will reflect it in his behavior, or he may leave.

There is one large national youth-serving agency, for example, which has found that, on the average, members retain membership for only one year, and another for two years. Need-meeting is the crux of personality growth and social education. Group-services agencies cannot afford to be haphazard about the needs and interests of members. Social injury may result whenever members are served by trial and error methods, and time and money may be risked in such planless operations. The prime principle here is that the social service through group process begins at intake. Some who come for service seek it with anxiety, fear, ambivalence, a sense of anticipated rejection or interpersonal shortcomings. They find it difficult to present themselves directly into a group or an activity and hence are lost between registration and the door leading to the activity. Such people need help and support to enter and the giving of this support is partially the function of intake.

The agency must be personalized. The agency may appear to be cold and impersonal to many people who need it the most, but when such a person meets a staff member who is warm, friendly, concerned and understanding, he can begin to cope with his feelings.

Meaningful relationships begin at intake, for it is through the intake worker initially that the agency communicates its sensitivity to the person's needs and its willingness to help. One of the important aspects of intake in casework is that the intake process is, in a sense, a sample of what the applicant may expect in subsequent interviews. This is not as true in groupwork, but it is possible for intake to be a sample of the helping process and agency function which differentiates it from a solely recreation program. Security for the applicant grows from knowing at least one staff member who is a symbol of helpfulness. The enabling process begins at intake and the channel for help is opened here.

Group-services agencies do not always interpret their function and purposes to an applicant but a new member is entitled to know the ideological bias and the cultural values within which he will be expected to operate. A failure to interpret the agency may result in a resistance to it at a later date, unreadiness to grow within it, and the feeling that one has been duped. The initial stage in the helping process must begin at intake within an atmosphere of freedom which encourages self-determination. The agency is obliged to interpret its function and policies in order to help the member to organize himself to articulate with the agency or to withdraw. Self-determination for the member is predicated on known options and it is at intake that the agency tells the applicant what it has to offer.

Whether only this part or all parts are handled in one session at the point of initial contact is for each agency to decide. There is no prescription which dictates that intake be restricted to one interview. Sound practice may indicate the contrary. A further step in interpretation of function is related to whether this agency and its services are for this applicant. It may not be what he wants or needs, he may not be ready to use it effectively, or the agency may not be ready or able to provide what he needs or wants. There may be other agencies or services that are more suitable for him. Few, if any, agencies can be all things to all people and, if a service is to be really meaningful, its focus must be sharper than universality and more specific than that of a service geared to a broad range of normality.

Many people are not ready for a group experience and will not profit from it. Many are unable to face sharing, surrendering some personal autonomy for the good of a group, or revealing themselves. Some may be seeking therapy or have personal needs that are more than the agency can meet. On the other hand, some people are contagion carriers and can infect others who are emotionally susceptible. The intake process makes it possible for the applicant to choose the service and for the agency to indicate that it is or is not the proper one for the individual. The agency may not accept every applicant for service. This calls for skillful interpretation and the agency has a responsibility to those it cannot accept. There may be situations wherein persons will be engaged in intake for some time or be seen several times in order to work this through. For some people, it may mean referral to a more useful service, such as counseling, and for others it may mean acquainting them with community resources such as public recreation programs or adult education classes.

It follows that an agency must have clarity of purpose and a precise concept of function. It is inherent that these functions and purposes be clear in order to guide method and concomitantly to utilize personnel appropriately. Group-services agencies are not in the business of serving the recreational needs of the community. While members have options, make choices, and are helped to achieve their goals, agencies are not to be expected to deal with all needs, all interests, or all people. The service is bounded by the function of the agency and it is within that function that members can be self-determining. Agencies must limit function and thereby delimit their clientele and define their services, and through intake proceed to do their unique job by serving their members well. Group services will never justify themselves unless they demonstrate clarity of function and of boundaries so that they can perform competently and do what is required of them. Some people seem to feel that group-services agencies do and should serve anyone who comes and in the way each one wishes. Such a premise, if followed to its logical conlusion, reduces the quality of service and does not ensure specific help to the members. An agency must have a stance so that agency and members may have a basis for transaction.

Careful intake procedures help an agency to know who its members are and thereby provides the data for over-all program design. Such data can help the staff devise new programs, eliminate some and modify others. This evaluative procedure should be repeated regularly in order to keep the service vital and flexible. It also provides some of the information which is necessary for policy-making. Careful analysis of composite information secured through intake is useful also for planning staff training.

Social service through group process begins at intake. No one learns a great deal about a person in an interview or two, but a worker can certainly gain valuable understanding of social functioning by observing the behavior of an applicant at intake. The provision for an adequate intake procedure is an administrative function and the administration must provide the setup, space, and staff time to do it. However, if intake is unrelated to the program, if it is not recorded adequately, and if there is no follow-up, it can be only partially effective. The data must be relayed to the staff to be used by them.

A Suggested Procedure for Intake in a Group-Services Agency

No suggested procedure can be assumed to apply to all agencies. This outline is for the purpose of illustrating the principles discussed above.

A new applicant usually is seen first by a receptionist. A temporary membership card can be issued at this time and there may be a discussion of the available activities, time schedule, fees, and how one locates things in the agency in order to provide a beginning sense of security and belonging. Some agencies tend to confuse what the receptionist or membership secretary does with intake, but usually most of what is done at the outset is registration, and this is a clerical operation which involves the filling out of an application, payment of fees, and congenial conversation. An intake worker should be highly skilled, with special training for the job, but in many settings the membership workers have no training for intake, are clerical workers and may be volunteers.

If it is considered feasible or useful, the applicant may be given a tour of the facilities with some interpretation of what is or will be going on in the rooms. It is suggested that the filling in of long forms, interest finders, and face-sheet data come much later in the process, perhaps after the applicant has had an opportunity to use his temporary card once or twice, but, of course, this may not be appropriate in all instances. The next step would be the intake interview itself, conducted by either a person who has that as his main function or by a member of the staff of the appropriate division.

The intake worker explores feelings, reasons for wanting to join, readiness to participate, interests, friends, and experience. He observes carefully the applicant's posture, ease, seeming anxieties and fears, strengths and skills, defenses, mannerisms, and modes of adaptation in an interpersonal interchange. It is quite important to gain some impression of the applicant's self-image and his hopes and aspirations. The success of an intake interview lies in how much understanding of the person a worker can gain through the process. It is not necessary or desirable to ply the person with questions because if a worker establishes an atmosphere of warmth and acceptance, and can be at ease, the applicant can be encouraged to relax and talk naturally. More can be learned by allowing the applicant the freedom to express himself than by interrogating him. The worker must, of course, observe carefully, and skillfully guide the interview with a minimum of direct questioning.

The worker interprets the agency function and philosophy on the basis of the interview, and a tentative program for the applicant may be drawn up. The initial intake session may take a half hour or more; it may be broken into two sessions with a trip between, or it can be on different days. At this time, the applicant may be given an enrollment slip for each activity he selects to support him to attend it as his right, or an arrangement may be made for him to come to the membership office and be escorted to the activity, and be introduced to the worker in the group. This may be supplemented by observing the new member in a lounge or games room, at a party, in a trial visit to a class, or in a short-term trial group.

Beyond identifying data, forms need not be filled in until some time has been spent in exploration and discussion. By this time, a relationship has begun to be established. The applicant is beginning to feel that the intake worker is interested in him and is there to help him. Much of the face-sheet data will already have been volunteered in the general discussions and the applicant will not have been tensed up by a battery of questions or questionnaires. If questions are personal, they are resisted strongly; enough can be observed and discussed to serve the purposes of intake, and to begin individualization through the methods which we have been describing. The opportunity to interpret the agency function in more detail and to begin a contract comes when the applicant begins to ask questions.

It is doubtful that an applicant, even though adult, should be handed any form to complete himself. It is significant that he be involved in his becoming a member but, to that end, questions should be factual and nonthreatening. Experience seems to confirm that interest finders completed by applicants are almost useless, and questions that ask "why" produce cliché answers. Forms which are used as schedules for an interview with open-ended questions seem to be more productive. Material which deals with feelings, needs, or other emotionally charged matter may be better left to be recorded after the applicant leaves, and only factual data committed to writing in his presence. The record should contain an analysis which can be used by the professional staff. This should include observation of significant behavior during the interview, estimated risk if any, suggested program based upon needs and interests, estimates of adjustment and predicted role, prognosis, and also a plan for follow-up.

There are ways to decrease dropping out between intake and entrance into the program and although this is not specifically part of intake procedure, a few will be mentioned. One can use an intake committee of members who call applicants and conduct them individually into the program, help them feel at home, and give them an initial bridge into the agency. There can be home visits to younger members, introductions to staff and members by the intake worker, follow-up interviews after the first few experiences to discuss and resolve any difficulties. One can assign a staff member to follow up an applicant so as to be sure he has found the program he wants, and also it is recommended that a record be kept of dropouts from activities as soon as they occur to permit an immediate contact to find out why. The new-member banquet or meeting is used by some associations but it may threaten shy members beyond endurance.

One method of facilitating the use of intake records is to file them by date in a current drawer and require that staff members initial them within a specified period of time to indicate that they have read them. A refinement on this is to require that staff members add comments on the file monthly to indicate that the applicant has been followed, to test the accuracy of the prognosis, to record what has happened with him, and to note progress. In this way the staff can operate as a team and follow a consistent approach. This also ensures that no one falls between the supports, and allows for a procedure for staff consultation when indicated. Another less elaborate system is to send summaries of the intake record to staff members concerned. Club leaders should not be expected to collect face-sheet data again. Such a procedure weakens the relationship instead of strengthening it.

There are some practitioners who will object to these intake procedures because they are time-consuming. Whether intake is more time-consuming than a hit-or-miss approach to our work has not been researched. However, time and again, groups may be at a standstill, movement of individuals retarded, and time wasted in redoing what was first done on a guess. Such problems might have been avoided if intake had been done properly. Wastage in turnover and dropouts alone would justify the investment in intake. When service to an individual in unplanned and unscientific, it tends to take more time than when there is methodical preparation.

Some agencies that function seasonally find it worthwhile to spend the first few weeks on careful intake even before planning the administrative setup for opening. Often program design can be altered better to fit the clientele.

It must be restated that intake without clear definition of agency function is only half effective. It should be clear that the intake worker is not a salesman for the agency. He is a helping person who uses special skills, accepts the applicant, assesses his needs and, with some understanding of his motivations, help him to plan a program so that he may have the most useful and appropriate service and may use it most appropriately.

NOTES / READINGS

Sallie Churchill, "The Use of Social Group Work Method as a Diagnostic Tool in Interdisciplinary Evaluation of a Disturbed Child," *American Journal of Orthopsychiatry*, Vol. 35 (1965), pp. 581–588.

Helen Northen, *Social Work with Groups* (New York: Columbia University Press, 1969), pp. 86–115.

Helen H. Perlman, "Intake and Some Role Considerations," *Social Casework*, Vol. 41 (April, 1960), pp. 171–177.

Aaron Rosenblatt, "The Application of Role Concepts to the Intake Process," *Social Casework*, Vol. 43 (January, 1962), pp. 8–14.

Frances H. Scherz, "Intake: Concept and Process," *Social Casework*, Vol. 33 (June, 1952), pp. 233–240.

Phyllis Rolfe Silverman, "A Re-examination of the Intake Procedure," *Social Casework*, Vol. 51 (December, 1970), pp. 625–634.

Frances B. Stark, "Barriers to Client-Worker Communication at Intake," *Social Casework*, Vol. 40 (April, 1959), pp. 177–183.

14

❖❖❖❖❖❖❖❖❖

The Task-Oriented Group

The task-oriented group is one in which the achievement of a group product or decision is the important objective and this supersedes the growth of the members. The group usually forms around tasks rather than interpersonal relations. It is often time-limited, the members often are appointed or elected, and it is formed generally for a specific function or charge. Task groups that predominate in group services are committees, councils, boards, neighborhood or block clubs, and the like. Committees, councils, and neighborhood or block clubs will be discussed in this chapter, but policy-making boards will not as they are a part of administration.

Committees

The groupworker with his understanding of group process and his skills is called upon constantly to work with committees. A committee is a group and, as such, provides a group experience for its members, but it is a group which is formed to accomplish a charge; it is a task-oriented group. A groupworker does not work in the same way with a committee as he does with a growth-oriented group. I have defined task orientation to mean the achievement of a goal that is external to the growth or the enhancement of the social functioning of the members. A treatment group has a task to be sure, that of helping the members to get well or to find themselves, but this is not a job on behalf of an organization. It has been written that a friendship or natural group in a youth-serving agency, where the purpose is developmental, requires tasks to focus the efforts of

323

the members. I agree, but here the presence of a task is a means to an end, the end being the fulfillment of the members.

Committees are an integral part of organizational life and have been studied by several disciplines, but little has been written about the group process in a committee or about the function of a group-worker in committee work.[1] The primary emphasis in the literature has been on the committee as part of administration. However, a groupworker works differently to implement the function of the agency in serving the members than he does with policy-making bodies where he acts as a resource, an administrative assistant, and as a clerical aide in the meeting. In the case of the administrative committee, the worker fulfills his function through his participation in the administrative process. In an effectively administered agency, he is involved in staff deliberations, is party to the formulation of policy through channels of communication within the administrative structure, and is part of the process of drafting policy by passing on his knowledge and expertise to the policy-making bodies. When he works with such bodies he is part of the circulatory process by which direction flows downward and experience and information flow upward in helping to determine policy. In this functioning, the groupworker is not practicing groupwork but is an extension of administration.

At the service level, the worker is required to carry out policy through program. As a groupworker, he is not part of the formulation of policy with member committees in the same way as when he functions as a part of the ongoing administration of the agency. With the former he is a social worker, an educator, or group counselor, with agency functions and goals, and professional obligations to fulfill to the members. The writings of the authorities in this field are neither clear nor sharp on the distinctions, and when discussed under headings such as "Work with Committees," the differences in worker involvement usually are left to the reader to clarify. The function of the groupworker with committees is clouded also in the writings by an anticipated conflict between the committee chairman and the groupworker. Since their functions and roles usually are defined poorly and seen to overlap at many points, it is implied that the worker may find it difficult to know when and how to move. I hold that these positions are complementary and the roles are reciprocal.

If the chairman of a committee is competent and skilled, and operates within agency function and policy, the role requirement for a groupworker is minimal. The position of a chairman is a function of the group, and he is part of the group and its structure, but not so with the groupworker. The groupworker is within the social system but he is not a member of the group. The two work together toward common goals, the groupworker performing the function of enabler so that the group and the chairman can fulfill their responsibilities and achieve the committee task. Where the chairman and the worker understand their respective functions and the expectations each has for the other, the situation is ideal and works very well. This mutual understanding and its sanction by the committee group should be part of the contract.

As a complementary functionary, the worker uses himself as a group leader only to the extent that there is need; that is, if the chairman is not functioning or no other member is performing the leadership role. However, the worker's primary obligation is to help the chairman and the members to perform their roles. If they do not, the worker acts only to prevent the committee from floundering, or prevent the possibility of the task achievement being thwarted while he teaches the chairman and members how to conduct themselves in their roles. The chairman should stimulate interaction that will serve to unite the group and help the members to work together as a unit; he should help the committee understand the charge, be committed to its goals, and develop stratagems for carrying out the task; he should help to develop a climate of satisfaction in working together on the task, and pleasure in each other's company; he should help the members listen to and appreciate each other's contributions; he should help the members participate and express themselves; he should help in the structuring and timing of the work through assignments, delegation, and accountability, that is, he should help to organize the work. The chairman also should help the committee to evaluate its progress and achievement. It is the worker's job to complement the chairman and help him to carry out these duties. A groupworker carries a chairman's duties only when this is necessary to the enterprise. Obviously, he has the function of training the chairman in the sessions as well as outside of the meetings.

With member committees, it is clear that the chairmanship duty is to conduct the meeting so that the committee accomplishes its purpose in the most effective manner possible. The worker may question, stimulate, be a resource, and help the committee to evaluate its decisions and assess its operation. The chairman is not a tool or a puppet; he is a partner, and the two must work together to carry out the job.[2] Therefore, the worker does not usurp the chairman's position or role, but strengthens or weakens his own leadership in inverse relationship to the chairman's ability to fulfill the chairmanship responsibilities.

Social agencies, associations, schools, and similar settings utilize committees for specific purposes related to carrying out the function of the social institution, its philosophy, and its policy. Such committees are brought into being to carry out a special job, to provide a training ground for committee work, to provide for member involvement in policy-making and program-planning, and to provide an ongoing group experience related to the objectives of the agency. Committees generally should be used to get a job done, and that goal has a higher priority than any other. The practice of using committees to provide a social groupwork experience, to meet a member's needs, or for treatment is not sound in either youth-serving agencies or in the usual group-services setting. It is viable in institutional settings, residential treatment setting, correctional centers and the like but, and this is an important *but*, for circumscribed purposes only. Such committees are useful to offset the institutionalization that these settings foster, to counteract dependency, and to afford the members an opportunity to feel that they have some control over their environment and their lives. The important point to be recognized is that the assigned task may not be fulfilled well, or it may be postponed in the interest of the growth experience it provides, whereas a true committee, by definition, is a social invention for getting a job done. Committees are work groups in which persons pursue a course of collective thinking toward creative action. I contend that a group task is only a means to an end in growth groups and treatment groups, whereas in a committee, the end is the job to be done and the committee is the means. Committees that are used, therefore, as part of program-planning are supplementary to the treatment aspects or the group-counseling. While no hard-and-fast line can be drawn dividing these distinctions, I hold that committees are different from growth or treatment groups. This does not imply that in committees there is a disregard for human values, personality growth, or a denial of social objectives, but it places a different emphasis or priority on a worker's method in working with a committee as contrasted with working with other groups wherein the timing and program can be varied to meet the interests and the needs of the group members.

Committees should be constituted only when the job to be done can be accomplished best through group thinking and cooperative action. If the job to be done is central to the purpose of the committee and its other goals are dependent on that one, it becomes obvious that the job must be done or all else fails. If, for example, a teenage planning committee is to plan and run a social and it fails to carry it off, the benefits of the committee to the entire membership are in doubt, the teenage group at large suffers, and little has been accomplished. Purpose, therefore, whether growth, treatment, or task accomplishment, determines the approach. When working with a committee, the worker allows opportunities for treatment to pass in the interest of the achievement of the task.

Jennings has helped to clarify the differences between the group which is bonded for interpersonal reasons and the group where the focus for being together is a task which is external to the social functioning of the members.[3] She uses the term psyche to describe the first type of group and socio for the latter. A group that is organized primarily for growth or interpersonal relations is a psychegroup. The medium in this group is intimacy or relationship while in the sociogroup it is the problem or the job. In the psychegroup, the members talk privately and in confidence—they reveal themselves—but the sociogroup is geared to its job and hence it limits discussion about personal problems and is not private or confidential because it is responsible or accountable to its main body. The psychegroup is concerned with problems that involve the members deeply in respect to interpersonal relationships, happiness, and social adequacy with emphasis on one's role performance and the emotional satisfaction of need. The sociogroup is concerned with the needs of the total organization of which it is a part, and the tangible results of action. The psychegroup does not function within a set agenda or an inflexible charge; the sociogroup must function within its instructions and job assignment since failure or success is objectively demonstrable. The psychegroup is less diverse in background and objective, and so communication is easier than in a sociogroup where the members are not chosen for homogeneity of psychological predispositions.

Different kinds of needs are dealt with in these different types of groups. All persons must have psychegroup experience somewhere in their lives or they will endeavor to utilize sociogroup experiences to fulfill those needs to the detriment of the task achievement and often to the impairment of the other members. Sociogroups develop hierarchical structures which may be productive but are not necessarily healthful or nutritious for the members. On the other hand, sociogroups are said to be more productive and efficient when the basic human needs of the members are met. In any social situation, people perform better if their needs such as acceptance, recognition, security, and the like are being met in that environment. Maslow holds that these fundamental needs must be satisfied before a person can be creative and self-actualizing and, therefore, in the context of a committee, the meeting of the basic needs of the members is to facilitate their performance in that committee in order for it to fulfill its task.[4] Admittedly, the distinction being made is a matter of degree and emphasis, but it is important nonetheless.

A person can perform on a committee at an intellectual level, with constricted *affect,* and with formalized interpersonal relationships, not needing to reveal himself or to be concerned with feelings. One could even suggest that reliance on feelings, a self-centered use of the committee to meet one's own needs, or too friendly a social atmosphere could block the committee process.

Committee morale is not as much a matter of individual need-meeting as it is an agreement on explicit goals, agreement that its leadership can help the committee achieve its task, and agreement that the means employed will achieve the ends. In this context, an individual's needs are often sacrificed. A semantic problem arises in the way the word need is defined. Basic needs that are essential for health and growth may not be synonymous with learned needs, acquired needs, or social needs. Moreover, neurotic needs can also operate to keep people at jobs that thwart their growth and development. As a general rule, it is believed that people flee from social situations where their basic needs are not met. As a matter of fact, this is far from being universally true. Once again, not all groups are good for their members, not all group experiences are growth-producing, and not all efficient organizations meet the needs of their human components.[5]

Where a committee is formed by a worker or an agency as a medium for groupwork and not as a work group that must complete a job within a time limit and be held accountable for it, or where the job to be done is considered secondary to the personal development of the committee members, there is little difference between a committee or a club in an agency, and hence little difference in the method a groupworker uses. There are minor differences such as: a charge to the committee is substituted for a group goal and the committee has to make the charge its goal, the committee is accountable to the main body while a club group is accountable to itself alone, success or failure is more easily evaluated in a committee than in a group, and a committee may be legitimately smaller or larger than a growth or treatment group. I do not recommend that committees be employed as psychegroups or that workers endeavor to develop them into psychegroups. I do not regard intimacy as one of the elements of a task-oriented group. The effort spent on solving personal problems in a committee takes away from the time and energy which should go into the committee work. Self-revelation and self-seeking in a committee are blocks to committee function.

It must be restated here that functional social behavior depends upon the fulfillment of basic human needs; that it is the concern of the chairman and the worker to see that these needs of the members are not frustrated, and that the structure and the impinging environment of the committee provide for the meeting of the basic needs of the members. However, in working with a committee, the concern of the worker is with the personal needs of the members only as they are related to the proper operation of the committee and the achievement of the goal of the committee. If the work of the committee can be facilitated only by meeting a member's abnormal needs, the worker may address himself to it. Anxieties, fears, unresolved psychic conflicts, or personal hangups often may have to be dealt with to free a member so that he can function effectively on the committee. Helping the group to resolve conflicts, guiding interaction, and creating harmony are related primarily to the committee job and to the accomplishment of its goals.

Where the job to be done is paramount and the group members' emotional development is secondary, the functions of the worker are as follows:

In a committee, the task is assigned, and the worker helps the group know what the task is and to select appropriate ways to carry it out. The bond in a committee is based on a commitment to the task, hence the worker does not encourage ingroup feeling but instead he facilitates the transfer of loyalty to the entire group of which the committee is a part. The committee is a subgroup and should not be a clique which sets itself off and away from the parent organization. Satisfaction should come from doing a good job in relation to the function and goals of the entire project and operation. Group-member committees are not formed to serve themselves and, although they may do their own job well, they still can be out of alignment with the operation of the organization. It is the function of the worker to help them adjust any mismatching that may occur between committees and their parent bodies.

It is possible now to generalize as a proposition much of what has been said above. The worker's function with a committee is to help the members to fashion a system that is efficient and effective for accomplishing the committee assignment. This means, of course, the development of structure, processes, and function. In this context, then, the worker focuses on relationships within a social system; he is working with the system and not with the individual members. The system which he helps to develop and to function is designed to produce. If a committee operates effectively and progress toward its objectives is good, the members will receive basic satisfactions which come with accomplishment. The worker is aware of what committee success means to the members and what motivates them to work.

Unlike a friendship group or many treatment groups, a committee has time limits, and the worker helps it to organize, structure itself, and set priorities in order to be efficient and to complete the job as required. A committee must be helped to accept its imposed goal or to seek a readjustment of it from the main body of which it is part, since it may not alter unilaterally the charge to it. The worker helps the committee, which is not autonomous, to function within the principle of the delegation of authority and to limit itself to its authority, to accept its accountability, and to report back. Policy-making or executive committees have more leeway in defining their own goals but they must operate within a framework of sanction and remain accountable also.

A committee does not have the right to appropriate funds for its own use or pleasure. A program committee which has run a series of successful parties for the entire membership may not decide to give itself a dinner out of club funds as a reward for its hard work. A committee works on behalf of its organization and not for itself, and the funds belong to the club. The worker helps the committee to gain status for its contribution and this facilitates its progress.

While members must gain satisfaction and enjoy working on a committee, and the meetings should not be dull or boring, the atmosphere should be that of a work session. There is less need here for cycles of release or relief from tension than there is in a treatment group, and no need for play as there is in a development group. The worker helps the chairman draft the agenda, plan and carry out the meeting, and together they constitute a team. The worker gives administrative help with securing and setting up the room, the meeting time, the sending of notices, and the like. He and the chairman set the atmosphere which provides a tone for the committee that is warm and friendly but also conveys the understanding that there is work to be done. The atmosphere which is set should make it possible for the members to feel free to speak and work together. In committees, as in other groups, basic trust, autonomy, and purpose must be resolved before the committee is able to function most efficaciously. However, the degree of trust is not comparable to that required in a treatment group where members are to reveal themselves, nor is the battle for autonomy as crucial, although committees do resist superimposition and domination. Initiative and concomitant purpose are crucial issues and must be achieved if a committee is to be free to be creative and innovative in thinking collectively.

The chairman, if there is one, defines the purpose of the group, but if no chairman has been selected, the worker defines the purpose. When committees fail, often it is because they were not clear as to their purpose or function. Here is an excerpt from a record which illustrates the way a worker performs.

As the worker, I called the meeting together and outlined the purpose of the committee. I indicated that this was a planning committee set up to plan a program for the Young-Adult Department for Friday nights. I told them that the committee was responsible to the Young-Adult Council and, therefore, had to work within its policies as well as the policies of this Y. I outlined the areas which we would be discussing; namely, the types of programs, dates, and participants, the mechanics and publicity, but that they had nothing to do with refreshments or tickets. These would be handled by other committees but we would deal with program. I indicated that within the area of program their work would depend upon their imagination and initiative. I told them that the first Friday for which we were responsible would be November 3rd. I asked them how they reacted to this charge.

The chairman and worker remind the group of the time limits. This must be done as regularly as is necessary and the same applies to other aspects of reality. The worker helps the committee decide about officers, their responsibilities, and other aspects of structure. The worker interprets agency policy and also may set limits. For example:

I said that I realized that forcing any group to do something which it was opposed to was not good, but that agency policy had to be considered. I pointed out that the Y was not in a position to open the Friday program to the public as it does not run a public dance hall, but if it wished to run one, which I did not think it did, the law requires a license. If the committee wished to ask for a change in this policy, which it had a right to do, there were channels for making the request, but we could not change it on our own or disregard the policy.

The chairman points up the direction of the discussion and helps the committee focus on the topic. Where he does not, the worker helps. For example:

"Mr. Chairman, are the members interested in the idea of a speaker and dancing also, or is the idea to eliminate dancing this week?" Or, "Mr. Chairman, we seem to agree on having a special dance theme—can we decide on the theme now?"

Provision should be made for a method of follow-up on committee assignments. For example:

"Who is going to contact Mr. Jones, Mr. Chairman? Had we better ask someone to be responsible for that, set a deadline, and ask him to call you, or me if he can't reach you, to report on what success he had?"

The worker seeks to prevent the chairman from hurrying matters through without adequate discussion or in violation of democratic process, and makes every effort to prevent domination of the committee by the chairman. He seeks to encourage everyone to speak, to participate in the deliberations, and to take part of the responsibilities. He assists the chairman to set limits on members who monopolize, wander off the topic, and block movement in the group.

The worker, as I indicated earlier, helps members meet their special needs to the extent that this is essential to the functioning of the committee. In this he uses himself, the group, and group interaction. Here is an example:

Jane complained to the worker that she and John do everything on the committee. "Now we have to run out the publicity." Worker asked what was the matter with the publicity chairman. Jane said he did not send out the material soon enough. Worker suggested that she confer with the publicity chairman before she take it upon herself to send out her own material. Worker tried to point out that Will likely had plans, and that he would be getting the material out. Worker told her that she had no reason to encroach upon his job and if he was not doing it properly she could bring it up at a meeting or discuss it with the president. Worker is going to have to work more closely with Jane for she needs to begin to verbalize her reasons to dominate and control the program. Until she realizes her motivations or has her satisfactions provided in other ways, Worker does not think she will be able to be effective on this committee.

When the meeting began, George took the chair. He called the meeting to order and quickly outlined the agenda, asking for additional items. Jane immediately launched a tirade against the whole committee in general and Will in particular. Once she had done so she seemed ready to proceed with the meeting.

The worker may have to limit a dominant, indigenous leader if he is blocking the group, manipulating it, or using it for his own ends. For example:

Worker's role has been a dual one, helping George by supporting him and limiting him. Worker realizes that this is an area of potential conflict with George for George fears that the Worker might take control of the program away from him. This control is important to George for it gives him status and recognition. George can function more effectively as a leader. Worker talks over every move with George and makes suggestions primarily by asking George what his plans and suggestions are first. Worker is careful not to threaten George.

The worker acts as a resource person and helps to broaden and vary the committee's working as well as to perfect its mechanics. As a resource person, he tries to help the committee work out its problems by identifying blockings.

The worker seeks to prevent the committee from becoming a clique by directing the group back to its constituency for authority, and by indicating that the committee is not there to run programs of interest to itself specifically but those that interest the group members. He also attempts to help the members see that a committee is a device for pooling knowledge and interests and coming up with a group effort for the good of the entire group, and not to serve a vested interest or a select section of the membership.

The chairman and groupworker keep the group working on the job to be done, keep the goals before it, and enable the committee to move forward. In part, this is done by breaking the job down into small units of work, helping the committee to select and define methods, assist in the decision-making process, and work toward eliminating blocks. The worker seeks to provide an experience in collective thinking.

The worker helps the chairman learn how to chair and how to lead and, in addition, he helps train all of the officers. In doing this, he must clarify specifically his own role as that of helper and facilitator. He helps the chairman to see and assume his responsibilities to the group, to understand the committee structure, and to apply the functioning of the democratic method. As indicated earlier, there are variables in the chairman's potentials and in the level of group development which inform and alter the worker's performance. He helps the chairman prepare an agenda, plan for the meeting, and use procedure appropriately. It is essential that the worker and chairman meet regularly to plan together and to evaluate the work. During the committee meeting, the worker supports, helps, enables, and clarifies when asked and where needed. He does not take over the chairmanship or deprive the chairman of his status or initiative. The officers are helped to see their responsibilities, foresee and handle detail, and avoid damaging failure. The worker resists attempts by the committee to push its own responsibilities onto him.

The worker helps the committee carry its plans into action and assists in the execution of the program to the extent that this is needed. The worker helps the committee evaluate itself and its results. He gives support, status, and recognition, but at the same time helps it to look realistically at its failures, try to find the reasons, correct them, and thereby select better methods of doing the job.

The worker helps the committee to relate its work to that of other committees by providing channels and suggesting their use. He helps it report back to the main body, and make suggestions and recommendations to facilitate its own job. The worker helps the committee terminate when it has completed its assigned job or tenure.

It is important that a committee see not only its segment of work, but also be helped to see the relationship of its work to the total enterprise and to gain satisfaction from it. It is helpful also if the chairman and worker, in summarizing each meeting, point out what has been accomplished at that meeting so that satisfaction accrues from group productivity.

The success or failure of a committee is measured by its ability to accomplish its objective, that is, produce through socially acceptable means. There are discernible factors which inhibit productivity in committees and which require the attention of the groupworker.

Some Barriers to Committee Productivity

1. Differences in degree of involvement among the members.
2. Differences in experience.
3. Differences in ability to comprehend subject matter.
4. Insensitivity to real interests of others.
5. Personal antagonisms.
6. Personal rigidity.
7. Failure to assess accurately where the group is.
8. Failure of communication.
9. The pace of the meeting is too fast.
10. The committee is not oriented to time limits.
11. The committee members have preconceived expectations.
12. Members operate in a manner which conflicts with group goals.
13. Inability of members to perceive their own role.
14. Inaccurate perceptions of reality.
15. Personal interest or fear.
16. Inability of committee to evaluate its own success or failure and profit from its own experience.

In the beginning stages of the committee's development, the committee members experiment to test trust and to determine what will give one status in the group. Often, it is felt that talking a good deal or sounding knowledgeable will promote them into positions of leadership and recognition. Other members may be afraid to speak lest their contributions be regarded as foolish and thus they will lose status. As long as committee members are looking over their shoulders wondering what others will think of them while they strive for status, group productivity suffers. The worker helps by giving status for contributions to collective thinking and praising members who help the group move toward its goals. There is acceptance and recognition given by him for all contributions but those that help the committee are given specially reinforcing rewards.

Committee productivity is curtailed when members use the committee for the meeting of personal needs rather than the fulfillment of group goals. The worker helps by dealing with the necessity for meeting personal needs, as discussed before, in relationship to the committee function by giving recognition when behavior is group centered and limiting behavior that is not. The worker can help also by assisting members to gain awareness of their behavior and by assisting them to see what roles they play. This is accomplished through feedback, the use of a group observer, and through an analysis by the group of its behavior. A committee should be helped to ascertain what blocks its progress.

The groupworker can help members talk to the group rather than to the chairman or the worker. He can help by asking that words be clarified, seeking for meanings, and acting as a communication bridge. He can help resolve semantic problems, and solicit working agreements on terminology so as to avoid misunderstandings.

The worker can help to integrate subgroups or cliques into one committee by gaining agreement on goals and means. He can help reduce any feeling of competition for his approval by being fair and impartial. He can assist in the decision-making process. He can help by working through "idea possessiveness" of individual members. He can help the group see that, whereas every idea is important, only those ideas that contribute to group productivity are really useful to the whole committee.

The worker helps by filling roles which are needed but are not being filled by others, such as initiating, seeking information, giving information, encouraging, and integrating. At all times the worker helps by focusing attention on the job and the democratic method in the conduct of the committee.

An Illustration of a Program-Committee Meeting

AGE: Adults
SETTING: Group-Services Association
SESSION: Third

The meeting was called to order by the chairman. The committee has conducted several meetings during the current year. The meeting they had scheduled for the second Thursday of the month had been postponed, requiring the committee to meet this evening as a replacement.

The chairman opened the meeting, apologized for the confusion in communication resulting in the cancellation of the last meeting. Some discussion resulted, ranging from "What is the regular meeting night?" to "I thought we always met on the second Thursday." Staff member suggested that a letter be sent to all committee members specifying that the second Thursday of each month is "the" committee meeting night and that reminder notices be simply reminder notices. The chairman agreed that this might solve the problem and asked that this be done.

The chairman then asked for a report of the current adult informal education program. Staff member presented an over-view of the present program, including related problem areas and highlights. Committee reaction was mixed with regard to the content of the program, amount of staff time required, priorities, importance to total center effort. Staff member related the amount of staff time available, the amount of time required, and the need for additional volunteer assistance if the program was to continue to grow. A detailed summary of growth during the past few years was made, both in numbers of participants and in earned income, and the effect that this had on the entire center operation.

A committee member said that she had a program idea. Some discussion began about income produced, about why a course was offered, and in general the committee broke into many small groups. Program idea was lost until the staff member asked during the general confusion what the person had in mind. Attention refocused on the person and the idea was presented. No action was taken.

The committee chairman suggested that there was a real need for a subcommittee to be concerned solely with Informal Adult Education. A member was appointed as the subcommittee chairman.

A report of the Retired Persons Program was presented by the committee member representing that special activity. Staff was asked to supply the statistical detail. A complete review of the program was made with specific respect to the purpose of the group and the results which had been observed.

The committee chairman reviewed the forum program conducted by the Golden Branch. It had been suggested that such a program be established to focus on local community problems and interests. Staff was asked to make a report on a previous venture in this direction a year and one-half ago with a local community civic organization. The Center Board, it was reported, had agreed to supply a meeting place one evening each month on a one-year trial basis. The civic organization was to plan, conduct, publicize and coordinate the actual program. One program was conducted, with some degree of success, but no additional meetings were scheduled. No further interest was shown by the civic group.

The chairman indicated that he had discussed the project with a fellow member of the committee and a member of the staff and suggested that the center pursue the forum idea. He suggested that one of the committee members become chairman of the forum committee. This was declined. Another member suggested they think about who might chair the subcommittee. Staff suggested they develop a list of potential chairmen tonight. This was done. A guide to persons wanted on the subcommittee was proposed. The chairman asked staff to contact the first-choice candidate to seek his acceptance. Staff refused on the grounds that this was a function best performed by a lay leader. Some discussion resulted and it was decided that the chairman would make the first contact.

Worker's Comments on the Meeting

This regular meeting is scheduled monthly—however, this particular meeting is a makeup meeting. Present were the committee chairman, two female members, and two male members. Also present was the staff person responsible for this committee—a part-time woman who works about 22 hours a week. Also present was the Center Executive who was asked by the chairman to be present to observe.

Major Tasks. To work with the members of the staff in developing a program for adult members of the center designed to meet identified needs and interests. To evaluate program and related practices to ensure that the programs are relevant to the purpose of the center and fall within the range of organizational goals. The immediate tasks were:

1. To review the present adult informal education program.
2. To effect some changes in committee structure.
3. To consider a change in an established program unit.
4. To introduce a new program.

Goals. To work with staff in resolving problems within the scope of the committee responsibility; to review the work of the center and to plan future programs with staff. Goals of the staff were to make the members of the committee familiar with the problems which result in the conduct of adult program; and to involve the members of the committee in the work of the center.

Blocks. Committee structure is extremely loose and informal. This often leads to great periods of wasted time.

Assets. Board will not perform committee function, therefore, the responsibility to get the job done is placed squarely in the hands of the committee.

Delegate Councils

There are many opportunities for the use of delegate councils in group services. For example, recreation and informal-education agencies frequently have "house councils" made up of representatives of various clubs and activities in the agency. Often departments such as teenage or young adult have their own councils. Many camps use camper councils or section councils for planning the intergroup activity of various units or sections of the camp. Councils are also an integral part of decentralized associations such as the Boy Scouts and similar national organizations. In large cities, one finds inter-agency councils, youth councils, and club councils. Councils are used also in hospitals to foster patient government as well as in community operations such as block clubs and neighborhood organizations. The delegate council is part of our societal system and political philosophy, and should be studied and used consciously and purposefully to accomplish the ends best suited to it as an organizational instrument. The delegate council is not valid merely because agencies use it or because it seems to be a thing to have. It should not be used as a device to permit articulate groups to let off steam to avoid embarrassing the administrative staff, nor should it be a debating society. The delegate council is a sensitive instrument which, when used properly, fulfills a most important role in group and community life.

A groupworker often is called upon to render professional service to a delegate council. It is important that he understand the difference between how one works in a growth-oriented group, a committee, and a council. The function of a groupworker with a council becomes sharper for the worker if he remembers the basic difference in functions between a committee and a council. A committee is a group of people appointed by a parent body to accomplish a particular job. The committee is responsible and accountable to the parent body. All of the members of the committee are responsible also to the parent body. A committee member, however, once appointed to the committee, is free to use his own discretion as to how he votes. He is bound to function for the benefit of the entire membership but is not bound to ask it how he should vote on a given issue. In addition, a good committee member gives up the vested interests of any subgroup with which he is affiliated and, once on the committee, is concerned with the interest and benefit of the total membership. A committee is the instrument of all of the members to be used to accomplish a desired job as part of the structure of the parent body. A committee may be an operating group, an exploring or investigating group, or a planning group. The function of the groupworker with a committee has been analyzed in the preceding section.

A delegate council is a secondary group, organized to carry out the goals of the many groups which are represented on it. Nevertheless, group methods are applicable to it, and a groupworker is equipped to serve as a professional worker with a delegate council although, in this setting, he uses his skills differently from the way he would use them with a growth-oriented group or a committee. The delegate council is responsible for and accountable to all the groups that it numbers in its constituency, but the council member is responsible primarily to the group that he represents. The council member has a dual responsibility—first to his group and then to all the groups in concert. The council's unique role is integrative. The council is not appointed by a parent body but by a number of groups or organizations. The council member acts as a representative of the special interest that appointed him and, therefore, he does not renounce his vested interest on the council but maintains it as his guide to his functioning. His first loyalty is to the group that sent him. He does not vote on his own and how he pleases, but for his group, and although his group is concerned ostensibly with the total good, it is devoted also to its own benefit which can be derived from the council. The council member is not a free agent who uses his own discretion; he is a delegate, a representative, who votes as his own group would have him vote.

As the council process evolves, it is hoped that the groups represented on the council will mature and be able to submerge their self-interests into the interests of all, and subscribe to general goals. In this respect, groups can develop a social sense, even as one hopes that individual members of groups may be helped to submerge their personal interests into those of the group and function for mutual interest. This is a goal and objective of the process, but within it the worker must recognize the autonomy of the constituent groups.

It might be said that council membership is a more advanced step on the ladder of social maturity. Within the social group, the member, through meeting his own needs and the needs of others, learns to relate himself to his fellow group members and to adjust his interests to theirs, eventually seeing the group goals as prior to his own in relationship to the group endeavor. In the committee, he finds his functioning dependent upon a maturity sufficiently developed to subordinate himself to the benefit of a larger and less personal membership, where he must think in broader social terms, and satisfy his personal needs by achievement related to the committee goal. In the delegate council he is called upon to relegate himself completely to the role of a representative, able to function in interpersonal relations with a number of other representatives who are perceived as separate personalities, but who at the same time are also symbols of entire groups. He must take on the personality of his own group, think as his members think collectively and represent their interests, and in that capacity interact with other people who also are acting in a representative capacity.

The delegate must be able to curb himself and function within the strict limits of his understanding of his group's wishes, and also check his impatience to get things done while he returns to ask his group for instructions. The role that the group asks him to assume may be contrary to his own inclination and to his own personality or needs, and yet he must represent his group faithfully and skillfully. This calls for both personal security and mature perspectives.

The Function of Delegate Councils

Delegate councils definitely have a place in social-agency function. They are an administrative tool that is useful in providing agency members an opportunity to participate in decision-making and it would be difficult to construct a device that would allow members of an agency to function within a democratic framework without considering constituencies. An alternative to such councils is to set up a structure whereby all members vote for all representatives at large. While this allows greater participation, it weakens accountability, and may also result in a failure to ensure that all factions and points of view are represented and included in the decisions. A properly operating delegate council assures constant communication between the council member and the desires of his constituency, and also makes sure that many points of view or organized interests are heard and considered. The question of how to represent the unaffiliated agency members presents a problem and the soundest solution seems to be to permit those persons to have the status of a constituency with the right to choose delegates-at-large to represent them. These delegates-at-large should be voted for by the unaffiliated members only and be responsible as delegates to them.

The question of constituencies is peculiar to each setting and situation. Should the council include interest and activity groups or only clubs and other similar organized associations? If a council is composed only of clubs, it is actually a club council and, therefore, its powers should be limited to matters of concern to its constituent groups. In some settings and neighborhoods, organized clubs or associations may represent a power elite and, in many instances, councils made up of these organizations do not represent truly the general membership or public. This is a fault to be avoided in the use of group process in organizational and neighborhood-development work.

Delegate councils afford a splendid opportunity for the training and teaching of participatory democracy and representative government through experience. Both council delegates and members of affiliated groups can come to understand the complicated structures of representation and democracy which function through the consent of the governed when the council is properly constituted and functions well. Councils have no way of effecting their decisions other than by the consent of the organizations that belong to it. They have no control over the internal operation of autonomous member groups. The suspension or withdrawal of a group does not enforce a council directive; its power rests on agreement, good faith, and the commitment of its constituent groups to the well-being of all of the people who belong to all of the groups of the council. In some instances, there is an exception to this when the professional staff or the administration of the sponsoring agency is constituted as a higher authority which can enforce council-made policy. In such instances, it is incumbent on the worker to explain agency policy and goals before or during the debate so as to avoid nullifying the democratic process by exercising a veto power later. It can be justified where the council is part of agency administration and its policies are extensions of agency policies.

Delegate councils can provide a medium for the planning and execution of programs which are too large for any one organization to undertake. They become a medium for intergroup festivals, leagues, exhibitions, carnivals, city-wide programs, and other mass activities as well as social-action programs. Such councils are practical and effective devices for neighborhood work such as community-action projects. Because they involve the groups in a council-group process, activities such as these can be more successful and meaningful than if they were promoted and run by the staff or even were products of committees. Because they represent many viewpoints, they guard against limited participation and clique control.

The major functions of a council are those of planning and policy-making, and less often that of operating. However, any programs that it does carry out are relegated to committees which may be considered as operational arms. An intergroup program requires that planning and policy-making be the media through which member groups relate to each other. The largest part of a council's activity, then, is planning and it should understand clearly that this is its role.

Councils provide excellent training groups for indigenous leaders who later will be able to take their places on boards, administrative committees, and otherwise assume important positions on agency and city-wide planning bodies. Such training is an important function of social agencies. The training is not only in the actual skill and knowledge of council work, but also in attitudes toward the giving of time and service for community betterment. Social agencies are being called upon to combat that cynicism and disillusionment caused by an unpopular war, a series of manipulated political conventions, and the effects of unbridled industrial expansion. There has been a decrease in voluntary effort in the organized social services, and a withdrawal of youth from established media. The concept of service, community development, and the dedicated involvement of people in the social problems of the day should be included as goals of group-services agencies, and the delegate council is a step in that direction in agency practice.

The Use of Delegate Councils

It is of great importance that groupworkers analyze carefully their motivations for developing a council, relate it to agency function and find its appropriate place in the over-all structure. It is vital also for the membership to be ready for such an experience if the council is to prove successful. The groups that are represented on the council must have achieved a degree of maturity as groups before they can function within a council format. Where organizations are beset with internal problems and are having trouble moving toward their own goals, they have little energy left for intergroup activity. Group members who are unable to find meaningful relationships within their own groups will be unable to grasp or cope with the complexities of council functioning and it is essential that council delegates experience the meeting of their own needs within their primary groups so that they will be free and able to use themselves in a representative role. A council experience is an advanced step in group life, and the groups must be ready for council participation by successfully developing healthy groups and committees that are schooled in the more fundamental forms of group government.

The administrative responsibility allocated to the council, by like token, must be in proportion to the age and experience of the group members and what is appropriate for them to handle. Matters that require professional judgment, staff execution, or board action are not within the competence of a member council. The planning of program with staff guidance is usually suited to youth councils, but such councils often are not competent to legislate on matters of safety, fire regulations, total budget, and such matters. It should be obvious that their functions and responsibilities differ from those of staff, and it is vital that a council know the limits of its authority. The use of contract here is similar to its application in other groups, and the purpose for which the council is formed is equally relevant.

Although it is easy to see that the responsibilities that have been discussed require some successful group experience, a community of interest, and sufficient knowledge and emotional security to understand the role of a representative, many neighborhood organizers in community-action programs, as an example, have failed to appreciate the importance of these requisites. It is doubtful that one finds such maturity in junior groups. Councils are suitable for youth groups if the members have had previous successful group experiences. It is dubious that a wide age range is conducive to. adequate communication between groups or to a community of interest. Some agencies, camps, and neighborhood organizations can point to exceptions to these operating principles, but close examination may reveal that such so-called councils function as committees, that they are only sounding boards for program ideas conceived by staff, and that they do not perform a planning or policy-making function. For similar reasons, neighborhood councils, especially those developed recently as part of federal grant programs, have experienced rough going. These will be discussed in the last section of this chapter.

An effective council develops when the agency decides that there is a job to be done that can be done best through a council format, that the organizations to be included are ready for a council, that the agency or sponsor is willing to delegate some of its power and authority to the council, or that a council format is being demanded by the membership and the agency is willing to have one. To superimpose a council on the membership or the neighborhood when they have neither the desire nor the interest for one may not serve a useful purpose. Interest and desire should be developed first through suggestion, exposure, or involvement in programs that are appropriate to a council format. To permit the establishment of a council, even though requested, when there is neither readiness nor maturity is equally inadvisable. One cannot assume that it is preferable to let people find out for themselves that they are not ready to handle council responsibility because this may result in a slowing of the maturation process as well as inhibiting the motivation to become involved in decision-making in the future. To set up a council which has no job to do or has only artificial or superficial issues with which to cope will result in frustration, in the council's militant pressure on the agency, or in development of negative attitudes about agency management. To sponsor a council when the administration is not willing to delegate power to it is deceptive and results in the expected reactions to such provocation.

If a council is to be used, it should be regarded as an important instrument for performing tasks that are needed, and once that is agreed, the agency must surrender the authority and responsibility commensurate with the tasks to be performed by the council. Councils should not be treated as paper bodies. There is danger in playing at democratic processes as members may become frustrated and disillusioned with the experience, surmising that the problem is a weakness inherent in democracy rather than in its improper use by the agency. This engenders disrespect for democracy and, in some instances, a swing to a contrary ideology. This, sad to say, is evident in the attitude of many young people in this country today, and is an indictment against our social institutions. Agencies that sponsor councils must be ready to grant them status to a level appropriate to their designated functions and to delegate the power to them to do the job. Councils that are permitted to be review bodies, rubber stamps, and lifeless organisms disintegrate, become listless, and develop scapegoating, arguing and power politics. Also, where a council is given to understand that it has an important role but it is not permitted to fulfill it, education for democracy is reversed. This situation develops, too, when the area of responsibility has not been defined clearly and therefore seems to encroach on staff or board responsibility, or where limits are applied as broad, operative guides to council action after council decisions are finalized rather than being set up in advance.

Council Formation

When all of the requisites discussed above have been met and a council is to be formed, the agency has to define clearly its function and the scope of its authority so that the groupworker can begin properly his relationship with it. The groupworker assigned should be a senior staff person who can lend prestige to the beginning council, he should be related to the constituent groups as part of his regular job responsibility, and he must have authority to carry the responsibility at whatever level is required of him. It is to be expected that the groupworker will have working relationships with groups, organizations, and members who meet in the agency or that make up the group life of the neighborhood, and that he will visit, observe, and supervise club and neighborhood workers.

If one is to develop a council within an agency or association, the first steps in its organization are interpretation, planning, and consultation with the club workers. If there are no club workers, then planning should include the group presidents at the outset. If group representatives are the first people called to a meeting, one can anticipate such difficulties as the club workers feeling left out and inadequate and reacting negatively, the clubs or groups not understanding fully the function of the council and if they consider it to be unimportant, not sending representatives, the sending of low-status and inadequate persons as representatives, the representatives who are sent coming without instructions or the authority to act, and when the representatives return from the council meeting not being asked for a report or being prevented from giving one. It is essential that the club workers understand the council format, its function, and the role they must play to help make the council meaningful and useful to their own group.

The next step in the formation of a council is to interpret it to the groups that will be invited to join and it is advantageous to do this, group by group, with the members of each one, giving them ample opportunity for questions. If the groupworker fails to do this, and he explains the council only to the representative, the representative may not convey the message adequately or may not have the status to interest the other members. This is true equally when working with neighborhood or block clubs. If the groupworker leaves the interpretation to the club worker or organization president, often it means that the presentation of the idea of the council is deprived of the status of the worker and the club worker can make just another routine matter of it. In addition, the interpretation may differ in each group, depending upon the understanding and skill of each club worker or president, and often they feel that it is just another chore not directly related to their group program and hence they may slight it. Follow-up may be left to the club workers or officers to handle, but the club workers and presidents must be sold on the idea of a council and kept informed constantly of its program if they are to be effective. Where the club workers are paid staff persons, adequately trained, the groupworker who is responsible for the council may give more responsibility to them, work through them, and leave more of the interpretation to them. Where they are volunteers, inexperienced, or indigenous, the groupworker should take the responsibility.

A most important obligation for the club worker or president is the selection of the representative to the council. Unless the group realizes and accepts the importance of the post which they are about to elect or appoint, they may choose the least appropriate person. This is an easily recognized pattern of group life. Each group sees its own problem as all-important and is reluctant to send its most useful people to an intergroup council. However, the group reduces its own leadership resources by so doing and adds an additional burden to a heavily loaded official. It fears that its representative will become so involved in the council and its committees that he will have little time for his club duties, which often happens. When a council has high status and the position of representative is seen in that light, appropriate people are chosen as delegates. It is the job of the club worker or neighborhood worker to help the groups appreciate this, evaluate the position and role, and choose wisely.

All too often, groupworkers find themselves with councils of low-status persons who are isolates in their own groups. These people, of necessity, seek to use the council as a primary social group for the satisfaction of their personal needs. Such a council will fail in its objective and lose what little status it might have.

When the representative is chosen, it is important that both the group and the representative understand what constitutes a delegate. They should know that a delegate is supposed to carry out the wishes of the group, that he is expected to report back to the group on all activities and decisions of the council, and seek advice and instructions from the group on what stands he should take on these matters. It is preferable that this phase of interpretation evolve into a discussion of representative government and procedure rather than become a lecture by the worker. It is to be hoped that every member of the group will know and understand the concepts so that the council can operate properly and smoothly.

If the council has authority delegated to it as part of the job it has to do, its importance or status will rise and the interest of the constituent groups will go up in proportion to it. It is difficult to interpret intangibles to people, and the idea of democracy through representative government is most intangible. Frequently, groups will prefer to risk their futures on the decisions of staff whom they perceive to be fair rather than on those of a council of peers whom they mistrust. It is difficult also to interpret the fund-raising possibilities of a council to the groups. It takes a good deal of maturity to understand the value of a large-scale program to raise money, for example, for equipment for the agency or for use in common. If such a project is related in some way to the needs the members feel, then its value becomes apparent immediately to everyone. It is only later that a council may mature to the point of rendering service to others. The type of authority that raises the status of a council is the control of certain facilities, funds, or jobs, or the formulation of rules and regulations. A council must feel that what it does matters and that it has a direct say in things that affect the groups and the members of the groups.

Where importance is placed on the council, club presidents tend to want to be the council delegate. This is not an advisable practice, and the reasons why this is not so should be interpreted carefully to them. The two main reasons are that the obligations of the presidency are heavy, if carried properly, and both positions therefore are too much for one person to carry, and also that leadership should be dispersed throughout the group and not monopolized by one dominant person. The president should be helped to see this and be willing to entrust the important post of delegate to another member.

Past presidents tend to make good council representatives and their selection helps to provide an antidote for the letdown feeling people have when they relinquish the presidency and have no other role to perform. Their group experience has prepared them for council responsibility.

Sometimes a council can be afforded status by the choice of its meeting place. If there is a room available which generally is not used by the groups and it can be used by the council, the members interpret this to mean that the staff or sponsors think that the council is important. If an important person is present at the first meeting, this also will raise the tone. Such a person might be the executive of the agency, a board member, a person from the metropolitan office, or a member of the city council or legislature whose function would be to welcome the delegates, launch the council, and wish it success.

It is of the utmost importance in the first session that the function of a council be explored thoroughly and, as part of this discussion, that the groupworker define its scope and the limits of its authority, the channels for communication, and his function as the worker. The vital points to be made in this connection are that a council is an instrument to make it possible for groups to work together for the benefit of all, and that intergroup relations should be mutually satisfying. It is advisable to point out that no matter how well the representatives get along together, it is not as important as how well the constituent groups and their members can learn to work together. In the first session, the groupworker will point out the meaning of being a representative, the obligation of reporting back to the group all that transpires, and receiving instruction from the group on how to vote and what proposals to make. It is well also to lay the foundation for the development of social goals, social action, and positive attitudes toward projects that have service motives.

Unlike the social groups which I have discussed earlier where the worker minimizes structure, structure is important for a council. The worker can help the council develop a structure that is suitable for carrying out its functions and also to understand its structure. Where there is a prime obligation to get a job done, even though process and means are to be considered always, it is essential that the mechanics for facilitating the job be developed early. If the council has to wrangle about structure and procedures later when its time and effort should be devoted to its tasks, its work will be slowed and its satisfaction limited. It is to be remembered that the means and processes conspicuous in social groupwork with growth-oriented groups are not used so readily by a worker in a council because the focus is not on interpersonal relations but on intergroup relations. As part of structuring, it is usually advisable to have a written constitution and bylaws which govern the council's activities and define the rights of all concerned. While the representatives may trust one another and feel that they do not require a set of rules, the group members are not in the same face-to-face relationship and must have clear criteria for intergroup business as well as for settling disputes.

Questions of the numbers of representatives and the interchangeability of delegates are important aspects of structure. Issues will arise as to whether each group, regardless of size, should have the same number of delegates or whether the number should be predicated on the membership of each group. These are matters to be determined on the facts in each instance. Generally, it is preferable to have two rather than one delegate to protect against absences and also misinterpretations by one delegate when he reports back. The question of votes is knotty also. If there are two or more representatives for each group, is the group entitled to all of its votes even when a representative is absent, and can the vote be split between them, or do they vote as a unit? It is well if the worker can help the council and the groups understand the importance of regular and continuous representation, so that the delegate is a designated person and not just any group member who happens to be free or wants to come. It is obvious that the representative is useful only if he attends all meetings and knows what is going on. Some groups get into the habit of sending more than their allotted quota, insisting that the excess will not vote. This is a dangerous and slovenly practice because power blocks develop, intimidation or threat can be implied, and suspicions become aroused. The worker can help to enforce an agreement that only official delegates and alternates may attend meetings. The practice of having an alternate, however, is widespread and workable.

The Groupworker with the Delegate Council

It is important for the groupworker to interpret his own role adequately so that he is accepted for what he is and the expectancies the delegates have for him are sound. His role as enabler, resource, and helping person should be clear. He must know and understand the groups that are represented and the council delegates so as to be able to assist the council in its functions. It is part of his job as an enabler to help the individual representatives perform effectively as delegates. Their individual needs are secondary to the development of intergroup relations. The worker concerns himself with individuals, as discussed in the section on committees, only to the extent that it is necessary to facilitate the activity of the council.

The groupworker helps the council learn how to conduct its business, and as part of this function assists the council chairman and officers with their jobs. He helps the council move along toward its goals with emphasis on the will of the constituent groups at all times and sometimes he may have to ask the chairman not to permit a vote if there has not been time for the representatives to go back to their groups for instructions. The worker facilitates the group bond of the delegates in the council to the extent that is necessary to do the job and give the members a satisfying experience. The loyalties of the council members should be directed first to their groups and then to the council. The council should not be permitted to become more important to him than his own group.

Wilda said that it would be nice if all the council members could go skating together. She suggested the coming Wednesday night. Julie and Harry said they could not make it. Worker suggested Saturday so that the group members could come as it was not a school night. It was decided to have it on Saturday, but for council delegates only.

Such a plan, although it seems harmless enough, excludes the group members and destroys the important understanding that the council exists only to serve the groups and to promote intergroup activity. Wilda is making the council a primary group.

The worker is a resource person; he is called upon to suggest and stimulate programs suitable for intergroup activity, help the council plan such activities, and help the delegates get their groups solidly behind the council projects. Special care should be taken to avoid conflict in program or dates with the constituent groups. For example, if the council is preparing a gala affair for a given night, it is obviously a poor idea for a member group to hold a dance around the same date. This becomes a matter of interpretation for the worker and is one of the reasons why it is suggested that the worker be related to the groups belonging to the council. The council should not plan activities that compete with the groups either. Where a council plans a series of dances and each group generally has had a big dance every year, the delegates should be helped to see that the traffic may not bear so many similar affairs and that the group programs have precedence. It is also a bad idea for the council to sponsor any event that traditionally one of the groups has sponsored. Difficulties may arise when drama programs, athletic events, and similar activities are not considered carefully by the delegates.

The worker must help the groups to have integrity in the choice of their activities and to support their council. It is a serious sign of weakness when council representatives vote for a particular event and their group members fail to attend. It is part of the worker's job to interpret to the council members that a vote for an event means that the group members intend to support it. This is a unique aspect of intergroup work that requires the special attention of the groupworker. Another problem to avoid is a failure of the council members themselves to attend events that they have planned. This is a sign of serious malfunctioning of the council and needs the attention of the worker to diagnose the cause or to call upon the council to look at its own operation and to correct it. In these instances, the crux of the matter lies in the understanding that the council and the total membership of all of the groups are one. Part of learning to practice democracy is the lesson that one's representatives are not separate from the constituency to be regarded as "they," but are alter egos to be regarded as "we." The "we" feeling of individuals which is the bond in a group, in a council should be a "we" feeling of groups, and the groups must be helped to see that although the council is a separate entity, in fact it is an embodiment of themselves.

One of the principal causes of these difficulties is faulty reporting to and from the groups. This is an area which needs help from both the groupworker and the club workers. The initial help may come through a discussion by the council members of how to report back, with an analysis of why some delegates and their groups fail to handle it properly. Sessions can be spent on how to make reports and how to interest the group members. Role-playing can be used as well as tape recorders. Help also can be given within the constituent groups by impressing the club workers and presidents with the importance of reporting back, and by the worker asking when he visits the groups whether the delegates are reporting, or asking that they report at this time and soliciting questions about the council business. The flow of information is facilitated if the minutes of the council go to the groups. If this is not the practice, the groupworker may provide notes for the use of the club workers, or report on council activities at staff meetings of the club workers, or discuss the council in supervisory conferences. Through these same channels, groups can learn whether their delegates are attending meetings regularly and whether they are doing their jobs. If their delegates are not attending council meetings, it may become necessary for the worker to let the groups know, but it is preferable for this to be done in the first instance by the secretary of the council. Reporting or keeping the groups informed is facilitated when a council gives wide publicity to its functions, activities, and plans through bulletin boards, a house organ, open meetings, and speakers. Periodically, a meeting of all of the members of the groups to give sanction to a vital issue or to approve a large expenditure will develop interest and give vitality to the council.

It is recommended that council delegates draw upon group members for assistance in carrying out council projects as this broadens the base of participation. It can be done by granting all the chairmen the power to include group members and by using people other than council members to fill various jobs in connection with all projects. Subjects which must be reported back are issues requiring the instruction and approval of the groups. It does not include matters of procedure and the minutiae of running the meetings of the council. Groups do not have the time nor should they be asked to conduct the business of the council. They should be asked only to discuss the vital matters of intergroup concern.

I suggest that a groupworker who works with a council ought to visit the groups to ascertain their interests and points of view firsthand. A knowledge of their goals will help the worker assist with the formulation of council goals. Such knowledge provides the worker with the information he may need to help a delegate or when a delegate is absent. It may become necessary, from time to time, for the groupworker to interpret groups to each other and help them to see each other's point of view. He must be objective and neutral.

The groupworker records council meetings and other pertinent data, interprets agency policy to the council, and interprets council positions to the administration of the agency. These functions apply equally to neighborhood councils under civic auspices. Some councils have a tendency to think that they are serving the agency but the worker should interpret to them the fact that the council is there to serve the people and that anything it buys, conducts, or does is for the benefit of the members or neighbors and not for the benefit of the agency, its staff, or board. This interpretive job should not wait until an issue arises but should begin with the negotiation of the contract and must continue throughout the life of the council. The question of council treasuries arises in this connection. Many councils raise money for operating expenses and socially motivated projects. This money does not belong to the delegates nor does it belong to the groups on a prorated basis. It belongs to the group members in common, held in trust by the council to be used for the purposes for which it was raised. Where no specific purpose is stated, some general purpose must have motivated the fund-raising. However, the worker should encourage the council to state a purpose and not raise money just for the sake of fund-raising. The accumulation of money in the treasury can result in trouble. It is important to remind the council members that their purpose is to serve the groups and the members of the groups because sometimes, when councils run intergroup projects with fund-raising objectives, they forget the primary purposes and begin to regard the fund-raising as the goal.

A council serves to broaden the outlook of each group beyond its own immediate concerns and program. Groups can become so ingrown that they forget that they belong to an agency or a sponsored community project. For example, camp cabin groups sometimes can become so group conscious that they lose camp loyalty. A council should provide a channel for all groups to see beyond themselves to the broader endeavors through group interaction.

To achieve these ends, the worker helps the council evaluate its program and each of its projects regularly. The evaluation process is important; it is also useful to refer the delegates back to their groups to ask them to evaluate council program and in this way involve the entire membership and assure the intergroup aspect. The council might consider also its effectiveness in serving all groups and devote some attention to recruiting groups that do not send delegates. It may need help from the worker to do this and while he will interpret the council to these groups which do not send delegates or participate, it is up to the council to devise ways to attract all groups to join.

The groupworker helps the council with routine administrative matters, and the extent of this help will depend on the age and ability of the council members to manage their own affairs. Arrangements, the seating of delegates, the provision of facilities, notices of meetings, follow-up telephone calls, minutes, and securing equipment are all functions of council members. The responsibility for the execution of these details should be assumed by the delegates and other members, and it is part of the worker's function to help them to accept their responsibilities and do their jobs. Whether the worker should call the delegates to remind them to attend meetings is a fine point on a continuum. He has to give careful consideration to his motives and objectives, and analyze the situation. It may be better to work through the officers of the groups or the officers of the council, but in any event, his decision to act must be supported by a diagnosis of why the delegates are irregular in attendance. There are realistic factors, such as: the delegates are employed, are busy and forget, or teenagers are not reliable, or it is a cultural pattern in the neighborhood. It is the worker's responsibility to see that attendance is maintained, but his choice of method requires that causes be assessed and consequences weighed.

It is good practice to avoid any agency action that will bypass the council when the program contemplated, advice sought, or job to be done would fall appropriately within the council's jurisdiction. Where the council is not used appropriately, its status drops, the members feel that they are not being recognized, and the groups begin to bypass their own delegate body, defeating the purpose for which the council was established. If representative democracy is to be demonstrated and practiced, the agency and its staff, as well as the members, must use the instrument. The lesson becomes meaningful when this is observed.

Some Frequently Encountered Problems in Delegate Councils

1. The groups do not understand the function of the council.
2. The groups do not see the value of working with other groups.
3. There is no intergroup setting of goals.
4. The groups are striving for prestige, power and status, and use the council as a stage for power politics.
5. The groups are not mature enough to appreciate their role in its totality.
6. The groups are too involved in their own problems to care about larger issues.
7. The groups do not understand the function or role of the groupworker and seek to use him for their own ends.
8. The groups think that they are doing the agency a favor by participating in council affairs.
9. The groups do not understand representative government and choose delegates unwisely.
10. Intergroup communication is blocked.
11. The to-and-from process wherein delegates report back to their constituencies for instructions is not operating.
12. Limits are poorly defined.
13. Authority has not been accorded to the council.
14. The club workers and presidents are not involved in the intergroup planning.
15. The council fails to plan ahead.
16. The council structure is not appropriate to its function.
17. The council delegates either do not understand the nature of representation or are not mature enough to fulfill that role.
18. The job does not require a council format and might better be done with some other mechanism.
19. Procedures are faulty.
20. The groupworker does not know how to work with a council and treats it as a growth-oriented, primary group.

How to Work with a Delegate Council

The following points are intended to summarize the principles discussed in this section.

The groupworker's focus as he works with a council is on the relationship between groups rather than between individuals. He sees the process that unfolds as one in which large numbers of people are involved and affected through units that have unique characteristics of their own. These units are the group constituencies and it is the function of the groupworker to guide the process so as to facilitate harmonious cooperation among them. In social groupwork, for purposes of the growth or treatment of people, the groupworker must understand the behavior of the individuals who comprise the group. His understanding of the member groups is an additional and paramount factor in working with and helping a council.

The delegates in a council are symbols of the groups they represent. The worker helps the delegates not to be themselves but to be accurate symbols of their groups. This is different from his functioning with primary groups as delegates must be enabled to separate their personal opinions from those of their groups and to function as alter egos of their constituencies. It is enabling at a secondary level also as the worker helps a delegate act as a representative because it is through this process that the groups are enabled to interact to achieve intergroup goals. It is important that the groupworker helps the council to move in the direction of goals set by the groups.

Everything that is done in the council must be seen as being done by groups and not by individuals, but the delegates nonetheless are people who have needs, personalities, beliefs, behavior patterns, and perceptions. They will, therefore, act in their own idiosyncratic manner in the council but they must be trained to represent the members of their groups and to act on their behalf. The groupworker functions on three levels simultaneously. He enables a council made up of delegates to function as an intergroup, while also appreciating them as individuals, and at the same time he must understand the groups which they represent. As people, the delegates must gain recognition and status for their achievements, feel that they belong and are accepted in the council in order to be free to act and be creative and, at the same time, get sufficient satisfaction to attend meetings and perform as expected. Their basic needs must be met sufficiently to permit them to carry their roles, but on the next level the groups must gain recognition, status, and satisfaction also from the intergroup experience.

The groupworker teaches democracy to the group members

through delegates who demonstrate a representative form of government. This chapter is not the place to debate the pros and cons of representative government versus participatory democracy. The demonstration will be successful if the groups' expectations are met, but if the groups' needs and interests are not fulfilled, the desired learning does not take place. The meeting of these requirements is vital to the whole process but the meeting of the personal needs of the delegates is secondary. Their personal needs should be met in their own primary groups.

The bond that is to be sustained in the council is the "we" feeling of each group in its affiliation to the council; it is their council but the bond of the delegates must be limited to that concept. The council is in danger of becoming a primary group or an ingroup if delegates form bonds within the council apart from the intergroup. In council work, program is used as a tool to effect intergroup bond and resultant activities; program is not valid if it does not further intergroup interaction. Programs that include dances, mass activities, leagues and the like but do not involve the council in intergroup thinking and planning which results in intergroup cooperation are not justifiable. The process is more important than the resultant activity, and the activity at all times should reflect and foster intergroup action rather than mass action. It is preferable for council action to have a service component through which the groups can carry out socially desirable programs and social action too ambitious to be handled by any one group alone.

The groupworker plays a vital part in fostering reporting back so that the constituent groups themselves are actually involved in planning. The worker assists in developing policy with and imposing limits on the groups as well as the delegates. The worker assists in developing a structure through which the groups can interact and act successfully. He assists in the process of selecting delegates and to do this he must relate himself to the groups themselves, either directly or through club workers and officers. He must go beyond working through the delegates on occasion until such time as the delegates are able to be accurate symbols, sensitive to their own groups' interests and desires. The groupworker need not work with the groups if the delegates are mature and can perform the representative roles. Councils in agencies and neighborhoods rarely achieve this degree of perfection and, therefore, the worker is always involved in teaching.

The groupworker assists with administrative detail, educates council officers, instructs club workers, and helps to provide the machinery for the operation of the council. He helps interpret groups to each other and mediates so that they may understand the positions of each other. He helps define council function and policy, agency function and policy, and the over-all goals. He helps the groups sift out and identify blocks to achievement and devise methods to overcome them; he helps them evaluate their work.

The worker is a bridge of communication between agency administration and the council. He helps groups and the agency use the council effectively and appropriately. He functions within the accepted concept that a council is a device to accomplish certain tasks, teach democratic method, and provide a medium for intergroup action. It is his obligation to enable the council to move in these directions, to achieve the goals the groups have for the council and to meet the needs of the groups through a guided and purposeful process.

The process of intergroup action is as important in council work as group process is within a group. A groupworker can foster and guide this process if he learns and understands how to function with a delegate council, bearing in mind that the delegates are not individuals but symbols of groups and yet that they behave as individuals while they perform as representatives. He is there to help them learn how to be representatives and to help groups learn to work with other groups. Thus, the intergroup process is a group process on a secondary socio-level. A groupworker who uses methods that are appropriate to other purposes or to primary groups when he works with a delegate council will be committing a serious error.

Neighborhood Councils and Block Clubs

Whether neighborhood organizations and neighborhood groupwork are conducted to effect social goals and social change, to render and achieve limited social work service objectives, or to enhance the people who serve on neighborhood committees and councils is a moot point. Community organizers tend to regard the organization of neighborhoods as means toward improving the community and the success of these programs in the antipoverty program, community-action programs, model cities, and similar projects is evaluated in terms of the achievement of social goals. Social settlements have considered that their clients are neighborhoods and communities, and not individuals. In their view, changes in the social system will accrue to the benefit of the residents but the point of leverage and the entry are in the system. Other social workers have contended that the objective of neighborhood organization is the development of the people involved and, while they do not denigrate the achievement of social change, the focus, diagnosis, and approach remain oriented to individuals and families.

There is disagreement also about the underlying philosophy of neighborhood work. Those who are elitists hold that social planning should be in the hands of the educated, the successful, and the expert. They contend that there is no evidence to support a claim that decisions made by the people who live in a blighted area are better than those made by experts, or that they know what is best for themselves, or even what they want. Popularists believe that people make better decisions than do experts, and that people should be involved always in decisions that affect their lives. Social group-workers believe, as an inherent part of social work, that the people must be included in the planning; it is a principle of practice. I believe that the involvement of people in decisions that affect them is more than an act of faith. This judgment is not based upon whether the decisions that are made are better than those that an expert would make, or on the pragmatic premise that the effective execution of the decisions is facilitated when they take part in the planning. I believe that decision-making and planning in improving one's life space are ego-strengthening, raise one's self-image, give one a sense of adequacy and competence, and provide essential exercises in the mastery of one's environment.

White writes that needing to feel effective is a primary, biological endowment. It is met by successfully dealing with the environment. He indicates that one aspect of reality, in ego terms, is the endeavor to make real changes in external circumstances. Competence comes from cumulative learning as one gains skill in being effective in dealing with surroundings through action. This is crucial to the adaptive process; it is the opposite of a feeling of powerlessness and its concomitant sense of a lack of self-respect. Competence is the capacity to interact and master the environment and it is the cumulative result of one's whole history of transactions with the environment.[6] Self-image and security rest on social competence and self-esteem springs from what a person can make the environment do as well as the feedback from others because of what he has accomplished. It is debilitating to feel that one has no power to influence one's world, and the result of such a feeling of being helpless and manipulated leads to apathy and a sense of worthlessness, or frustration and anger. The effect is infantilizing, and in some people it can result in dependency or apathy, while in others it can lead to hostility and anger which some internalize and direct at themselves and others act out against society.

Goffman has written that total institutions take away or corrupt those things which in a civil society give a person some sense of power over his world. They destroy his sense of autonomy, undermine his sense of self-determination, and divest him of any feeling of freedom of action.[7] An analysis of the centralization of decision-making and power away from the local level will give convincing evidence that communities in America are more like total institutions in this context than autonomous civil units. Political decisions are made in national and state capitals, policies about interest rates and the flow of currency are made in banking centers, educational policy is made in state education committees, merchandising and consumer products are decided upon by the home offices of big business, and church policy is laid down by high officials. There are only a few matters and concerns that are subject to control in the neighborhood and those that are impinging, such as housing, pollution control, adequacy of electricity and fuel oil, and consumer protection, are being controlled from afar. This is the situation in both rural and urban America today. It is evident in middle-class and fashionable areas, but it is many times more evident in the ghetto and in neighborhoods where welfare recipients reside.

I have said elsewhere in this chapter that committees and councils are instruments for accomplishing social tasks, and the worker uses group methods differently with them than he does with growth-oriented and treatment groups. The neighborhood council and club are exceptions to the rule. Neighborhood organization and neighborhood groupwork share the objectives of community organization; namely, social change, the reallocation of resources, the arousal of the residents to an awareness of their social problems, to the development of self-help, and to working for a redistribution of power. Traditionally, community organization does not include in its objectives the provision of direct social services or the growth and enhancement of the residents, but neighborhood groupwork does regard social goals and the development of persons as interrelated and interdependent, and the reasons why they must go together are obvious. It is axiomatic that we are not interested in developing viable groups or healthful communities as ends in themselves, but because they are the *sine qua non* for healthy and happy people.

Neighborhood councils or clubs that exist to serve the community must have members who are functional and mature enough to be able to serve on behalf of others. Community organization holds that it deals with people who are on committees and councils, not to serve themselves but to serve on behalf of others, i.e., the recipients of service, but neighborhood groupwork works with the neighbors who are, in fact, the recipients of social service. They are both planners and clients at the same time. These people usually have not had the life experiences, the social supports, or the resources to equip them to serve on committees on behalf of others, or to carry the role of a representative. They lack—and this is neither a slur nor disrespect for them—training in conducting group business or the psychological stability to handle these roles efficiently. Many people who have been deprived, or who hurt, or who are exploited, tend to find it difficult to empathize or consider the needs of others before their own, find it hard to postpone gratification and adhere to rules.

In the previous section on delegate councils I said that delegates must be mature, that they must have constituencies, and that they should have successful primary-group experiences. The rank-and-file adults in a disintegrating neighborhood rarely have these prerequisites. Neighborhood workers usually invite institutional leaders, or so-called leaders who represent small segments of the neighborhood and, in doing so, they miss the voice of the man-in-the-street who may not belong to identifiable or recognized formal groups such as churches, business or civic organizations, or prestigious social strata. Councils composed of status leaders, self-appointed spokesmen, or the officials of institutions usually do not represent the people, and workers who compose such councils are not preparing or educating the "common man" to take responsibility for making decisions and especially those that affect his life. One of the purposes in neighborhood groupwork is to educate and train the residents in democratic self-government and another is to give them the experience and practice that is necessary for them to be effective in community action. For these purposes to be achieved, the residents also must be helped to mature personally. These are some of the reasons why social goals and personal development are inseparable in social groupwork with neighborhood groups.

Groups of adults that are formed for community action and social improvement are not therapy groups; the members are not in need of treatment. Those few who might need treatment should be helped to get to clinics, social-treatment agencies, or psychiatric community-health centers. The community committee, neighborhood council, or block club is not to be used or diverted into a treatment group. They are developmental and task groups and have several foci as such. As I have stated, they help the members develop social competence so as to be able to fulfill their roles as planners and decision makers on behalf of the neighborhood. They are helped to learn how to act as mediators, negotiators, and organizers. They do undertake to render social services or to carry a variety of community-action programs. The groupworker acts as an educator and trainer for the officers and also the members; he is an adviser, guide, stimulator, and morale booster. He encourages and motivates; he listens, empathizes, suggests, and helps to channel frustration and anger into socially effectual action. He keeps the objectives in focus for the members and helps them to set priorities, assess consequences, and evaluate methods. The groupworker is a reflector of reality.

It is essential that the worker not lose sight of the fact that the members are human beings. They are not tools to be manipulated nor are they expendable in the interest of social action. A purpose of importance equal to the development of the members as citizens and social change agents is their development as people. One rationale for this is that it is compensatory. It is also an aspect of habilitation and the development of potential, and the important targets are self-image, self-respect, and a sense of adequacy. Inherent in the development of these attributes are trust, autonomy, initiative, industry, and identity, all of which are recognizable as the developmental tasks of the ego. In previous discussions I have stressed the discovery of self as a prime objective in groupwork; in this phase of work I am emphasizing the development and maturity of self. The stress on freedom which is so vital in treatment is essential in this context also but must be coupled appropriately with limits and social reality. These people are responsible for community change, service, and the enhancement of others as well as being responsible to themselves. They must be free, but free within boundaries of the social good, and hence the concept of a matching model for groupwork practice has great relevance here. The members are involved in an enterprise wherein they are seeking to reconstruct impinging environments to provide the quality and quantity of nutrients that they and others require, to facilitate the fulfillment of human potential, and to be conducive to the maximum realization for all individuals; and while so doing, they are enhancing their own social functioning. These endeavors proceed simultaneously and in tandem and are illustrated in the following excerpt.

Several months after the Elton Community Council was formed and its officers elected, the council was approached by a small group of residents who requested action regarding the unsightly appearance of a junked-car lot and the practice of the owner of leaving wrecks on the street. Robert Ray, the chairman, presented the complaint to the council, and the members agreed that this was a legitimate task for the council to undertake. They voted to do something about it and asked Ray to contact the owner.

Mrs. Ray said she would be glad to go see the owner with a committee of women. The worker said that the approach should be an official one and would have more weight if an officer represented the council.

The worker made his comment because there is a tendency in this neighborhood for the women to dominate and prevent the men from developing their sense of manliness. Mr. Ray was unemployed and needed a sense of adequacy, and he was a passive man who was willing to allow his wife to run things. The worker also thought Ray would lose face if Mrs. Ray assumed leadership in the council.

The worker suggested that the president go. Ray said he would and asked the worker to accompany him and the worker agreed. At the prescribed time, the worker met Mr. Ray and was surprised to see that Mrs. Ray was with him. Ray explained that Mrs. Ray drove the car.

When they arrived at the lot, Mr. Ray introduced the two and himself and said he was sure that Fulton, the owner, was interested in the neighborhood. He proceeded to relate the complaint of the residents and the council's decision and asked Fulton if he would be willing to cooperate. Fulton said he agreed that the neighborhood looked like a junk yard and that was why he did not bother to keep his lot in better shape. He said if the neighbors really cared about looks they should start with their own lots. Mrs. Ray looked like she was about to answer but the worker caught her eye and she refrained.

Mr. Ray said Fulton could begin to clear his frontage as an example. Fulton laughed and said he thought the council ought to sponsor a neighborhood cleanup drive as an example. Ray said that was a good idea, he would tell the council. He said it could be a deal. Could he tell the council that Fulton would tidy his lot if the council sponsored a neighborhood cleanup campaign? Fulton laughed loudly and said Ray was a shrewd bargainer. Mrs. Ray remained silent but looked surprised.

On the way home Ray said, "We are going to do great things in this council." Mrs. Ray agreed. Ray then said, "I'm going to hit Fulton for a truck for the cleanup." The worker said he had done a good piece of business this morning.

The council did sponsor the cleanup, Fulton provided a truck, and the officers had their pictures in the paper showing them with shovels. At a later meeting, Johnson, the vice-president, said that since his picture had been in the paper people showed him more respect and even his son was impressed.

The groupworker has the added function of timing, pacing and sequencing, and of assessing the changing primacy of objectives. The successful accomplishment of small gains in the early stages builds hope and confidence in the members and readies them to risk further. The emergence of trust and a sense of autonomy which evolves from some degree of mastery and freedom from domination by the worker allow creativity to emerge in setting goals. These steps pave the way for industry and productivity in a culture which may have had little reverence for work. These involvements provide a basis for identity and a sense of pride in who one is. The sequence is one in which, as competence and confidence grow, more difficult projects can be assumed, and as experience and accomplishments multiply, competence and confidence grow. Care must be taken to avoid domination and exploitation of the committees or councils by chairmen or indigenous leaders. This difficult job must be undertaken by the worker; the functions that a groupworker must perform with adults who are socially immature and needful require consummate skill and inordinate patience. They call for a delicate balance of promoting autonomy and encouraging the members to do things for themselves while giving advice and guidance and setting limits.

The extent to which the worker can act as mediator, expediter, advocate, and broker must be weighed ever so carefully so as not to deprive the members of these experiences and the sense of competence while guarding against failures and frustrations. The worker gives support, lends a vision, takes a back seat to allow the members to get the credits, and constantly helps others to take responsibility and play their roles skillfully. Emphasis is on social goal, the responsibility to others and self, and performance. Group method calls for exploration and explication of social values, and is characterized best as being experiential under guidance. The process has been likened to the rolling of a hoop by a boy. He sets the hoop upright, steadies it, and taps it smartly to start it on its way in the right direction. So long as it rolls on course, he does not touch it, but if it deviates, he gently guides it with light pressure on either side. As it slows down and long before it falters, he propels it again. If it accelerates too rapidly or speeds up going downhill, he retards it by holding it back and he does this also if he sees an unsettling obstacle in its path. Should it encounter a block such as a rock or curb, he will ease it over the rise with a boost, rarely if ever carrying it. If it falls he will certainly have to take some of the blame. Careful aiming, guidance, and propulsion will keep it rolling smoothly. When it rolls, he watches approvingly but keeps his hands off. The analogy breaks down at this point because the groupworker should teach the hoop to roll itself.

NOTES / READINGS

1. See Mary K. Kendrew, Nathan Nackman, and Evelyn Holsey, "Some Dynamics of Committee Interaction," *Social Work*, Vol. 6, No. 2 (April, 1961) pp. 94–98.

2. Gordon Hearn, project director, "A Study of Decision-Making in Girl Scouts Board of Directors" (Berkeley, Calif.: School of Social Welfare, University of California, June, 1953). (Mimeographed.)

3. Helen H. Jennings, *Leadership and Isolation* (New York: Longmans Green Co., 1943).

4. A. H. Maslow, *Motivation and Personality* (New York: Harper, 1970, 2nd ed.).

5. Daniel Katz and Robert Kahn, *The Social Psychology of Organizations* (New York: John Wiley & Sons, Inc., 1966).

6. Robert W. White, "Ego and Reality in Psychoanalytic Theory," *Psychological Issues*, Vol. III, Monograph II (New York: International Universities Press, 1963).

7. Erving Goffman, *Asylums, Essays on the Social Situations of Mental Patients and Other Inmates* (Garden City, N.Y.: Anchor Books, Doubleday & Co., Inc., 1961), p. 43.

15

❖❖❖❖❖❖❖❖

T-Groups, Sensitivity Groups, and Encounter Groups

T-Groups

In the last twenty-five years, the use and popularity of sensitivity training has burgeoned. Warren Bennis, a psychologist, estimates that better than six million people are participants in encounter groups of various kinds in this country. Some people newly come to this movement believe that the theories and techniques of sensitivity training in groups were developed at the Esalen Institute at Big Sur, founded in 1961. Sensitivity training and practice had their inception in group dynamics and are based on the original work of Lewin.[1] He had been studying small groups at the University of Iowa and later established a research center at the Massachusetts Institute of Technology in the nineteen forties. The T-group originated with Lewin in 1946, and flowered in the National Training Laboratory in Group Development which was founded in 1947 (now called the N.T.L. Institute of Applied Behavioral Science) sponsored by the National Education Association and conducted annually in Bethel, Maine. Major work on small-group theory was continued by Lewin and his followers at the Research Center for Group Dynamics of the University of Michigan. Gradually, the T-group was focused more on interpersonal relations with less emphasis on leadership training and democratic decision-making. Currently, there is a stress on self-actualization and individual development. Today, there are many other centers that are offshoots of this training program throughout the United States and Canada.[2] The important theorists and developers, in addition to Lewin, include researchers

Bradford, Benne, Ronald and Gordon Lippet, Shepard, and others.[3] The momentum for these programs came from Lewin's interest in studying the way in which small groups work.

Group dynamics is a name which was given to the study of small groups. It was not a practice or an applied field; it was and is a research endeavor. As time went on, some of the techniques which were developed within this small-group research were put to use and have evolved into a variety of human-relations training programs. Those persons who were and still are associated with the National Training Laboratory and some of its satellites are serious and ethical scholars who have devoted themselves to the rigorous study of small groups. The persons who lead groups under these auspices are trained, and are guided by professional standards. There are many people, however, who attend a two- or three-week institute as participants and then proceed to conduct sensitivity groups.

A short time after World War II, group-dynamics researchers were asked by a branch of the Armed Services to investigate the dynamics of combat teams on bombers, small naval craft and the like for the purpose of devising ways of improving the human relations among the men and between enlisted men and officers. These crew members depend upon one another to survive, and a line of command based upon authority did not seem to produce cohesive and compatible teams. Men who were forced to live together on a submarine or corvette in close quarters for weeks on end under tension, or who were stationed on isolated outposts, became short-tempered and hostile to one another and jeopardized the lives of others as well as the mission itself.

The study projects which were conducted by Lewin and his staff evolved into programs which applied what was learned in the research and at that time became known as Human Relations Training. Further work produced insights into specific areas of group life, such as leadership functions in groups, and subsequently in workshops conducted by the researchers; these learnings were applied and were termed Leadership Training Institutes. These were the forerunners of the encounter groups of today, known also as sensitivity training. Sensitivity training is primarily a form of verbal encounter. The institutes were well planned, predicated on theory, the teams were well trained, and the results were carefully evaluated. As much cannot be said for many of the programs that are operating presently. The purpose of the T-groups, an abbreviation for training group, was for the participants to observe and study group dynamics.[4] It is a laboratory method in which the study group itself is the group under examination.[5] As part of the study process, the members become sensitive to others, to their own behavior and how they affect others, become aware of how small groups work.[6] As the sensitivity of the members increases, it becomes possible for them to experiment with new behaviors by which they influence people, gain favorable response, and achieve personal goals. Hence, the training group is a laboratory in human relations; it was not conceived of as therapy. The laboratory at Bethel built in several teaching aids and safeguards, such as good food and group living, lectures on theory, demonstrations, the skills-training group which teaches the participants how to handle themselves in group situations, the catharsis group which allows them to blow off steam, evening sessions devoted to social-change tactics, recreation, and the availability of therapists should they be desired. Current versions of T-group practice under other auspices have not provided these facilitating supports and rely on the T-group itself to accomplish the goals.

The legitimate programs are predicated on several theoretical premises. They rest upon the assumption that learning is achieved best when thinking and feeling are combined with experience and practice. This is a basic premise in groupwork also. A second premise is that attitudinal and behavioral changes occur more readily when the participants are involved in making decisions which affect them; also a basic premise in groupwork. A major assumption rests upon a feedback control system; behavior changes as persons learn how they behave in response to others, and vice versa. Dimock notes that the training program withdraws the participant from the security of his usual surroundings and places him into a new reference group, the T-group. This creates anxiety; it also uses the T-group as a source for new norms of behavior and psychological safety. Dimock writes that "these new functions of the T-group give it unusually powerful opportunities to influence behavior as members react to group pressures and conform to group standards."[7] This can pervert a major belief in the democratic process held by Lewin and his early associates, Ron Lippet and others. Dimock observes that the traditional T-groups are concerned about participants experiencing democratic values of group decision-making, but that many of the current groups (encounter, human potential, Gestalt, etc.) center around the trainer and his actions.

The T-group as a modality has been adopted in a multiplicity of settings and for a wide variety of purposes. Industry uses it to help executives get along better with co-workers and also to train for leadership functions. It uses it also to assess organizational problems, increase production, and alleviate tensions and friction. Governmental departments use it to train personnel in better approaches to working with the public and with members of other disciplines, and to help employees accept change. Educational institutions use it to foster better relations, to "cool it," and to do almost anything else that they have not been able to do successfully with traditional methods. The churches use it ostensibly to foster better human relations and as a substitute for group counseling. National associations use and promote it, seemingly as a shortcut or quicker way to achieve the aims of the organization, sometimes because the members request it, and sometimes because a staff member has attended a T-group as a participant and believes that this is the answer to people's problems.

I find that the newer hybrid versions of the T-group have been most strongly espoused by those organizations which are rigid, authoritarian, and hidebound, while most recent participants in encounter groups are seeking freedom, spontaneity, and intimate, interpersonal relations through a group experience. We will examine several versions of encounter groups.

The T-group, in its authentic form, conducted by a person who knows what he is doing, and within the context of sensitizing people to group dynamics and the behavior of individuals in groups, follows a fairly standard process. There is a trainer and co-trainer, the group numbers between fifteen and twenty, the duration is of several weeks, and the members take turns acting as group observers. The trainer opens by making it clear, either verbally or by his behavior, that he will take no directional responsibility. He states no purpose and sets no contract, he divests the group of authoritarian control and gives it liberty to do what it wants to do. The members are not introduced to each other and they are urged not to identify themselves by occupation, status, or other social symbols. The lack of structure creates great anxiety, confusion, dependency, and anger. Those participants who need structure argue for a chairman, an agenda, and stated goals, and there are attempts to chair, to choose a chairman, to suggest bylaws, and the like. Others argue for the process, that is, for an experience in human relations free of institutionalized structure.

The lack of a resolution of the conflict results in an attack on the trainer either for not telling them what to do, or because he did make a suggestion. Based on things that the participants may have heard about T-groups, there is a preconceived notion that the culture supports an attack on the trainer and a demand that people tell what they think of each other. The interaction becomes sharp for three reasons: a reaction to frustration, a preconceived idea that this is supposed to happen, and license which is used by some to hurt. Some members become frightened, some become belligerent and vituperative, and some withdraw, but willy-nilly, the members are forced to reveal themselves, their modes of adaptation, and their coping patterns. Attitudes emerge, defenses are shown, and emotional biases are revealed. The group displays all of the attributes of a diagnostic group and the first stages of groups in general— random behavior and testing, a demand for structure, and a reaction against an authority figure which, in turn, exacerbates peer rivalry.

It is not by chance that the T-group is like a diagnostic group because its purpose is to study group process. As I said earlier, when people are in a group situation and there is no structure or direction, anxiety rises and people act in accordance with their habitual responses and coping mechanisms. Such an environment provides an opportunity to study behavior. Since most of the participants know that this is an objective of a T-group, members begin to comment on what is happening, the observer feeds back the group dynamics and the assistant trainer provides some guidance in the explication of the group process. The method is a familiar one involving awareness through feedback and participant observation.

The members have been put in a situation in which they have revealed themselves to others. There is fear and a lack of trust, but the climate seduces some members to talk about their past histories or present anxieties. Having done so, a coalition develops which demands that others do the same; and if they resist, they are prodded by being asked what they fear and why they cannot trust, and are made to feel uncooperative and deviant. Members do express feelings and react to anxiety by the familiar patterns of fight, flight, dependency, or pairing; however, relationships within the group are not discussed as yet because a real group has not developed and, therefore, that topic is not a safe one. Feelings run high and are released by direct attacks on one or several members in addition to or in place of the trainer.

The dynamics are not the same as those in the groups I discussed earlier in the book where trust was developing and hence people began to risk and test mutuality. Here the climate is one in which mistrust runs so high that one who has inadvertently revealed himself needs to know about others for self-protection. The thought is, "If you can hurt me because I am now vulnerable, I can also hurt you if I know about you; therefore, I must force you to reveal yourself and then you had better not attack me." The proponents of T-group method believe that the fact that negative feelings are expressed early in the meetings indicates an attempt to test the group's freedom and trustworthiness. I believe that it happens because it is easy to express one's anger when one is anxious and afraid and also because it is dangerous to express liking openly for another, which is subject to being misconstrued in our society. There must be trust in order to be able to approach others and to request closeness.

The proponents believe that trust does develop and because of this, usually by about the end of the second week, the members ask for and are pushing for "good and welfare," each person taking his turn at being told by every other member how he is perceived, how he comes across, and what people like and dislike about him. This is by no means a unanimous desire of all the members. Often those who do not want such an experience are put under great pressure to agree to it. There are several personality characteristics operating here: some people who have a sadistic desire to cut and criticize in the name of being frank and helpful, some who fear being criticized and seek to handle the fear by asking for it, and those who are secure and honestly feel that it would help them to know what their best friends will not tell them.

It is true that people who are in pain and show it or admit it are dealt with kindly. The frightened and anxious ones appeal to the group and usually the group members show warmth, acceptance, and support. Those who hide behind a façade of braggadocio, or who seemingly are self-confident or aggressive, tend to be attacked. Many people are told unpleasant things about themselves of which they were never aware. There is great impatience in the group with defenses and masks, and generally speaking, there is a group culture or norm which evolves that enforces frankness and demands encounter. In many ways, the group climate and mores resemble a Synanon group, which has been characterized as a group of people who engage in discussion to find truth. This includes truth about oneself, one's motivations and defenses, and the games one plays even if that truth is unpleasant to hear. Unlike Synanon groups, however, the frankness and feedback in many T-groups is not motivated necessarily by a desire to help others or to develop mutual aid.

There are merits to what happens in T-groups and there are positive values in the method. Theoretically, participants in T-groups are reasonably well adjusted and have the ego strength to deal with knowledge about themselves. The group members do learn group dynamics in a laboratory and can see the stages of group development, can examine how leadership develops, norms evolve, a group culture comes into being, the effects of group pressure on individual behavior, status and power dynamics, and the like. Participants can and do experiment with new roles, changed behaviors, and learn how to exert leadership and influence. They can learn also how to eliminate blockages and facilitate group movement. Members do acquire sensitivity of various kinds; become sensitive to group processes, learn when and how to perform group functions, enact roles, and fill role gaps. They become sensitive to cues which are keys to communication, and learn how to observe and respond to the messages of others. Most participants become more sensitive to their own behavior and how it affects others, and how their own actions result in the frustration or achievement of their own goals and need-meeting. The method, then, teaches human relations, group functioning, how to be a group member, leadership functions, and sensitivity.

Post-meeting reaction sheets which are filled out at the end of each session often are tabulated, summarized and presented visually at the beginning of the next session. People can compare their own perceptions, reactions, and performances against the combined judgment of the others, and this can facilitate self-correction, but it can also produce conformity. For people who are motivated to change and can change, the T-group provides the feedback which is difficult to acquire elsewhere, makes the participant reveal himself and look at himself; that is, "makes" used in the sense that a Christmas club makes a person save. The group culture reinforces acceptance of self, the sanction to express feelings, and authenticity. One assumes that the intensity of the experience—and it is intense—develops a bond, a fabricated intimacy like a summer romance and, therefore, the frank criticism is constructive because it occurs in the context of mutual concern. For some people, the T-group experience is the rare occasion in which they can feel that they belong to a human group and can taste the flavor of intimacy. A group that goes through an ordeal develops morale and cohesion. I do not believe that most T-groups achieve a stage of intimacy. I am certain that the weekend T-groups and other similar short-term sessions do not even approach a stage of group caring, but that does not mean that they have no value.

T-groups, because of the climate of confrontation, tend to facilitate a closeness which may not approximate love but which does promote human interaction. They cut through the pastimes, routines, and games, and they press for being oneself and for learning to accept oneself even though some of these processes are brutal. There is a growing body of opinion which holds that helping professionals are too gentle and subtle. One of the persistent myths in counseling is that the counselor may drive the client into a break if he is direct and confronts. Professionals persistently underestimate the strength or overestimate the fragility of clients. Perhaps the very frankness of the T-group is refreshing because it is not hypocritical, offers no double-bind, and tells it as it is. The T-group does not hide behind a polite lie and, therefore, does not allow the member to run, rationalize, or excuse himself. Albeit, this is usually true also of a therapy group. If the member wants to do so, the T-group allows him to try on new role behaviors, to do exercises in altered patterns, and to test the consequences of new coping devices and modes of adaptation. Generally, the group will reward positive changes and reinforce them, thereby assisting the member to stabilize new habits of interpersonal relations.

Some Cautions

A good trainer will not allow anxiety to rise beyond the capacity of the members to handle it. He will prevent attacks on members that will destroy or breach defenses too early or will leave people unprotected. He will not condone either sadism or masochism which have no constructive potential. A trained groupworker will sedulously avoid being seduced into dominating or exploiting the group no matter how strongly the members press for it. The same principle applies when working with a T-group as with a treatment group; namely, that when the group members do not improve their behavior or when it worsens, it is related to something unhealthy in the worker which is interacting with the members' hangups. The worker who is free of sarcasm, sadism, seduction, fear, and the need to dominate can function in an atmosphere of truth. One of the frightening dangers in current T-group practice, and in many current encounter groups, is that the trainer is not such a person.

There are other less serious dangers in T-group and sensitivity-group training. Frequently, the changes in behavior are impermanent and the experience does not run long enough or has not had stabilization built in. Some people are revealed and gain self-awareness but the hangups are not worked through and there is a need for follow-up and for competent help for these people. This is true, especially, where people who are not strong or who have latent emotional problems which can be brought to the surface as a result of the experience come into T-groups. These dangers are inherent in the method, and there are also some other problems which are not insurmountable but which do plague practice.

For example, the group very often tends to become a tyrant and although the worker does not control, the group controls rigidly. This negates the freedom which is stated as being there but, in fact, is denied. Another danger lies in the group dealing gently and giving status to people who conform, are quick to adapt, and who do not stand up for their own beliefs. Persons who do not have strong identifications become good group members easily. The group tends to give its attention to the persons who are opinionated and dogmatic. Another weakness lies in a climate of pseudo-intimacy, and although it appears to be a human interchange, it very often is just a game or a role-playing enactment.

The T-group or laboratory method has been adopted and elaborated upon by a plethora of group programs. These have proliferated because of feelings of isolation and alienation in contemporary life, and a need in many people to have a human experience. These groups are partially an expression of an existential point of view, but also are a seeking for treatment for sufferings and yearnings that is not available through any other form of service. By gap theory, therefore, since there is no place to go for group experiences that alleviate feelings of alienation, the encounter groups flourish. It has become a means of dealing with tension and a possible resource for finding authenticity and fulfillment. More than that, encounter groups provide an opportunity for one to become a part of a human group even if only for a moment. It is a place to communicate, to be validated, to be touched, and to confirm one's existence. It is a place to seek and perhaps to find acceptance, freedom, an intimate interpersonal relationship, and oneself. The fact that the encounter-group development has grown so rapidly and become so large is an indictment of the group-services agencies, our educational system, and, in the final analysis, the family.

Encounter Groups

It is well to restate the fact that the T-group was designed to study groups, gain skills in interpersonal relations, and to develop sensitivity. But sensitivity groups become more than verbal interchanges; they act out, as we shall see. The new form of encounter groups is entered into for personal gain; to find favorable response, interpersonal intimacy, and authenticity. For many people who receive benefit, it accomplishes some of these purposes, but for others who are seeking therapy, consciously or unconsciously, it is disappointing. Many of these groups are being conducted by people who lack qualifications, personal and educational, to provide either kind of service, and while some good is done, some harm is done also. There is an assumption made, which is open to debate, that openness and frankness are therapeutic; for some people they may not be. For some, the encounter group is a means of being "turned on" and it can have deleterious effects, especially if the worker also is caught up in the "turn on." There is an assumption too that the free expression of anger, the so-called scream within, is beneficial. This is not true universally either.

The usual procedure in an encounter group is to begin by helping the participants relax and get over shyness and inhibition. Most people fear looking ridiculous and risking rejection. There are different techniques used to loosen up people, such as directing them to shout, wave arms, jump in place, and march. It is at this point that I must enter a strong objection because a stranger, one who is ostensibly the leader, is giving orders. He calls every move and the members follow his orders meekly. They walk, stop, sit on the floor, and so forth on command. It is possible to purchase a set of tapes for do-it-yourself encounter groups wherein the commands are given by the speaker on the tape and everyone acts out the scenario. This entire process is antithetical to the avowed purpose of freedom and authenticity. I contend that there can be no growth when autonomy is violated in so flagrant a fashion.

The members are directed to walk about the room and look at each other to achieve eye contact, and to communicate nonverbally. After ten minutes of such encounter, people are asked to shake hands, later to touch another's face, and then to embrace. Some groups now are asked to pair off, sit on the floor, and study each other. Other workers go even further and deliberately request hostile, negative acting-out; others ask the members to do silly or childlike things such as make faces, walk in unusual ways, act like cats, dogs, or other animals, and form grotesque statues. Theoretically, these exercises produce exhilaration and a group feeling and one can thereby experience the joy of release. Obviously, some people become very anxious and are traumatized. Failure to follow the instructions results in censure, embarrassment, and isolation. One is encouraged to admit feeling uncomfortable but to perform anyway.

Having negotiated these simple steps, the group proceeds to more intimate encounters such as leg wrestling, arm wrestling, falling and being caught by a fellow member (a demonstration of trust), nose-rubbing, and gazing into the eyes of the other. Other groups that are farther out are encouraged to touch each other and explore. The body-contact exercises lead to emotional contact which includes making verbal choices of friends, telling people why you do not like them, expressing truths about "whitey" or one's professor to his face, or talking about oneself. Encounter groups range all the way from circumspect value orientations to those that espouse complete freedom from social or moral proscriptions. There are those movements where the members are seeking freedom from overly restrictive superegos and want to be able to develop social competence that will allow them to be comfortable in groups, in usual social intercourse, and to function without constant embarrassment and fear. These people are looking for human warmth and a chance to interact on a person-to-person level. In classical terms, they are seeking to resolve the conflict between wish and fear in favor of being able to operate on enabling solutions, in favor of wishes but within a context of the realities of social norms and expectancies. These are to be differentiated from those people who are seeking thrills, and are attracted and excited by the prurient potentials that exist in license, non-self-responsibility, and sexual satisfaction under the guise of truth, science, and psychology. These latter groups are the ones that move from the exercises I have been describing to nudity, touch-and-feel, eroticism, and other forms of self-expression.

Some workers discourage any sexual expression while others encourage it. For those people who are seeking such stimulation and attend very permissive groups, perhaps no harm is done. For those with genuine problems or hangups, guilt, shame, and disappointment can ensue. From the theory sections in this book one can deduce that encounter groups can isolate some people, scapegoat others, exploit some, and play upon the weaknesses of others. For many people, the entire experience is superficial and does not begin to meet their needs. I am talking about those lonely people who need to be accepted and loved and who cannot withstand the letdown when the group ends, or those who sink into despair when they find themselves back where they started, or even worse, that they have been used. These groups lend themselves to exploitation and manipulation.

Some people are making a life-style out of going to encounter groups because this is the only way they can be in a group or because it releases inhibitions within that group climate which they cannot achieve elsewhere. Some enjoy the emotional battering and it is a way to assuage guilt, and for others it can be their moment in the spotlight; for still others, it is the channel for releasing unbearable hostility. For some it is the "club," and for those who can afford it, it is like a weekend at a resort.

The encounter group idea, per se, has merit. Like any such device, the right group is good for the right person and the wrong group can be tragic. The worker is crucial, and sad to relate, in encountering's present faddism there are few good ones around. The groups ranging from those which are formed to effect release and find an existential climate for self-actualization, to and including those that frankly advertise their sexual character are in contradiction to the model of groupwork described in this book. The encounter group usually demands emotional conformity and is a restrictive and autocratic climate. It insists upon prescribed behavior, feelings, and communication, and it punishes those who will not or cannot comply. Although it is a paradox, the fact is that the usual encounter group denies freedom, and will not countenance the emergence of a true self. Like many other current movements that profess an allegiance to doing one's own thing, it is tyrannical and dictates just what that thing should be. I believe its popularity is based on the security which its format affords, the simulation of a family with an autocratic parent who loves one, and siblings who tell it to you like it is, professing that they act only in the interest of you, their brother. People are seeking a family and this type approximates the one that is most familiar to most people. Since intimacy is comparatively scarce in the experiences of those who are most attracted to encounter groups, the role-playing of intimacy in the groups has a great appeal; and if one hurls oneself into the role-playing, one can almost have the illusion of the real thing.

T-groups, sensitivity groups, and encounter groups have developed some strategies, tactics, and techniques that have merit and that I have incorporated in the method I have presented in this book. Why then have I included so many negatives when describing it? Because most of the practitioners are not qualified and many are not guided by any standards of professional ethics; because encounter groups, exclusive of T-groups properly conducted, are dominating and deny freedom and hence curtail growth; because they do not respect the individual's right to be himself.

Encounter groups usually have no contract, the members do not function for the mutual benefit of each other, there is no agreement against exploitation, and they are permitted to become manipulative. They do not last long enough for basic trust to develop and are certainly of too short a duration to achieve intimacy, hence the intimacy that is portrayed is role-playing. People can be attacked, their defenses breached; they can be damaged and also can have their hangups reinforced through interaction with people and workers who use them. Persons who break under the pressure are not protected or referred for help; some people come for therapy, think they have had therapy, and are disillusioned and disappointed to find no benefit after the group ends. Finally, in the farthest-out encounter groups where license and acting-out are encouraged and condoned, some people experience guilt and shame while others are reinforced in using people as commodities for their own pleasure or satisfaction.

For the hundreds of people who find what they want, who get an experience that helps them understand themselves, and who find some answers to interpersonal problems, the encounter group is perhaps the only place available to achieve these results. They are lucky indeed. The T-group, in the hands of a skilled trainer, under proper auspices, and with supportive group activities described, helps many people in many ways. One cannot fault a method because some who employ it misuse it or lack ethics, as the same criticisms can be directed against therapists. This, however, does not negate the viability of the method. If the positive attributes of the encounter group could have been found in social agencies and institutions, the chances are that the popularity of the private groups would not have grown. This does not mean that T-groups, sensitivity groups, and encounter groups conducted by universities, churches, schools, or youth-serving agencies are good by virtue of the sponsorship. Some of them are very destructive and many sins against people are committed with the best of intentions. Neither do I mean that because a group is conducted by a minister, a schoolteacher, a psychologist, a social worker, or a professor it is free from the dangers I have cited. Enough has been said in this book about the worker to make it clear that credentials are not a substitute for competence, that techniques are not a substitute for stance, that knowledge of group method is unique and essential, and that the person who conducts a T-group, sensitivity group, or encounter group must have training in that methodology.

For those who attend these groups with high hopes and are victimized, their experience duplicates the worst features of our society, and for them it is a human tragedy. There is a crying need for our agencies and associations to provide opportunities for good group experiences.[8]

Reprise

This text for groupworkers began with a quotation from *The Redemption of Democracy*, a portion of which bears repeating now.

But if, as cannot but be the case, civilization and higher probity are possible only when they grow from morally responsible individual nature, and then only as far as the individual is allowed freedom of co-responsibility and joint decision on a universally valid basis—if this is so, then there is only one thinkable conclusion. The conclusion is to resist the temptation toward all-powerful machineries of coercion, even though it be in the interest of so-called progress, or would make that progress easier. The conclusion will be that we had far better give up such supposed progress than expose ourselves to the mortal peril of a coercive system.

NOTES / READINGS

1. Kurt Lewin, "Frontiers in Group Dynamics," *Human Relations*, Vol. I (1947), pp. 5–41.

Kurt Lewin, "Frontiers in Group Dynamics II," *Human Relations*, Vol. I (1947), pp. 143–153.

2. R. T. Golembiewski and A. Blumberg, eds., *Sensitivity Training and the Laboratory Approach: Readings about Concepts and Applications* (Itasca, Ill.: F. T. Peacock Publishers, Inc., 1970).

3. Leland P. Bradford, J. R. Gibb, and Kenneth D. Benne, eds., *T-Group Theory and Laboratory Methods* (New York: John Wiley & Sons, Inc., 1964).

4. Catherine P. Papell, "Sensitivity Training: Relevance for Social Work Education," paper presented at the Council on Social Work Education, Seattle, Washington, January, 1971.

5. Edgar H. Schein and Warren G. Bennis, *Personal and Organizational Change Through Group Methods, the Laboratory Approach* (New York: John Wiley & Sons, Inc., 1965).

6. This can be traced back to the work of Trigant L. Burrow reported in "The Group Method of Analysis," *Psychoanalytical Review*, Vol. XIV (1924), pp. 268–280.

7. Hedley, G. Dimock, "Sensitivity Training in Canada: Perspective and Comments," *Canada's Mental Health*, Supplement No. 69 (September–October, 1971), p. 4.

8. Suggested References:

Jack R. Gibb, "The Effects of Human Relations Training" in *Handbook of Psychotherapy and Behavior Change*, A. Bergin and S. Garfield, eds. (New York: John Wiley & Sons, Inc., 1971), pp. 839–862.

A. Burton, ed., *Encounter: The Theory and Practice of Encounter Groups* (San Francisco: Jossey-Bass, 1969).

Jane Howard, *Please Touch: A Guided Tour of the Human Potential Movement* (New York: McGraw-Hill, 1970).

L. Soloman and B. Berzon, eds., *The Encounter Group: Issues and Applications* (Belmont, Calif.: Brooks-Cole, 1970).

W. G. Dyer, ed., *New Dimensions in Group Training* (New York: Van Nostrand, 1970).

Index

Christians, 21
churches, and T-groups, 366
client, and public assistance
    agency, 37–39. *See also* agency
    intake process
coeducational groups, 64
cohesion, concept of, 215
committees, 58
  as barriers to productivity,
    334–35
  in task group, 323–37
commune, 21
community action, 359
"community of obedience," 101,
    103
"community of will," 103
communication, 63, 118–24, 209–11
    theory, 25
    written, 21
community, and neighborhood or-
    ganizations, 358
compromise, and decision-making,
    222
Comte, Auguste, 21
conflict, and group life, 128
conformity, 111, 116–17, 190
contract, 156
  and group termination, 287
  making, 137–38, 161–68
  and social relationships, 164–68
  use of, 179–80
Cooley, Charles, 24
correction groups, 31, 182
corrective settings, 40–41
Cottage Six (Polsky), 300
Council on Social Work Education,
    146, 147
councils:
  requisites of members, 342–43
  treasuries, 351–52
  uses and types of, 338
  see also delegate councils
crisis intervention groups, 43–45
  procedure for, 275–76
crisis theory, 44
cultural heritage, 29

decision-making:
  as basic skill, 49
  as group process, 216–20
  groups, 35
  in neighborhood councils, 358

decision-making (*cont.*):
  procedure, 220–22
  process, 213
delegate councils, 337–56
  formation of, 344–48
  function of, 340–42
  groupworker and, 348–53
  how to work with, 354–56
  problems in, 353
  use of, 342–44
delinquency, 300–2
democracy, 202
  contract and, 163
  in delegate councils, 354–55
  in groups, 65
  process of, 28–29
development, requisites for
    healthy, 23
developmental groups, 42–43, 58,
    79. *See also* growth and devel-
    opment groups
developmental tasks, 60
deviant roles, 104–5
diagnostic group, 35, 66
dignity of man, as basis for social
    work, 23
Dimock, G., 365
double-blind messages, 210
dramatics, use of, in program,
    229
Durkheim, Emile, 24, 25
Dymond, R. F., 104
dynamic homeostasis, 128–29

educational group, 35, 59
educational institutions, and
    T-groups, 366
ego function, 48, 98
elitist philosophy, 22, 357
empathy, 98, 211
encounter groups, 364, 366, 371,
    371–75
enhancement goal, 139
environment:
  group as, 53–54
  manipulating, 279–80
  relation of group to, 129
  validating, 212–13
equifinality, 130
Erikson, Erik, 60, 234
Erikson, Kai, 104
Esalen Institute, 363

Maloney, Sara, 61
manifest goals, 139
married groups, 64
Maslow, A. H., 27–28, 327
mass activities, in use of program, 241–72
mass program:
 requisites for, 269–72
 values of, 242
Massachusetts Institute of Technology, 363
Mayans, 21
Mead, George, 25, 54
mediating model, 294–96
meetings, first, 81–88, 156, 161–68. *See also* group development
mental health, 22, 25
metacommunication, 120, 150
methods:
 and acting-out adolescents, 299–309
 for groupings, 310–13
 definition, 146–47
 mediating model, 294–96
 for problem-focused group, 299
 and transactional analysis, 296–98
 see also groupwork
Michigan, University of, 363
milieu:
 group as, 53–54
 use of, 191–92
Mills, Theodore, 71
minority members, social role and, 101–2
"mixed transactional model," 232
Mobilization for Youth (MFY), 43, 300
motivation, 27, 123, 137
Mudgett, Margaret, 61
Murphy, Gardner, 54
music, use of, in program utilization, 230, 235
mutual identification, 24. *See also* mutuality
mutuality, 137, 140, 173, 278
 and social control, 214
 in social relations, 24

national associations, use of T-groups, 366

National Education Association, 220, 363
National Training Laboratory in Group Development, 363, 364
N.T.L. Institute of Applied Behavioral Science, 363
National Association of Social Workers (NASW), 147
 Practice Committee, 40
natural friendship groups, 43
natural groups, 57
need-meeting, 27–31
 and group services, 316
 and position, 91–92
 resource, deprivation of, 30
needs, 34, 48
 and committee groups, 328
 and program activities, 232
 in reference group, 46
 see also need-meeting
neighborhood councils, 356–62
networks, group, 55
norms, 22, 68, 70, 81, 113–16, 122, 163, 217
nurturance, 178

"offering stage," 155
O'Gorman, Ned, 79
open-house activity, 260
orientation, 81–83

Parents of Exceptional Children, 39
parents' groups, 39–40
parliamentary procedure, 202. *See also* democracy
party programming, 262–63
peer groups, 157, 287
person and role, interrelationship of, 103–6
"person-in-the-situation," 54
personality, 22
 and social system, 24
 see also self
physical force, and problem behavior, 280
Piaget, Jean, 115–16
popularist philosophy, and neighborhood work, 357
position, 90–92
 and feedback, 128
 in group structure, 68

task-oriented group (*cont.*):
  neighborhood councils and block
    clubs, 356–62
  structure, 108
  termination of, 283–84
technique, definition of, 146–47
teen canteen, 242–43
teenagers:
  and lounge program, 248–49
  parties for, 257–66
  see also adolescents
themes, group, 55
Thomas, Edwin, 192
tool concept, 54
traditional group, 216
T-groups (training), 363–71
transaction, 107, 126–27
transactional analysis, 296–99
transference, 67
treatment goal, 22, 139–40
treatment group, 35, 41, 58, 79,
    155, 157, 164, 168, 172, 173,
    182, 202–3, 214, 217, 223
  principles for composing, 60–64
Trecker, Harleigh B., 79

tribe, 21
Tropp, Emanuel, 295
trust, 30, 67–68, 110, 134, 212
  and program selection, 234
  worker, and development of,
    154–68

unit, group as, 54–55

validation and reality-testing,
  211–213
values, 22, 70, 81, 116–17
  use of, 196–201
Vinter, Robert, 153–54, 230–31, 295

Weber, Max, 24
White, Robert, 27, 357
Wilson, Gertrude, 118, 228, 232
Wiltse, Kermit, 38
worker, *see* Groupworker

young adults:
  dances for, 266–68
  groups, 64
  and lounge programs, 248–49